GW01149097

Handbook of Salary and Wage Systems

Handbook of Salary and Wage Systems

Second edition

**Editor: Angela M Bowey
Advisory Editor: Tom Lupton**

A Gower Handbook

© Gower Press 1975
© Gower Publishing Company Limited 1982

All rights reserved. No part of this publication may be reproduced, stored in a retrieval system, or transmitted in any form or by any means, electronic, mechanical, photocopying, recording, or otherwise without the prior permission of Gower Publishing Company Limited.

First published in Great Britain by Gower Press Limited 1975

Second edition published by
Gower Publishing Company Limited,
Croft Road, Aldershot, Hants, England

**Printed in Great Britain by
Biddles Ltd, Guildford, Surrey**

British Library Cataloguing in Publication Data

Handbook of salary and wage systems.
— 2nd ed.
1. Wages — Great Britain
I. Bowey, Angela M.
658.3'2'0941   HD5017

ISBN 0-566-02261-3

Contents

List of illustrations	xii
Acknowledgements	xvi
Notes on Contributors	xvii

Part One: THE CONTEXT OF WAGES AND SALARIES

Editor's Introduction	1
1 Facets of Wage and Salary Administration	3
Angela M Bowey	
Aims of this handbook	3
Work assessment and job design	4
Payment levels	4
Designing a payment system	6
Other considerations	7
2 The Social Context of Work	9
Tom Lupton	
Pay systems	9
Conflicts about outcomes—and the social context	11
Pay structures (conflicts about outcomes)	13
3 Government Policy and Payment Systems	19
Angela M Bowey and Richard Thorpe	
Impact on incentive schemes	19
Impact of policy on differentials	25

Impact on wage bargaining	28
Case study one	30
Case study two	33
Conclusions	35

4 The Structure of Collective Bargaining in Britain — 37
Andrew Thomson

The development of bargaining structure in Britain	41
The statistical profile	42
British bargaining structure in an international context	46
Efficiency in bargaining structures	48
Conclusions	52

5 Installing Salary and Wage Systems — 55
Angela M Bowey

The strategy for change	57
Criteria the new system must meet	60
The features of the new system	60
Supporting changes in the organization	61
Implications of the changes for other groups	61

Part Two: JOB CONTEXT AND MEASUREMENT

Editor's Introduction	63

6 Job Design and Work Organization — 65
David W Birchall

Job rationalization	66
Job enlargement and work rotation	70
Job enrichment	71
Semi-autonomous group working	72
Discussion	73
Case studies of job restructuring in practice	74

7 Techniques of Job Evaluation — 77
Jack Butterworth

The principle	78
The four main techniques	78
New techniques	83
Performing the job evaluation exercise	85
Pricing the grade structure	86
Summary	87

8 Sex Discrimination and Job Evaluation — 89
Patrick Walker and Angela M Bowey

Formulating a job evaluation scheme	90

Contents   vii

Different types of job evaluation scheme	92
Take care who is left out of the scheme	98
Implementing a job evaluation scheme	99
Appendix: The legislation	101

9 Work Study, Method Study and Work Measurement   105
E G Wood

The historical background to work study	105
The objectives of work study	107
Method study	108
Work measurement	112
Using work study data	115
The practical implication of work study	117

10 Productivity Measurement   119
Richard Thorpe

The meaning of productivity	119
The complexity of measurement	120
Still the need for a measure	126
Total productivity measures	131
Significance of the market position	135
Significance of organizational location	137
Productivity planning	140
Industrial relations	141
Conclusions	143

Part Three: ESTABLISHING THE RATE FOR THE JOB
Editor's Introduction   145

11 Relating Wages to Job Evaluation and to Work Measurement   147
Jack Butterworth

Subjectivity of job evaluation and work measurement	147
Job evaluation	148
Work measurement	153
Summary of effect of job evaluation and work measurement	157

12 Comparability   159
Angela M Bowey

Statutory and informal usage of comparability	160
Methods of making comparisons	162
Comparing pay	167
Problematical implications	168

13 The Strategy and Tactics of Bargaining   173
Andrew Gottschalk

Objectives of bargaining	173
Developing a negotiating strategy	174
Analyzing and selecting negotiating tactics	179
Preparing for bargaining	180

Part Four: SALARY SYSTEMS
Editor's Introduction — 185

14 Salary Bands and Salary Progression Curves — 187
Lawson K Savery

Wage surveys	187
Designing salary bands	189
Relationship between bands	192
Methods of salary progression	193
Relationship to performance	194
Progression curves	195
New employees	196

15 Performance Appraisal and Review — 197
David Cameron

Objectives of performance appraisal and review	199
Procedures for appraisal and review	201
Management by objectives	207
The appraisal interview	213
Assessing employee potential	220
Assessment centres	226
Management development	229
Salary review	230

16 The Hay Guide-chart Profile Method — 235
W F Younger

Meeting the needs of employers and employees	235
Development of the Hay guide-chart profile method	236
Installing and using the system in practice	239
Summary of objectives	247

17 Incentive Bonus Schemes for Managers — 249
Michael White

Why have incentive schemes?	249
Major types of management incentive schemes	250
Key questions	252
Technical problems in management incentives	259

18 Selecting a Salary System — 265
Michael White

Need for systematic approach	265
The appropriateness of a system	266
Matching remuneration to motivation	271
Cost-effectiveness in remuneration systems	275

Part Five: WAGE SYSTEMS
Editor's Introduction — 283

19 Payment by Results Systems — 285
G H Webb

Straight piecework and flat day rate	285
Payment of a bonus reward	287
Geared schemes	293
The economics of PBR schemes	293
Practical illustration of a successful PBR scheme	295

20 Payment by Time Systems — 297
Anne G Shaw and D Shaw Pirie

Introduction	297
Philosophy of time-based systems	300
Why choose a time-based system?	301
Operational points	303
Some implications of adopting a time-based system	305
Summary	306

21 Status, Effort and Reward — 309
Dan Gowler and Karen Legge

What is status?	310
Effort and reward	311
Status as rank	312
Status as ascribed social position	314
Status as achieved social position	316
Conclusions	318

22 Bonuses Based on Company Performance — 321
Fiona Wilson, Sally Haslam and Angela M Bowey

Principal objectives of company-wide bonus schemes	321
Types of scheme	322
Advantages and disadvantages	325
How to design and implement a scheme	326
Added value schemes	329
Scanlon plans	333
The payment system	334
Case study of a Scanlon plan	337

23 Selecting a Wage System	349
Angela M Bowey	
Background to the study	350
The production process and associated behaviour patterns	351
The payment structure	353
Follow-up	360
Conclusion	361
Part Six: EMPLOYEE BENEFITS	
Editor's Introduction	363
24 Employee Benefits for Managers and Executives	365
Richard Cockman	
The total benefits/salary package	366
Basic types of benefits	367
'Status' benefits	368
Security benefits	370
Work benefits	372
Key benefits	374
Summary	375
25 Employee Benefits for Non-managerial Staff	379
Richard Cockman	
Statutory benefits	380
Security benefits	381
Welfare benefits	383
Conclusions	385
26 Company Pension Schemes	387
Michael Pilch	
Objectives	387
Types of benefit	388
Legislation	390
Designing schemes	393
Paying for pensions	394
Sources of advice	395
Part Seven: ADMINISTERING POLICY AND PLANNING	
Editor's Introduction	397
27 Operating, Developing and Adjusting Reward Systems	399
John F Percival	
Monitoring in the short term	400

Adjustment and development in the medium term	403
Wage and salary audits	407
Taking action	410
Summary	412

28 Budgetary Control of Salaries and Wages
Anthony G Hopwood

	415
The technical framework of budgeting	416
Using budgets as targets	419
Managerial uses of budget reports	422
The way ahead	425

29 Survey of Sources of Information
Anthony Barry

	429
Official statistics	429
Pay agreements	432
Surveys	432
Comparability—the CSPRU	435
Other sources	435

Index 439

Illustrations

Tables

3.1	Changes in proportions receiving payment by results 1974–80	20
3.2	Extent of coverage of different types of incentive schemes in 1977	24
4.1	Bargaining structure in the private and public sectors. Males, 1978	45
4.2	Differentials in gross weekly earnings of covered over non-covered workers, by agreement types, 1978	50
8.1	Example of discriminatory job factors	94
8.2	Example of less-biased job evaluation factors	95
8.3	Example of discriminatory factor weighting	97
10.1	Percentage of wage-earners paid under systems of payments by results, 1938–79	126
10.2	Domestic billing and collection of water charges	128
10.3	Comparison of costs for alternative staffing levels	129
10.4	Investment decisions—reprographics	130
10.5	Typical added value calculation	136
10.6	Resource productivity and measurement	139
12.1	Key events in comparability	165
14.1	Analysis of 452 salaries	188
15.1	Percentage usage of different types of performance appraisal and review schemes	203
15.2	Weights applied to factors	205
15.3	Example of employee's overall rating	206

22.1	Simple example of an added value bonus scheme calculation	331
22.2	An alternative added value bonus scheme calculation	332
22.3	Simple example of a Scanlon plan calculation	333
22.4	Scanlon plan standard ratio—basic calculation fiscal 1978	340
22.5	Calculations (October 1978–March 1979)	341

Figures

3.1	Influences on the instability of differentials	27
4.1	Centralisation of union-management structure related to level of bargaining	47
5.1	A model showing behaviour patterns and the factors influencing behaviour in a garment factory	57
7.1	Evaluating total rate for any job	81
7.2	Scattergram	86
9.1	Process chart symbols	110
9.2	Multiple activity chart	111
9.3	Critical examination technique	111
10.1	Inputs and outputs which may be constituents of a productivity measure	121
10.2	Areas of activity which could contribute to improved company performance	132
10.3	Interrelated factors which influence productivity	133
10.4	Organizing a company for productivity improvement	142
11.1	Scattergram to show relationship between present rates of basic pay and job scores	149
11.2	Line of best fit applied to scattergram	150
11.3	Pay grade boundaries on scattergram	151
11.4	Payment for points scheme	151
11.5	Scattergram showing the relationship between job ranks and present pay	152
11.6	Distribution of work performance related to earnings	155
11.7	Graph showing specified wage/performance relationship	155
11.8	Rationalized pay structure	156
11.9	Rates of pay following introduction of measured daywork	156
13.1	Continuum of strategies for bargaining	174
13.2	Emphases for a negotiating strategy	176
13.3	Scheme for analyzing tactics	181
13.4	Matrix for discussing tactics	182
13.5	Scheme for considering concessions	182

14.1	Pay scales: decision where to set mid-point, maximum, and minimum lines	190
14.2	Pay scales superimposed over the scattergram of actual earnings	190
14.3	Enlarged pay scales superimposed over scattergram of actual earnings to try and encompass all jobs within the boundaries of the pay scales	191
14.4	Constructing salary bands	192
14.5	Methods of salary progression	193
14.6	Another form of linear increments	194
14.7	Salary band graded according to performance	194
14.8	Increments graded according to performance	195
15.1	Extract from a rating form	205
15.2	Review of present performance	211
15.3	Assessment of present performance	212
15.4	Overall performance rating	213
15.5	Overall performance appraisal and rater's general comments	213
15.6	Example of a form used in an 'open' scheme	218
15.7	Concluding section of performance appraisal and review document	219
15.8	Factors for managerial success	222
15.9	Methods used in the identification of management potential (N=236)	224
15.10	Use of psychological tests	225
15.11	Bell's grid for results of assessment tests	228
16.1	Relationship between numbering pattern, step value and percentage increase (copyright HAY–MSL 1974)	237
16.2	Hay guide-chart for evaluating know-how	240–1
16.3	Hay guide-chart for evaluating problem solving	242–3
16.4	Hay guide-chart for evaluating accountability	244–5
16.5	Scattergram of actual base salaries plotted against job units showing line of central tendency	246
17.1	Who should be included in the scheme?	253
17.2	Whose performance to use as the basis?	254
17.3	What kind of performance measurement?	256
17.4	What form of incentive payment?	257
17.5	Using graphs to show incentive relationships	261
18.1	Key choices for salaried staff remuneration schemes	267
18.2	Build-up of remuneration preference analysis	274
18.3	Factors affecting the promotion resources available	279
18.4	Commonly occurring promotion situation	280
19.1	Simplest form of PBR–straight piecework	286
19.2	Flat day rate	286
19.3	Superimposition of straight piecework and flat day rate curves to find fair day's rate of pay	287

19.4	Effort rating scales	287
19.5	The form of bargain in terms of personal abilities and bonus opportunity	288
19.6	Distortion of presumed relationship between effort and reward—ie wages drift	288
19.7	Basic steps in establishing a time study standard	293
19.8	Geared bonus system	294
19.9	Unit cost curves	294
19.10	Example of a layout of a successful PBR scheme	295
20.1	Main types of payment by results by time studies	298
22.1	Common output and input measures	327
22.2	Comparison of main productivity measures	328
23.1	Hourly earnings (averaged over 6 weeks) of female staff (in pence per hour)	354
23.2	Average hours worked per week	355
23.3	Assessment of suitability of different proportions of incentive pay	357
23.4	Reject rates in the factory before and after the change in the payment system	361
23.5	Garments manufactured per week before and after the change in the payment system	362
26.1	Limits on pensions	391
26.2	Limits on lump sums	392
26.3	Limits on death benefits	392
27.1	Pay data from assembly department	401
27.2	Pay and operational data from assembly department	401
28.1	How the under-estimation of fixed costs results in budget bias	419
28.2	Relationship between degree of budget difficulty and task performance	420
28.3	Relationship between degree of budget difficulty and task performance when the budget is used in a punitive manner	422

Acknowledgements

Grateful thanks are due to the people who helped prepare this second edition: to the new authors and those who updated their chapters; to Marianne Campbell and Betty McFarlane, who kept the typing under control; and especially to Lawson Savery and Christine Reid for all their work on the literature for this edition.

Notes on Contributors

Angela M. Bowey (Editor and author of chapters: 1, 3, 5, 8, 12, 22 and 23) is Professor of Industrial Relations at the Strathclyde Business School, University of Strathclyde. She is also a member of the Scottish Economic Council, a part-time Commissioner on the Equal Opportunities Commission, arbitrator for ACAS, Director of the Pay and Rewards Research Centre at Strathclyde Business School, and Editor of *Management Decision*. Previous posts include technical assistant (mathematics) working on the design of nuclear power stations; assistant lecturer in sociology at Elizabeth Gaskell College of Education; researcher and later lecturer on the Manchester Business School staff. Professor Bowey has advised numerous companies on wage and salary administration and written several books and many articles, including: *Job and Pay Comparisons*, co-authored with Tom Lupton, Gower, 1973; *A Guide to Manpower Planning*, Macmillan Press, 1974 and 2nd edition 1977; *Wages and Salaries*, co-authored with Tom Lupton, Gower, 2nd edition 1982; and *The Sociology of Organisations: Case Study Analysis*, Hodder and Stoughton, 1976.

Tom Lupton (Advisory Editor and author of The Social context of work) is Director and Professor of Organizational Behaviour at Manchester Business School. Previous posts include Head of the Department of Industrial Administration at Birmingham CAT (now Aston University) and Montague Burton Professor of Industrial Relations at the University of Leeds. Professor Lupton has written several books including *Job and Pay Comparisons*, Gower 1973, and *Wages and Salaries* (Gower, 2nd edition 1982) both co-authored by Angela Bowey. He is a consultant to several companies.

Anthony Barry (Survey of sources of information) is an industrial journalist and a former Editor of *Incomes Data Services*, a fortnightly publication covering collective bargaining and industrial relations law. He has worked on the editorial staff of several publications, including *Business Management, Times Review of Industry* and *The Engineer*, and as Editor of *Personnel Management*. Mr Barry holds a Bachelors degree in Economics and Modern History and has written numerous articles in various management journals.

David Birchall (Job design and work organisation), is Director of Graduate Studies at Henley, The Management College. He obtained a PhD for a study of the relationship between job attributes and employee attitudes. He has been a Senior Research Fellow in the Henley Work Research Group since 1974 and undertaken action research into both mass production and office settings. His recent publications include *Tomorrow's Office Today—Managing Technological Change*, Business Books, 1981.

J. Butterworth (Techniques of job evaluation; Relating wages to job evaluation and to work measurement) is Professor and Head of the Department of Management Studies at the University of Leeds. Prior to this he was Senior Lecturer and Director of Post-Graduate Studies at The University of Manchester Institute of Science and Technology. Mr. Butterworth has acted as a consultant to a large number of organizations in the public and private sector and is author of *Productivity Now*, Pergamon Press, 1968.

David Cameron (Performance appraisal and review) is Reader in Organisational Behaviour and Deputy Convener of Research at Strathclyde Business School. Before joining Strathclyde University, Dr Cameron gained considerable experience in industry as a personnel manager, works manager and general manager. Formerly in charge of the Business School's MBA Programme, he is a Fellow of the Institute of Personnel Management and a Member of the British Institute of Management. He undertakes consultancy in the United Kingdom and overseas.

Notes on Contributors

Richard Cockman (Employee benefits for managers and executives; Employee benefits for non-managerial staff) is Managing Director of Cockman, Copeman and Partners Limited, consultants in financial incentives and employee benefits. Prior to this he was General Manager with Business Intelligence Services Management Advisory Service, after a period as Marketing Executive with Phillips Petroleum Products. Mr. Cockman has contributed various articles on share schemes and employee motivation to newspapers, and financial and trade magazines.

Andrew Gottschalk (The strategy and tactics of bargaining) is Lecturer in Industrial Relations at the London Business School and visiting Professor in Industrial Relations to the European Institute of Business Administration (INSEAD, France). He is manpower adviser to Continental London Ltd and his many publications include *Bargaining for Change,* George Allen and Unwin, 1974 and articles in management journals on negotiating and industrial relations.

Dan Gowler (Status, effort and reward) is University Lecturer in Management Studies (Organisational Behaviour) and Fellow of the Oxford Centre for management studies. Mr. Gowler read Economics and Social Anthropology at Cambridge on a mature student state scholarship, having previously spent fifteen years in industry, most of this time employed by an oil company. He is joint editor with Karen Legge of *Managerial Stress,* Gower, 1975 as well as many other books and articles on a range of subjects including the supply and mobility of labour, wage payment systems and job satisfaction.

Sally Haslam (Bonuses based on company performance) is a Research Assistant in Organisational Behaviour at the Manchester Business School. She spent some time working in personnel management. She holds a degree in Business Studies and a Masters degree in Manpower Studies. Her present work involves action research in the areas of wage payment systems and labour turnover.

Anthony G. Hopwood (Budgetary control of salaries and wages) is the Institute of Chartered Accountants Professor of Accounting and Financial Reporting at the London Graduate School of Business Studies and Professor of Management at the European Institute for Advanced Studies in Management, Brussels. Educated at the London School of Economics and the University of Chicago, he has also served on the staff of the Manchester Business School and the Oxford Centre for Management Studies. Professor Hopwood is the author of *An Accounting*

System and Managerial Behaviour, 1973 and *Accounting and Human Behaviour*, 1974, and numerous articles in professional and research journals; he also serves as Editor-in-Chief of the international research journal *Accounting, Organizations and Society*. In 1981 Professor Hopwood served as the American Accounting Association Distinguished International Visiting Professor at various institutes in the USA. In addition to his research interests, he also works as a financial and management consultant to a number of major British and European enterprises.

Karen Legge (Status, effort and reward) is Senior Lecturer in the Department of Social and Economic Studies at the Imperial College of Science and Technology, and Joint Editor of *Personnel Review* and the *Journal of Management Studies*. She has carried out intensive field studies on wage payment systems, labour turnover, personnel management and the evaluation of change. Her publications include joint editorship with Enid Mumford of *Designing Organisations for Satisfaction and Efficiency*, Gower, 1978; joint editorship with Dan Gowler of *Managerial Stress*, Gower, 1975, and *Power, Innovation and Problem Solving in Personnel Management*, McGraw Hill, 1978, as well as many articles and essays in the areas of labour economics and industrial sociology with particular reference to the operation of reward systems and internal labour markets and the evaluation of planned organisational change.

The late *John F. Percival* (Operating, developing and adjusting reward systems) was Principal Consultant with P-E Consulting Group Limited where he worked for eighteen years. Prior to this he worked with a domestic appliance manufacturer as a Graduate Apprentice. Mr. Percival held a Masters degree, was a Civil Engineer, a Fellow of the Institution of Production Engineers, and a Member of the British Institute of Management and of the Institute of Management Consultants. He was author of several articles in various journals and magazines. It was with sadness that we learned of his death after he had prepared his chapter for this book.

Michael Pilch (Company pension schemes) is a Director of Noble Lowndes and Partners Limited. He holds a Bachelor of Arts degree, is a Fellow of the Chartered Insurance Institute and the Pensions Management Institute, and Vice-President of the National Association of Pension Funds. He is co-author, with Victor Wood, of *Pension Schemes*, Gower, 1979, and a number of other works on pensions and retirement.

Lawson K. Savery (Salary bands and salary progression curves) is a lecturer in Industrial Relations and Personnel at the Western Australian Institute of Technology. Dr. Savery studied for his doctorate in Economics at the University of Western Australia after obtaining his Master's degree in Industrial Administration from the University of Aston in Birmingham. He spent many years in industry from student apprentice in a foundry to works manager at a fastener producing plant. Dr. Savery is a Chartered Engineer, a Member of the Institute of Production Engineers and is on the Western Australian Industrial Relations Society Committee. He has written several papers on industrial relations and has worked as a consultant in personnel and organisational development and has lectured on these subjects to many organisations in Western Australia.

Anne G. Shaw (Payment by time systems) is Life President, having recently resigned her chairmanship of, The Anne Shaw Organisation Limited. After graduating from Edinburgh University she was awarded the Scholarship for European Women at Bryn Mawr, USA, where she obtained a post-graduate Social Economy Certificate. Having spent two years in the USA as Personal Assistant to Gilbreth Incorporated Management Consultants, she returned to England as Chief Supervisor of women, and Motion Study Investigator at Metropolitan Vickers. Miss Shaw is a Fellow of the Institution of Production Engineers and has been President of the Institute of Personnel Management, Chairman of the Management Consultants Association and a Member of the Lord Robens Committee on Safety and Health at Work.

D. Shaw Pirie (Payment by time systems) was until recently Managing Director of The Anne Shaw Organisation Limited. After graduating from Glasgow University with a first degree in Mechanical Engineering he joined the Anne Shaw Organisation as a Management Consultant. He then moved to the Graduate School of Business Administration at the University of California to study behavioural training and then to Harvard University, specializing in management development. On his return to England he became Director and Company Secretary of the Anne Shaw Organisation. Mr. Shaw Pirie is a Member of the Institution of Mechanical Engineers and of the Institution of Production Engineers. He is currently sailing his boat around the world.

Andrew Thomson (The structure of collective bargaining in Britain) is Professor of Business Policy at Glasgow University. He was educated at Oxford and Cornell Universities and spent five years with Lever Brothers as a Brand Manager. He came to Glasgow in 1968 as Lecturer in Applied Economics and was appointed to the Chair of Business Policy in 1978. Professor Thomson has published books on grievance procedures, labour law and public sector bargaining and has a major interest in wage and bargaining structures. He has twice been visiting professor at the University of Chicago Graduate School of Business.

Richard Thorpe (Government policy and payment systems and Productivity measurement) is a teaching company Fellow, lecturing at Glasgow University in the Department of Management Studies. He gained his interest in incentive schemes as a work study practitioner devising and installing incentive schemes in a public sector organization, and later as Factory Manager in a small manufacturing company in the Scottish highlands. Prior to moving to his present post, Richard Thorpe worked as Research Fellow at the Pay and Reward Research Centre at Strathclyde University.

Patrick Walker (Sex discrimination and job evaluation) is Principal of the employment section of the Equal Opportunities Commission. This section is responsible for producing guidance notes on all aspects of employment including codes of practice from the Commission. He commenced work in the textile industry in 1954 and trained as a Work Study Officer. He was appointed District Secretary of the former Amalgamated Weavers Association at 25 years of age, and became Industrial Assistant at Head Office prior to being appointed Assistant General Secretary of the Amalgamated Textile Workers' Union in 1974. He was a Member of the Industrial Training Board, The Narrow Fabrics General Industrial Council, The Industrial Economic Development Council, The NEDO Joint Textile Committee, and The Industrial Research Council. He also served on many T.U.C. Committees. He was responsible for initiating a number of job evaluation schemes in the textile industry prior to joining the Equal Opportunities Commission in January 1980.

G. H. Webb (Payment by results systems) is Director of Research with the Engineering Employers' Federation. He gained experience in industry, as a designer, consulting engineer, production manager and management consultant. Mr. Webb is a Member of the British Institute of Management, of the Institution of Mechanical Engineers, the

Institution of Production Engineers, the Institution of Works Managers, and the Institute of Personnel Management.

Michael White (Incentive bonus schemes for managers and Selecting a salary system) is a Senior Research Fellow at the Policy Studies Institute. He worked in industry in the 1960s and then in management research at the Oxford Centre for Management Studies, and at Ashridge Management College. He joined the Policy Studies Institute in 1979. He holds a degree in Psychology from London University and a doctorate in Organizational Behaviour from Lancaster University. His publications include five books and numerous articles for management journals.

Fiona Wilson (Bonuses based on company performance) is a Research Assistant in Organizational Behaviour at the Manchester Business School. She gained a degree in Psychology and Sociology from Leeds University and then a Masters Degree in Organization Studies from the same university. Before her appointment at MBS, she worked in the steel industry mainly in industrial relations. She is presently involved in action research in companies.

E. G. Wood (Work study, method study and work measurement) is the Director of the Centre for Innovation and Productivity at Sheffield City Polytechnic. He has had considerable experience in industry and in management consultancy in a wide variety of companies. Mr. Wood holds a Bachelor of Commerce degree, and is a Fellow of the British Institute of Management and a Member of the Institute of Management Consultants. He is the author of several books including *Bigger Profits for the Smaller Firm, Costing Matters for Managers and Added Value – The Key to Prosperity* (Business Books) and has written many articles for management journals.

W. F. Younger (The Hay Guide-chart profile method) is Chairman of Hay-MSL Limited, Chairman of Hay Communications, Chairman of MSL Group International Limited and a general partner of Edward N. Hay Associates. He is also Chairman of Kalamazoo Limited. He worked in the personnel field in the zinc and tobacco industries before moving into management consultancy. Mr. Younger has a first degree in Commerce, is a Companion of the Institute of Personnel Management and a Member of the Institute of Management Consultants. He is a past Vice-President of the Institute of Personnel Management and is a Member of the Institute's National Committee on Pay and Conditions of Employment. Mr. Younger has written various articles for magazines and newspapers.

Part One

The Context of Wages and Salaries

Editor's Introduction

The field of wage and salary administration contains many facets, and difficulties are sometimes experienced in linking these together. The first of the five chapters in this section considers the inter-relationships between such activities as job evaluation, job comparison, work study, merit appraisal and others in order to provide a framework for the chapters in other sections. The second chapter examines the links between procedures for wage and salary administration and the social context of work. For example, how do the experiences, home background, wider social relationships and other features of the social context impinge on behaviour at work, and thereby on the operation of wage and salary systems?

Chapter 3 considers the political context within which wages and salaries are set, and in particular looks at the effects of government policy in the incomes field on the jobs of wage and salary administrators.

Another major contextual influence on pay is the structure of collective bargaining whereby pay is negotiated. Chapter 4 considers the framework of bargaining structure in Britain, and the effects of multi-employer, single employer, company level and plant level negotiation.

When changes are made in salary or wage systems, and particularly when new systems are introduced, special attention needs to be paid to the context into which the changes are to be introduced. In the fifth chapter the results of experiences of introducing these kinds of changes in many companies is condensed into some guidelines which have been shown to be effective if applied in the right way and in the right circumstances.

1
Facets of Wage and Salary Administration

Angela M Bowey

Aims of this Handbook

Wage and salary administration is complex and subtle, and littered with techniques designed to reduce the complexity for the administrator and cope with the subtleties. This handbook brings together descriptions of the most important techniques that are available for coping with the major tasks of the wage and salary administrator, and shows how and when these may be used.

One of the biggest difficulties in the past has been the tendency for each proponent of a technique to make the claim that their method will solve the problems of all organizations. Hence, incentive payment schemes, measured daywork, management by objectives, etc, have at times been sold as the answer to everyone's difficulties. This leaves the salary and wage administrator with very little guidance as to which will be most effective in his organization.

Research has shown that the nature of the situation into which a technique is installed has a very large effect on the results obtained. This handbook attempts to point out the kinds of situation for which each technique is most suitable, or at least the changes which would need to be made to a situation to make it suitable for that technique. Where the latter approach has been taken, the reader should take care that the changes suggested would not cause difficulties for other areas or objectives of his organization.

There are so many techniques, designed to cope with a number of closely interrelated facets of wage and salary administration, that it may be useful to begin by describing what those facets are and precisely how they interrelate; and also to point out where each technique fits into this overall framework.

Sections 2–6 deal with different aspects of the wage or salary scheme itself, and the activities which may need to be performed in order to operate it.

Work Assessment and Job Design

There are many systems of payment which attempt to relate earnings to the work done. But before any such system can be used it is necessary to assess that work in some way. This can be done either by comparing the nature of the work (eg Is it heavy work? Does it carry a large amount of responsibility?) with the work done in other jobs in the organization to produce a hierarchy of jobs to which different pay levels are then attached; or by assessing the rate at which the employees are working and rewarding them at different rates corresponding to their different rates of working. The first method involves job evaluation; the second involves work measurement. In many organizations both techniques are used to produce a hierarchy of basic payment levels with varying performance-related bonuses in addition.

A closely related activity to work measurement, which often includes the study of methods of working, is job design. Research has suggested that alternative principles of job design are appropriate in different circumstances. The types of job-design principles currently in use are job rationalization (ie the reduction and simplification of human tasks by the introduction of more sophisticated and automated machinery); horizontal job enlargement (ie increasing the number of tasks which form part of an individual's job); vertical job enrichment (ie increasing the employee's responsibility for planning, control, etc); and autonomous group development (ie creating unsupervised teams of employees with responsibility for coordinating themselves). Each of these has different implications for the type of reward system which would be appropriate and for this reason job design should be considered in conjunction with reward system design.

Payment Levels

Once the jobs have been assessed, sums of money must be allocated to each job. There are three different considerations here. First, the mechanics of assigning different amounts of money to different positions in the jobs hierarchy and to different standards of performance.

Second, consideration of the absolute levels of pay which should be given when pay in other organizations is taken into account. Third, the process of negotiation between the management and the union about levels of payment.

The technicalities involved in converting job-evaluated rankings into differences in payment levels vary according to which system of evaluation has been used. Most of the procedures involve drawing scatter diagrams of present payment levels plotted against evaluated positions, and from this a 'best-fit' line may be sought for relating pay under the job evaluated scheme to the scores from the evaluation. These scores may take the form of an assignment to a grade, a total number of points, a rank order position or, in some unusual cases, an actual sum of money. In each case, some jobs are likely to be currently paid more than the scheme recommends, and others less. It is usual to raise the pay of those who are indicated as underpaid, possibly in a number of steps if a large sum is involved; and to hold steady the pay of those indicated as currently overpaid, until their position relative to other jobs has been put right. There are obvious difficulties here in relation to the motivation of those employees, and increases will occur in the total earnings bill for some years even if the employer is successful in holding back the pay of the overpaid. Because of these problems and others which have been discussed at length elsewhere (Lupton and Bowey, 1974) job evaluation should only be introduced into situations where it is necessary, and not simply because it is used in other organizations.

There are also complexities involved in converting the results of work measurement or work study (where these are used) into sums of money. The timings obtained (or sometimes, where direct observation is not used, the predetermined times) must be converted into allowed times for the work, incorporating allowances for recovering from fatigue, visits to the toilet, drinking beverages, contingencies which may arise to hold up the work, etc. These figures must in turn be related to an increasing scale of payment corresponding to increasing rates of working. In some cases further refinements may be added to take into account jobs on which the individual can only affect his performance for part of the time, eg the man who feeds and unloads a machine, but has little to do whilst it is running and no control over its rate of operation. In these cases 'process allowance' payments are often made as a means of compensating for the limited opportunities to earn bonus payments. Successes with 'process allowance' payments have been very limited and such schemes should be regarded with caution.

Both the allocation of different pay levels corresponding to the job evaluation procedure and the determination of the way the bonus scheme will operate if there is one, beg the question of what the absolute level of pay should be. Some guidance on this can be obtained by looking to the payments made to similar operatives in other companies, and there is a precise procedure which can be used where it is thought desirable to make accurate comparisons. Collective bargaining is a major determinant of the absolute levels of pay, as it is here that the expectations of employees and of managers are brought into line, and the differences narrowed until some figure which is accepted by both parties is arrived at.

Designing a Payment System

When wage payment systems are being designed there are a number of major principles on which certain well-known types of payment system are based. These are payment by results systems, payment by time systems (such as measured daywork), and company-wide incentive systems (eg the Scanlon plan, added value plan or certain other types of productivity bargaining). In addition, there are rewards for status which are frequently overlooked in the literature (payments for skills, responsibility, qualifications, experience, social 'standing' in the community, etc). There are also techniques which can be used for deciding which type of payment system is appropriate to a particular situation.

The design and administration of salary systems usually involves different procedures. Work study is not a method that is normally applied to salaried employees, although it is often thought desirable to try to motivate them to perform their jobs better. Management by objectives and merit appraisal are two techniques that are commonly used to try to achieve this aim. With management by objectives, the employee and his superior agree a set of objectives for the coming year, and the individual is given a salary increase at the end of the year which is partly determined by how well he has succeeded in achieving those targets. Variations of the technique, eg shorter review periods and group-targets rather than individual ones, have been developed to try to overcome some of the difficulties experienced with such schemes. Merit appraisal techniques are similar but less formal, and the setting of targets is not usually part of the scheme. Each salaried employee under such a scheme, is reviewed annually and advised about his progress during the year. Training needs may then be pin-pointed, and promotable individuals identified. Sometimes salary increases are based on the appraisal, and sometimes not.

This kind of activity is closely akin to the task of identifying the potential for further development and promotion of the individuals in the organization, a task which needs to be closely coordinated with any manpower planning activities which are occurring within the organization.

When a salary system is being designed, there are a number of decisions to be made about its characteristics. The first is whether there should be bands in the total salary range paid, such that the people in a particular grade are all paid somewhere within the appropriate band, depending on individual merit. If so, how many bands, and should they overlap one another or not? The second is whether there should be salary progression curves, which will determine the rates at which individuals are given increases in salary to progress them through the bands. And should these be straight lines or geared; should there be more than one curve so that the most able employees can progress faster than others; should there be bars to progression beyond which an individual cannot advance without satisfying some specified criteria?

The other questions to be considered are whether some form of job evaluation procedure should be used for ranking the salaried jobs; and whether some form of motivator should be incorporated into the salary system in order to encourage high performances?

Whether one is considering a salary system or a wage system, the administrator will need to pay attention to the benefits which employees receive in addition to their wage or salary—in particular their pension rights and fringe benefits. What alternative types of pension benefits are there? How do they affect the employee? How might they be funded and administered? What impact do fringe benefits have on employees, and how can the company be sure that the benefits it gives are valued by their employees?

Other Considerations

Finally, there are matters to be considered which do not necessarily involve changes in a wage or salary system. There are the problems of coping with an existing payment system, of ensuring that minor changes which become necessary are made and that the payment system remains reasonably well coordinated with the other control procedures in operation in the organization. Changes in government policy towards incomes will also need to be taken into account in monitoring the system, along with changes in the EEC and in Europe which may eventually affect what happens in this country. The company may desire to have an overall wage or salary policy, and this too, may require careful consideration on the part of the salary and wage administrator.

These are the kinds of questions and issues which are considered in this handbook, and advice is offered from people who are specialists on the particular topics they have covered.

References and Further Reading

ACAS *Advisory Booklet no 2: Introduction to Payment Systems*, ACAS, London, 1980.

Bowey, A. M., 'Tailor-made payment systems and employee motivation', *Management Decision*, Spring, 1972.

Compensation Review—a quarterly journal produced by the American Management Association.

Lupton, Tom, and Bowey, A. M., *Wages and salaries*, Penguin, Harmondsworth, 1974 (revised 2nd edition, Gower 1982 forthcoming).

Wood, A., *A Theory of Pay*, Cambridge University Press, 1978.

2

The Social Context of Work

Tom Lupton

Conflicts frequently occur as a result of the working of pay systems and pay structures; and they are of three, related kinds:

1. Conflicts about *rules*.
2. Conflicts about *procedures*.
3. Conflicts about *outcomes*, when the rules and procedures are practised.

These conflicts and their origins will be examined in more detail below. First, it is necessary to define rules, procedures and outcomes as they relate to pay structures and pay systems. From this discussion the influence of the social context on the design and administration of pay arrangements will become apparent.

Pay Systems

The *rules* of a pay system say how effort (energy expended or skill applied, for example) is to be related to reward (pay or perquisites). The rules of a *simple piecework system* might, for example, state that for every component completed to a given standard of quality the reward to the operative is 33p. *Incentive bonus schemes* have more complicated rules. Here is a typical example:

> Every increment of measured performance between 100 and 133 performance points will be paid at the rate of 14.573p per point.

Performances above 133 will be paid at a rate of 15.35p per point, up to 140, when bonus ceases to be paid at all.[1]

Measured daywork schemes have similar rules, specifying the measured performance which must be regularly maintained by the operative in return for the rate for his or her grade of work. In this case, the rules will also say what the penalties are for falling short of the (contracted) performance standard.[2]

The *procedures* of a pay system say how the rules are to be administered. To ensure that an operative is, in fact, paid 33p for every completed component in a piecework system, completed work must be recorded systematically. The record will usually be checked by management to make sure that no more than the correct number of 33p's are paid out.

Procedures for reporting faulty materials, tools that will not work etc are common. These ensure that the allowances specified in the rules are correctly calculated and paid to the operative. The procedures may also require that the reporting be done at certain times by certain people.

The outcomes of the application of the rules via the procedures could be that bonus earnings are bigger (or smaller) than they were expected to be (or than some people desired) or that performances are better (or worse) than expected, or than some people or groups might have desired.

Dissatisfaction with a pay system usually starts when the outcomes are thought by someone to be undesirable; it quickly shifts to a consideration of the procedures and rules, which may then be altered with different (desirable) outcomes in mind.

Later in this chapter I shall enquire how it is that the rules which govern pay systems, the way that they are arrived at, and the processes by which they are distorted or are deliberately changed, in practice, reflect, and are linked to, the social context. First, however, I wish to consider the rules, procedures and outcomes of *pay structures*.

The *rules* of a pay structure might say, for example, what combinations of scores on a number of factors such as skill and physical effort, or what particular characteristics, such as time span of discretion, or quality of decisions made, will qualify a job for a particular pay grade.[3] In a particular case it might turn out, on detailed inspection, that the job, 'fitter's mate', needs little skill, demands few responsibilities, and little physical effort, so it is placed in Grade 4 along with jobs that have similar 'scores' on these factors.

The job, 'instrument technician', would probably score high on 'responsibility', 'discretion' and such like, and for that reason be placed in a higher grade than the job, 'fitter's mate'. The rules of a pay structure simply say how many grades there are to be, what the pay will be for each grade, and what the criteria are for placing a job in a grade.

The *procedures* of a pay structure will always include directions to be followed when the jobs are changed, or when, because technical arrangements are altered, individuals are asked to transfer to different jobs. For example, although the rules governing the rate for a job in its grade may remain unchanged, an individual moving from a higher-graded to a lower-graded job may qualify for his previous rate for, say, six weeks after the transfer.

As with pay systems, dissatisfaction starts with *outcomes*. Managers might think that too much 'grade drift' has occurred—that is, the population in higher-paid grades has increased unduly, as a result of transfers, and too many persons in lower grades are in receipt of 'temporary' higher pay for the same reason. The remedy suggested might be to alter the rules for evaluating the jobs, or the procedures governing transfers.

Conflicts about Outcomes—and the Social Context

Here are some examples of conflicts about outcomes which are commonly observed.

1. In a measured daywork scheme managers complain that operatives are not performing as they contracted to perform in return for the regular pay for the grade. The operatives, for their part, argue that, because of shortcomings in production administration, they are unable to reach contracted performance and/or that it is unreasonable to expect them to do so in the circumstances.

In this case, there are a number of aspects of the social context which exert influence. In the first place, the duty to keep contracts once they have been agreed, which is learned during the individual's schooling and family experience, is invoked both by operatives and managers.[4] Both parties also invoke the notion that, if the conditions under which a contract is made change in such a way as to place either party at a disadvantage then the contract should be rewritten.

In the second place, the measured daywork contract is uneven. Managers deploy sanctions for breach of the contract—for example, disciplinary action and subsequent dismissal—which are more powerful than those deployed by workers. To be sure, unions can help workers to equalize the power, but unions cannot monitor every detail of the contract every minute of the day on the factory floor. Managers have more opportunities to do that. Many of the problems associated with measured daywork arise from unevenness in the power to exert sanctions for breach of the contract that relates effort and reward. This unevenness resides in the relationship of the parties to ownership of the plant, the machinery and other tools, and in the legal powers that ownership confers—a very significant aspect of social context.

2   In an incentive bonus system managers complain that workers do not seem to be responding well to the opportunities for extra pay that the system offers for greater effort. Workers point out that the extra pay is not enough to reward them adequately for the extra effort to be exerted.

It could turn out, on examination, that in this case the rules specify that every increment of extra effort above a certain performance level is paid at a progressively diminishing rate. It might also turn out that the proportion of incentive pay in the total earnings of workers is low, so that the increments add little to total pay. It may be that workers just feel that the standards set (or proposed) by work-study engineers are difficult to achieve and that any attempt to push beyond standard is very difficult and, for the pay, hardly worth striving for.

There are two contrasting views of the effort-reward bargain here. The view of the managers (sometimes labelled the 'logic of efficiency') is that they have to protect themselves from the consequences of their own errors of commission or omission, in such a way as to prevent workers from exploiting 'loose' performance standards to make large earnings for little effort. This is expressed in the 'geared' bonus curve. The low proportion of 'bonus earnings' in total earnings is designed as a further safeguard. The logic of efficiency says that managers must exert control to ensure that workers exert effort commensurate with the money rewards they receive, and to prevent them from getting as much as they can for as little effort as they can get away with (managers often assume that workers behave in this way). This logic of efficiency combines 'getting a fair day's pay for a fair day's work' (which is a moral aim), being efficient by controlling costs (which is an economic aim), and developing a good design for control (which is a 'professional aim').

The workers are probably guided in their own behaviour by a different concept of the effort-reward bargains. In their view, perhaps, the effort specified or proposed by management (or agreed between management and union officials) may be thought to give inadequate allowance for shortcomings which the workers cannot, are not permitted, or perhaps do not wish, to remedy. Workers may also regard the specific effort levels as leaving little allowance for enjoying the social interactions with workmates which help make bearable what might otherwise be a dull and repetitive existence.

Other interpretations could be put on this case. The reader who tries one of his own will find that he cannot avoid explaining why there should be differences in the way various groups interpret the effort-reward bargain. Inevitably, he will have to turn to such factors as social class, education, occupation, economic level, social aspirations, political ideas, family background and age, and also influences such as technology, supervisory structure and the design of managerial control systems, which help shape relationships on the job.

The practical resolution of the problem again lies in the design of the rules and procedures, and it seems to go without saying that a set of acceptable procedures would have to take account of these factors. For example, the rule governing the gearing of the 'bonus slope' might be changed, and the rules governing payment for time spent waiting, and the procedures for arriving at standards of performance. Any designer of payment systems would do well before making changes to take full account of those aspects of social context mentioned above. Later chapters in this book give examples of how this might be done.[5]

It might be enlightening to think of a pay system as embodying certain assumptions about the social context in its rules and procedures rather than to think of it as some separate device having a social context that influences it. Whether a payment system works well or not—that is, whether it fulfils the aims of its designers, and satisfies those whose performance it is set up to influence—will surely hinge on how accurately its rules and procedures reflect the values, preferences and expectations of the participants, be they workers, managers, work-study engineers or inspectors. Conflicts will inevitably arise in the process of designing and operating a pay system because of differences arising from social class position, previous education, the demands of the educational role, and the age, sex and family status of these participants. The rules and procedures must take account of such differences.

The pay system is also a device for handling some of the conflicts, since it can be seen as a means of offering compensation for some of the satisfactions than an individual might expect from a job but which the job itself cannot provide, as for example, in repetitive, short-cycle, manual operations.

Pay Structures (Conflicts about Outcomes)

These general considerations also apply to pay structures. However, the rules and procedures of a pay structure reflect a different range of social values and expectations, not values about effort and what will release it, but values about the relative worth (expressed in cash) of different occupations. There can, of course, be much conflict about this, as the following example shows.

3   One outcome of a careful study carried out jointly by a manage-

ment/union team concluded that three jobs A, B and C each carried out by groups of women in the same workshop should be graded for pay purposes in the rank order C, B, A. This upturned the traditional order causing resentment, especially in groups A and B.

The explanation of the outcome lies in the selection and weighting of the factors used to determine the rank order. Young women were usually recruited for job C, which required agility and energy as well as considerable skill and responsibility for quality. After a few years, these women were 'promoted' to job B which paid more, used much the same skills, but was less physically demanding. If they stayed until middle age, or left to raise children and returned, they were promoted to job A which was a sedentary job demanding less skill.

The criteria used to re-rank the jobs did not include age, and weighted skill, physical effort and responsibility for quality very high. The resentment felt was not just general 'resistance to change' but a reaction to the neglect by the evaluators of strongly held convictions, which the old order embodied, that:

1   The young ought to defer to the old.
2   The young ought to be asked to contribute the energies and skills that their youth endows them with.
3   The young women ought to settle for less cash because they are young and have fewer responsibilities, and because they are not fitted either to carry the responsibility or to spend wisely.

If these were not the convictions held, then how can the persistence of the A, B, C pattern over many years be explained?

It can be seen, therefore, that pay structures and the conflicts they engender, are a reflection of social agreement and disagreement about how jobs should be ranked and rewarded, and they are also devices for attempting to resolve those differences. Proposers of schemes for national pay structures are convinced that there is widespread agreement about the ranking of jobs. So much so they say that we need only evaluate all jobs in terms of some straightforward, accepted criteria to ensure an end to arguments about pay relativities.[6] Similarly, advocates of job evaluation systems of various kinds sometimes make similar claims for their usefulness as preventers of social conflict.[7]

Many of the chapters in this handbook are devoted to practical methods for designing pay systems and pay structures. The expositors of these methods rarely make fully explicit their assumptions about social context. This chapter has been less explicit about the methods and more about the social context. Having explained the links between pay systems, pay structures and social context, it is now time to examine the implications of those for the design and administration of pay systems.

From what has been said so far, it would surely follow that an absolutely necessary first step in the design process would be to ascertain what the expectations, preferences, aspirations etc, are of the various participants to such matters as the effort-reward relation or job ranking. Just as important is to ascertain what some participants (eg workers) perceive the preferences, expectations, etc, of others (eg managers) to be.

It is not enough to accept general statements, like, 'Workers are only interested in money'; 'Managers have only one aim: to get costs down'; 'Everybody accepts that responsible jobs merit higher pay'. Instead, careful enquiries should be made to find out what particular categories of participants in particular situations value and prefer, and to seek evidence about the extent to which these are likely to change. Methods exist to help one discover such values and preferences systematically and they are not particularly difficult to administer.[8] In the absence of these methods, and of people capable of administering them, a 'straw' canvass of experienced people and careful observation are better than nothing as a means of ascertaining what people prefer, and what matters give them concern. What must be avoided at all costs, however, is the making of prior moral judgements about these preferences and concerns. The observer must not make statements such as, 'They ought not to be doing that' or 'That is a bad attitude'. People must and do make judgements, the process is not objectionable but the timing may be. It is the judgements that are made before the facts have been investigated that are hazardous, and often productive of conflict.

I have been referring to the necessity of taking account of social context in the design and redesign of pay systems and pay structures. If I have given the impression that I think of design as a backroom exercise in which clever men, after having taken account of all the relevant information, proclaim their answer to eager participants, nothing could be further from my mind. The design of a pay system or a pay structure is itself a social process—a process involving people in cooperation in pursuit of an aim. Those involved could be exclusively specialists and, properly guided, they could take into account the social context and arrive at a near acceptable design, but it is surely more economical, and more conducive to arriving at a satisfactory and acceptable design, if all the participants or their representatives are involved in the process. This is not a plea for participation for its own sake, but merely an argument that if the job is to set up rules and procedures, and if rules and procedures are to take full account of the social context, then as many aspects of that context as possible should be involved in the process, either by the personal presence of the carriers of values, preferences and concerns or by inputs of information describing those items, or both.[9] The advantage of doing things this way is to reduce the element of surprise (surprise at unanticipated outcomes that is) and also, perhaps, to avoid the difficulty and expense of removing 'eroded' systems every few years, which commonly happens. To make sure of this another element is needed: continuous joint monitoring of rules and procedures.

To sum up, certain rules and procedures of pay systems and pay structures in their social context produce undesirable outcomes. The reason for this is that the rules and procedures do not represent the social context as it is expressed through individual and group preferences and concerns. To the extent that the rules and procedures do represent and continue to represent current preferences and concerns so will the pay system/structure resist erosion. Therefore it is essential that the preferences and concerns are treated as highly significant design parameters. This can best be done by joint information gathering, design and subsequent control; joint in the sense that everyone whose work will be affected will be represented. How this can best be done is best worked out to suit the circumstances of a particular case. It is never easy, and the stringent main requirements for managers who must initiate it and for workers and unions involved are

1 Specialized knowledge of pay systems and structures
2 Skill in working with groups
3 Knowledge of research method
4 Knowledge of the social context as here defined.

At present most firms and unions must rely initially on consultants to bring some or all of these skills in. They would be advised to make sure that they themselves are well trained in them for the future.

Notes

1 For other examples, see Chapter 19.
2 For a fuller discussion of the characteristics of measured daywork, see Chapter 20.
3 These matters are dealt with in detail in Chapter 7.
4 Gowler has discussed the effect on young female operatives' attitudes to a MDW contractual scheme, of their membership of families of fishermen, whose employment conditions are dominated by legally enforceable contracts. (Unpublished paper.)
5 See especially Chapters 5, 7, 17 and 23.
6 For a discussion of this point see Angela Bowey and Tony Eccles 'Relativities, national job evaluation, and collective bargaining', *Journal of Management Studies* February 1975.
7 See Chapter 7 for an example.
8 I refer, of course, to the methods evolved by social scientists. For a useful discussion of these methods see John Madge, *The Tools of Social Science*, Longman.

9 For a more detailed presentation of this argument see T. Lupton, 'Organizational change—top down or bottom-up management', *Personnel Review*, volume 1, number 1 (Autumn 1971). See also Chapter 5.

References and Further Reading

Lupton, Tom, *On the Shop Floor*, Pergamon Press, Oxford, 1963.
Lupton, Tom, and Tanner, Ian., 'A self-regulating pay structure' *Personnel Review*, 1980.
Robinson, D. (Ed.), *Local Labour Markets and Wage Structures*, Gower, London, 1970.
Urry, J., and Wakeford, J. (Eds.), *Power in Britain*, Heinemann, London, 1973.
Warmington, A., Lupton, Tom, and Gribbin, Cecily, *Organisational Behaviour and Performance*, Macmillan, London, 1977, esp. Part II.
White, M., *The Hidden Meaning of Pay Conflict*, Macmillan Press, 1980.

3

Government Policy and Payment Systems

Angela M Bowey and Richard Thorpe

This chapter considers the effects which government policy in relation to incomes over the past decade has had on wage and salary administration at company and local levels.

It considers how the jobs of wage and salary administrators have been affected by the experiences of recent years; the impact on differentials and on wage bargaining; and the effects of a cyclical pattern of incomes policies (on-off, on-off).

A key problem associated with government policies in the pay area is that they are designed at national level with priorities in mind such as controlling inflation, improving the UK position in international trade, maintaining credibility with the international monetary fund, etc. But they can only achieve these objectives through the way in which they affect wage and salary administrators' actions and decisions. And not enough attention has been paid in the past to the way such policies have affected the work of these specialists. This account, which includes the case histories of two very different companies, is an attempt to provide this kind of knowledge and insight.

Three areas of wage and salary administration have been especially affected in recent years. These are the administration of incentive schemes; the administration of differentials; and wage bargaining.

Impact on Incentive Schemes

In view of the labour government's policy of restricting pay increases which were not justified by a self-financing productivity scheme, it is not surprising that there was an increase in the numbers of employees receiving incentive payments between 1974 and 1979. Table 3.1 shows the overall increases for different groups.

Table 3.1

Changes in proportions receiving payment by results
1974–1980

Manual men

	1974 %	1975 %	1976 %	1977 %	1978 %	1979 %	1980 %
In all industries and services	41.4	41.2	37.9	36.8	42.3	44.0	42.3
In manufacturing	43.4	40.9	39.9	39.5	45.0	47.0	45.6
In non-manufacturing	39.2	41.5	36.1	34.3	39.8	41.1	39.4

Non-manual men

	1974 %	1975 %	1976 %	1977 %	1978 %	1979 %	1980 %
In all industries and services	7.9	7.3	7.6	7.2	10.6	12.9	12.0
In manufacturing	8.2	8.5	8.6	7.9	15.3	18.0	19.8
In non-manufacturing	7.7	6.8	7.3	6.9	8.8	11.0	9.0

(Source: New Earnings Surveys)

The figures result from quite different changes occurring within different industries. In several parts of the public sector preparation had been underway for some years to introduce work measured payment by results schemes on a large scale for manual workers. In the health service, coal mining, water authorities and local authorities, for example, decisions had been made (in some cases as far back as the late

1960s) to introduce incentives. Two problems had been identified in the 1960s in certain public sector industries—low pay and poor productivity; and it was hoped that by introducing work measured incentive schemes (which had previously been more common in private sector manufacturing) both of these problems could be partially corrected.

The managers responsible for installing and administering these schemes had varying degrees of faith in their likely effectiveness. There were many who said that productivity was so low in their organization that any scheme which measured effort (however inaccurately) and encouraged employees to work harder, was worth introducing for its initial impact on productivity levels, even though they recognized that because of the nature of the work the scheme would be full of loopholes and open to abuse. A minority held to the view that people are motivated to work better primarily by financial incentives; and a larger minority were opposed to the introduction of these schemes which they believed to be inappropriate to the nature of the work.

An example of the kind of problem involved in the application of work measurement to service sector jobs was the case of workmen digging and then filling in holes in the road. The time allowed for such a job was calculated according to the area and depth of the hole and the kind of ground to be dug. But the teams worked in widely dispersed locations, and it was impossible to have a work study officer or supervisor on hand to examine every hole after it had been dug and before it had been filled in. Reliance had to be placed on the workman's description of how deep and how difficult the hole had been. This is tantamount to asking him how much bonus he thought he should get for it.

But most of these public sector schemes at least had a long gestation and preparation period, and were introduced by people who on the whole believed this was the best way to proceed. Even so, there were some groups for whom hastily drawn up schemes had been rushed in prior to the imposition of an incomes policy on 11 July 1975. For example, one public sector corporation hastily botched up an incentive scheme for craftsmen so as to prevent labourers on bonus earning more than skilled men. The skilled men, who previously had refused on principle to be involved in bonus payments, recognized the danger of being left behind when the new stage of incomes policy came into force, and accepted the scheme.

A different picture emerged in the private sector, especially in manufacturing industries, where there had recently been a steady decline in the use of incentives until August 1977, when Stage III of the Labour Government's incomes policy was introduced. This allowed an overall increase in a company's wage bill of not more than 10%, but allowed extra payments above this level if they arose as a result of a self-financing productivity scheme. This encouraged a swing in favour of incentive payment schemes quite out of line with trends in previous years (see Table 3.1). In the first months of Phase III many schemes were put together hastily and rushed in, as a means of raising pay with little thought for the suitability of the schemes. Between 1977 and 1979 the responses of management audiences at seminars on the subject of self-financing productivity schemes to a question about the main reason for their current interest in introducing a self-financing productivity scheme changed considerably. This was not intended originally as a rigorous study, and the categories of answers offered to between 100 and 150 managers in each of the 3 years were not mutually exclusive. But the increase from 1977 to 1978 in those who expected to derive productivity benefits from the schemes (from 43% to 60%) and the corresponding decrease in those who were merely interested in finding a way to pay their employees more money (from 43% to 26%) indicated a trend towards greater faith in the power of incentive schemes to motivate employees. Also the difference between 1977, when not one person said their main reason for considering incentives was because people were motivated by money, and 1979 when over 30% gave this answer, was striking.

The growth of support for the view that it is right to share the benefits of improved productivity with employees (from 9% in 1977 to 27% in 1979) probably reflected the frequency with which profit sharing and added value sharing schemes were introduced between 1977 and 1979. They had the advantage of being fairly quick and easy to instal, requiring no work study and only limited extra work for managers or administrators of the schemes. Also a number of major consultancy companies and writers drew attention to the successes of companies which had introduced added value schemes years earlier.

The advantages and disadvantages of added value schemes are discussed in Chapter 22, but it is worth pointing out that this was the first time performance-related bonuses had been used on a large scale for such groups as production managers in Britain. Indeed, a few years ago most employers would have said they were against such an idea 'in principle'. An added value scheme highlights the contribution all those working for an organization can make to company prosperity, rather than focusing on shop floor manual workers as the only source of improvements in productivity. But in many cases the added value bonus was too complicated to calculate and too remote from the influence of individual employees for it to act as an effective motivator of better performance. Whilst many companies produced figures on the basis of which they justified paying bonus, our interviews and studies showed many cases where the scheme was quite ignored by employees as far as any effect on the way they worked was concerned.

This whole four-year period (1974-78) resulted in an increase in the extent of incentive schemes in Britain, but also a definite undermining of both their effectiveness and of management and union faith in them.

The next few years will see a move away from incentives, at least in the private sector and especially in organizations with a short lead time on changing policy direction and implementation. This is already evident in the figures for 1980 shown in Table 3.1.

Incentives have been undermined because so many schemes were introduced primarily to increase earnings, and it became incumbent on management to ensure that the increase was paid. This meant that the motivational effect of the incentive was missing. The theory behind incentives is that employees will work better or harder to earn extra pay, and will not receive such bonus pay if they do not. But if a bonus is used as a way of raising pay or as a negotiated pay increase then the employer faces a dilemma if it is not earned. In many cases employers went to considerable pains to ensure this would not happen; and in other cases where it did happen, employees were angry that the company withheld what they saw as their rightful pay increase. In one case which we studied in detail the employees threatened strike action because their added value bonus was not due to be paid. In the face of this threat the management paid the bonus, as did some other companies in a similar situation. This has contributed to a situation in which employees in many organizations see bonus pay as a fixed level pay increase, and not as a reward which varies with effort. It may be some years before the latter idea can be reinstated, if at all.

A second way in which the power of incentives to motivate has decreased arises from their decrease as a proportion of total pay. During those periods when incomes policy allowed flat rate or percentage increases in basic pay but not in bonus pay (or no additional increase in bonus pay) then, as shown in the example below, bonus pay became a smaller proportion of the total.

Basic pay before increase (say) £50: bonus pay £16: bonus as percentage of total = 34%.
Basic pay after increase £56: bonus pay £16: bonus as percentage of total = 29%.

During periods between incomes policies (such as 1974) basic pay rose dramatically and bonus earnings did not keep pace. And during Stage III (1977-78) when incentive payments were allowed over and above the pay norm, many new schemes were introduced but employers were on the whole cautious of large bonuses and introduced schemes designed to pay between 5% and 10% of total pay in self-financing productivity bonuses.

Also, the complexity of the incentive situation in many organizations increased substantially. Some companies installed added value schemes or waste saving schemes or absentee reducing schemes on top of existing payment by results schemes. During the four years of incomes policy they went through stages of paying wages comprised of basic pay, unconsolidated stage one supplement, unconsolidated stage two increase, shift premiums, overtime pay, payment by results bonus, and self-financing productivity bonus. The complexity and the frequency of changes led to some companies abandoning their explanatory handbooks for employees; and one company we studied even gave up trying to explain the payment system to new recruits.

These kinds of changes in the administration of incentive schemes were accompanied by an array of changed attitudes and expectations in relation to incentives which will not easily be reversed.

It may be useful to include in this section some figures on the extent to which different kinds of incentive schemes were in use for different groups of workers as indicated by a special section incorporated in the 1977 New Earnings Survey. The last line shows the figures from our survey of newly introduced schemes. These figures indicate that

Table 3.2

Extent of coverage of different types of incentive schemes in 1977

	Individual incentive %	Group incentive %	Company incentive	All incentive schemes
Men				
Manual	14	12	2	28
Non-manual	3	1	1	5
Women				
Manual	15	6	1	22
Non-manual	2	1	0.5	3
Strathclyde Survey of new schemes	23	43	21	100

(Source: New Earnings Survey 1977)

company wide incentive schemes have not been widely used in Britain (less than 2% of all manual workers received them); but if the 63 companies in the Strathclyde survey are taken as an indication of a trend in newly introduced schemes, then there has been a growth in their use relative to other kinds of incentive scheme, and a decline in individual incentives.

Since the change of government in 1979, the Conservative government's policy has been to avoid any direct involvement in company decisions about pay, so far as possible. In the public sector, where the government is also the employer, this has proved difficult, as discussed below. But so far as incentive payment schemes are concerned, there has been no government policy influencing management decisions one way or the other.

The decline in the use of incentives, as indicated by the coverage figures for 1980 shown in Table 3.1, reveals that employers have been taking incentive schemes out. Apart from non-manual men in manufacturing, where the coverage continues to grow (perhaps due to them being included in company wide schemes which may still be replacing other kinds of incentives) there was an across the board reduction in coverage. Our view is that this decline in the use of incentives, especially of the individual payments-by-results type, will continue unless a change of government policy encourages their use yet again.

Impact of Policy on Differentials

Differentials have become a key issue for wage and salary administrators over recent years. No sooner have one group received an increase to satisfy their demands or their sense of grievance than another becomes agitated that they have been left behind and demand that their differential be restored. Whatever stability in differentials once existed has been lost and we have a never ending spiral of negotiations in which attempts are made to restore the most favourable former position for each group.

Before considering the effects this has had on the jobs of wage and salary administrators, it is worth reviewing some of the possible causal processes which have produced it.

Manual workers and particularly militant trade unionists no longer accept a 'correct' hierarchy of differentials derived from management's prerogative to make these decisions. This may well be part of a larger social change whereby the 'right to manage' is being superceded by the 'need for effective management'. In recent years the challenge has related increasingly to the differentials between jobs. Research has indicated that employees are more concerned about the differential between themselves and some other nearby reference group (geographically and in pay levels) than they are about the fact that the company chairman is earning three or four times as much as they are.

We have now reached a stage where it is impossible to satisfy expectations of all groups because differentials and relativities have fluctuated so much in recent years that each group has a different perception of what is fair and of their own position in the hierarchy. Figure 3.1 shows diagramatically some of the main influences which have produced this situation, with the causal and historical processes flowing from left to right.

This instability and uncertainty has contributed to the tendency for income increases to escalate. It has also created serious problems within organizations where lack of flexibility to make adjustments to pay in the past and the differential impact of certain phases of incomes policy on different groups of employees has resulted in a structure of differentials which does not match management or employee perceptions of what is fair and rational. Moreover, added to this there has been so much disturbance that former definitions of a fair structure of differentials are impossible to re-impose and powerful groups such as the unskilled workers in some industries are in many cases determined that a situation more favourable to themselves should be achieved and maintained.

The impact of the recession, the high level of unemployment, and the genuinely difficult financial position of many companies in 1980 and 1981 has produced a situation where pay increases have been lower than in previous years. This is consistent with the Conservative government's policy of encouraging employers to give increases in pay which they could afford, rather than contribute to their financial difficulties by paying more. The corollary of this, is that when the surviving companies come out of the recession and some begin to make excellent profits again, their employees will seek pay rises as large as the company can afford, so producing even wider discrepancies in pay for similar work between employers.

In the unstable pay situation of the 1970s it is no surprise that the Comparability Commission and the Civil Service Pay Research Unit were seen as possible sources of help with setting pay levels relative to other organizations, and job evaluation was increasingly installed to establish an internal structure of pay levels. There are many problems with comparability and job evaluation, as discussed in Chapters 7, 8 and 12. But in the confused and conflict-ridden position regarding levels of pay which many companies have found themselves facing in recent years, these techniques do provide some kind of solution, albeit at the cost of other kinds of difficulty. Job evaluation has consequently been used increasingly in Britain and knowledge and skills in applying and administering job evaluation have become an increasingly important part of the job for wage and salary administrators. In 1968 the National Board for Prices and Incomes conducted a survey and found that only 9% of the organizations in their sample had introduced job

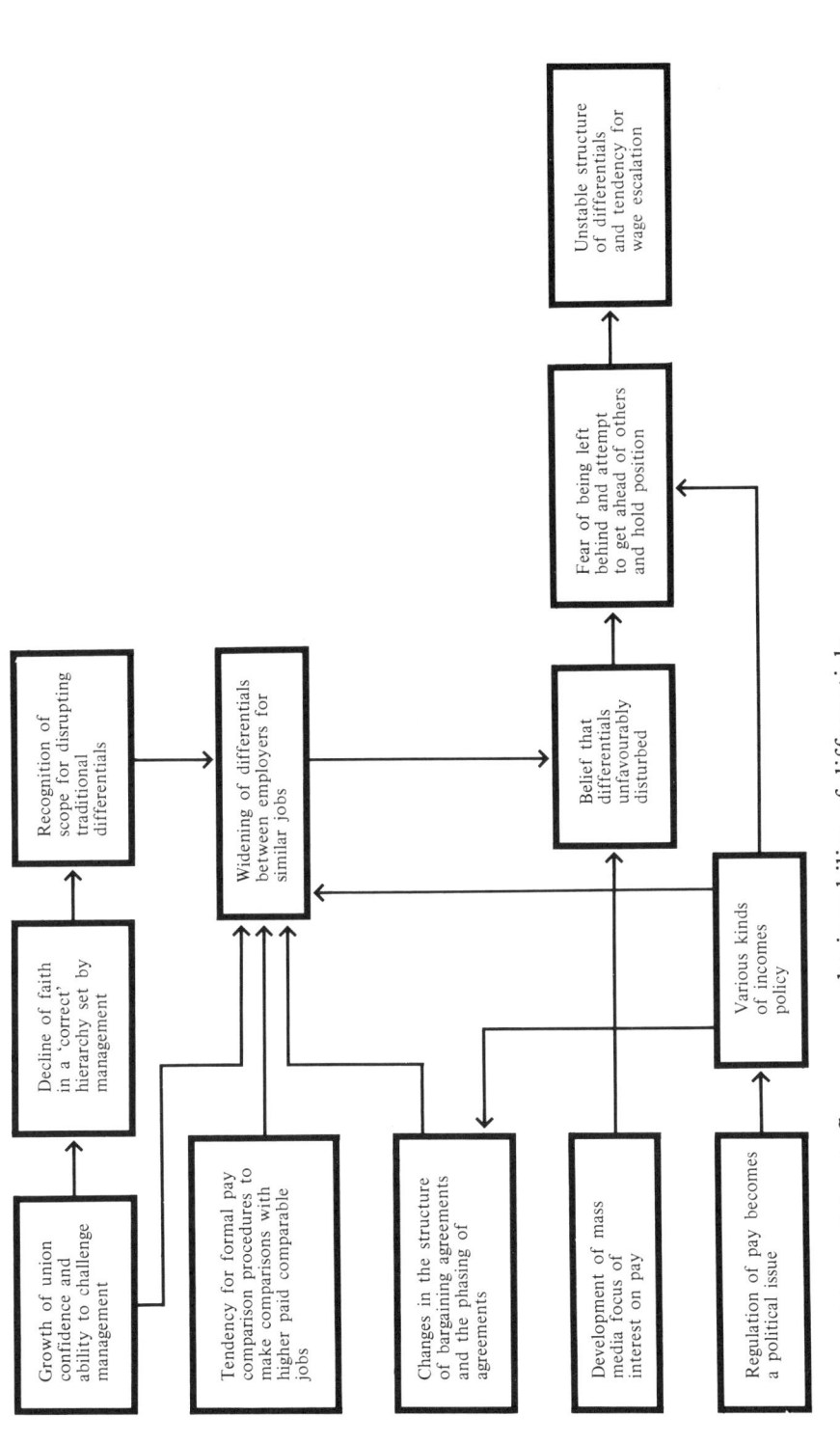

Figure 3.1. Influences on the instability of differentials

evaluation, and these were predominantly the large organizations. But in 1973 the British Institute of Management conducted a similar survey and found 63% of organizations had introduced job evaluation. Another BIM survey in 1977, this time of smaller organizations only (under 2,000 employees) showed that even here 46% had introduced job evaluation.

An indicator of how much difficulty has been caused for wage and salary administrators by the two areas just discussed, incentive schemes and differentials, can be taken from the 1978 annual report of the Advisory, Conciliation and Arbitration Service. This shows that of all the cases referred to arbitration during that year, 85% involved pay issues, and 96% of those cases as John Lockyer explained related to 'issues concerning bonus payments, grading issues, overtime payments and other disputes mainly affecting small groups of workers usually at plant level'. (Lockyer, 1979).

A number of companies studied by our research team in 1979 had found an increasing reluctance at plant level to make decisions about subsidiary issues relating to pay and conditions, such as those which made up such a large proportion of the cases which eventually went to arbitration. This reluctance arose from uncertainty about the implications of their decisions in an incomes policy climate, and fear of the consequences of their decision being used as a precedent for a domino effect series of disputes throughout the company. Its consequence was that these large companies found more and more issues being passed up the organizational hierarchy for decision, and the eventual decision maker being a person further and further removed from local knowledge about the issues involved. This centralization of decision making was not a welcome development for several reasons. It produced delays in the decision making process; it produced, in some cases, a lower probability of the decision being acceptable to the employees; it overloaded senior managers; and it took away some of the autonomy of managers at local level.

Impact on Wage Bargaining

The process of wage bargaining has changed considerably over the past twenty years. It is no longer the case that employees are prepared to forego wage increases when their company or their industry or the nation as a whole are doing badly. The best that management negotiators can achieve, except in very rare, extreme circumstances, is a smaller increase than usual. On the whole the threat that a company will go bankrupt if a particular pay claim is pursued is either not believed (because the same threat was made before and the dire consequences never happened) or not cared about (either because redundancy pay and social security benefits take the sting out of the fear of unemployment or because those who press for increases are in a short supply situation and do not doubt their ability to find other work). Employees have come to expect an increasing real income from year to year. They fear that future incomes policies may leave them behind in relation to the pay of other reference groups and some groups have made a concerted effort to improve their relative pay position.

On the management side, there are few rewards for negotiators who take a firm stand and bring about a strike sooner than settle for a high wage increase. On the contrary, such a manager is likely to face considerable personal criticism and stress, both from his colleagues, the media, and his bosses; and from the men he subsequently has to go on working with, whose cooperation he will need on future occasions.

On the trade union side, there are pressures to increase membership and to gain national political power by being seen as one of the most militant unions, successfully demanding high wage increases for their members. Like shop floor workers and white collar workers, many of them have lost their fear of consequent closures and unemployment, and are anxious not to be left behind in the pay round nor 'boxed in' by incomes policy. They have developed improved strategies of industrial action, such as strikes by small groups of key employees or at peak periods, and banning overtime or working to rule in key areas. These strategies are very harmful to the operations of the organization but cause very little trouble to the union. And there is a belief amongst many union negotiators that free collective bargaining means what it says—that they are free to bargain for whatever they can get from their employers.

These changes have produced a situation in which it is difficult to see what pressures exist for holding down incomes increases. It is unrealistic to expect that eventually so many companies will have gone bankrupt that managers become afraid of generous settlements and unions develop a real fear of closures and unemployment. Which brings one back to the expectation that there will be a return at some point to a system of statutory controls over the rate of increases. In 1968 the Labour Party brought in its 3.5% ceiling on wage increases to bring down wage settlements which were currently running at 8.8% per annum above the previous year. At the end of 1972 the Conservative government brought in a wage freeze to bring down wage increases from an annual rate of increase of 17%, and in 1975 the Labour government brought in its £6 per head supplement for those earning less than £8,500 as a means of bringing wage increase rates down from the 29% level they had reached.

In this kind of situation there are special problems for wage and salary administrators. They have to make decisions about modifications to differentials, about pay rises for key groups who are hard to recruit, about introducing or taking out bonus schemes, job evaluation, and pay scales, in a situation fraught with uncertainty about how far ahead they can expect to be operating under free collective bargaining. They have to make decisions and justify them to unions and employees without the explanatory power of either an incomes policy which ties their hands or a consensus about the dire consequences of extravagant payments. They need skills of sensitivity and compromise in relations with employee representatives to make judgements about the kind of settlement which will most likely be accepted and the extent to which employees are prepared to take industrial action in response to alternative levels of the 'final offer'. They have difficulty making forward plans either for wage and salary policy or for wage and salary costs.

In short, the uncertainty of the stop-go kind of experiences of incomes policies in Britain has produced a situation in which wage and salary administrators are encouraged to act in a fire-fighting, ad hoc way, responding to opportunities and crises as they arise, rather than planning and pursuing a professional approach to their responsibilities. Those organizations which have weathered the changes and more or less steadfastly pursued a planned policy over a number of years have found themselves swimming against the tide of opinion at one point and with it the next; and sometimes blocked from pursuing their policies for years at a time.

These, then, are the general changes which have affected the jobs of wage and salary administrators. The following brief accounts describe what happened over the years 1974-78 in two particular companies, one which coped fairly smoothly with the problems and one which ran into many problems.

Case Study One

This very large company employed over 20,000 employees covering several industries and many different sites. The policy of the industrial relations division was to maximise local autonomy, and there were consequently different shift arrangements in different divisions and even at different sites within the company. Some parts of the organization adhered fairly rigidly to national agreements reached by an employers federation; others supplemented employers federation agreements with local bargaining; some negotiated nationally on a company basis; and some negotiated purely locally. Payment systems varied from sophisticated work measured payment by results through to fixed hourly or daily rates.

Because of the industries it operated within and its market characteristics the company needed to achieve the following objectives:

1 A good well motivated labour force willing and able to respond to seasonal pressures and/or rapid technologically-based change.
2 Continuous operation in many divisions of very expensive capital equipment.
3 Sufficient supply of skilled and qualified employees.

With these objectives in mind, the company had a central policy on personnel and industrial relations which incorporated the following considerations:

1 To attract and keep the right calibre of employees the company should pay high wages and salaries.
2 To recruit and motivate skilled and qualified staff a structure of 'good' differentials between grades was needed.
3 To ensure effective management and cooperation for high productivity there should be as much local autonomy as possible in personnel and industrial relations issues.
4 To assist local management there should be a fast and helpful industrial relations information service from the centre.
5 To ensure adaptability there should be as much flexibility as possible at local level on wage issues.
6 To ensure advice and information from the centre was appropriate, the industrial relations function at head office should understand and have good relations with the trade unions.
7 To avoid jealousies between sites incomes policies should affect all sites equally, and be adhered to.

Very positive efforts were made by the company's head office to specify its objectives and to pursue a planned policy in the industrial relations field.

The Company during Stages I and II, 1975-77

The flat rate increase of £6 in Stage I and the 5% with a £2.50 to £4 minimum of Stage II had the effect of narrowing the differentials for skilled workers within the company. This caused some problems of recruiting, retaining and motivating skilled workers. These stages also allowed for no increases in shift premiums and overtime pay, and consequently the company claimed there was a measurable decrease in the utilization of their expensive plant and machinery, due to the relatively less attractive rewards from overtime and shift work.

But the biggest problem for the wage and salary administration staff was the process described above whereby decisions tended to be pushed up to head office which according to the company's policy should have been made at local level. This undermined the company's policy of maximizing local management autonomy, and consequently, it was felt, reduced efficiency. It also reduced the need for highly experienced management at local level as the number of decisions they made decreased.

However, the company continued to pursue its policies as far as was practicable, and there were no major disputes during this period.

The Company during Stages III and IV, 1977-79

At the start of Stage III there were differences between sites on the issue of whether the Stage I and II supplements should be consolidated into basic pay at this point, and the extra costs taken out of the 10% allowed under Stage III. Some wanted to move this way in order to simplify the complex wage structure; others wanted to take the maximum advantage of the 10% increases, and wait for an opportunity later to consolidate the earlier supplements. The group faced problems also in finding suitable self-financing productivity schemes for its many sites. The company did try to encourage schemes which related bonus pay to measured improvements in productivity, but this was not always possible.

It was recognized that an added value scheme would be the simplest to install; but it was considered that in a fast changing technological environment it would be too difficult to separate labour productivity from the productivity of capital, and the scheme could get very quickly out of hand. The installation of bonus schemes by traditional methods of work measurement was impossible at some sites because of a shortage of work study engineers. During Stages I and II work study engineers had been to some extent switched from traditional work measurement activities to method improvements projects and O & M work.

Another problem was that in some areas there already was high productivity and it was very difficult to see how this could be improved. Although performance based schemes could be installed in these areas, the government policy required all schemes to be self-financing, and this was a difficult requirement to fulfil. Lastly, there was the problem of applying incentives to staff areas where they had never been introduced before. Staff were distrustful of incentive schemes, and to some extent considered that they carried connotations of lower status.

Bearing these constraints in mind incentive schemes were designed to meet local needs and problems, relying heavily on local management to design and install them, with advice and help from head office. All of these schemes had a 'cut off' at 10% and were put in for a two-year period only. These constraints were designed to safeguard the company from schemes getting out of control and becoming too large a part of the wage packet. Three main types of scheme were introduced:

1 *Factories*: In the factories and where payments by results were already in operation an additional bonus was introduced related to

gross earnings. This bonus was designed to monitor and improve weak points in a factory, say, absenteeism, or wastage, or even buying out tea breaks.
2 *Engineering*: Where there were work study staff available in engineering, performance related incentives were devised in the traditional way. Alternatively a system of Rated Activity Sampling was used to install them as speedily as possible. There is always a degree of error in this last procedure, depending on the number of samples taken, but because of the 10% limit and the two-year life this was not regarded as a serious problem.
3 *Staff*: Staff were put on an added value scheme. All staff received the same dependent upon company performance. To some extent even though there were misgivings about the scheme, the company found they could measure productivity in this way, even though the bonus was not closely associated with individual performance.

Conclusions on Company A

This example of a well organized company demonstrates the advantages of having a policy and carefully monitoring the effects of any enforced pay policy on both company performance and conformity with the policy. In this way a return to policies tied to planned objectives for the company can be made more easily when the policy is lifted, and the company will not stray too far from its intended direction in the industrial relations field.

Case Study Two

In complete contrast to the previous large enterprise this small engineering factory made heavy weather of coping with incomes' policy. It ran into several confrontations with the workforce in which the incomes' constraints of the day played a key role, and finally produced an 'all out' strike.

The company employed about 700 employees, 20% staff, 20% skilled manual workers, and 60% semi-skilled female workers. Situated on the outskirts of a large industrial conurbation, the company was in the machine tool industry, a precision manufacturing trade employing skilled labour and having large capital investments in plant and machinery.

Until 1975 this had been a non-union company, with 95% of the work force not belonging to any union, and with communications and consultations operating through a works council, a system which had worked fairly smoothly for 25 years. Individuals were elected to the works council from different constituencies within the factory, and these nominees elected a 'senior member' who met regularly with the managing director. In this way urgent matters could be dealt with swiftly and only those issues which needed fuller consultation were left for the full works council. This changed in 1975, and it was management's theory that the local district union office had 'planted' one or two people in the factory in 1974 with instructions to unionize the plant.

The Company during Stages I and II, 1975-77

In 1975, just prior to the introduction of Stage I, the union demanded a £10 wage increase on behalf of the workforce. Since under the Stage I regulations this was not allowable, the claim was reduced to £6 payable as a lump sum, rather than (as the policy dictated to firms with settlement dates prior to 1 August) at £4 now and £2 in February 1976. The company stated the pay guidelines and re-affirmed its intention to stay within them. The union then called an all-out strike. This being the first official strike in the history of the company was a very sad affair for management and workers alike.

The two sides reached a compromise whereby the company agreed to pay the whole sum immediately if the Department of Employment approved. The management, unlike the workers, fully expected that the Department would refuse to allow this immediate payment, which they did. The workers returned to work but they had gained nothing and there was a festering bad feeling and serious worsening of industrial relations. The management explained the strike to our researcher in terms of a strike ballot which had been tipped by only three votes and repeated reports of intimidation of workers by the union. Since the time of the strike the company has been plagued with strikes and stoppages. Efficiency has dropped and the company has been losing orders.

The increases in basic wages paid under Stages I and II exacerbated a process of decay of the company's incentive bonus scheme. The firm had always applied increases in basic rates negotiated nationally by their employers federation, but had not made corresponding changes to the bonus rates earned. This rigid adherence to national agreements and equally strong opposition to letting the piecework times drift had created a situation under Stages I and II where the incentive was eroded still further. The management's attitude to this erosion of the incentive element in pay was that a bonus scheme only motivates people to improve their performance during the first three to six months of its life. Thereafter they control their rate of working to a set level and there is no point in maintaining high levels of incentive pay.

As a result, fall back rates (ie basic pay) were increasing steadily and creeping up the effort score scale. Each new increase in basic pay meant that bonus pay only became applicable beyond the point on the effort scale corresponding to that higher level of pay. So those employees whose performance level was below this new level would receive an increase in pay up to the level of the increase, but those performing just above it would notice no difference except that their colleagues were able to work much slower for hardly any difference in pay. The effect of this situation was so serious that on one occasion after management had tried to lift the low performance of certain workers through training, 120 of the high performers suddenly dropped their performance below the fall back level. Their complaint was that their higher performance was not reflected proportionately in their pay. They had to work very hard to earn pennies more than their neighbours.

The management's reaction to this claim of unfairness was to accuse the workers of defrauding the company by withholding performances due to the company. They warned that unless they returned to their original speeds they would have the new basic ignored and would all be paid what they earned under the original scheme. For support they argued that the workers were not conforming to the employers federation agreement and that therefore their action constituted industrial action without having gone through the agreed procedure. The workers returned to their old performance levels, but the month of November saw a 20% drop in output.

Conclusions on this Case

The change in industrial relations climate in this company seems to have bewildered its senior management, and their resort to a kind of conspiracy theory to explain the reactions of their workforce produced actions which exacerbated rather than improved the situation. Undoubtedly there was more to the events than was revealed to us in these interviews, because we did not have the opportunity to study the processes of change in industrial relations as they were happening. But there can be little doubt from the way in which things developed that the company embarked on a feud with its workforce, and acted under Stages I and II to incorporate the allowable increases in ways which contributed neither to motivation nor to good industrial relations. During Stages III and IV they attempted to install a company wide bonus scheme based on the number of units of work in total production divided by the clock hours taken to produce them. At the time of our study the union had lodged a claim for a 30% pay increase and the two sides were locked in negotiation.

Conclusions

These two examples have, we hope, shown in a little more detail how some of the problems described earlier affected two particular companies. Should there be another incomes restraint policy in the foreseeable future, it is to be hoped that it will be one which manages to achieve its objectives without damaging the attempts of those salary and wage administrators who are attempting to pursue planned and rational policies. This will require very careful consideration of the ways such a policy may affect local level situations.

References and Further Reading

Armstrong, M. and Murlis, H., 'Salary Administration', *BIM Survey Report* no. 36, 1977.

Behrend, H., *Incomes Policy, Equity and Pay Increase Differentials*, Scottish Academic Press, 1973.

Blackaby, F. (Ed), *The future of Pay Bargaining*, Heinemann, 1980.

Brittan, S. and Lilley, P., *The Delusion of Incomes Policy*, Temple Smith, London, 1977.

Brown, W.A., 'Incomes Policy and Pay Differentials', *Oxford Bulletin of Economics and Statistics*, volume 38, February 1976.

Brown, W.A., 'Engineering Wages and the Social Contract, 1975-77', *Oxford Bulletin of Economics and Statistics*, February 1979.

Daniel, W.W., *Wage Determination in Industry*, PEP no. 563, 1976.

Dean, A.J.H., 'Incomes Policy and Differentials', *National Institute Economic Review*, no. 85. August 1978.

Department of Employment, *'New Earnings Survey'*, HMSO, 1973-80. (annual volumes).

Henry, S.G.B. and Ormerod, P.A., 'Incomes Policy and Wage Inflation: empirical evidence for the U.K. 1961-77', *National Institute Economic Review*, August 1978.

Lipsey, R.G. and Parkin, J.M., 'Incomes policy: a reappraisal', *Economica*, 1970.

Lockyer, I., *Industrial Arbitration in Great Britain*, IPM, November 1979.

Midland Bank Review 'A future for an incomes policy?' *Midland Bank Review*, Winter, 1980.

National Board for Prices and Incomes, 'Job Evaluation Report and Supplement', no. 83. HMSO 1968.

Wilson, B., 'Creating and Sharing Wealth—the Added Value Approach', *Employee Relations* volume 1. no. 1, 1979.

4

The Structure of Collective Bargaining in Britain

Andrew Thomson

Bargaining structure has been a central preoccupation of concern about the machinery of pay determination in Britain since the report of the Donovan Royal Commission on Trade Unions and Employers' Associations (1968). Perhaps the most evocative recent statement of the problem was made by the Confederation of British Industry in its proposals for reforming pay determination (1979):

> The situation is made worse by the fragmented nature of our bargaining system. It is fragmented vertically in that collective agreements can be made at the industry level, company level and the plant—groups of employees may bargain at all three levels. It is fragmented horizontally since employees in the same company or industry who normally make comparisons with each other may be split into several bargaining units. Frequently, each bargaining level or unit has a distinct settlement date to itself. So an employee may be covered by two or three agreements each with a separate date of implementation, while employees working side by side may settle pay awards at different times of the year . . .
>
> . . . Often there is competition between bargaining units, especially if they are represented by different unions. Different bargaining levels can be used by unions to obtain higher pay awards than can be justified on productivity grounds. A good example is of domestically negotiated bonus arrangements being eroded by nationally negotiated minimum rates. Each level may be stable in itself, but the combination disrupts rational pay structures and enhances the importance of pay comparisons.
>
> The inflationary effect is increased when fragmented bargaining

produces 'leapfrogging' between different groups of workers. If one group gets an increase another group will try to restore its relative position. The temptation to leapfrog is especially strong because the bargaining round lasts the whole year. Those who bargain late in the round will seek larger pay awards than those who settled earlier. In the next round the latter inevitably try to catch-up with the leapfrogging that went before, so adding a new twist to the inflationary spiral.

Fragmentation is the outcome of the long, uninterrupted development of collective bargaining. It arises from the presence of several unions in an industry or plant, and from the growth of shop floor power . . . In some industries there is near anarchy as small groups strike without warning, and in defiance of their officials and of agreed procedures.

With irrational bargaining structures . . . it is not surprising that employees often use their industrial power in ways that are ultimately self-destructive. There is little incentive for the individual to place his long-term good above short-term gains. Bad structures reinforce bad attitudes. And bad attitudes cement bad structures.

From the above quotation it is clear that the institutional structure within which pay is determined has a considerable influence upon the outcome. However, it is probably necessary to define the concept of structure rather more clearly, since it is a multi-dimensional term. Perhaps the most extensive definition of structure (Department of Employment 1971) identified four different dimensions:

1 Bargaining levels, or the points within a system at which collective bargaining takes place.
2 Bargaining units, or the specific group of workers that are covered by a particular agreement.
3 Bargaining forms relating to the degree of formality of an agreement.
4 Bargaining scope or the range of subjects covered by collective agreements.

This chapter will be concerned primarily with bargaining levels and to a lesser extent with bargaining units; we shall not consider bargaining forms or bargaining scope to any significant extent. However, the above definition, extensive as it is, does not adequately convey the dynamic impact of bargaining structure upon pay determination, which relates to the inter-relationships between bargaining structures, which in British terms are often called parity or comparability relationships.

Finally, from the perspective of public policy, it might be suggested that any structure is desirable which maximizes productivity and the degree of participation of the employees, whilst minimizing wage inflation and the degree of overt conflict. However, these objectives frequently tend to be mutually contradictory in practice. While the outcome in public policy terms of the Donovan Commission's (1968) various considerations was their recommendations for at least the private sector to consolidate bargaining structure at the level of plant or company, it cannot be said that successive governments have had any very clear policy of what to do about implementing this, and indeed insofar as legislation and governmental action has impinged on the area, it has done so in a confused and contradictory way. Indeed it can be said that the policy of all the groups mentioned, with the possible exception of groups of employees, has been responsive and by default rather than by initiative and intent.

It is the contention of this chapter that bargaining structure can significantly affect pay and in this sense is an independent variable within the party determination process rather than as some have argued, a transmission mechanism through which other forces are channelled but without any independent impact upon the process or the outcome by itself. It follows from this assertion that bargaining structure confers power, and for any given change in structure one party is likely to gain power relative to the other. At least to a considerable extent, the parties are therefore likely to see decisions on bargaining structure as being of a zero sum kind. It is by no means always obvious however just what are the considerations which should be taken into account in developing a strategy of bargaining structure or indeed how these considerations should be weighed (Beaumont, Thomson and Gregory 1980).

It may help however to sketch some of the considerations of benefit and disadvantage in bargaining structure from the point of view of the parties. For employees there is a logical goal in moving to that structure which provides the highest pay and the greatest opportunity to influence the work environment for the individual or workgroup. Many workers have only a limited knowledge of, and a purely instrumental attitude towards, the national union; for them the occupational or departmental workgroup is the primary unit of identification and the shop steward or convener the personification of the union. The fragmentation of collective bargaining in Britain which took place in Britain in the decade or so before the Donovan Report of 1968 was largely a result of work groups seizing the opportunity afforded by full employment to assert new supplementary bargaining units which best reflected their own power and their own aspirations. This process and its results were evocatively described by Fox and Flanders (1969):

> Work groups capable of mobilizing the necessary power have broken through a relatively larger area of regulation and imposed a relatively smaller one more favourable to themselves. And when faced with gaps in the normative system in respect of certain of their aspirations, groups with sufficient power have introduced their own. In both situations the revision and creation of norms has

been improvised and piecemeal, has rested on a very small area of agreement and has not been related to larger units of regulation. This splintering of the normative order within the establishment and the piecemeal, hotch-potch additions to it, all determined by the accidents of power distribution rather than by agreed principles of any sort, has greatly increased the probability of disorder and loss of control . . .

The employee or workgroup perspective may well not be the same as that of the unions, for which there were at least traditionally perceived advantages in taking labour out of the sphere of competition and therefore having standardized wage levels within the area covered by the particular product markets. Unions must in any case take a rather wider perspective than the workgroup; what is good for the workgroup may not be the optimum for all the union's membership, even within a similar industrial or occupational grouping to that in question. Unions may also have different structural objectives to the workgroup; to maintain cohesion as an organization necessitates a coordinating role and unions may be unwilling to forego this in such a key area as collective bargaining. But democratic pressures from below have often meant that unions have given free rein to workgroups, taking less account of wider labour and product market factors wherever workgroups are sufficiently powerful to stand on their own feet. This has usually been feasible where product markets are oligopolistic or where there are controls on entry to the labour market, as through a system of craft apprenticeship. Where both types of market are competitive, the traditional union approach of taking labour out of the sphere of competition still operates. In practice, however, there was little planning of this strategy, since the fragmentation of collective bargaining in the 1960s largely took unions by surprise, and they were slow to respond in terms of their own organizational structures.

For employers there are conflicting philosophies. On the one hand there is much to be said for linking pay directly with productivity, and this points to decentralized bargaining. One of the great weaknesses of the traditional British system was that it imposed a similar rate of pay on all employers in the industry, regardless of their ability to pay or the productivity they obtained in return for such payments. Highly profitable employers could not, except by indirect means, pay more to obtain good quality workers, and rates tended to be set in order to keep the most marginal firms in business. On the other hand, as many British employers have found to their cost, there are considerable problems of control in highly decentralized bargaining, since once fragmentation has begun it tends to have a spillover effect on other groups, leading to jealousies, leapfrogging, and parity claims within the company. This may lead to a situation where power, conferred by the accident of technology, and which may only reflect productivity to a very limited extent, can become the primary determinant of pay.

The Development of Bargaining Structure in Britain

To understand the structure of pay bargaining in Britain today, it is necessary to understand how it developed historically. The broad origins of bargaining structure arose in the district agreements of the later part of the 19th century, of which there were essentially two types. One was for the skilled trades, where the unions sought to impose their working rules, especially those relating to apprenticeships, on the employers. The other type was in the highly competitive industries producing a homogeneous product where lack of regulation encouraged wage cutting amongst employers. But perhaps the most significant feature was the lack of desire of either side to bargain or indeed to have any joint institutions at plant level. Managements were concerned with maintaining their prerogatives, while unions felt that 'works' unionism could mean employer domination and in any case their primary objective was to achieve standard conditions within the locality. Before the First World War collective bargaining was still conducted largely on a district-wide basis, but from that time the desire of both unions and employers to eliminate competition from low wage districts tended to widen the area of collective bargaining to the industry level. This tendency accelerated during the war as a result of national wage awards, and continued from the 1920s when the implementation of the recommendations put forward by the Whitley Committee, and encouraged by the governments of the period led to the formation of national joint industrial councils in a large number of industries. The interwar period was the high water mark of the 'traditional' system in which the vast bulk of bargaining was at industry level.

However, in the postwar period the position changed radically when as a result of full employment and the lack of any coherent industrial relations machinery at plant level, workgroups became able to exploit both their own power and the competition between employers for labour in the way described by Fox and Flanders. It was in fact the trend towards unregulated shop floor bargaining that was central to the Donovan Commission's (1968) analysis of the problem of the British industrial relations system. In their view:

> Britain has two systems of industrial relations. One is the formal system embodied in the official institutions. The other is the informal system created by the actual behaviour of trade unions and employers associations, of managers, shop stewards and workers. The keystone of the formal system is the industry-wide collective agreement . . . The informal system is often at odds with

the formal system. Actual earnings have moved far apart from the rates laid down in industry-wide agreements; . . . disputes procedures laid down in industry-wide agreements have been subjected to strain by the transfer of authority to the factory and workshop. The bargaining which takes place within factories is largely outside the control of employers associations and trade unions.

Accordingly the Commission urged the reform of bargaining structure, in particular a change in the relative importance of the different levels of negotiation, ie they argued for more bargaining at the middle levels of negotiation, below the level of the industry, but above the shop floor. This recommendation has been the focus of public policy since that, although the actual articulation of policy has been limited, to put it mildly.

The Statistical Profile

Moving on to describe the present structure of bargaining in Britain, the Donovan Commission was also the first body to try to measure the extent of different types of structure. As pioneers in the quantitative measurement of bargaining structure the Commission had to derive its estimates on a piecemeal basis, collating from a variety of sources data prepared for other purposes and of mixed quality. Since the Commission's central concern was with the declining effectiveness of the industry-wide agreement they categorized industries according to the extent to which actual rates of pay followed or diverged from those specified in the relevant industry agreement. Five categories were defined:

1. Where actual pay (excluding overtime) for most workers was thought to be well in excess of the nationally determined rates. This accounted for most of manufacturing and covered some 10.75 million employees.
2. Where this was true for substantial groups but not for the majority of employees. This related to construction, textiles, mining, and railways, covering some 4 million employees.
3. Where industry-wide rates were followed but overtime added around 50% to average earnings. This was the case for some 0.5 million workers in road transport and shipping.
4. Where industry rates were generally followed and were not supplemented to the extent of Category 3. This covered some 4.5 million workers, mainly in the public sector.
5. Some 4 million workers, mainly in services, who could not be classified.

To give a statistical picture of the pattern of bargaining structure of more detailed scope than that of the Commission poses an awkward dilemma. Comprehensive coverage of the labour force, including its industrial, regional, sex and occupational dimensions, requires a large, national sample, such as the New Earnings Survey. On the other hand to capture the many subtleties and complexities which characterize bargaining structure in practice requires data gathering related to the detailed circumstances of the individual firm, such as that recently carried out at Warwick University. The conflicting nature of these objectives is reflected in alternative types of data which are more easily juxtaposed than synthesized, and we shall look briefly at each.

The Warwick Survey

The Warwick Survey is based on a very detailed investigation in 970 establishments in manufacturing only, each supplying a minimum of 50 workers, into many aspects of the system of industrial relations at the plant and shop floor level (Brown and Sisson 1979, Brown 1980). The central focus in the Warwick approach is the distinction between multi-employer and single-employer bargaining as the most important level of pay bargaining, with the latter subdivided between multi-plant and single establishments agreements. The main insight to emerge from the data is the importance, for manual and non-manual groups alike and across a wide range of industries of single employer, single establishment bargaining on pay. This is the most important level for 45.9% of all manual employees in the sample, as against single employer, multi-plant bargaining for 21% and multi-employer, industry-wide bargaining for 17.1%. Among non-manual workers single-employer, single establishment bargaining has virtually identical importance, (45.5%), while multi-employer industry-wide bargaining is of much less importance (7.2%) and single-employer, multi-plant (26.8%) and 'no bargaining' (14.7%) of greater importance.

Establishments are further grouped by their number of employees into five size categories, ranging from 50-99 to over 1000. Among both manual and non-manual workers clear gradients emerge in the relative importance of the alternative levels of pay bargaining with establishment size. Single employer, single establishment bargaining is the most important category at all size levels, for both manuals and non-manuals, although it reaches its maximum importance (involving 54% of manuals and 50% of non-manuals) in the size-group 500-999 employees, then diminishing somewhat in establishments with over 1000 employees. Single employer, multi-plant bargaining is the category which increases most strongly with size, doubling in importance between the size group 500-999 and the over-1000 group, to affect 32% of manuals and 38% of non-manuals in the largest group. The multi-employer category, on the other hand, both in the form of the industry-wide agreement and of Wages Council loses ground as establishment size increases, as does the 'no bargaining' category.

The Department of Employment New Earnings Survey

This is one of the larger annual surveys of pay and terms of employment available in any country in the world, based on a 1% random sample of the total employed labour force, yielding over 170,000 returns. On two occasions, in 1973 and 1978, the survey has included a special question on bargaining structure: 'Please indicate the type of negotiated collective agreement, if any, which affects the pay and conditions of employment of this employee, either directly or indirectly', with four mutually exclusive categories defined: national agreement only; national agreement and supplementary company/district/local agreement; company/district/local agreement only; no collective agreement.

Considering first the coverage of collective agreements at any level, before turning to the individual agreement types, the most striking feature of the results reported in the survey for 1978 is the pervasiveness of coverage by collective agreements and its comparatively high level across each of the major groups in the labour force. An overall coverage rate of 68.9% is recorded among full-time adult employees, ranging from 77.1% among male manual workers through 70.4% among female manuals and 66.2% among non-manual women to 59.0% among non-manual males. Moreover the coverage of collective agreements outstrips the extent of unionism in the economy by substantial margins; according to the estimates by Price and Bain in 1974 union density in the total labour force was 50.4%. This difference between agreement coverage and union membership is however not too surprising in view of the continuance of broadly-based industry arrangements where employer membership of an employers' association is the determining factor in coverage.

Two other interesting patterns merit a brief mention. Coverage rates in general are lower in England, slightly higher in Scotland and significantly higher in Wales. Within England a clear regional gradient exists, with the lowest rates in the South-East, somewhat higher in the Midlands and highest of all in the North and North-West. Similarly, coverage rates increase steadily across the age range up to 60 years, except among white collar men where the profile is flat. Both regional and age group coverage rates reflect the industrial and occupational distribution of the employees in them, but the differences are too great to be explained by these factors alone, suggesting that other, perhaps sociological, factors may also be at work.

Perhaps the most important distinction in structure is the difference

Table 4.1

Bargaining structure in the private and public sectors males 1978

	National plus supplementary %	National only %	Company district and local %	No agreement %
Managers				
Private	8.5	7.7	10.5	73.3
Public	11.3	76.7	2.7	9.3
Professionals				
Private	11.1	7.4	15.8	65.7
Public	12.9	80.0	0.9	6.2
Intermediate non-manuals				
Private	8.8	10.6	18.3	62.3
Public	12.8	82.7	1.1	3.3
Junior non-manuals				
Private	18.7	12.9	14.9	53.3
Public	9.7	86.8	1.1	2.3
Foremen				
Private	21.0	20.8	18.5	39.7
Public	19.3	70.0	5.5	5.2
Skilled				
Private	33.1	24.8	15.3	26.7
Public	27.4	65.1	3.5	3.9
Semi-skilled				
Private	30.5	19.1	18.2	32.2
Public	17.1	78.4	1.1	3.4
Unskilled				
Private	23.0	29.6	14.7	32.7
Public	28.2	66.6	2.0	3.1

Source: Derived from New Earnings Survey

NOTE: The definition of public sector employees is those in any industry covered by one of the listed public sector agreements or in one of the public sector MLH's, namely nos. 101, 311-3, 384-5, 601-3, 701-2, 707-8, 872, 874, 901, 906. This was the NES definition in 1973, and for the sake of comparison we used the same definition in 1978 even though the NES had updated their own definition.

between the public and private sectors as illustrated in Table 4.1. This table for simplicity deals only with males, but the pattern for females is similar. The public sector comes predominantly within the 'national only' category for all socioeconomic groupings, but especially within the higher occupational ranges, whereas in the private sector the most important category is 'national plus supplementary' for manual grades, while a large majority of non-manuals are not covered. Thus, in overall coverage, the public sector coverage is over 95% while the private sector has only two-thirds of manual workers and one-third of white collar workers covered. In some private sector industries, such as agriculture, distribution, finance and miscellaneous services, even male manual coverage falls below half, although in some parts of these wage council arrangements take the place of collective bargaining.

Turning more specifically to the differences between bargaining categories, 'national only' agreements are strongest in the public sector and some relatively small-scale industries such as construction, textiles, clothing and furniture, although these latter also contain elements of the other categories, probably in the larger companies. The 'national plus supplementary' category is strongest in manufacturing and especially in engineering and paper and printing. This category has arguably changed considerably in the last decade or so, with the industry level part of the bargaining playing a declining role to the point where it performs only a very limited role for most companies (Brown and Terry 1978). The 'company district and local' category is essentially the category recommended by the Donovan Commission for the private sector. It is the largest category for male manuals in chemicals, food, drink and tobacco, and other manufacturing industries, and grew between 1973 and 1978. It is probably true, however, that a considerable part of the 'national plus supplementary' category has in practice much the same latitude in pay determination as those in the 'company district and local' category, so that the apparently small overall size of the latter does not necessarily mean that Donovan has been ignored. Indeed there undoubtedly has been a great amount of consolidation of structure at the local level, giving greater control to employers than a decade ago. Nevertheless many companies still have considerable numbers of bargaining units, often based on occupational groupings and rivalries, and as the earlier quotation from the CBI attests, these can be very disruptive.

British Bargaining Structure in an International Context

Bargaining structures in an international context are almost as difficult to classify as in Britain; they vary enormously within countries as well as between countries, and it is by no means easy to give a thumbnail sketch of national structures. However, Figure 4.1, produced by OECD, compares the level of bargaining to the structure of the parties. As can be seen, there is a strong tendency for the degree of centralization of employer and union organization to be related to the level of bargain-

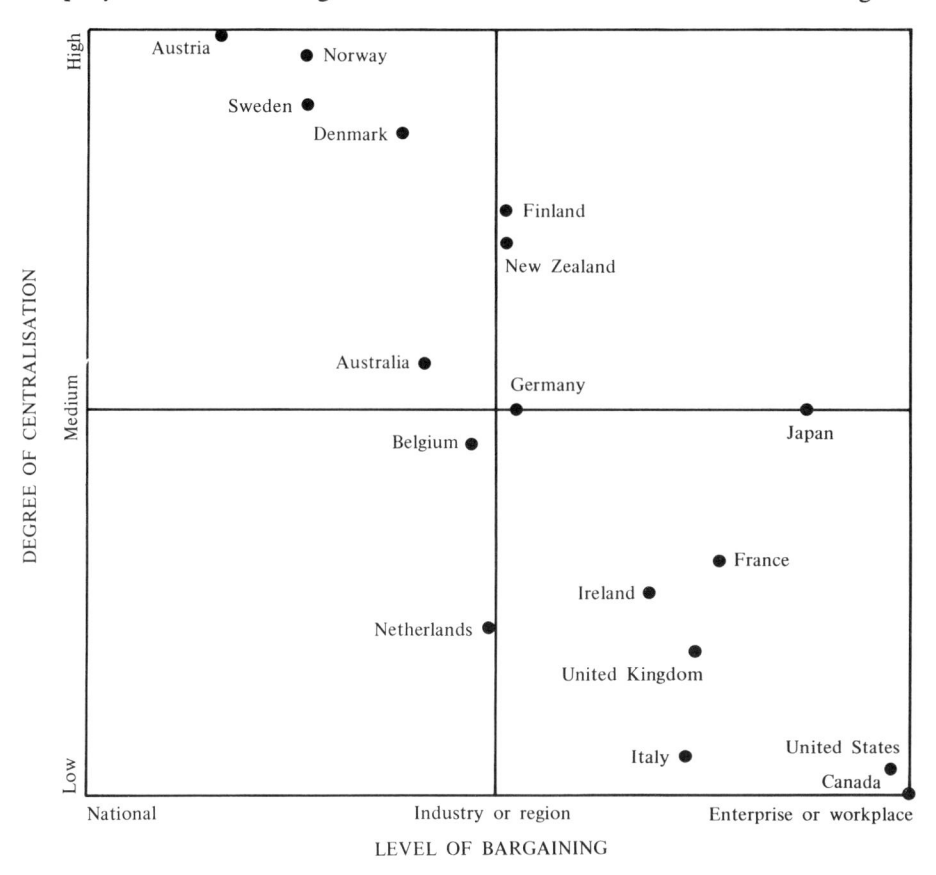

Figure 4.1 Centralisation of union management structure related to level of bargaining

ing, ie power is decentralized within the parties when bargaining is decentralized, and vice versa. This is only to be expected since the parties tend to focus their own organization at the point where the key decisions are made. But why these differences in structure between countries, which, as Clegg (1976) noted, has a very powerful impact on the whole industrial relations system? The reasons are numerous, but include early bargaining patterns in many countries, the willingness of employers to form coalitions, the form of divisions between unions, the role of state policy, and the nature of product markets at the time bargaining developed. It is noteworthy that Britain appears by no means extreme, although the figure cannot encompass the diversity or the sharp divisions between the formal and informal systems in Britain. It is doubtful if any other country has experienced the same degree of fragmented workshop bargaining, although it is by no means unknown elsewhere.

The above indicates that there are diverse forces at work; it is worth noting that economic forces have had only a limited influence in shaping bargaining structure on a world wide basis, in spite of the significance which is assumed in the very limited (and largely American) theory. On the other hand there are signs of economic forces imposing changes in direction, mainly to provide some greater extent of plant or company decision making in accordance with different local circumstances in those countries with centralized bargaining, and conversely some move towards consolidation of structures in countries with decentralized bargaining. In all countries governments have sought more influence on the end outcome of bargaining, usually through some form of corporate state council for tripartite discussion in the countries with centralized bargaining or intermittent incomes policies in the decentralized countries. There are forces for change in all countries, often pushing in several contradictory directions at the same time. What may well be developing is a more explicit alignment of particular decisions with particular levels; most countries have an informal, if not always a formal, multi-tiered structure, although the definition of which decision and which level is uncertain everywhere.

Efficiency in Bargaining Structures

International comparison of structures inevitably leads to questions of relative efficiency, although the notion of efficiency itself raises issues of what criteria are appropriate and in whose interests efficiency should be judged. Possibly the best exposition of alternative models of structure has been that of Ulman (1974), writing a few years after Donovan and in an international context, but nevertheless embodying many of Donovan's implicit arguments. Ulman postulated two models, 'A' and 'B', and evaluated them in terms of their potential for generating and controlling inflationary pressures.

Model A 'involves the negotiating of wages, fringes, and some work conditions between the company and one or more national unions, the latter connecting the company-wide wage settlements in an industry via pattern bargaining. Working conditions and, to a lesser degree, some pay questions are also negotiated at the plant level with local unions; and local and national unionists are sequentially involved in grievance handling'. Ulman saw this model, generally prevalent in the US manufacturing sector, as giving management 'an arrangement designed to connect the wage-setting and productivity-determining activities as closely as possible', and as permitting the national union, for its part, 'to perform vital and highly visible services for local officers and members alike in processing their grievances and policing the contract'. Model B, on the other hand, 'is characterized by wider separation of the centres of decision-making and more overlap in the determination of pay. Pay is determined by formal industry-wide bargaining and again, less formally, at plant level by management activity either unilaterally or under pressure from shop stewards or local shop committees; the company-wide level tends to drop out as a visible locus of wage determination. The role of the national union in the determination of non-pecuniary conditions and in the disposition of grievances is minimal; those functions tend to be discharged by management and/or local work groups, as in the determination of local wage supplements, and also by legislative enactment and labour courts'.

Ulman concludes by arguing '(a) that connective bargaining (under Model A) might make for less inflationary and less restrictive settlements, and (b) that under certain circumstances, company-level bargaining (under Model A) need not result in fatter settlements than industry-wide bargaining (under Model B)'. This result would be because 'the closer linkage of working conditions, security, grievance settlement, and wages makes Model A a presumptively more 'efficient' system of industrial relations than Model B'.

Ulman's alternative models and his argument were implicit in the report of the Donovan Commission and its recommendations that the bargaining structure in Britain should be reformulated to emphasize much more strongly bargaining at plant and company level. It was argued that only at these levels could many of the decisions being made on a fragmented and informal basis be regularized and brought under the control of the institutionalized parties, and there was a clear presumption that this would provide a more efficient system of bargaining and would thus contribute to reducing what were seen as the inflationary pressures of the system.

However, Ulman's argument was dependent on a fairly high degree of independence in decision making for company or plant units. He accepted that for pattern-based bargaining to be adopted in its entirety would prevent the connecting of the 'wage-setting and productivity-determining activities as closely as possible', which he saw as one of the key aspects of the efficiency of his model. Given the use of 'orbits of coercive comparison', the possibilities of 'whipsawing' or 'leapfrogging' on the basis of institutional union power rather than productivity would limit or even reverse the gains to be made from linking pay and productivity in the original bargaining unit. It was this possibility which doubtless led Ulman to add the caveat of 'under certain circumstances', which he did not further define, to his claim that Model A need not result in fatter settlements than Model B. It was also this fear of the inflationary potential of decentralized bargaining that has led writers of diverse political viewpoints to criticize the Donovan recommendation of plant or company bargaining.

It is difficult to measure the efficiency of bargaining structure empirically, but the New Earnings Survey does indicate that there probably are returns to workers for decentralized bargaining. As Table 4.2 indicates there are higher differentials for manual workers in the

Table 4.2

Differentials in gross weekly earnings of covered over non-covered workers, by agreement type, 1978

		% differential over non-covered workers for			
		All covered workers	National agreement only	National plus supplementary	Company or local only
Males:	Manual	9.9	6.1	11.1	17.8
	Non-manual	−2.5	−2.1	−4.0	−2.6
Females:	Manual	17.6	13.4	22.2	20.3
	Non-manual	22.8	25.0	23.5	6.1

Source: Derived from New Earnings Survey

two decentralized categories, although the situation is less clear for non-manuals, largely because many of the most highly paid non-manuals are not covered by collective agreements in the private sector. The apparent returns to decentralization must also be qualified by possible structural factors such as size of unit and product market dimensions, or performance factors such as productivity and workforce quality. Nevertheless a similar pattern is found in the United States, and it is not unreasonable to conclude that there is an industrial relations effect, probably caused by the whipsaw possibilities of decentralized bargaining. A related issue is that it is much more difficult to operate a successful incomes policy under decentralized bargaining; indeed the recent spate of incomes policies were primarily introduced as a result of the wage drift resulting from fragmented bargaining in the early 1960s.

It does not, however, necessarily follow that decentralized bargaining is inflationary, because as Ulman noted higher wages may be offset by higher productivity. This was the argument underlying the productivity bargaining movement of the late 1960s, strongly encouraged by the Prices and Incomes Board. Although doubts have been expressed about the outcome of productivity bargaining in many instances, it did emerge that successful productivity bargaining needed to be conducted at a decentralized level.

A third dimension by which efficiency might be judged is the extent of conflict generated by a particular bargaining structure. In terms of time lost there is no doubt that decentralized structures generate more conflict. The United States and Canada, in spite of relatively low levels of unionization, have amongst the highest levels of time lost through strikes. This is not mainly due to the frequency of strikes but their length, since strikes tend to be fought on a calculative, economic basis. By contrast, where arrangements are centralized, the high costs of a strike, and the different views likely to emerge amongst both sides as it continues may lead to greater inhibitions in allowing strikes to break out.

The final dimension of efficiency, if efficiency is stretched to include political as well as economic goals, is the opportunity for employee participation in company operation. Under very centralized industry wide or economy wide arrangements, it is clearly difficult to permit much direct employer participation, but less evidently it is also difficult to achieve participation in certain issues if the bargaining structure is too decentralized. As the TUC put it (1973):

> Major decisions on investment, location, closures, takeovers and mergers and product specialisation of the organisation are generally taken at levels where collective bargaining does not take place ... On the one hand local and plant bargaining do not affect planning and investment decisions, and on the other, national agreements are not concerned with the management decisions of individual firms.

Industrial democracy in the sense in which the Bullock Report conceived it inevitably concentrated on the company level, and this happened to coincide with attention in collective bargaining increasingly becoming focused on economic and bargaining issues which could also best be decided at company level. This new focus is in sharp contrast with a previous vacuum at company level in British industrial relations arrangements. The Bullock recommendations for company based industrial democracy could also, through the proposed Joint Representation Committee of all company unions, perform the useful function of providing the unions with a ready made vehicle for company bargaining.

Conclusions

As can be seen from the above discussion, there is no easy definition of bargaining structure which will meet the various objectives; all that can be hoped is that there will be a nationally evaluated tradeoff between them. But bargaining structure will remain a vital aspect of any improved industrial relations system, and as the Donovan Commission noted, the onus of action is on the individual enterprise even though national leadership is also urgently required. Having begun this chapter with a statement by the CBI (1979) on the problems of structure, it is perhaps appropriate to finish with the CBI's five-point set of guidelines:

1. There should be the minimum number of bargaining units consistent with the structure and organization of a company or industry.
2. The bargaining unit should comprise all those employees who share a common interest and who would be able normally to claim comparable concessions from employers.
3. There should usually only be separate bargaining units where there is a significantly different employment package. A single bargaining unit will normally cover many different occupations and thus rates of pay, the objective being to ensure that differential relationships between common interest groups are maintained.
4. Bargaining can take place at more than one level, with different bargaining units for each. Where flexibility through multi-tier bargaining is desirable there should normally be clear separation of those items of the employment package bargained at each level, with no item bargained at more than one level and only those items for which flexibility is required bargained at the lower level.
5. Arrangements for accountability and endorsement should be clear to ensure bargaining retains credibility at all times.

References and Further Reading

Beaumont, P.B., Thomson, A.W.J. and Gregory, M.B., 'Bargaining Structure', *Management Decision Monograph*, no. 3, 1980.

Brown, W.A., 'The Structure of Pay Bargaining in Britain' in Blackaby, F. (Ed), *The Future of Pay Bargaining*, Heinemann, London, 1980.

Brown, W.A. and Sisson, K., *The Changing Contours of Collective Bargaining*, British Universities Industrial Relations Association Conference 1979.

Brown, W.A. and Terry, M., 'The Changing Nature of National Wage Agreements', *Scottish Journal of Political Economy*, June 1978.

Clegg, H.A., *Trade Unionism under Collective Bargaining*, Blackwell, Oxford, 1976.

Confederation of British Industry, *Pay: The Choice Ahead*, CBI, 1979.

Department of Employment Manpower Papers no. 5, *The Reform of Collective Bargaining at Plant and Company Level*, HMSO, 1971.

Fox, A. and Flanders, A., 'The Reform of Collective Bargaining: From Donovan to Durkheim', *British Journal of Industrial Relations*, July, 1969.

Thomson, A.W.J. and Hunter, L.C., 'The Level of Bargaining in a Multi-Plant Company', *Industrial Relations Journal*, Summer, 1975.

Trades Union Congress, *Industrial Democracy*, TUC, 1973.

Ulman, L., 'Connective and Competitive Bargaining', *Scottish Journal of Political Economy*, June, 1974.

5

Installing Salary and Wage Systems

Angela M Bowey

One of the aims of managers in organizations is to control or influence the behaviour of the people in that organization, to ensure that the required activities are carried out to an acceptable standard, that responses are made at the right times in the right way, that the behaviours of different people are coordinated, etc. There are many control systems operating in an organization to achieve such ends, eg financial control, production control, stock control, information control, quality control, budgetary control, maintenance planning, manpower planning, work study, job evaluation, incentive bonus systems.

All of these control procedures may be operating within the same organization, all influencing the behaviour of the same population of individuals; and in addition, those individuals have aims and interests of their own which affect the way they respond to the situation. Until recently, it was common practice for the experts in any one field to design the control procedures for their specialism without reference to any other aspects of the organization, and in some specialisms and some organizations this still occurs. The results, all too frequently, were that the operation of one control procedure caused serious difficulties in other areas.

For example, the editors were asked to advise a company on their industrial relations situation, which was gradually worsening and so had become a cause of concern to their senior managers. The centralized planned maintenance system which had been installed was one cause of the discontent, as it had broken down long-standing working practices from which the men had derived satisfaction and a greater sense of safety in a fairly dangerous environment. The management's reaction was to insist that the maintenance system was a separate issue from industrial relations, and one on which the researchers were not experts and therefore should not comment.

Another example of this tendency to 'compartmentalize' organizations is described in Chapter 28. Organizations which have salary systems incorporating merit increases based on the achievement of budgetary targets can run into difficulties when the target system has been designed by financial experts and is rigidly adhered to by production managers without regard to the variations in circumstances.

Behaviour in an organization is simultaneously influenced by a variety of control procedures and personal interests, and since the system for paying salaries or wages does, and is usually intended to, influence behaviour, it follows that it will have implications for many other areas of the organization. It is for this reason that when plans are made to change a salary or wage system, the system designers need a very thorough understanding of the way the organization is currently operating, and of all the factors which are influencing the behaviour of the people concerned. Unless this knowledge is obtained, it is impossible to predict the behaviour which will result from any particular change in the system. As Tom Lupton said, 'How can you plan a route to take the organization from A to B, unless you know where A is?'

The following technique has been developed as a result of experience in changing payment systems in a large number of organizations.

The first stage is information gathering. One technique for obtaining the necessary information is to investigate the ways in which the people concerned perform their jobs, and in particular to note any activities which cause difficulties for other groups of employees or which have adverse repercussions on the output of the organization, and the reasons for those activities, ie 'What is going on here?' and 'Why?'. This information can usually be obtained from discussions with the people concerned, and the other groups such as their managers, subordinates and the adjacent departments who interact with them. From this information (which needs to be validated by reference to statistics and other objective evidence) a model can be drawn, showing all the important factors influencing behaviour and all the significant patterns of behaviour. An example is shown in Figure 5.1, which refers to the case study described in Chapter 23. When this has been drawn, it is possible to identify the factors which the new system will need to change, and the repercussions that any proposed change may have on other areas.

Producing a model such as that shown in Figure 5.1 should form part of the first stage of any plans to install a new wage or salary system. There are five major issues which need to be considered when such plans are made. These are:

1 The strategy for change.
2 The criteria the new system must aim to meet.

Installing Salary and Wage Systems 57

3 The characteristics of the payment system which are to be changed and/or the features of the new payment system.
4 The changes in other control procedures or activities which will be necessary to support or be compatible with the new system.
5 The implications of the changes for other groups of employees not directly involved.

The Strategy for Change

The reward system is a major mediating mechanism between the requirements of those planning the organization and the desires and interests of the employees. Some characteristics of certain types of payment system will contribute towards the greater satisfaction of the

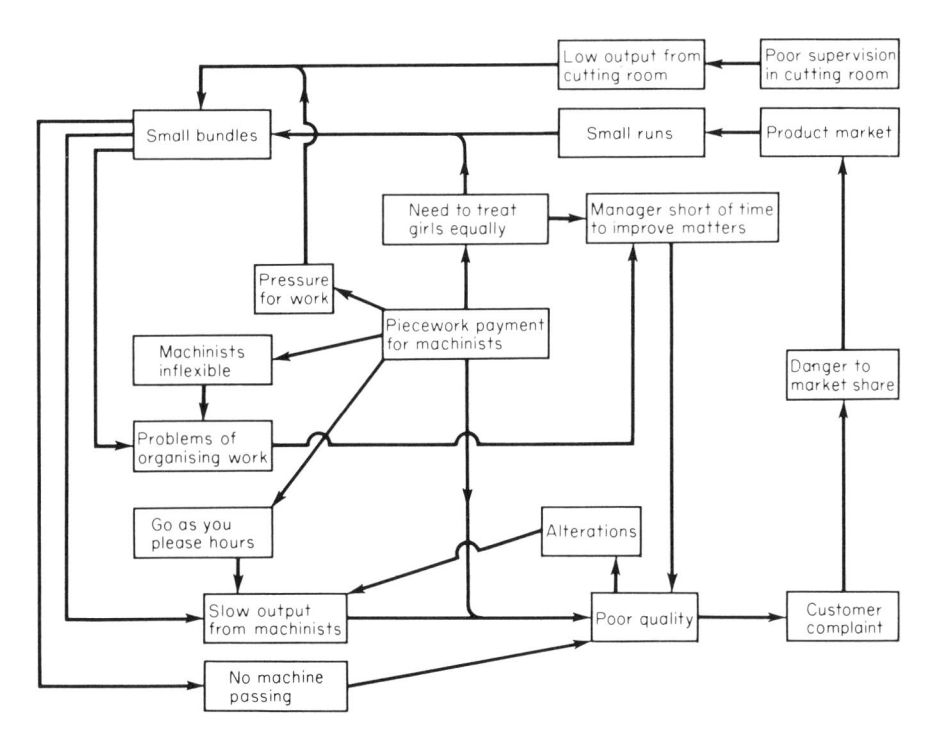

Figure 5.1 A model showing behaviour patterns and the factors influencing behaviour in a garment factory

employees, and some characteristics of some payment systems will encourage the desired behaviour on the part of those employees. There are an enormous number of different permutations of the various features of payment systems and no reason to believe that one cannot be found which contributes significantly to the benefits to both company and employee (discussed in Chapter 23).

It will be rare for an organization to be so small and simple that one individual can understand all the interests involved and integrate them into a suitable payment system. That was what the author did in the garment factory illustrated in Figure 5.1, but even there another procedure would have been preferable had the company been prepared to spend the time and the money on a larger exercise, and had the predominant managerial style been reconcilable to a 'participative' approach.

In most organizations in Britain, particularly those large enough to have wage and salary administrators, the interests of the various groups are so complex, and the extent to which they are prepared to trust another, particularly a manager, to adequately represent their point of view is so limited, that it is almost imperative for long-term success with a new payment system, that those groups are involved as participants in the design of the scheme. In the author's experience this is by far the best way of proceeding.

An additional consideration is the time and resources that would be required for the management to investigate the situation in sufficient detail to produce an adequate model of what is currently happening in that organization. Even then, it is doubtful whether managers could understand the perspectives of other groups, or indeed whether those groups would be prepared to reveal their interests and informal activities to a manager.

It is for these reasons that the setting up of a group of people representing the senior management, the employees to whom the new system is to be applied and any other groups (such as supervisors and work-study officers) who may be affected by the changes, is strongly recommended. This group can then ensure that all interests and problems are taken into account when the description of the present situation and its shortcomings is prepared. In addition, once this group has worked through the exercise of designing a new scheme, even though the resulting scheme may not be precisely the one management would have liked, it will at least have the commitment of all the parties who are going to be affected by it. There is nothing so damaging to a new control procedure in an organization, as most managers will know, as the alienation of some important group such as the supervisors from that procedure at the very start.

Another difficulty which can arise with this kind of exercise, is that a great deal of effort may be put into designing a new system and enthusiasm and commitment generated, only for some more senior figure to decide not to implement the plans. This can have damaging effects on industrial relations, and undermines the willingness of employees to make a contribution to planning on later occasions. It is important therefore to seek support for an exercise such as the redesign of a payment system from the most senior and the most powerful people in the organization, and if possible to involve them in the exercise so that they understand what is being done and why.

Once the new system has been designed, a useful change strategy is to select one section, group or department, and implement the changes on a small scale as a pilot exercise. In this way, the parties concerned can be reassured that the new scheme will have the effects that were expected and no unexpected adverse effects that would make it undesirable. Since the scheme has been designed with the participation of the employees, then there will usually be benefits to them from the scheme. Once these have been demonstrated, the acceptance and speedy installation of the scheme should follow.

A frequent problem with installing payment systems, particularly those requiring a work-study involvement, is that the employees are not committed or enthusiastic towards the new scheme and consequently employ delaying tactics. It might then take many years to complete the installation and the system may never operate satisfactorily. Because situations may change (due to changes in the product market, the labour market, technology, union organization, etc) it is often desirable to update a payment system. If its very installation takes five years, the difficulties for the administrator of knowing which sections are at what stage and which need what updating adjustments, are so enormous that they are likely to be postponed. Eventually, they may build up to a point where the system, although not yet fully installed, is already unsuitable and needs a major revision. Commitment towards and involvement in the design and monitoring of the system can shorten the time taken to install it once the planning stage has been completed.

In relation to joint working parties of any type, it is very easy for the members of a working party to get out of touch with their constituents in the organization and to be seen as 'collaborators' who have been 'brainwashed' into thinking like the management. To avoid this, attempts should be made to involve those who have representatives on the working party in exercises which bring to their notice what is going on and reassures them that their interests are being taken into account. This may be done through a programme of interviews (with joint management-union pairs of interviewers, or just union interviewers) to sound out opinions; by questionnaires to check particular points; by invitations to 'anyone who wishes to state their point of view' to talk to the working party or a subcommittee of it; or by periodic large-scale meetings at which the work done so far is explained and opinions and discussion are invited.

Once a model or account has been agreed which describes the present problems with the payment system, the following points will need to be considered.

Criteria the New System Must Meet

What are the objectives which it is desired that the new payment system should meet? These should be apparent once the present situation and the likely situation in the future have been examined. They may include some or all of the following, plus others specific to the particular situation of the organization:

1. To enable the employees to earn a good or a reasonable salary or wage.
2. To pay equitable sums to different individuals, avoiding anomalies.
3. To be understandable and acceptable to the employees and their seniors.
4. To reward and encourage high quality work.
5. To encourage employees to accept transfers between jobs.
6. To encourage employees to accept changes in methods of working.
7. To discourage wastage of materials or equipment.
8. To encourage employees to use their initiative and discretion.
9. To encourage employees to develop better methods of working.
10. To reward and encourage high levels of output.
11. To discourage and lead to a decrease in overtime working.

It is then possible to examine the effects of different types of salary or wage system on these criteria (Lupton and Bowey, 1974).

The Features of the New System

The decisions must then be made as to whether the new scheme should contain an incentive element, how rapidly should that incentive increase and in response to what activities on the part of employees (effort, output, machine utilization, contribution to profit, costs saved, profit improvement, value added, merit, etc)? How much of the total pay should the normal incentive payments make up? What unit should calculations be based on (individual, group, section, factory, whole company, etc)? How many grades should there be, and what should be the pay relativities between them? And what should be the absolute levels of pay be? Advice on answering these questions is the aim of this handbook, and later chapters will prove useful at this stage.

Supporting Changes in the Organization

Any change in a salary or wage system may require changes to be made elsewhere in the organization. For example, the introduction of an effort-related incentive bonus scheme may require the work-study department to be strengthened and enlarged. The introduction of measured daywork would require more and better trained first-line supervisors. Many systems, and in particular the introduction of management by objectives (MBO) into a salary system, may require better measurement and recording procedures to be introduced. A procedure for updating the salary or wage system may also be desirable. These points are discussed more fully in later chapters.

Implications of the Changes for Other Groups

Once the plans have been drawn up, the implications of the proposed changes for those groups of employees who are not directly involved should be examined. It may, for example, prove to be desirable to include in the scheme some other group of employees not originally considered. Plans may then be set in motion for involving those people in an exercise to see whether the scheme is acceptable to and suitable for them.

It is likely that the earnings levels of other groups may need to be adjusted in order to maintain differentials with those involved in the new scheme. Any loss of privilege that will result from the changes should be examined carefully and plans made for coping with the readjustment problems.

This done, the stage is set for the implementation. If a working party was set up to design the new scheme, it can continue to have a useful role throughout the implementation as a monitoring and disputes-settling body; and beyond that, perhaps with a circulating membership, it may prove very useful for long-term monitoring and adjustment of the wage or salary system.

References and Further Reading

Bartlett, A., and Kayser, T., *Changing Organizational Behaviour*, Prentice-Hall, Englewood Cliffs, 1973.
Brooks, E., *Organizational Change: The Managerial Dilemma*, Macmillan, 1980.
Clark, P.A., *Action Research and Organizational Change*, Harper and Row, New York, 1973.
Golembiewski, R.T., *Approaches to Planned Change. Part 1 and Part 2*, Marcel Dekker, 1979.

Lupton, T., and Bowey, A.M., *Wages and Salaries*, Penguin, Harmondsworth, 1974 (revised 2nd edition, Gower, 1982, forthcoming).
Marchington, M., *Responses to Participation at Work*, Gower, 1980.

Part Two

Job Context and Measurement

Editor's Introduction

An important feature of any payment system is the set of rules which determine how much pay each individual shall receive by comparison with others in the same organization. Two factors may be used to determine these differentials—the nature of the work done and the amount of effort the individual puts into his work.

When evaluating the nature of the work done it is usually considered necessary to pay more money for jobs which are more important or more senior in the organization. Responsibility for example is often taken as a major justification for such differentials, and the more responsibility a job carries the more it is paid. Decisions about payment differentials of this kind can be made by subjective judgement on an informal basis; or a more precise procedure can be used which specifies exactly which aspects of the work are to be taken into account, and where more than one aspect is considered, how much weight is to be given to each by comparison with the others. There are many job evaluation techniques which can be used in this way and in Chapter 7 the most commonly used procedures are described. But even with the most precisely defined procedure, there are still subjective judgements implicit in the design of the technique (such as which aspects of work are to be taken into account and what weights are to be assigned to them). There is no science in job evaluation,—it is a procedure for formalizing a subjective decision process which if it is not formalized can sometimes produce troublesome anomalies and discontent. But an inappropriate or over-rigid job evaluation scheme can produce serious problems also. The reader should guard against claims that any job evaluation procedure is non-subjective.

Before jobs can be evaluated, however, decisions must have been made about the design of jobs in the organization. All formal job evaluation procedures involve an examination of job descriptions, and in many cases this affords the management an opportunity to rationalize and re-design some jobs. Obviously the way a job is designed and its boundaries of responsibility will affect the evaluation it eventually receives; but decisions about job design should take account of many other factors, and Chapter 6 is concerned with the problems involved in job design and the various different approaches which can be adopted.

In addition to differentials based on the nature of the work, it is often the case that further differentiation between employees occurs as a result of payments for effort or amount of work done. Work study and work measurement are methods of determining how hard an individual is working and of relating all types of work to a single effort rating scale. The most obvious use of work study techniques is in payment systems in which some portion of pay is related directly to effort rating. However, there are many situations where this kind of scheme is inappropriate, but where work study techniques can still be used to compare the 'effort content' of some other index (such as number of parts produced) to which pay is related. Work study, work measurement and the related activity of methods study are described in Chapter 9. Chapter 10 addresses the difficult question of how we can measure productivity. The difficulties involved in finding a measure which can be used to make comparisons across time, between organizations, or between societies are considered. However great these difficulties, there are still situations in which such a measure is of vital importance.

6

Job Design and Work Organization

David W Birchall

Work study has an important part to play when new payment systems are to be introduced. Method study can be employed to determine the 'best' way to do the work technically; time study facilitates the determination of the time required to carry out the task. The job designer has an important role at this stage since it is also necessary to make decisions about other aspects of the job such as the relationship between the man and his machine and the composition of the workgroup. There are a number of different principles which are currently used for the design of jobs and work organization and in some cases they have different implications for the kind of payment system which is appropriate.

Many organizations are continually attempting to increase operational efficiency through making better use of their human resources but, unfortunately, in some cases the wider implications of the changes which have been introduced have been overlooked. Jobs have been rationalized, mechanized and automated in order to increase the competitiveness of the organization's operations. Often the effects upon both the person performing the job and his relationship to that job have been ignored. Factors external to the organizational environment, eg the effect upon the individual's aspirations and expectations resulting from increased educational standards, have also often been disregarded. Even though these changes have often been accompanied by increases in earnings they have also been criticized for increasing 'boredom' at work, which in turn is said to have resulted in growing absenteeism, labour turnover, grievance activity and even sabotage. Attention is often focused upon assembly line jobs although these problems are not confined only to blue-collar workers.

Job design and work organization is concerned with the specification of the contents, methods and relationships of jobs to satisfy technological and organizational requirements as well as the social and personal requirements of the job holder. In addition to the functional and operational requirements of the job those responsible for job design must consider two related aspects—ie the physiological and physical environment, and the organizational, social and personal aspects. The prediction of man's responses to both the physical and physiological demands of work have been widely researched and data are available to aid the job designer. Ergonomists have refined research techniques to the extent that machines may now be designed to meet the physical requirements of man. Training programmes can also be devised to equip man for the task. This chapter, however, discusses the organizational, social and personal aspects of jobs where techniques are less well developed.

Job Rationalization

Early theories of job design and work organization were based upon two concepts, ie the division of labour and the model of man as a rational economic being. Taylor (1947) suggested that management, in order to improve efficiency, should undertake all of that work for which it is better equipped than the operative, particularly all the planning and organizing activities. He argued that rules, laws and formulae devised by management were likely to be superior to the judgement of the individual worker. The worker therefore was to be given little scope for the use of initiative and was rather seen as an adjunct of the machine. The division of labour was seen as creating jobs for which unskilled labour could rapidly be trained. It was further assumed that man calculates the actions which will maximize his self interests and that he then behaves accordingly. His main motive in working was assumed to be monetary gain. Emphasis was placed upon the use of selection procedures, methods improvement and financial incentives to improve efficiency. This desire to achieve greater worker efficiency also appears to have considerably influenced the early work of many industrial psychologists. Investigations were carried out into the effects of factors such as physical conditions and rest pauses upon monotony, boredom and fatigue, in order to determine the optimum conditions for maximum worker output.

High product demand and competitive pressures have brought about technological developments which in many industries have transformed the traditional craft structure. Following rationalization, jobs which formerly were undertaken by craftsmen using skills and knowledge acquired through long experience in that job, are deskilled and consequently capable of being undertaken by lower skill workers. Whilst former craftwork demanded the application of both mental and physical skills, mechanization and job rationalization has, in some cases, produced jobs which make high physical demands on workers but which require little mental and physical skill. In automated processes such as chemical refining, machines have largely replaced manual labour and the production worker is engaged on mental rather than physical activity in a job which is basically equipment monitoring and control.

If the job designer's sole objective is technical efficiency the workers would be assigned simple tasks to be performed using predetermined methods. Reduced work complexity also simplifies operator training and facilitates worker transfer between jobs. In consequence work is often repetitive, lacking variety and requires limited skill and ability. The methods of working are predetermined and the worker has little opportunity to change his work method. The division of the task often makes it difficult for the worker to perceive the relationship of any one work activity to a meaningful and worthwhile end product. In addition the work pace may be mechanically controlled, so that the worker's freedom of movement and social interaction may be restricted.

Many observers have reported high job rationalization to be associated with high levels of expressed boredom. Lack of task variety has been found to be related to both job dissatisfaction and undesired worker behaviour; on the other hand, some researchers have pointed out that such jobs appeal to some workers. Mechanically repetitive jobs have been seen often to leave the mind free to 'wander' and 'daydream'. Where opportunities for social interaction are available they may compensate for monotonous work. Such work is generally highly predictable which may contribute to a worker's feelings of security. It has been observed that paced repetitive work seems to be a source of positive motivation to some workers who may be 'pulled along' by the inertia inherent in such repetitive activity. Furthermore it has been suggested that the repetitive nature of the work does not necessarily interfere with improved morale when the product is attractive, when workers can take pride in an unusual kind of skill and when the 'pull' of the process is not interrupted by excessive pressure for quantity, by unwanted interruptions from outsiders or problems regarding incoming materials and equipment. To other workers, however, the pacing effect associated with certain machine and manual-assembly processes would appear to be a source of some dissatisfaction.

The extent to which the worker is able to control his own work activities also appears to influence job attitudes and behaviour. In highly rationalized work the operator has little control or responsibility, factors which seem to relate to the level of job interest expressed by workers. Also of importance in this relationship is the extent to which the individual feels the desire to satisfy, through work, higher order needs such as personal achievement and social status.

Some investigations (eg Walker and Guest, 1952) have suggested that these 'undesirable' characteristics of highly rationalized jobs, eg work pacing, lack of variety in tasks performed, lack of worker freedom and control, little use of skills and abilities and low responsibility, are causes of job dissatisfaction and undesired worker behaviour. However, other researchers (eg Goldthorpe, *et al.*, 1968) have reported contrasting findings, eg those workers who expressed the least favourable attitudes to work were less likely to seek alternative employment and that both pay level and security had an important influence on such decisions.

Although opinions on the effect of jobs and work upon the job attitudes and behaviour of employees vary considerably it will be argued here that there are certain job and work attitudes which have on the whole desirable effects and should therefore be taken into account in the design of any job.

These desirable job attributes are considered to be:

1 The level of variety.
2 The extent of repetitiveness.
3 The degree of attention with accompanying mental absorption.
4 The level of responsibility for decisions, the discretion present and the degree of accountability.
5 Employee control over his/her own job.
6 The presence of goals and achievement feedback.
7 Perceived contribution to a socially useful product.
8 Opportunities for developing friendships.
9 Where dependent upon others for task achievement some influence over the way the work is carried out.
10 Perceived skill utilization.

In certain circumstances rather than focusing upon the design of each individual job it may be more appropriate to consider the design of the workgroup and its activities. Membership of a workgroup can have certain positive benefits for the individual. We have already referred to the need for social opportunities at work. When tasks are interdependent membership of the group at least assists in sustaining communication and developing an understanding between team members. Beyond this the workgroup may develop to a stage where standards of cooperation are enforced and mutual help and support is available. Membership of a workgroup can also have positive benefits where the work is particularly stressful since support from others experiencing similar problems can help overcome the difficulties. Focus on the group task can also facilitate the development of a complete and meaningful task where subdivision of the work to individuals would result in a series of fragmented activities.

The following guidelines are suggested for the design of workgroup activities (based on Schumacher, 1976):

(a) Primary workgroups should include between 4 and 20 individuals.
(b) The primary workgroup should have a designated leader who is accountable for the group's performance.
(c) The group should be responsible for activities which make up a complete task.
(d) Wherever possible the group members, through their supervisor, should be responsible for planning their own work.
(e) Members should have the opportunity to evaluate their performance compared with the standards.
(f) All the skills necessary for satisfactory task achievement must be present within the group.
(g) Reward systems should be designed to support group behaviour.

The emphasis when applying these guidelines is upon defining the tasks and responsibilities of the workgroup rather than each individual job. Individuals within that group then are afforded the opportunity to develop with other team members their own role within that group. Objectives for the group must be clearly established but the means for achieving them then become the responsibility of workgroup members. The size of the group is an important consideration. If too few tasks are assigned to the group there will not be sufficient flexibility within the range of activities to enable staff to develop a variety of roles. Also social opportunities will be more restricted. As the group increases in size agreement will be more difficult to attain and fragmentation of the group more likely. Group performance over time can be improved if members are involved in both the planning and evaluation of their own work. This can lead to an increased knowledge of the work and its relevance to the organization in total as well as increased understanding of how best to organize the workgroup.

Involvement in monitoring performance also gives an opportunity for members to improve problem-solving skills. Additionally it gives individuals the feedback about their contribution which has been frequently referred to as an important element in the motivation process.

In order to provide more of these desired attributes in jobs which were previously over-rationalized, use has been made of several distinct approaches to change. The first two, job enlargement and job enrichment, focus upon changing individual jobs. The third, semi-autonomous group working, focuses more upon designing the group activity in a way which permits group members to decide their own work organization within the boundaries of the overall task.

Job Enlargement and Work Rotation

Job enlargement and work rotation have been used as a way of increasing variety in highly rationalized jobs, the objective being to relieve the monotony associated with such work and by so doing alleviate any possible boredom.

Work rotation is the movement of employees between different tasks on either an obligatory or a voluntary basis. As well as increasing job interest due to changes in the environment, skill requirements and job content, work rotation is claimed to provide the 'managerial' advantage of increasing the employees' skills and, therefore, their flexibility. In many cases wages have been increased in order to facilitate the introduction of the change and/or in recognition of the employees' higher skill level. In such a situation it is important that payment systems be related to the individual's skills and capacity for performing the different tasks rather than to the individual job. Problems may be created if the rotation is compulsory since constant changes in the pattern of social interaction may interfere with group development, and in addition some workers may prefer to remain on one familiar job. (An example of the application of work rotation is presented as Case number 1, below).

Job enlargement stems from the addition of one or more related tasks. It may be achieved by introducing more frequent changes in the products being manufactured, eg through a reduction in the batch size. Benefits are said to include reduced employee fatigue, reduction in boredom and broadened work skills. Critics of the technique argue that the extended job is usually only composed of multiples of the original task and that often nothing is added that will contribute to increased employee job satisfaction and motivation.

In practice benefits reported from exercises involving the enlargement of assembly line and similar work have often been operational rather than behavioural. Productivity and quality have increased in many such cases, hence costs have been reduced. Where assembly lines have been reduced in length it has been possible to introduce model changes more smoothly. Where jobs have been enlarged it has often been easier for the employee to perceive the value of his contribution to a meaningful and worthwhile end-product. Job satisfaction, absenteeism and turnover have improved in several cases. In other cases job enlargement has been necessary where previous work systems were inappropriately applied.

When jobs are enlarged it is necessary that the system of payment is related to the skills and abilities utilized. Where potential benefits to the company may result from those changes workers are likely to resist their introduction unless they too gain financially. (An example of the application of job enlargement is presented as Case number 2, below).

Both job enlargement and work rotation have limited value with regard to improving the motivational content of jobs since such changes generally concentrate upon increasing the physical variety in jobs. The motivational impact of increased task variety is restricted since workers soon become familiar with enlarged jobs. Other desirable job attributes suggested earlier, eg employee control, decision making, responsibility and accountability, are not considered when jobs are only 'enlarged'.

Job Enrichment

Job Enrichment is generally applied with the purpose of increasing the motivational content of jobs by giving the employees greater opportunity for achievement and recognition. Horizontal job enrichment involves changes to the immediate work to enable the employee to exercise more control over his working speed and use more of his skills. Vertical job enrichment is aimed at increasing employees' involvement in the organization and/or their jobs, eg by providing increased participation in company policy-making; increased job responsibility; increased involvement in the process; and increased opportunity for training and advancement. A vertically enriched job may therefore be seen as one which includes responsibility, achievement, recognition, advancement and growth as well as providing autonomy, variety and task identity.

In some cases where horizontal enrichment has meant the modification of conventional assembly lines, or similar systems, to individual or small group assembly both worker behaviour and productivity have improved. Workers on restructured jobs have greater control over work pace, they can readily observe their contribution to productivity and have increased task variety. Changes in which the worker has also been assigned greater responsibilities, however, have generally proved to be more successful. These additional responsibilities have included such duties as setting-up the machines, inspection and maintenance as well as, in some cases, the authority to deal directly with service departments, suppliers and customers when queries have arisen. (An example of vertical enrichment is described in Case number 3, below).

Whilst in many cases job enrichment, in particular vertical enrichment, has led to some degree of success in improving workers' attitudes and behaviour, generally little consideration has been given in these changes to the role of the work group. For example, where individual assembly has been adopted there has tended to be a lack of opportunity for social interaction in addition to task independence, which, in one case at least, was the primary cause of failure. In several other instances disputes arose where the level of payment was not adjusted to take into consideration the employees' additional responsibilities. Also, where piecework incentives were operating, satisfactory changes were often difficult to implement.

Semi-Autonomous Group Working

Semi-autonomous group working involves the creation of formal functional workgroups which have some degree of autonomy and responsibility within a defined area. The objective of such changes is to make available opportunities for both 'enriched' work and group development. The organizational changes necessary when such workgroups are established may affect considerably the role of first line supervision.

Membership of a workgroup offers many potential benefits to the individual. Employees may gain greater confidence through recognition of important skills, through the development of social skills, through opportunity to exercise influence and assume a leadership role, whilst the group may provide an individual with support, encouragement, protection and security. Such benefits may derive from membership of various types of informal or formal groups but successful outcomes appear to be more likely where there is task interdependence between members of a formal functional workgroup.

It is often difficult to build into the jobs of individual workers those attributes which were earlier identified as desirable in well-designed jobs. The need for close coordination often prevents the delegation of complete task responsibility to individuals. The group task, because of its greater content and complexity, is more likely to provide a satisfactory basis for the allocation of responsibility and discretion than the smaller and less complex individual task, whilst this larger group task is more likely to provide conditions appropriate for goal-setting. Apart from the socio-psychological benefits of group membership, which may in any case derive from informal group membership, it can be argued that the existence of formal functional workgroups facilitates the establishment of production targets and standards, provides greater opportunity for work variety and facilitates adaptation to change. The determination of work targets and schedules, and the measurement of performance against such standards is easier for larger operational units than for individual tasks or for separate workers.

Voluntary work rotation within the group can provide increased variety for the group members who participate. Flexibility can be achieved more easily within the semi-autonomous group enabling disturbances caused by such things as product changes, absenteeism and machine breakdown to be more easily accommodated. It, therefore, appears that through semi-autonomous group working the worker is more likely to experience desired job attributes than as a result of either the enlargement or enrichment of individual jobs. (An example of semi-autonomous group working is briefly described in Case number 4, below).

Where increased levels of group autonomy are to be introduced it is essential that the organizational climate is conducive to such changes. Information systems which facilitate goal-setting, feedback and performance measurement are essential. Opportunities must also exist for the employee to attain those goals which he considers to be of importance, eg increased earnings, promotion, social integration. Payment systems must be related to group activities rather than based upon competition between group members. Premium wage systems related to the group's output are particularly suitable. The introduction of semi-autonomous groups has often been accompanied by wage agreements— the group of workers sharing in the benefits resulting from the changes. In several cases the employees involved have been given 'salaried' status. The modified role of first line supervision must be clearly established, and attention paid to the motivation of both first line supervisors and lower level managers, since experience in some organizations has shown that these personnel are likely to feel threatened by the changes.

Discussion

Job design and work organization has in the past been dominated largely by cost considerations, comparatively little attention having been paid to the needs of individuals. Job enlargement, work rotation, job enrichment and semi-autonomous group working have been suggested as possible techniques for providing the job attributes which are thought to be desirable.

The most ambitious experiments have given rise to the creation of semi-autonomous groups of workers with considerable responsibility, little direct supervision and opportunity to participate in policy- and decision-making. This solution appears to be particularly suitable where the work is such that it must be performed by a group, eg manning process plants and machine supervising. Assembly-line reorganization has also proved successful where the effects of machine-pacing have been removed and groups established to undertake the work. The enrichment of individual jobs, whilst not offering all the advantages of semi-autonomous group working, is particularly useful where grouping of tasks is not practical, ie one employee is capable of completing the total job. Such possibilities exist in both white-collar and blue-collar situations—jobs can be redesigned both to increase employee responsibility and provide greater 'closure'. Where technological constraints exist which prohibit the introduction of enriched jobs, either through semi-autonomous group working or changes to the job of the individual, greater variety can be added to the job by either enlarging the tasks performed or rotating workers.

In many organizations new payment systems have been introduced at the same time as jobs and work organization have been restructured. When the objective of the job changes is greater worker involvement, the employee may have greater job responsibility and control. These aspects of a job are not easily measured using traditional time-study methods. Consequently payment by results schemes where measures of task performance are based upon time-study data may be inappropriate for these restructured jobs. In such cases new payment systems have often been negotiated which either exclude incentive payments often giving workers 'salaried' status or incorporate incentive schemes closely related to achievement of the group's formal goals as in the case of premium wage systems.

Case Studies of Job Restructuring in Practice

Case number 1: Volvo car assembly (Sweden)

One example of the many work rotation programmes operating in this company involves 20 people out of the 32 engaged in the 17 different working operations required in the internal and external sealing and insulation of car bodies. Internal sealing, in particular, is very tiring since those carrying out the work are obliged to adopt uncomfortable working positions inside the body. Work rotation takes place once per day with the exception of the 6 engaged on internal sealing who rotate hourly. The pattern of rotation was determined by the foreman in consultation with the employees. After agreement was reached a period of training was begun to enable each team member to familiarize himself with all the jobs carried out by his team.

It is claimed that the changed work pattern has contributed to improved work attitudes and a greater understanding of the total work process. Complaints concerning muscular pain which may result from the persistent use of the same muscles have reduced. Quality, absenteeism and turnover have also improved since work rotation was introduced but many factors, both internal and external to the organization, affect such variables.

Case number 2: an appliance manufacturer (USA)

Assembly of the 5 different models was formerly undertaken on an 8-station assembly line with a work-cycle time of about one minute. It was considered essential that inventories be minimized in order to maintain low investment in stocks and consequently manufacturing batch sizes were low and there were frequent disruptions due to model changes on the line. This led to technical problems in maintaining the balanced allocation of work to the individual stations.

The enlarged jobs were performed by 4 teams each comprising of 2 workers. A female operative assembled the lower half of the assembly which was mainly electrical components whilst a male used mechanical tools and fixtures to assemble the hardware in the upper section. This new method resulted in a 24% reduction in assembly labour costs.

Case number 3: machine operators (IBM: USA)

The jobs of machine minders working on slicing equipment preparing silicon wafers for integrated circuits were enriched. Workers who previously were rotated among all the machines were given the responsibility for 2 machines. Maintenance training was given to each worker following which they became responsible for the minor maintenance of the 2 machines. Each operator was given the authority to decide when to replace the slicing blade. A performance feedback system was developed to provide daily quality information to the operator. Improvements in performance were recorded, maintenance costs were reduced and employee attitudes improved.

Case number 4: process operator's job (UK)

The work of 16 process operators was modified from the initial routine job of monitoring equipment and making slight adjustments to one with much greater responsibility and group autonomy. Operators were allowed to fix their own breaks and arrange cover amongst themselves. Panel operators, rather than foremen, were to make the decisions on whether to run batches of finished products into stock tanks; batches which were as specification were to be put to storage without further reference to supervision. Operators were encouraged to raise maintenance job cards themselves and pass them direct to maintenance. Finally, each operator was made responsible for 2 plant efficiencies over which he had some measure of control.

The first two changes were introduced successfully. No evidence of errors of judgement were found concerning 'go/no go' decisions on batches. Operators were reluctant, however, to raise maintenance job cards and supervisors reluctant to delegate the responsibility. The fourth change proved difficult to introduce because of problems carrying out the calculations and reluctance on the part of the operator to accept the added 'chore' and therefore it was eventually abandoned, even though it had shown benefits such as the earlier spotting of leaks.

Factors beyond the control of the experimenters influenced attitudes, performance and turnover. Rumours about plant closure led to an increase in labour turnover from 20 to 100% over the year and the redesigned jobs being performed by a succession of raw recruits. Evaluation of the change was made difficult but the works manager reported that at least no losses or disadvantages were attributable to the job redesign and that in more favourable circumstances he felt that it would be successful.

References and Further Reading

Birchall, D.W., *Job Design—a Planning and Implementation Guide for Managers*, **Gower, 1975**.
Birchall, D.W., *Tomorrow's Office Today—Managing Technological Change*, London, Business Books, 1981.
Davis, L.E. and Taylor, J.C., *Design of Jobs*, Hamondsworth, Penguin, 1972.
Goldthorpe, V.H., Lockwood, D., Bechhofer, F. and Platt, J., *The Affluent Worker: Industrial Attitudes and Behaviour*, Cambridge University Press, London, 1968.
Legge, K. and Mumford, E., *Designing Organisations for Satisfaction and Efficiency*, **Gower, 1978**.
Mumford, E. and Henshall, D., *A Participative Approach to Computer Systems Design*, London, Associated Business Press, 1979.
Paul, W.J. and Robertson, K.B., *Job Enrichment and Employee Motivation*, Gower, **1970**.
S.A.F., *Pay Reform in Sweden*, Sweden, Sweden Employers' Confederation, 1977.
Schumacher, C., *Principles of Work Structuring*, London, British Steel Corporation, 1976.
Taylor, F.W., *Scientific Management*, Harper and Row, New York, 1947.
Walker, C.R. and Guest, R.H., *The Man on the Assembly Line*, Harvard University Press, Cambridge, Mass., 1952.

7

Techniques of Job Evaluation

Jack Butterworth

Job evaluation is the term used to describe both the principle and the family of techniques currently recognized as being essential basics of a rationalized wage and salary structure. The principle of job evaluation is to evaluate different jobs using the same yardstick, and thus to produce a rank or hierarchy from which can be seen the relative importance of any job to another. Essentially the job and not the job holder is evaluated. Adhering to this principle, in some cases only nominally, are the techniques used to produce the ranking of jobs, the job grades and subsequently wage rates. Several distinct techniques using different yardsticks for measuring job content have been developed and applied with some success. Traditionally, the more widely used techniques have been classified into analytical and non-analytical depending on whether the job as a whole is considered without breaking it down, or whether the job content is analysed and each factor identified is then considered (National Board for Prices and Incomes, 1968).

Over the past twenty years new concepts have been evolved, notably by Jaques and by Paterson (Paterson, 1972), to enlarge the range and knowledge of job evaluation. Concurrent with these developments, the growth of management consultancy services has resulted in a need for easily applied and readily accepted techniques. To satisfy this demand some of the larger consultancy groups have devised their own distinctive brands of job evaluation, usually based on the traditional techniques.

The Principle

The principal purpose of job evaluation is to rank jobs as a basis for a pay structure. It aims therefore to compare all jobs under review, using common criteria to define the relationship of one job to another. It is essentially concerned with relationships not with absolutes. Putting the principle into practice becomes fairly easy once a policy outlining this approach has been prepared and circulated to all those involved. It should be remembered that job evaluation is concerned only with that part of the total wage which is paid for satisfactory performance in the job (ie the basic rate). For more than satisfactory performance a merit rating scheme may be applied. Indeed, any form of bonus scheme is entirely separate from a job evaluation exercise. Job evaluation is a process of analysing and assessing the content of jobs in order to place them in an acceptable rank order which can then be used as a basis for a remuneration system. It stresses the importance of being systematic in approach. Written job descriptions enable discussion to be based on what actually happens in a job, not what people think happens or what the job was five or six years ago. Jobs are compared using common previously defined criteria so as to increase the objectivity and consistency of the evaluation. The whole process is one of systematically relating jobs one to another by examination of the importance or difficulty of a job. It can be seen that jobs previously rewarded for historical performance or conditions which no longer appertain will not have as high a placing in a new wages structure based on job evaluation as at present.

Wage and salary structures have a vital and direct bearing on people's performance at work. In many cases the structure could be improved by the introduction of an effective job evaluation scheme. Following the description of the principle in general, an outline of the technique, together with the advantages and disadvantages, will illustrate the principle in practice.

The Four Main Techniques

Four main methods of job evaluation are in use: ranking, grading or classification, factor comparison and points rating. The first two are usually described as non-analytical, while the latter two are termed analytical. Points rating is the most common type of scheme in Britain and the USA; followed by grading or classification, ranking and factor comparison in that order. Taking the four methods with widest application, all except factor comparison may be applied to manual, staff or managerial employees, though the methods vary in their suitability for different situations.

Ranking

This is the simplest method and the easiest to apply. Essentially a job description is prepared for each job to allow the duties, responsibilities and necessary qualifications to be identified. These descriptions should be agreed by both management and union representatives as being accurate representations of the jobs. 'Key' jobs are chosen which will adequately cover the whole range of jobs and these are compared with each other to produce a ranking of key jobs. The remaining jobs are compared with the appropriate key job and inserted into the ranking. Once a complete ranking is achieved, it is divided into a number of grades by choosing positions where, of two jobs, one is held to have a job content of much higher quality than those below. Pay levels or ranges can then be allocated to each range.

A variation on the 'comparison of jobs' step is to use the paired comparison approach of comparing each job with every other one in a sample of key jobs. Each pair is considered independently by several judges. Usually, the judges must base their decisions on a limited number of factors to be considered within the job. A rank order is produced, grades determined, etc. Currently this technique is being applied by consultants under the name of the direct consensus method. In this method two points are scored for a preferred job and one point for tied jobs. Total points allocated determine the ranking. A further refinement is the calculation of a coefficient of agreement between judges which should be greater than 0.75. If less, then the judges are asked to justify some of their decisions with reference to the selected factors. It is claimed that this will usually result in final agreement. There are statistical and other problems with this quantified approach to ranking (Clegg, 1980).

Advantages of the ranking method are its simplicity and easy application in small units. Cost of installation is low and the ranking is flexible in that further jobs are readily incorporated. It is relatively crude but it avoids the hypocrisy of seeming to be scientific; is easily understood by those affected and makes only low demands on time and administration. However it becomes impracticable in large units where a more detailed analysis of the components of a job is required. Its biggest drawback is the complete failure to measure the difference between jobs; it can only show that one job is more difficult than another, but not how much more difficult. The assessors also have difficulty in explaining why they have ranked a series of jobs in a certain order.

Another major drawback is its dependence on existing attitudes towards the ranking of the jobs, which does not allow therefore for any systematic correction of those attitudes where they are based on sexual discrimination. As the Equal Opportunities Commission has pointed out (EOC 1981), this kind of job evaluation is particularly prone to sexual bias.

Grading or classification

A number of grades are determined having recognizable characteristics. Grade definitions take into account discernible differences in skill and responsibility required by jobs in each grade. Job descriptions are then prepared for each job considered, and jobs allocated to the predetermined grades. Essentially the procedure is one of juggling with the actual jobs to relate them to the grades in order to get an acceptable wage structure.

Advantages of this method are that it is easy to apply to a small range of jobs, it is comparatively inexpensive and is readily understood by those affected. Also most workers have some rough conception of the general classification structure into which various jobs fall, and by using this a job description structure can be evolved.

A disadvantage of the method is the difficulty of writing grade descriptions. In practice, many classification systems have been based on job duties and responsibilities rather than on compensable factors. The method depends on assessors having an overall understanding of all jobs and is therefore not useful for scattered organizations. However, the main weakness in the method is the reliance on the judgement of the assessors, especially where complex jobs possessing many characteristics in widely differing degrees are concerned. Such jobs could well be allocated to several different grades. In a large range of jobs the scheme becomes unwieldly and inflexible, creating great difficulty in defining the grades. Nevertheless it has been successfully applied in the UK by several well-known organizations; for example, by the National Coal Board in 1955, when some 6500 jobs were identified as 400 standard jobs and reduced to 13 grades.

As with job ranking, this kind of job evaluation relies on value judgements about whole jobs, and is similarly prone to produce a sexually biased hierarchy of jobs (EOC 1981).

Factor comparison

The first of the analytical methods, factor comparison, attempts to rank jobs and attach monetary values concurrently. This method examines jobs in terms of the selected factors of which the jobs are thought to be composed. For manual workers the five factors normally used are:

1 Mental requirements
2 Physical requirements
3 Skill requirements
4 Responsibility requirements
5 Working conditions

Key jobs are identified which are capable of clear description and analysis in terms of the factors employed and which must display a sufficient range of variation under each factor. An additional qualification, not required by any other method, is that the pay rates for the key jobs must not be in dispute. Key jobs are examined factor by factor to produce a rank order for each factor. This shows the relative importance of each factor within each job. The proportion of the current wage rate paid for each factor is then established. When the results of the two exercises are compared and reconciled, a scale is prepared for each factor showing a range of cash values which may be allotted to any key job in respect of that factor. Other jobs are then evaluated factor by factor against these scales, the sum of all individual factor values being the total rate for any job. Examples are given in Figure 7.1.

Any further job, say one of routine inspection, can be allocated a rate for the job by considering each factor in turn and comparing it with the key jobs to find a place for the degree of that factor required.

Factor comparison has the advantage of trying to apply detached criteria in order to determine the relationship which an individual job has to another. If the scales can be evolved, very good results can be achieved. A major advantage is that the method requires a custom-built installation in each organization, and thus once constructed is in terms of the jobs themselves.

Key job	Basic rate	Skill M.V. R.		Mental requirements M.V. R.		Physical requirements M.V. R.		Responsibility M.V. R.		Working conditions M.V. R.	
Fitting	20	9.0	1	5.0	1	2.0	2	3.0	1	1.0	4
Welding	18	8.0	2	3.0	2	1.0	4	2.0	2	3.0	2
Fork lift truck driving	16	6.0	3	3.0	3	3.0	1	1.5	3	2.5	3
Labouring	14	4.0	4	2.0	4	1.5	3	1.0	4	5.5	1

M.V.—Monetary value
R—Rank

Figure 7.1 Evaluating total rate for any job

The basic disadvantages in the method are the very real difficulty in choosing key jobs where the basic pay rates are not disputed, and the arbitrary way in which existing wage rates are ascribed to different factors. Because the two distinct processes of evaluating jobs and determining money values are combined, the degree of detachment may be reduced and thus the acceptability of the scheme may be prejudiced.

Points rating

Devised by M.R. Lott in 1924, points rating analyses jobs in terms of factors. Factors are selected, eg skill, effort, responsibility, working conditions, etc, which are common to all or nearly all the jobs in an organization. These are the 'compensable' factors for which the firm is paying (Paterson, 1972). Each factor is defined and a weighting allocated to indicate its relative importance in the job. For example, using a scale of 200 points, skill may be allocated 60, effort 40, responsibility 60 and working conditions 40 points as a weighting. Within each of these main factors, subfactors are identified, defined and weighted in a similar manner to produce, for example, five skill subfactors with weightings of say 8, 10, 12, 14 and 16 points respectively. Each subfactor may then be further analysed into a number of degrees, with points being awarded for each degree up to a maximum of the total points allocated to that subfactor. Job descriptions are prepared for every job to facilitate analysis of the job and subsequent award of degree points. The sum of points represents its value relative to other jobs. When all jobs have been analysed in this way, a ranking by points enables an arbitrary number of grades to be fixed. Usually the number of grades fixed is about eight. As with the previous methods, key jobs representing the entire range are tried to test the factor, subfactor, and degree definitions and weightings.

The stability of the rating scales, once devised, tested and accepted, enables all changes of jobs and new jobs to be allocated grades without upsetting the placings of other jobs. Because of the amount of detail in definition down to degrees, it is fairly easy to achieve agreement on which degree fits the job requirements. Another advantage is that the processes of wage fixing and task evaluation are clearly separated. This plus the definitions enables the method to be more objective and consistent than the previous methods, and although by no means an accurate measure it does enable one to quantify the differential between jobs. It is the most readily adaptable of all methods and can cover a very wide range of jobs. Easily explained to those affected, the degrees allow ready explanation of points totals.

A disadvantage of this scheme is that the selection of factors, definition of degrees and weightings attached thereto involve many arbitrary and subjective elements, although the evaluation on these bases is more objective than other techniques. The large variety of job characteristics to be covered by a limited number of factors and degrees all require a long and costly series of discussions between management and employee representatives. Another disadvantage is the numerical rating scale which can give a spurious sense of accuracy to job assessment and cause arguments over minor job differences of little value. A further possible disadvantage is that the method's high degree of formality may also encourage rigidity.

New Techniques

From the comments on the four most widely used job evaluation techniques, it can be seen that as yet no one technique completely fulfils all the requirements that may be made of it. Each has advantages and disadvantages dependent upon the circumstances in which it is to operate.

More recently a further crop of techniques has appeared, some based on the same foundations as those described, and others based on new theories of what constitutes work, and for what one is paid when at work.

Job profile method

Devised by Urwick, Orr & Partners Ltd in 1960, the job profile method has three requirements. First, a group of clearly defined characteristics from which a company chooses those that are appropriate; second, a rating scale which deals not in points or money, but in levels of job demand; and finally, a weighting of the chosen characteristics specific to an organization. Six main job factors of responsibility, knowledge, work environment, physical aptitudes, mental aptitudes and social aptitudes are used. Each is further broken down, eg responsibility covers use of expensive resources, exercise of discretion, keeping of records and accountability for money, etc. For each of the subfactors, assessors are required to rate the degree of that subfactor required by ticking one of four categories, exceptional, high, moderate and low, for which scores of 4, 3, 2 and 1, respectively, are given. The scores are then weighted using the predetermined weighting (as in points rating), and a total score is obtained by aggregating all the subfactor scores. Grades are then determined arbitrarily as in points rating and pricing subsequently takes place.

This method is basically a streamlined version of a points rating method with the same advantages and disadvantages.

Guide-chart profile method

Practised by the Hay Company Ltd consultancy group, the guide-chart profile method, a form of points rating, covers a very large number of people in the UK. It is described in Chapter 16.

Time span of discretion

From the Tavistock Institute of Human Relations study at the Glacier Metal Company, Professor Elliott Jaques evolved a theory of work on which he based a job evaluation technique known as the 'time span of discretion'. This theory of work propounds that within any given job there is a prescribed content, those elements of work over which an individual has no authorized choice, and a discretionary content, in which the individual chooses how to do a job. Using this discretionary element to measure the size and quality of a job lends itself to quantification in terms of the maximum length of the span of time during which discretion has to be continuously exercised before the quality of the discretion becomes assessable—the larger the span of time, the greater the size or level of the work.

The concept of equitable payment is also used. Individuals are asked what payment is felt to be fair for the job at different stages in their career. By drawing a series of curves of length of time span against the felt-fair pay, any individual at a given age and length of time span can be allotted a wage. This series of curves allows a potential progress assessment of each person but requires a large amount of data and checking of an individual's performance plus continual updating when all pay levels rise. Although somewhat theoretical in approach and demanding in time and cost, this approach does provide a new insight into work—the quality of the discretionary work requiring decision making. The basic weakness of the method as a job evaluation technique is that it is mainly the person that is evaluated.

Decision band theory

Following on from Professor Paterson's theory of organizational grading which postulates that there are only six basic kinds of decision which define the whole range of jobs existing in the enterprise, the decision band theory has evolved. The six decision bands are:

1   Band E: policy-making decisions: typically policy decisions made by top management.
2   Band D: programming decisions: made by senior managers the decisions are within the limits set by the policy.
3   Band C: interpretive decisions: middle managers make decisions within the programming decisions.
4   Band B: routine decisions: skilled workmen make 'routine' decisions concerned with execution within the interpreted policy. They do not know 'why' something is done but are concerned with 'how'.
5   Band A: automatic decisions: the semi-skilled worker only concerns himself with 'how' to carry out instructions.

6 Band O: defined decisions: made by an unskilled worker. Only limited discretion, eg in rate of working.

Each band except O is divided into two grades making eleven in all. The upper grade of each band coordinates the work of the men in the lower level of the same decision band.

The method requires job descriptions detailing all duties in a job; each duty is then graded. The highest-graded duty fixes the grade of pay to be received. By showing what levels of decision-making are present throughout a job, attention is drawn to mundane duties which could be allocated to other jobs allowing extra time for more higher-grade duties. This is known as the economy of grading.

Simple to apply and easily taught, the acceptance of the principle to the exclusion of traditional factors remains the stumbling block to widespread application. Also within each grade some means of further differentiation may be necessary before acceptance by craft unions in particular.

Performing the Job Evaluation Exercise

It is imperative that a decision to use job evaluation be made at the top with a subsequent full announcement to all employees of company policy. The next step is to choose the personnel required. Consultants can often provide the outside expertise and authority needed to push a scheme through quickly and to appreciate the likely pitfalls more than local management, but if outside help is used the management may not readily accept responsibility for the running and consequences of the final scheme. If only company employees are used their familiarity with personalities and local background may well reduce the objectivity. Outside consultants in an advisory role is probably the best compromise.

Choosing company employees capable of writing job descriptions, carrying out the analyses and having a good general knowledge of work practices with sufficient objectivity creates a problem which may be solved by using middle management, eg manager, engineer, foreman, personnel manager, because experiments have shown that operators have difficulty in being objective, and lack a wide enough experience of jobs. However, where possible, operators should be involved in the evaluation, at least in as far as explaining their job to the assessors.

The method of job evaluation to be used will depend in part upon the industrial relations climate. Trade unions have their own favourite method, and officials having experience of it will almost certainly prefer that method to be used. On the other hand, where job evaluation has not previously been encountered, the employees may well accept management's suggestion of a technique. It is important at this stage to stress that in the long run regular meetings to explain developments and the technique to both employees and their representatives have proved to be worthwhile; and employees should, where possible, be part of the evaluating committee to raise queries at first hand. Depending on the method to be used, definitions, points allocations, key jobs and order of jobs to be evaluated should be decided jointly. Where employees are to participate in the writing of job descriptions and subsequent analysis, training will have to be given. As jobs are evaluated individuals will have cause to complain and a formal grievance or appeals procedure will have to be set up.

Preparing job descriptions often shows organizational defects such as overlapping of jobs, blank areas for which no one has responsibility, and the proportion of time spent on lower-grade tasks where in essence the job rate may be paid for higher-grade tasks (Paterson's economy of grading). A job description questionnaire covering job title, department, factory, departmental function, organization plus the factors of education, training, experience, etc. is useful.

Pricing the Grade Structure

Before trying to establish new basic rates, the relationship between present rates and the new grades should be shown. Usually this is done by drawing a graph of rate against ranking called a 'scattergram' (see Figure 7.2).

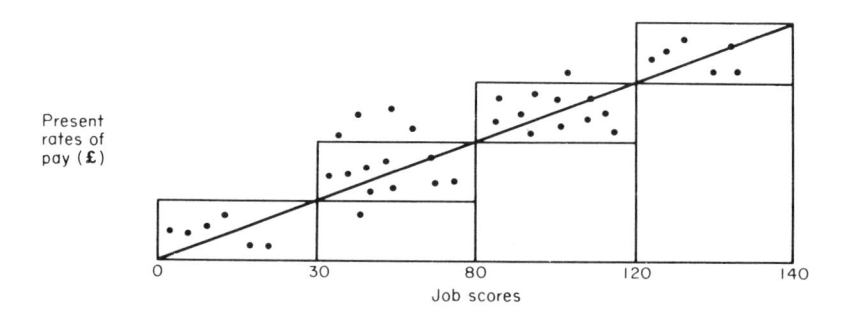

Figure 7.2 Scattergram

From the scattergram a line of best fit can be drawn which will reduce the discrepancy, if any, between present pay rates and a proposed pay rate. By using the method of least squares a wage curve can be plotted which will be the least cost to a firm. However, in practice it has been found that the wage curve has to be pitched above the majority of present pay rates to gain acceptance of the scheme, so that the introduction of job evaluation almost always increases the wage bill. Usually a basic rate is agreed above which each succeeding grade receives a similar increase. For example, with a basic at £40, there may be six senior grades, each receiving £4 more than the next lower grade, making grade rates of £40, £44, £48, £52, £56, £60 and £62. There is no reason why such steps should be the same, ie arithmetic. They could be increasing steps as the company may want to pay more than proportionately as the complexity of the job increases. For example, again a basic of £40 with seven grades; the first having a supplement of £4 and thereafter increasing by £6, £8, £10, etc, to produce rates of £40, £44, £50, £58, £68, £80 and £94. Naturally, the pay rates will be subject to negotiation.

A major problem to be solved is that of individuals' earnings which are too high to be encompassed in the pricing of the grades structure, since to do so would substantially increase all other pay rates. One solution lies in allowing the high earners to retain their present levels as personal allowances. No future increases are given to them until they are in line, while newcomers receive the new rate for doing the same job. As bringing it into line can take several years, dissatisfaction grows with those on the lower rate. An alternative is to offer a generous lump sum for the man to accept the new rate, though in practice it is difficult for anyone to accept a lower rate for doing the same job. A further alternative is to promote, or retire, where possible. Each case must be dealt with in the light of prevailing circumstances, and any, or all, of these possibilities may be feasible—especially if the difficulties have been thoroughly discussed over a period of time by the management and the men.

Summary

Although by no means scientific nor completely objective, job evaluation is a systematic means of rationalizing a wage or salary structure. The choice of job evaluation technique used will depend on the speed of application, cost of installation, acceptability by those affected, in fact a whole series of factors. This coupled with the fact that no one method has yet been universally accepted as being better than the others means that the choice of method depends upon the circumstances and parties involved in each individual organization. Despite many objections to the techniques the principle appears to be widely respected. The two main reasons for acceptance are the friction caused by anomalies, which arise when a payment structure develops without any guidelines, and the need for dealing with the changing structure of jobs as technology progresses.

With the advent of equal pay, job evaluation will loom even larger—as most firms have to integrate their male and female job rates in some justifiable manner. The next chapter deals with the problems associated with ensuring that a job evaluation scheme does not produce or perpetuate discrimination on the grounds of sex.

References and Further Reading

ACAS, *Advisory Booklet no. 1: Job Evaluation*, ACAS, 1979.
BIM, *Job Evaluation A Practical Guide for Managers*, Management Publications, London, 1970.
Butterworth, J., *Productivity Now*, Pergamon Press, Oxford, 1969.
Butterworth, J., and Shaw, C., 'Job Evaluation', *Advance*, Umist no. 10, (June 1971).
Clegg, H.A., *Standing Commission Pay Comparability Report* no. 9, HMSO, 1980.
IDS, *Guide to Job Evaluation*, Incomes Data Services, London, 1979.
Jaques, E., 'Taking time seriously in evaluating jobs', *Harvard Business Review*, volume 57, no. 5, September-October, 1979.
Paterson, T.T., *Job Evaluation: Volume 1 and Volume 2*, Business Books, London, 1972.
Thomason, G.F., *Job Evaluation: Objectives and Methods*, Institute of Personnel Management, London, 1980.

8

Sex Discrimination and Job Evaluation*

Patrick Walker and Angela M Bowey

Job evaluation is a system of comparing jobs to provide a basis for a grading and pay structure. The aim is to evaluate the job, not the job holder, but it is recognized that to some extent any assessment of a job's total demands relative to another will always be subjective. Moreover, job evaluation is largely a social mechanism which establishes agreed differentials within organizations.

The segregation of work into jobs performed traditionally by men or women is still widespread in industry. The rates of pay in the 'male' areas are usually higher than those in the 'female'. If there is no man employed on broadly similar work with whom to compare herself, a woman has no claim under the Equal Pay Act, unless she has been graded the same as a man under a job evaluation scheme as defined by the Equal Pay Act (see Appendix for further information on the legislation).

Non-discriminatory job evaluation should lead to a payment system within which work of equal value receives equal pay regardless of sex. A job evaluation cannot be expected to result in an even spread of sexes throughout the grades and the average woman's pay being equal to that of the average man, where women have been recruited in the past to the less skilled and less demanding jobs and not to the skilled or craft jobs. Only after decades of truly equal opportunities for training, recruitment and promotion would there be the likelihood of an even distribution of women throughout the jobs in an organization.

---

* Based on a handbook produced by the Equal Opportunities Commission.

This chapter draws attention to some of the practices which may (often unwillingly) introduce or perpetuate sex discrimination, and offers guidance on how to formulate, implement and maintain job evaluation schemes which are free of sex-bias.

Many schemes were implemented before the passing of the Sex Discrimination Act 1975 and prior to the present understanding of many of the implicit or hidden forms of sex discrimination, and therefore require review.

Formulating a Job Evaluation Scheme

Composition and Organization of Committees

It is recognized good practice in job evaluation to involve a representative sample of people from the spread of jobs covered by a scheme in discussions and committees, on the assumption that they are appropriate spokesmen for their own interests, *and* that a participative approach will ensure easier acceptance of the scheme and resolution of difficulties at an early stage. Although in some cases, women may be conditioned into downgrading their jobs, it could be equally true that male factory cleaners might be conditioned into downgrading their own jobs, and this is a poor reason to put forward for excluding them from being represented. A fair representation of women (in relation to their proportions in the workforce and in the jobs spectrum) in all job evaluation committees and discussions, is strongly recommended as a means of reducing the probability of sexual bias, and of being seen to be doing so.

In addition to any other training given, members of all the committees should receive training in how sex bias in job evaluation can arise and they should understand how their actions and decisions can produce such discrimination.

Research has shown that in general, chairmen of committees and especially of Job Evaluation Committees can be very influential in determining the outcome of the committees' considerations. It is therefore important that the chairman of all committees concerned with a job evaluation scheme should be selected not just for their knowledge of job evaluation and their acceptability to the various parties involved, but also because they are unbiased and concerned to ensure the procedures do not result in discrimination against jobs performed by women.

The Job Description and Job Analysis

Job descriptions written to an agreed format enable the jobs to be assessed according to a common standard. Forms or guidance notes should be provided to those who are writing job descriptions, containing a comprehensive list of elements which are factors in the jobs to be assessed. This will avoid the possibility of an unconscious bias coming into the evaluation at the job description stage. The job descriptions should contain at least the following information: job title; relationships at work (viz: the kind and degree of supervision received; the kind and degree of supervision given; the nature and extent of cooperation with other workers); a short summary of the primary functions of the job; a description of specific duties of the job showing approximate percentage of time spent on each and the extent of discretion or responsibility in relation to each; and the job requirements listed under the headings used for the subsequent job evaluation procedure (eg skill, responsibility, mental effort, physical effort). If subfactors are also to be used in the job evaluation procedure, these should also be indicated at the job description stage.

Where the format for preparing job descriptions differs significantly from the above, careful attention should be paid to whether the omissions or the additions are likely to result in aspects of jobs more commonly performed by women being underrated relative to other aspects of the spectrum of jobs.

The person or people given responsibility for the collation of the job descriptions should be trained both in the skills involved in preparing job descriptions and most especially in the importance of ensuring comprehensive descriptions which do not omit aspects of women's jobs nor over-emphasize those job characteristics which are missing from jobs typically performed by women.

The preparation of the job description involves at least three people; the employee who does the job or a representative employee, his supervisor or manager, and the job analyst or person responsible for the procedures. Close involvement of employees in the preparation of descriptions of their own jobs will benefit from their detailed knowledge of the job and help to ensure that important aspects of it are not overlooked. Involvement of the manager or supervisor is essential because of his responsibility for stating what is required of the job; but there is an important role for the job analyst at this stage in detecting any bias against a fair description of women's jobs and advising the manager accordingly.

There is a long tradition of using different titles for the jobs of men and women who are doing essentially the same work. This has frequently also denoted a status difference reflected in a pay difference which is based on sexual discrimination and not on the content of the work done. Job titles which are applied predominantly to one sex or the other and which have a counterpart applied to the other sex, should be very carefully examined and if they do not reflect a genuine difference in the nature of the work done they should be changed and the same title applied to both jobs. Examples of such discriminatory job titles are listed below:

Male job title	*Female job title*
Salesman	Shop assistant
Assistant manager	Manager's assistant
Technician	Operator
Office manager	Typing supervisor
Tailor	Seamstress
Personal assistant	Secretary
Administrator	Secretary
Chef	Cook

It is of course recognized that in some circumstances these different job titles are applied to essentially different jobs. They are only discriminatory where they are applied to the same job and result in different pay levels.

Different types of Job Evaluation Scheme

Some schemes consist almost entirely of drawing up a list of jobs in rank order (the 'felt fair' order for the organization). Job ranking and paired comparisons are examples of this approach. It should be borne in mind that *this type of scheme is particularly prone to sex discrimination* because where whole jobs are being compared (rather than scores on components of jobs) judgments made by the evaluators can have little standard basis other than the traditional value of the job. The rationale of such schemes is to reproduce in a systematic way a hierarchy of jobs which approximates to the 'felt fair' ranking of these jobs in the minds of the people working in the organization. But the sex of the job holder has been in many industries a factor contributing to the traditional place of the job within its organizational hierarchy. Removing this sexual discrimination is a break with tradition for which there is no provision in job evaluation procedures based on the 'felt fair' order.

Strongly engrained attitudes still exist about what work is appropriate to each sex and these attitudes can lead to acceptance of a grading and pay structure based unthinkingly on current and/or past practice, which can undermine equality of opportunity. Unless steps are taken to prevent it, job evaluation schemes can maintain a situation in which the jobs most frequently performed by women are regarded as having less value than those mostly performed by men. Examples of this would arise in situations where the job titles listed above were applied to workers doing essentially the same work.

The major alternative to schemes based on the felt fair order is schemes based on breaking the jobs down into job factors and evaluating their scores or their rank order on each factor separately before amalgamating the results into an overall rank order. Potentially such schemes can avoid sexual discrimination in the grading of jobs. But there are several points at which a bias related to the sex of the job holder can be built into the job evaluating procedures of this kind of 'analytical' scheme. Care is needed to ensure that this kind of sexual discrimination does not occur, and particular attention should be paid to the following points.

Pitfalls in Factor Choice

A factor is an element of a job which can be defined and measured, such as skill or mental effort, against which the jobs to be evaluated can be assessed. These factors are sometimes then broken down into sub-factors. Factor choice is crucial. Bad schemes can introduce selectively factors which will result in 'women's' jobs being placed unfairly at the bottom of the grading structure. Working conditions and physical strength are usually included in schemes covering manual workers; both these factors will appear in jobs performed by men. On the other hand, factors associated with work done by women, for example, manual dexterity and concentration, may not be used as factors at all. It is essential therefore that the factors chosen are representative of the whole range of work being evaluated. The example in Table 8.1 shows how two different sets of factors, one biased and one very much less biased, can produce different rankings for the same two jobs, the first set of factors being blatantly discriminatory.

This set of factors is discriminatory because it contains many aspects of the male job and very few characteristics which relate to the female job. Also some of the characteristics which relate to the male job are duplicated, for example 'strength required' duplicates to some extent 'sustained physical effort' with the result that a high score on one would very frequently be associated with a high score on the other. The same is true of 'lifting requirement' and 'strength required'. Note that the difference in scores on the factor 'experience in job' completely outweighs the more significant difference in the factor 'training'.

Compare Table 8.1 with Table 8.2 where the job evaluation factors are less biased. It is important to ensure that the set of job factors used incorporates all the important and relevant differentiating characteristics of all the jobs to which the scheme is going to be applied. It is important to check the factor scores of the jobs performed predominantly by female employees and if there are a lot of low scores and if the set of factors makes no provision for scoring aspects of the female jobs which reflect their value to the company, then the set of factors is discriminatory and should be changed.

Table 8.1

Example of discriminatory job factors

Factors	Maintenance fitter	Company nurse
(Each factor is scored on a scale from 1 to 10)		
(For simplicity no weights have been applied)		
Skill		
Experience in job	10	1
Training	5	7
Responsibility		
For money	0	0
For equipment & machinery	8	3
For safety	3	6
For work done by others	3	0
Effort		
Lifting requirement	4	2
Strength required	7	2
Sustained physical effort	5	1
Conditions		
Physical environment	6	0
Working position	6	0
Hazards	7	0
Total	64	22

Factor definition

Where large numbers of jobs are involved, factors are often broadly defined, so it is essential that proper descriptions are provided for the meaning of each factor. The definitions should be closely scrutinized to ensure that unjust sex bias does not occur. For example, length of service, if included in the definition of 'experience' could indirectly discriminate against women. It is not important if the job holder has twenty years service if the job could be learned in two months. Again,

Table 8.2

Example of less biased job evaluation factors

Factors	Maintenance fitter	Company nurse
(Each factor is scored on a scale from 1 to 10)		
(For simplicity no weights have been applied)		
Basic knowledge	6	8
Complexity of task	6	7
Training	5	7
Responsibility for people	3	8
Responsibility for materials & equipment	8	6
Mental effort	5	6
Visual attention	6	6
Physical activity	8	5
Working conditions	6	1
Total	53	54

such items can be compensated for outside the scheme. If 'numeracy' is a factor, a proper definition should be provided to avoid subjective judgments, for example, that women are less numerate than men.

Where scales are provided for measuring the factors (and this will usually be the case) it is important to ensure that the spread of scores along each scale is reasonably similar, so that the problem does not arise where some factors which have a wide dispersion of scores completely outweigh the degree of variance on other factors on which the spread of scores is narrower. In the context of sexual discrimination it is particularly important to ensure that factors which are characteristics of male dominated jobs do not have a wider dispersion of scores than factors which are characteristics of female dominated jobs. This point is illustrated in Table 8.1 where the widely disparate scores on experience in the job grossly outweigh the difference in training. Applying different weights to the different factors (which is discussed below) complicates rather than resolves this problem.

Factor Weighting

Once the important components of the jobs in an organization have been identified and converted into job factors with scales for measuring those factors, it will be recognized that they are not all equally important to the work of the organization. It is therefore normal practice to apply weights to the factor scores in an effort to reflect the relative importance of the various factors. A very important subfactor may be weighted even as high as 10% whilst an unimportant subfactor may be only weighted 1%. Deciding what these weights shall be is a highly subjective process and it is extremely easy for sex discrimination to appear in a job evaluation procedure as a result of discriminatory weightings being applied to the factors. Taking the example of the less discriminatory job factors used in the section 'Pitfalls in factor choice' the example in Table 8.3 shows how discriminatory factor weights produce a biased evaluation of the two jobs.

The first set of weights are biased because all the factors on which the male jobs scored highly have high weights and most of the factors on which the female jobs scored higher than the male job have low weights. It is unlikely that this particular set of weights could be justified by reference to the importance of these factors to the organization as a whole. The second set of weights is less biased because it is more likely to reflect the value of these various factors to the organization as a whole and does not unduly favour characteristics of male as opposed to female work. This set of weights widens the gap between the two jobs relative to the unweighted scores, and shows the company nurse to be a higher grade job than the fitter. The biased set of weights actually reversed the situation.

To avoid discrimination resulting from the weighting of factors, extreme weights (either very high or very low) should not be given to factors which are exclusively found in jobs performed predominantly by one sex, without very good reason.

An analysis showing the percentage of total points (after weighting) attributable to each factor should be compiled. This would assist in highlighting factors with heavy weightings and provide a relative comparison between factors. The factors with the heaviest and the lightest weightings should then be looked at again to ensure these can be justified and are not likely to penalize the jobs of one sex.

Benchmark Jobs

Most schemes involve the selection of benchmark jobs which are used as a standard because they are considered to be typical of a grade or group of jobs—against which other jobs in a scheme can be assessed. Discrimination can take place in the selection of benchmark jobs if they

Table 8.3

Example of discriminatory factor weighting

Factors	Unweighted scores		Biased weights	Weighted scores		Less biased weights	Weighted scores	
	Fitter	Nurse		Fitter	Nurse		Fitter	Nurse
Basic knowledge	6	8	7%	0.42	0.56	5%	0.30	0.40
Complexity of task	6	7	8%	0.48	0.56	15%	0.90	1.05
Training	5	7	7%	0.35	0.49	15%	0.75	1.05
Responsibility for people	3	8	15%	0.45	1.20	15%	0.45	1.20
Responsibility for materials & equipment	8	6	15%	1.20	0.90	15%	1.20	0.90
Mental effort	5	6	8%	0.40	0.48	10%	0.50	0.60
Visual attention	6	6	10%	0.60	0.60	10%	0.60	0.60
Physical activity	8	5	15%	1.20	0.75	10%	0.80	0.50
Working conditions	6	1	15%	0.90	0.15	5%	0.30	0.05
Total	53	54		6.00	5.66		5.80	6.35

do not represent a fair spread of the work done in the organization. Even this is not adequate where there are small numbers of female staff employed. In such cases it is important to ensure a representative sample of the female jobs are also included amongst the benchmarks as a means of ensuring that the job evaluation scheme takes due account of job elements which are peculiar to these predominantly female jobs, rather than continuing to rely on slotting the jobs of female employees into an evaluation procedure appropriate primarily to work of a different nature.

'Women's' jobs should not be excluded as benchmark jobs. It is commonly the case that the factors and factor weights to be used in a job evaluation procedure are derived by reference to a detailed study of the benchmark jobs. If 'women's' jobs are not included in the selection of benchmark jobs then it is unlikely that elements in their work will be fairly represented in the factors and factor weights which are chosen. In order to avoid sexual discrimination through job evaluation, it is imperative that a number of jobs representing the range of jobs performed predominantly by women be incorporated into the set of benchmark jobs which are used in the evaluation procedures.

Take Care Who is Left Out of the Scheme

Schemes may be specifically designed to exclude certain groups of workers, usually on the grounds that their work is too different from the main group of work. The problem lies in where to choose the cut-off point. It should not be chosen on the grounds that an evaluation may show a job to have been grossly undervalued in the past and to upgrade it would disrupt the 'felt fair' order (eg the job of personal secretary). Discrimination in the grading and pay of the jobs of female employees in many organizations has occurred or been perpetuated by their separation into a separate grading hierarchy with a separate job evaluation procedure, or none at all. Incorporating them within the same job evaluation scheme as the male jobs, provided that the job evaluation scheme is not discriminatory, will assist in the achievement of equal pay for equal work.

This does not mean that a single scheme covers all workers, but that as a general rule all groups should be included at the outset wherever practicable, and then good reasons put forward for any exclusions. Trade unions and employers should appreciate that problems can be created if bargaining units are used as the sole basis for the scope of jobs to be covered.

Implementing a Job Evaluation Scheme

Even if all the preceding points have been taken into account, discrimination can still occur when the scheme is introduced. This is the stage when grades or, in some cases, rates of pay are attached. Sometimes there are only a few points between similar jobs usually performed by men and women respectively. When the grades are allocated, the cut-off mark in the points scale should not be placed so as to deliberately segregate scores and thereby create male and female grades. The main result of this would be that having graded the jobs, grade differentials would occur leading to pay and status differentials which would amount to sex discrimination. The selection of grade boundaries, therefore, should be objectively based on the evidence provided by the evaluation, irrespective of the sex of the job holders.

Where analytical schemes are used which produce numerical scores for the jobs, grade boundaries should be placed only at points in the hierarchy where there is a gap in the scores. If for example a set of jobs produced the following scores; 56, 56, 57, 59, 60, 60, 61, 62, 64, 64, 72, 72, 73, 74, 75, 76, 76, then the grade boundary should fall roughly in the middle of the gap between the two clusters, at say 68 or 69, and not through the middle of either cluster. For schemes which do not produce numerical scores, grade boundaries should be set where there are discontinuities in the nature of the work.

Boundary Cases

Individuals may be re-evaluated if their jobs are very near to the boundary with a higher grade. If the original evaluation is confirmed, however, discretionary points are sometimes added to bring it into the higher grades. Care must be taken to avoid allocating points in a discriminatory way.

Red Circle Cases

Anomalies can arise in the payments system as a result of the job evaluation exercise. Some of the existing rates of pay may be above rates newly set for the grades appropriate to those particular jobs. 'Red-circling' is when the job holders maintain their current pay etc. and only when they leave the particular job does it revert to its evaluated rate. Alternatively, their pay can be phased into line with the rest of the grade by withholding or restricting future wage increases. Red circling should not be used on such a scale that it amounts to sex discrimination. If red circling results in men receiving a higher rate than women doing the same, or broadly similar work (or vice versa) this may give rise to an equal pay claim. The Employment Appeal Tribunal has held (Snoxell & Davies *v.* Vauxhall Motors Ltd. 1977) that red circling cannot be used as a defence if past sex discrimination is the cause of the difference in pay.

Appeals

Provision is normally made for a formal appeals procedure to deal with those cases where the employees believe their job has been unfairly evaluated. A representative committee is usually set up, and it is important that this committee should be trained both in job evaluation and sexual discrimination. The Appeals Committee members should not be prepared to condone sexual discrimination, and in particular the chairman should be someone with an interest in ensuring both fair evaluations and the elimination of sexual discrimination. All employees should be informed that care has been taken to ensure that the job evaluation procedure has not discriminated against employees of either sex, and that the appeals procedure can be used if they feel that they have been wrongly graded because of their sex or if they feel that the scheme has resulted in sexual discrimination in some way.

Appendix
The Legislation

1 The Equal Pay Act 1970
   (as amended by the Sex Discrimination Act 1975)

a) An equality clause is deemed to be included in a woman's (or man's) contract of employment when the woman is employed on work rated as equivalent with that of a man in the same employment.

Section 1 (5)

b) 'A woman is to be regarded as employed on work rated as equivalent with that of any men, if, but only if, her job and their job have been given an equal value, in terms of the demand made on a worker under various headings (for instance effort, skill, decision), on a study undertaken with a view to evaluating in those terms, the jobs to be done by all or any of the employees in an undertaking or group of undertakings, or would have been given an equal value but for the evaluation being made on a system setting different values for men and women on the same demand under any heading'.
c) In a case taken under the Equal Pay Act (the Act) referring to a job evaluation scheme, a tribunal would have to refer to Section 1 (5) of the Act which is set out above. In 1977, the Employment Appeal Tribunal, in the case of Greene and others *v.* Broxtowe District Council, held that, 'when there has been a properly constituted job evaluation study the industrial tribunal is bound . . . to

act upon the conclusion and content of the study. This can only be challenged . . . if it can be shown that there is a fundamental error in the evaluation study, or where . . . there is a plain error on the face of the record'. If such an error is found, the tribunal may then consider the application under the 'like work' provisions of the Act (Section 1 (4)).

2   The Sex Discrimination Act 1975 (SDA)

a) The SDA contains the concepts of both direct and indirect discrimination.
    i) *Direct Discrimination* is when because of her sex, a woman (or man) is treated less favourably than a man (or woman) is or would be treated in similar circumstances.
    ii) *Indirect Discrimination* is where an unjustifiable condition or requirement is applied equally to both men and women but where the proportion of women (or men) who can comply with it is considerably smaller than the proportion of men. It must also be to the woman's detriment that she cannot comply with the requirement or condition.
b) As yet no cases have been brought forward to test the application of the Act's concept of indirect discrimination in relation to the content or application of a job evaluation scheme.

3   The Central Arbitration Committee (CAC)

a) The CAC is empowered to examine pay and grade structures which are also job evaluation schemes. It can make a declaration to remove discrimination in collective agreements or employers' pay structures under Section 3 of the Equal Pay Act and give advice under Section 10 of the Act.
b) The Equal Pay Act, states that the CAC has the power to amend agreements and pay structures which contain provisions relating specifically to men only or to women only. It has sought to discover covert discrimination between men and women by looking at the distribution of men and women throughout the pay structure and at the relationships between pay rates for predominantly male and predominantly female grades.
c) The CAC's method is first to hold informal meetings with the parties and to give advice on how discrimination can be removed. This is often by the use of job evaluation techniques. The Committee then consider the results and make decisions. A recent High Court decision however decided that the only remedy open

to CAC was to raise the women's rate of pay to that of the lowest male rate.
d) The CAC is also empowered to decide claims on terms and conditions of employment under Schedule 11 of the Employment Protection Act. This can assist groups of workers suffering sex-based discrimination indirectly in that the CAC is able to consider claims that the wages of a group of workers are lower than the general level for the job in the industry in the district.
e) If an employer has Government contracts, any person or body can raise a question under the Fair Wages Resolution that terms and conditions are unfair. The CAC can then consider and if appropriate make an award to increase payments to workers.
f) The Disclosure of Information provisions in the Employment Protection Act require employers under certain circumstances to disclose information for the purposes of collective bargaining, eg grades and pay of a category of employees. The CAC may make a declaration that the employer should disclose.

References and Further Reading

ACAS, *Advisory Booklet no. 1—Job Evaluation*, Advisory, Conciliation and Arbitration Service, London, 1979.

Buckingham, G., *What to do about equal pay for women*, Gower, 1973.

EOC, *Job Evaluation Schemes free of Sex Bias*, Equal Opportunities Commission Guide 1981.

Fonda, N., Glucklich, P., Goodman, J., and Morgan, J., 'Job Evaluation without Sex Discrimination', *Personnel Management*, February 1979.

Malone, M., *A Practical Guide to Discrimination Law*, Grant McIntyre, 1980.

9

Work Study, Method Study and Work Measurement

E G Wood

Work study—the study of human work in all its contexts—is not a new concept. The application of analytical reasoning to simplify and improve the way work is carried out is as old as work itself. The need to estimate how long a job should take has existed for thousands of years. But the development of work study as a management technique is comparatively recent and its widespread application came only 20 years ago.

The Historical Background to Work Study

There is evidence that the monks of Rieveaux Abbey developed overall times for their building work during the Middle Ages. In the middle of the eighteenth century a Frenchman, Jean Perronet, studied the complete cycle of operations for manufacturing pins and took overall-timed studies. In 1792 Thomas Mason was employed at the Old Derby China Manufactory to use a stopwatch to observe the work done. He was sworn to secrecy, a practice now deprecated by managers and workers alike. About 1800, Robert Owen used time studies at his Lanarkshire mills to improve works layout and working conditions. Later, in the middle of the nineteenth century, Charles Babbage, the pioneer of the computer, carried out time studies, also in the manufacture of pins. In these early studies no attempt seems to have been made to break down the cycle of operations into elements. They merely recorded the overall elapsed time of production. However, Robert Owen's 'time allowed' included provision for relaxation and recovery from fatigue.

In the latter part of the nineteenth century, F.W. Taylor, the father of scientific management, evolved the principle of breaking a job down into detailed elements and then timing each element separately. He called this 'time study' and the technique, with refinements, is still the most widely used form of work measurement. Taylor also pioneered method study in his classic experiments on shovelling at the Bethlehem Steel Works. He tried to answer two fundamental questions: Which is the best way to do a job? and What is a fair day's work?

Another American pioneer of scientific management, Frank Gilbreth, studied bricklaying after realizing that each craftsman used a different method. He discovered that as many as 18 separate motions were involved in laying a brick. By analysing the movements he was able to reduce them to 5 per brick. Thus was born the technique of 'motion study' and Gilbreth, with his wife Lilian, set down the 'principles of motion economy' still in use today. They also investigated the problem of making allowances for and reducing the causes of fatigue.

Although Gilbreth and Taylor had the same objectives, they did not always agree. Taylor believed that time was the dominant factor; Gilbreth concentrated on improving methods and regarded the elapsed time as a secondary matter. Nowadays both method and time are regarded as equally important and inseparable.

The next major change came after 1911 when an American industrial consultant, Charles E. Bedaux, conceived the idea of the work unit to compare different types of work and as a basis for financial incentives. He called the work unit a 'B' after his own name. He also introduced the idea of 'rating' which acknowledged the fact that operators worked at varying speeds and effectiveness. Unfortunately, his system met with resistance from organized labour when it was misapplied by over-zealous managers, especially in the depressed years of the 1930s.

The Second World War brought pressure for increased productivity and work study received the boost of government support when the Production Efficiency Board was set up to run courses on motion study and to stimulate higher productivity in industry. After the war there was an expansion of management consultancy practices, mainly based on the application of work study. In 1957 the International Labour Organization published its now classic textbook *Introduction to work study*. In 1960, Russell M. Currie, Head of the Central Work Study Department in ICI, published *Work study*.

Since then, work study has gone from strength to strength. It has been applied not only in factories but in hospitals, shops, the Army and Navy, fire brigades, the police force, the Civil Service, the theatre and, last but not least, on the work-study practitioner himself.

The Objectives of Work Study

Work study has two objectives: first, to find a better way of doing a job; and second, to establish how long that job should take. Thus it consists of two interrelated techniques—method study to deal with the former and work measurement the latter.

The British Standard (1979) defines work study as:

The systematic explanation of activities in order to improve the effective use of human and other material resources.

Although it is convenient for the purpose of consideration and instruction to separate work study into the two main aspects of methods and time, it must be stressed that, in practice, the two techniques of method study and work measurement must be combined. Method improvement implies some form of time measurement in order to compare alternative methods.

In any situation where work study has not been used before, the typical picture is that much of the time and effort is wasted. This does not necessarily imply that there is a considerable amount of deliberate time wasting on the part of the average worker, whether on the shopfloor or in the office. Usually the worker works hard when he has the opportunity and the motivation. However, in practice, he does not always have the opportunity of working without interruptions of some sort.

In practice, time may be wasted waiting for materials because of inadequate planning or because the handling equipment is being used elsewhere. Time may be lost in waiting for instructions because the foreman is busy; waiting for the maintenance section to repair a machine breakdown; waiting for the storeman to issue materials and tools; or waiting for the machine to complete its cycle of operation. Each of these incidents may be small in itself, but over the working day they can add up to a significant amount.

Even when a worker is working hard, much of his efforts may be wasted. Excessive handling of materials and components is often the greatest waste of time and effort. Every time an item is picked up, put down or carried, it adds to the cost but adds nothing to the value. Other examples of wasted effort include:

1 Excessive changeover time due to poor batching of orders.
2 Excessive movement of materials and men due to poor layout.
3 Use of only one hand for productive work.
4 Machine speeds below optimum rate.

Method study reveals these sources of wasted effort and highlights the scope for improvement. Work measurement measures the extent of the hidden losses and establishes a fair target time for a better method.

Method Study

At one time it was thought that method study would find the 'one best way' of doing a job, It is now recognized that there may be several equally good ways of doing a particular job. Moreover, the concept of the 'one best way' implied that it could not be improved upon. Modern method study recognizes that there is always a better way, even for the job that has already been studied.

The procedure of method study is described in various textbooks, but practitioners know that they rarely follow the step-by-step routine exactly as it is laid down in the book. The practitioner applies the principles of method study automatically, just as a car driver changes gear without consciously thinking about the essential steps involved in carrying out the task. Nevertheless, it is essential to examine these steps in order to grasp the basic principles. There are seven essential steps in method study:

1 Select the job to be studied
2 Define the objectives
3 Record all the relevant facts
4 Examine the facts critically
5 Develop a better method
6 Install the new method
7 Maintain the new method.

Selecting the job to be studied

It may appear ridiculous to emphasize what appears to be self-evident, that before a job is studied it has to be selected. But it is all too easy to waste time studying jobs that are not worth looking at. For example, there is little point in launching a detailed investigation of particular production methods if the more important problem is the design or price of the product. The first step, therefore, is to obtain a broad picture and then narrow down the field by selecting those aspects which offer good scope for improvement. Bottleneck operations, or those involving excessive scrap, high cost or under-utilized plant; are often the jobs selected for method study. Shortage of skilled labour, excessive overtime working, poor morale or fatiguing work may also provide good reasons for selecting a job to be studied.

Defining the objectives

Again, an apparently self-evident question, yet it is surprising how often it is overlooked. Effort is put into an investigation without defining the purpose. Is it more output, better quality, lower costs, better delivery, greater safety, less scrap or what? Unless this simple question is answered, method study may produce a wrong solution, like a football team kicking the ball around without first finding out where the goalposts are.

Recording the relevant facts

This is where the trained work-study practitioner can blind the uninitiated manager with his fancy systems of recording the facts, using special charts and symbols. These are really quite simple, once you understand them. They are only a form of shorthand to save time and to make it easier to grasp the facts.

The charts used in method study are of two main types. First, there are charts indicating a sequence of events, known as process charts. Second, there are charts with a time scale, such as multiple activity charts which show the interrelationship of the activities of two or more workers or machines. Method study may also involve diagrams or models to record the relevant facts. Because these charts and diagrams can be fascinating in themselves, there is a danger of over-complicating the recording procedure and not getting around to achieving the results.

Using the special symbols shown in Figure 9.1 process charts record a sequence of events. Usually the first step is to construct an outline process chart showing only the main operations and inspections. The next step may be a flow process chart recording what the worker does or what happens to material; these charts show transport operations and storage, temporary or permanent. In some cases a two-handed process chart may be used to show the activities of the workers hands in relationship to one another.

Multiple activity charts are used when it is desirable to show the activities of a worker or machine in relation to other workers or machines. A simple example is shown in Figure 9.2 showing a worker attending two machines.

Although the flow process chart shows the sequence and nature of operations and movements, it does not show the path and distance of movement. For this purpose a flow diagram can be constructed, this being a drawing, substantially to scale, showing the location of the various activities and the routes followed by the workers, material or equipment. Process chart symbols may be included in the diagram.

Another aid to recording the facts is the string diagram, which is a scale plan on which a thread is used to trace and measure the path of workers, materials or equipment. The string clearly shows multiple journeys over the same path.

Examining the facts critically

Critical examination in method study questions the very fundamentals

Symbol	Interpretation	Description
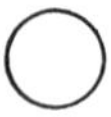 ◯	Operation	Indicates the main steps in a process, method or procedure
 ⇨	Transport	Indicates the movement of workers, materials or equipment
 ▽	Permanent storage	Indicates a controlled storage under some form of authorization
 D	Temporary storage	Indicates a delay in the sequence of events, eg between operations
☐	Inspection	Indicates an inspection for quality and/or quantity

When two or more events take place together, the appropriate symbols may be combined, eg a circle with a square in the middle = an operation including a subsidiary inspection

Figure 9.1   Process chart symbols

of existing ways of doing jobs. It asks two types of questions; the primary questions to indicate the facts and the reasons underlying them; the secondary questions to indicate the alternatives and thus the means of improvement. The questions are posed about the purpose, place, sequence, person and means involved, as illustrated in Figure 9.3.

Developing a better method

Usually this is the least difficult part of method study. By the time the facts have been recorded and analysed, the answers are obvious. Many managers and workers, even without the systematic approach of method study, could suggest ways and means of increasing the effectiveness of the jobs they are familiar with. Method study usually gives more and better ideas because it is so thorough. The main problem is not thinking up the better methods but getting them implemented.

Installing the new method

Installation should start even before the job is selected and studied. The cooperation of managers and workers should be sought to ensure that fears are allayed and that those involved can make a contribution to

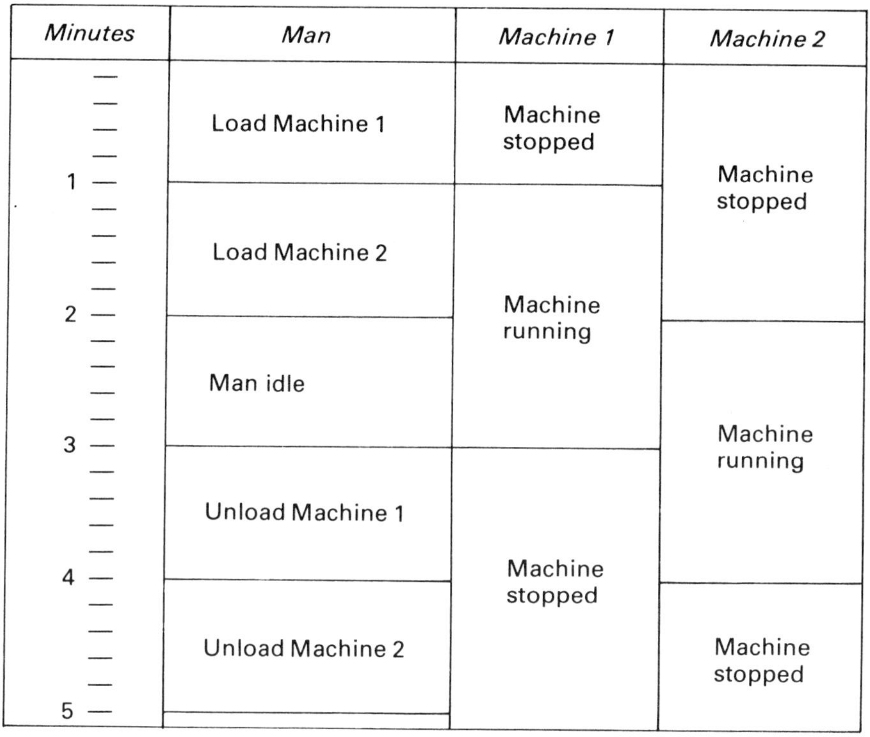

Work Study, Method Study and Work Measurement   111

Minutes	Man	Machine 1	Machine 2
1	Load Machine 1	Machine stopped	Machine stopped
2	Load Machine 2	Machine running	
3	Man idle		Machine running
4	Unload Machine 1	Machine stopped	
5	Unload Machine 2		Machine stopped

This chart clearly shows the under-utilization of the machines and the worker

Figure 9.2   Multiple activity chart

	Primary questions	Secondary questions
Purpose	What is achieved? Is it necessary? Why?	What else could be done? What else should be done?
Place	Where is it done? Why there?	Where else could it be done? Where else should it be done?
Sequence	When is it done? Why then?	When else could it be done? When else should it be done?
Person	Who does it? Why that person?	Who else could do it? Who else should do it?
Means	How is it done? Why that way?	How else could it be done? How else should it be done?

Figure 9.3   Critical examination technique

the new methods. Indeed, success is more likely to come from installing an improved method that is acceptable than by attempting to impose an even better method that is not liked.

Maintaining the new method

New ideas can stimulate enthusiasm but the novelty can soon wear off. Work study is a tool of management and it needs maintenance just as much as a machine tool or a motor car. Maintenance consists of periodically reviewing the working methods to ensure that the authorized procedure is being used, and to take account of any method improvements devised by the workers or management. Without such maintenance, an incentive scheme based on work study may drift, giving higher costs and earnings than originally envisaged.

Work Measurement

The aim of work measurement is to ascertain how long a job should take. This information can then be used for two main purposes. First, it can be used to look back to assess the level of performance in the past. Second, and more important, it can be used to set targets for the future. These should not be impossible targets, but realistic achievable targets for the average person.

Work measurement is usually thought of as something to do with stopwatches. It is true that the most commonly used form of work measurement, ie time study, does make use of stopwatches, but there are other techniques that do not require stopwatches, notably activity sampling and predetermined motion time systems (PMTS). These terms sound complicated but the techniques are quite simple.

Activity sampling

This technique consists of taking a sample of the activities and is based on the principles of statistical sampling as used in market research and opinion polls. By selecting and testing an adequate sample of people or activities, predictions can be made about the whole population. The degree of error should not be confused with the popular notion that opinion polls fail to predict election results. If the outcome depends on a narrow margin of 49:51 or 51:49, no poll can be sure in its prediction. In activity sampling, the margins are much less narrow. For instance, it can measure the proportion of time lost on machine breakdowns to quite acceptable limits of accuracy.

A number of 'instant' observations at random intervals of time are taken to see what types of activities are being carried out. The observation times should be chosen at random, using a table of random numbers, to avoid any bias in selection. On the basis of the sample results, the proportions of time spent on useful work, waiting time, idle time, etc, can be calculated. A simple statistical test is used to establish the size of sample needed for the required degree of accuracy. For example, 300 observations would suffice where the proportion of waiting time is 25% with limits of accuracy of ± 5%.

Predetermined motion time systems

In PMTS, instead of timing the job with a stopwatch, the work study man builds up a time from a knowledge of the method. He breaks the job down into very small elements of work for each of which the time can be read off a table of predetermined data. This information was built up by analysing cine films of many different jobs in order to identify the common elements. For instance, if one of the elements consists of reaching out through a distance of 50cms to pick up a small object, the time for this element is already known.

Until recently, the main limitation of PMTS was that it was only suitable for short-cycle repetitive work. It could take upwards of two hours to study a task taking only a minute to perform, though such a ratio might be economical if large numbers of workers are performing the same task. PMTS usually reveals substantial scope for improvement which may go unobserved in normal method study. Nowadays, there are several types of PMTS, some suitable for non-repetitive work such as plant maintenance.

Time study

In time study the first step is to break the job down into elements of work, usually of the order of less than one minute each. The elements are chosen for convenience of observation, measurement or analysis, using readily recognizable breakpoints, eg the end of a machine cycle, a change in the direction of motion of the hand, picking up or putting down an object. Some elements will be constant, ie the basic time will be constant whenever they are performed; other elements will be variable, ie the basic time will vary in relation to some characteristic of the product or process, eg dimensions, weight, quality, etc.

The next stage is to observe the elements of work being carried out and to record the actual time taken for each element. Although this process can be carried out by using an ordinary wristwatch equipped with a second-hand, the procedure is cumbersome. It means entering down the time at the end of each element then later subtracting the figures to find out the elapsed time for each element. It is much easier to use a stopwatch with a flyback mechanism so that the work study man can save himself the task of subtracting the figures. Also, most observers now use the decimal minute stopwatch which records in hundredths of a minute, thus simplifying the subsequent calculations.

In addition to recording the observed time the work study man also assesses and records the effectiveness of the worker. This process is called rating. The observer takes account of such factors as speed of movement, effort, dexterity, consistency, etc, and records his assessment of the actual rate of working relative to standard rating (designated 100) to the nearest five points, eg 85, 90, 95, 105, 110, 115, etc. Ratings below 75 are unusual and may indicate unfamiliarity with the job. Ratings above 125 are also exceptional, particularly over long periods of time.

Of course, rating is a subjective process, open to some degree of error. But criticisms of rating are often emotionally based. Most businesses rely on the subjective judgement of skilled employees, eg quality inspectors. The skilled work study man is trained to carry out the process of rating and his accuracy can be checked against other skilled observers and against films specially made for this purpose.

When the work study man has seen the operation performed a sufficient number of times (preferably at different times of day and done by different workers) he then derives the 'basic time' for each element by multiplying the observed time by the observed rating and dividing by 100. Any unusually high or low basic times may be discarded and the remainder used to calculate an average or median basic time.

An allowance for relaxation is added to the basic time to cover personal needs and also recovery from fatigue. The relaxation allowance varies with the nature of the work. For normal conditions it would be 10-15% but for strenuous work in hot noisy conditions it might be 50% or more. Finally, due allowance must be added for contingencies, ie small elements of work or delay which are uneconomical to measure. A typical contingency allowance would be not more than 5%.

The basic time plus the relaxation and contingency allowances gives the 'standard time' for the job. It should be noted that a standard time, usually expressed as standard minutes or standard hours, is not the same thing as an actual time. It is a unit of work consisting partly of work and partly of rest. It is the average time in which the job should be completed by a competent worker—not the best worker, but the average one. In many jobs the proportion allowed for relaxation and contingencies could be 20% or more, rarely less than 15%. This means that in an eight-hour day at least one hour is allowed to cover these factors.

Thus the standard time is an average achievable time, a realistic target. It does not demand a breakneck speed but a steady consistent pace that can be kept up throughout the day without undue fatigue, provided the appropriate relaxation is taken.

If the worker is attending one or more machines, the standard time may include an allowance for 'unoccupied time' to cover the periods when the worker is neither engaged on work inside the machine controlled time nor on taking authorized rest. Although part of the relaxation allowance may be within the machine cycle-time, some must be allowed outside it.

In multiple machine-minding, eg spinning and weaving, the standard time may include an interference allowance, or synchronization allowance, to allow for the loss of output when two or more machines are stopped simultaneously and are therefore queueing for attention. Similar allowances may be necessary in some forms of team work.

When the standard times (sometimes called work values) have been calculated, they are normally 'proved' by carrying out a production study of long duration—a day or more—in order to check that the various allowances are appropriate and that the basic times are valid.

Using Work Study Data

Standard times can be used to make a comparison between past performance and the expected future performance. The normal practice is to obtain records of output and wages for a period (known as the reference period) from the recent past. The period chosen should be typical of average conditions, excluding holidays, peak periods, etc. An assessment is made of the expected future level of output and allowance is made for any proposed increase in wages and other costs.

The results of a work study exercise can be illustrated by means of an example. Suppose that the work measurement shows that the standard time for a particular product is 40 standard minutes (SM). This means that over a working day of 8 hours a worker could be expected to turn out 12 items per day (480 min ÷ 40 SM = 12). (40 SM is less than 35 min of actual work because it includes at least 15% for relaxation and contingencies). Suppose also that the past records for the reference period show the following figures for a typical average week:

Attendance hours for 50 workers	=	2000 hours
Total wages at 75p per hour	=	£1500
Total output	=	1800 items

From these data the performance and costs in the reference period can be calculated as follows:

Total output in terms of standard hours = 1800 items × $\dfrac{40 \text{ SM}}{60 \text{ min}}$

Overall performance = 1200 standard hours

$$\text{Overall performance} = \frac{1200 \text{ standard hours}}{2000 \text{ clock hours}} \times 100$$

= 60 performance

$$\text{Wage cost per item} = \frac{£1500 \text{ of wages}}{1800 \text{ items}} = 83.3\text{p each}$$

$$\text{Wage cost per standard hour} = \frac{£1500 \text{ of wages}}{1200 \text{ standard hours}} = £1.25$$

Thus the records show that these workers have produced only 60% of standard performance (= 100). However this wide gap between the actual performance and the results achievable through work study does not necessarily mean that the workers were not working hard and conscientiously. It could be that a standard time based on the old method would be 60 SM, thus indicating an overall performance of 90 (1800 items at 60 SM = 1800 standard hours achieved in 2000 clock hours). The performance gap may be due partly to poor methods, partly to poor organization and partly to poor effort by the workers.

For the future, the achievable overall performance might be assessed at, say, 90, thus allowing a comfortable 10% for waiting time and other losses. In order to give the workers a share of the benefits of higher productivity, the future hourly earnings might be assessed at, say, 90p. (The extra 15p per hour might take the form of an incentive bonus). Thus the future output and costs would be:

Output in standard hours = 2000 clock hours at 90 performance
= 1800 standard hours

Number of items produced = $\frac{1800 \times 60}{40}$ = 2700 items

Total wages = 2000 hours × 90p = £1800

From these data the costs can now be calculated:

Cost per item = £1800 ÷ 2700 = 66.7p
Cost per standard hour = £1800 ÷ 1800 = £1.00

Thus the workers would receive a rise of 20% in hourly earnings and output would have risen by 50%, thus reducing costs by 20%. The savings in the reduction in cost per item go partly to the workers, partly to the management to cover the cost of devising and installing the new method, and partly to the customer in lower prices.

As well as facilitating a comparison between past and future performance, work measurement sets realistic standards against which current performance can be monitored day-by-day and week-by-week. In the example quoted above, management could check regularly whether the target performance of 90 was being achieved and to what extent waiting for materials, machine breakdown, trainees, etc, had been recorded as hindering performance. Since the standard minute is a common unit of measurement, all products and processes can be expressed in the same units thus facilitating comparison between departments and products.

Of course, such records do not in themselves run a business, but they provide a factual guide for management decisions. In particular they can help the foreman to organize his department so as to minimize avoidable waiting time and other losses. The performance records can be coupled to wage records to monitor costs and earnings. Thus the amount and causes of any excess costs can be revealed. For example, such records could show the costs of machine breakdowns and therefore help management to decide about replacements or better maintenance.

However, there are dangers in overcomplicating the figurework to the point where it is not readily understood or too late for action. Often it is sufficient to monitor the total output, the overall performance, the cost per standard hour and the average hourly earnings.

The Practical Implication of Work Study

Work study is traditionally associated with the shopfloor, but nowadays it can cover a much wider field than repetitive manual work. For instance, maintenance operations can be studied using such techniques as analytical estimating or basic work data (a form of PMTS). There are techniques for clerical work measurement and other special fields. Work study has been applied to selling activities, revealing an enormous scope for improvement in the utilization of the salesman's time.

The easy part of work study is carrying out the investigations and devising the new methods. Anyone of average intelligence can learn the rudiments of method study in a few days, though work measurement demands a longer training. The hard part of work study lies in getting the new methods willingly accepted, effectively installed and adequately maintained. This demands the cooperation of the people involved.

References and Further Reading

British Standard, *Glossary of Terms used in Work Study*, London, 1979.
Currie, Russell M., *Work Study*, Fourth Edition, revised by J.E. Faraday, Pitman/BIM, London, 1977.

Hamill, B.J. and Steele, P.M., *Work Measurement in the Office*: an MTM Systems Workbook, Gower, 1973.
International Labour Organization, *Introduction to Work Study*, 3rd (revised) Edition, 1979.
Whitmore, Dennis A., *Work Study and Related Management Services*, Heinemann, London, 1968.
Whitmore, Dennis A., *Measurement and Control of Indirect Work*, Heinemann, London, 1971.

10

Productivity Measurement

Richard Thorpe

For the last twenty years or more governments, academics, managers and trade unionists, have all stressed the importance of productivity, emphasizing to the nation its relationship with employment, standard of living and national prosperity.

The Meaning of Productivity

If indeed our standard of living and industrial competitiveness depend on increases in productivity then there needs to be a greater understanding of the constituents of productivity and which of these constituents need measuring, controlling and/or improving. There is increasing evidence that productivity does not necessarily mean the same thing to different people and its meaning, measurement and increase will depend very much on such factors as the state of the company in the market, the position of the person in the organization, and the time period over which increases in productivity are to be measured. By way of example, two years ago a team from the Pay and Rewards Research Centre at Strathclyde University studied the impact of a newly introduced self-financing productivity scheme introduced at an Iron Ore Preparation Plant in 1979. The employees were persuaded to accept this scheme on the basis of increased pay for increases in productivity. It was intended that all operators would share control over the process of ore preparation and if they could reduce the number of operational delays that occurred on the plant compared with an agreed datum then the whole workforce would enjoy a bonus.

Workers were not to be penalized for delays that could be attributed to poor maintenance or otherwise be seen to be the fault of management.

The research team interviewed employees and managers at the plant, and it soon became evident that the employees were keen to cooperate with the new scheme and obtain increased earnings whilst assisting management in seeking higher labour productivity. On answering questions as to what was most important to their job satisfaction, job security scored highly. For the men who operated and agreed the scheme it would appear the reduction of operational delays at the plant was the means by which they could contribute to productivity and so secure their jobs. However, at the end of 1980, the closure of this plant by the British Steel Corporation demonstrated that at a higher level within the organization, taking a broader, longer term perspective it was now considered that the productivity of capital was of more fundamental importance. Productivity potential lay, not at the blast furnace, but rather in the hands of the policy makers and salesmen whose markets had gradually declined.

Many writers, (for example, Novit, 1976; Currie, 1972) explain productivity in terms of the ratio of inputs to outputs with little further elaboration as to the number or nature of each, as in 'productivity is the quantitative relationship between what we produce and the resources we use' (Currie, 1972). Although such statements are acceptable in themselves, some elaboration and explanation is necessary to explain the nature of productivity.

First, it is important at the start to draw the distinction between production and productivity. Productivity refers, not to an increase in the outputs of a concern over a given period of time, but rather to an increase in the relative output from a given input. Therefore, to measure productivity there must be a measure of one or more of the inputs and one or more of the outputs of the system. An increase in productivity can be gained from an increase in some measure of a unit of output with the same units of input or a constant measure of the units of output from a reduced amount of inputs.

The Complexity of Measurement

Matters become complicated when the numbers and variety of inputs are taken into account as indicated in Figure 10.1. Some key factors from the environment are also shown. The inputs which have been given priority in many organizations' productivity measurement practices, have often been chosen with little regard to their degree of influence on the organization's overall performance (or productivity). The choice of measures of inputs and outputs has often depended on the perspective from which productivity is viewed. For example, from

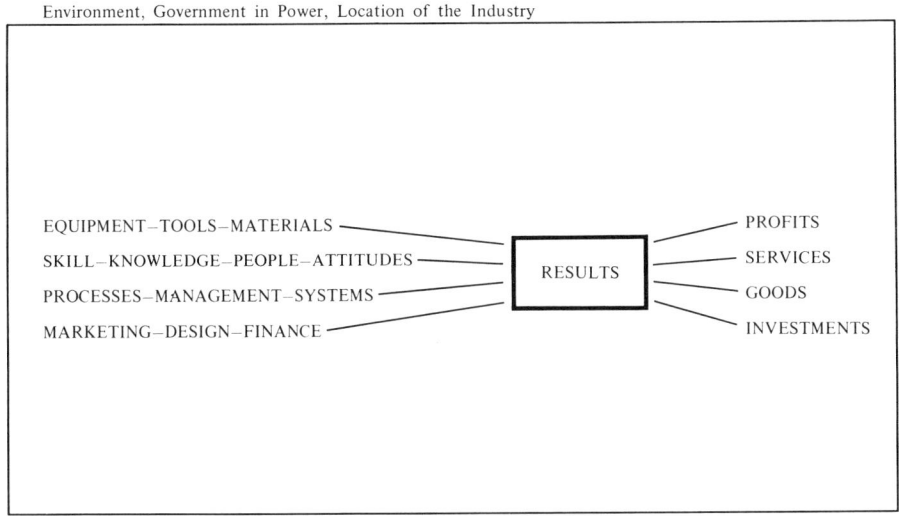

```
Environment, Government in Power, Location of the Industry

    EQUIPMENT–TOOLS–MATERIALS ─────╮         ╭───── PROFITS
    SKILL–KNOWLEDGE–PEOPLE–ATTITUDES ──┤ RESULTS ├── SERVICES
    PROCESSES–MANAGEMENT–SYSTEMS ──────┤         ├── GOODS
    MARKETING–DESIGN–FINANCE ──────────╯         ╰── INVESTMENTS

Local Culture, State of Industry, State of the Market
```

Figure 10.1   Inputs and outputs which may be constituents of a productivity measure

the engineer's viewpoint, units of material input divided into some unit of material output may be advocated as the measure of productivity. The financial accountant would be more likely to recommend that a unit of a financial nature be used, for instance capital employed related to some financial output such as profit. An economist on the other hand may take a different approach and emphasize labour input and output, measuring labour input via work study performance indices.

Partial Measures

Partial measures of productivity fail to take into account movements of other factor inputs and outputs. As has been pointed out by the BIM (1976), productivity measurement should involve more than just a measure of one or more partial inputs, as this does not take into account all the factor inputs in a given system. Another criticism of partial measures is that when measuring input and output, over what period does measurement become or cease to become, a valid determinant of productivity given that businesses are dynamic? It is to get around this problem that efficiency in productivity is a particularly useful concept as this tells how well resources at a given time are being used.

Efficiency can be divided into scale effects, increases in the quality of inputs, changes in techniques of production and improvements of the product. An increasing market brought about by mere population growth will permit higher productivity of many products as they become subject to economies of scale (Lipsey, 1979). A long production run provides for the substitution of more capital for labour, the opportunity to use better materials or to employ a better trained or more educated staff, and better organization of the factors of production can alone account for increases in productivity. It is for these reasons that productivity has been said to be a shorthand expression for efficiency, but although one of its components is efficiency the two cannot be said to be synonymous. In fact, there are continuing arguments on the precise definition of the words.

Localised Efficiency

Let us consider for a moment a company which decides to increase its productive capacity; reorganization of its factory may well, through better training and capital equipment, increase the output of the machine shop. It may be considered that efficiency has increased and in respect of the machine shop it may well have done so but it is not necessarily the case that productivity has increased when the company is viewed as a whole. Could productivity be said to have increased if output from this machine shop led to an increase in unsaleable stocks of finished goods? This happened in the case of a Scottish electrical manufacturer who after installing a productivity bonus scheme found that increases in output were not saleable. Redundancies followed; the localized increases in efficiency had led to an overall decline in organizational effectiveness. Similarly at a large engineering company studied in 1979, a researcher undertaking participant observation noted that localized efficiency did not lead to an effective result for the company. For instance, kit items needed for the final assemblies were prepared by the computer at night. All larger or heavier items for these kit lists were drawn from the central stores by night shift workers and brought up to be married with the smaller stores items, such as washers, nut and bolts, prepared during the day. All these small items were 'free issue' which meant that assemblers on the factory floor could draw what they needed from stock without paperwork. Each kit once complete would be sufficient to make one part of the final assembly. The job of the stores personnel was to take the computerised labels, stick them onto paper bags and fill them with the individual number of parts specified on the label. This job was extremely repetitive but was done fairly efficiently. However, the bags, carefully filled and stapled in the stores, once on the assembly shop floor were merely ripped open by the operator and in the majority of cases, the whole packet thrown in the bin. The reason for this was that these items, being divided into very small batches, were difficult and a nuisance to handle. The men working on a particular operation day in and day out knew their stock requirements for small parts by heart and found it far easier to maintain a personal stock of parts and replenish them when they became depleted, than to fiddle with handling small quantities of parts each time they received a new kit. However efficiently the job was done it did not lead in this case to increased effectiveness. There are a wealth of similar examples of lack of overall effectiveness as jobs become increasingly specialized and sight is lost of the organization's overall objectives.

Performance Indices

Performance indices, often also thought to be synonymous with productivity, are fraught with danger and can be misleading. Consider the two cases A and B below:

Case A: A worker works at a high effort rating (say 100 on the BSI Scale) but output is low due to ineffective, out-of-date methods and equipment. The result is that performance is recorded as high and productivity recorded as low.

Case B: A worker is unable to work hard due to a large proportion of his work being machine controlled. His effort rating is therefore low (say 50 on the BSI Scale) with the result that performance is recorded as low but productivity is recorded as high.

The above examples draw attention to the importance of a clear distinction between the meaning of efficiency, effectiveness, performance, and productivity. Taking the argument of efficiency a stage further, a preoccupation with efficiency and doing tasks either faster or better, may jeopardize flexibility and innovation which are the very hallmarks of long term productivity success. But recording and understanding the potential for improved productivity from all the input resources is a necessary step in assessing efficiency and this has relevance to productivity in all situations. This is of crucial importance in the search for an adequate means of measuring productivity. The establishment of productivity potential is in itself not an easy task and many factors come into play that may not at first be recognized, as discussed later in this chapter.

Comparisons

Productivity is often calculated by comparison and this practice is fraught with difficulties. Consider how the productivities of labour, capital and management in any organization are to be differentiated; each is closely related to the others. The precise dividing lines are difficult to draw. For instance, in a productivity bonus scheme studied at British Steel and based on reducing operational delays, the men were to be paid a bonus determined by the reduction in number of stoppages of the continuous operation. However, the bonus was not to be affected by any stoppages deemed to be due to equipment or management inadequacy. In this system arguments inevitably occurred when equipment failure was caused as a result of labour inefficiency (eg in clearing a blockage).

Other difficulties arise in assessing potential for productivity improvement when comparisons are made between different products or components. Financial analysts are keen to compare the rate of return on capital invested and use this as an indicator to advise on future investments. However, the rate of return from any company depends on such things as the life cycle of the product, the number of competitors in the market, the potential size of the market and the amount of capital invested. Is it then valid to compare the productivity in producing 100 tons of chalk with producing 100 tons of cheese in terms of the utilization of resources and the return on capital employed?

This argument can be extended to include comparisons between industries in different countries. Here, technological differences make vast differences to productivity and comparison is further confused. The scale of production will also have its impact on the validity of the productivity comparisons. Manufacture on a small scale may well be efficient and adequately meet the needs of small markets in a small economy. But when compared to large scale production for much larger markets its efficiency and productivity will appear low. As markets become increasingly world wide, countries and companies are forced to compete on the same terms with each other.

Concern for productivity is not always uniform. Consider the measurement of productivity potential in service industries, where measures of service are still difficult to define. By way of example, in an effluent treatment organization it was found that the productivity of different works was measured according to the amount of labour input per number of operations completed. Although variations between works were associated with the type of plant and equipment and age of the plant, they were also dependent upon the standards of up-keep demanded by the plant manager. Labour in the plants represented a high proportion of total cost and whereas one manager might wish to run a plant enhanced by smartly cut grass and well kept flowerbeds (a tradition amongst some of the older treatment plants) another had eliminated the flowerbeds in favour of concrete (easier and less costly to maintain). In this example, the concrete site did not look as attractive, but was highly efficient. When considering productivity a decision must be made about the level at which the subjective and qualitative factors are to be maintained.

The same argument applies equally well when considering the impact of culture on the maximization of the inputs/outputs relationship. Its importance should not be underestimated either in an international or a local context. In a study of a large primary process industry the local culture not only determined that young school leavers should enter the industry predominant in the locality but also that men were expected to work shifts. This tradition was accepted by men, wives and families and to some extent local amenities adjusted to suit this practice. Compared with another part of the country where shift working was not a usual and accepted part of the working pattern, productivity in a similar company in the same industry would be likely to be much lower. In another study, local culture had a major impact on productivity at a large engineering company in a rural location with a close knit local workforce lacking experience of other factory work and with very little conception of performance standards. Relationships between employees and management were casual and the pace of working was relaxed. Because this industry had no direct competitors within the United Kingdom and all its products were for government contracts, the impact of low labour productivity was not immediately obvious. However, in comparison with similar industries in other countries productivity could be seen to be low.

International comparisons are even more problematic. A large multinational company's subsidiary in Bolivia found difficulties in motivating its labour force to increase productivity. The parent company had noticed that by comparison to its other subsidiaries in different countries, labour productivity in Bolivia was extremely low, and various methods had been attempted to increase it. The traditional method of offering an incentive bonus for increases in output had failed to have any marked effect. On investigation it was found that the expectations of the town's population were so low that even to have a job was reward enough and there was little interest in earning more money by working harder.

Of course, these comparisons can go on ad infinitum and the message to be obtained is the extent to which local differences in culture, politics and attitudes impact on the production process. Special problems arise when one considers the extent to which they can be modified, are amenable to modification or as some writers have suggested and others queried, need to be modified (Schumacher, 1973; Hirsch, 1977). In India the bicycle is still the main means of transport and the Royal Enfield motor bicycle is still manufactured. In China dams and large capital projects are still built largely manually to provide employment for the population. Should they invest, however, in new capital equipment their potential for productivity in Western terms will not only increase but their rate of productivity growth will be dramatic as they will start from a low base. This highlights the dilemma of international comparisons of productivity.

Still the Need for a Measure

Notwithstanding the problems identified in productivity comparisons, companies and countries still find it necessary to measure productivity for a whole range of reasons.

Measurement is often required for productivity-related payments. In Britain today there is still a heavy reliance on the use of money incentives to increase labour performance, and indeed there has been a more or less steady increase in their use since the war in contrast to the USA (see Table 10.1).

Table 10.1

Percentage of wage-earners paid under systems of payments by results. 1938–79

Date	Percentage of all full-time manual men
1938	18%
1947	24%
1951	28%
1961	30%
1974	41%
1978	42%
1979	44%

Source: Ministry of Labour Gazette, New Earnings Survey, and The Department of Employment.

McCormick (1977) suggested full employment had raised the cost of supervisory labour, more of which is needed with other kinds of payment systems, and that this had caused the growth of incentive usage in Britain. But the difference between the USA and the UK is nevertheless surprising as both countries were subject to the same criticisms of incentive payment systems in the 1950s. One possible explanation is their repeated encouragement in Britain at times of wage restraint, as a means of increasing income above statutory limits. These payment schemes need a measure of productivity on which they can base the payment calculations.

There are special problems associated with the use of productivity measurement in this context, since it introduces into the procedures for measurement the financial interests of the employees whose work is being measured. It is common practice in many industries when work study techniques are used to measure productivity at 'normal workpace', for employees to work slowly, incorporating every detail of the correct procedure, whilst measurements are taken; and subsequently to obtain a false measure of productivity improvement by such devices as speeding up the machine (even by wrapping adhesive tape around a pulley wheel to increase its diameter, or feeding two products through a grinding machine back to back), missing out various steps, or developing other short cuts.

Another use of productivity measurement is to determine manning levels and here the concept of productivity potential becomes important. How hard are the employees currently working, and how many employees would be needed to carry out the work if they were all working at a standard pace? (see Chapter 9 for a discussion of work study techniques) Direct work measurement is often the tool used for measuring manual repetitive work and is increasingly coming into use for a greater variety of tasks.

Forms of indirect measurement, however crude, are also useful to determine the productivity potential of a given work site or to determine the appropriate establishment. Universities employ this technique widely and maintain strict staff/student ratios. This is a crude productivity measure, comparing one input—University lecturers, and one output—students.

An example of a more complex comparison is illustrated in Table 10.2. This large water authority took on the responsibility for direct water rate billing following local government reorganization in 1974. Unable to assess the establishment required to carry out this additional task, a study was instigated to assess performance and potential of the small team currently employed and to draw comparisons between sections undertaking the same tasks in different divisions. The index used was the number of completed assessments per employee in a given period. By way of judging potential, a work sampling exercise was commenced, comparing the work done by these employees with those in other divisions. It was evident that employees could handle approximately 25,000 assessments per head, at their present work rate. Their potential, however, was in the order of 30,000 assessments per head, assuming they worked at standard performance. After a review of the present and original proposal for staff increases made by the trade union, an evaluated proposal was put forward for negotiation. It represented a saving of some £15,000 with a reduction of 4.5 in the size

Table 10.2

Domestic billing and collection of water charges

The comparison of South Eastern Division with others.

	Division	Staff	Records	Assessments per head
Site 1	South Eastern (year 1)	15	292,000	19,500
Site 2	Nevis (year 1)	21	420,000	20,000
Site 3	Cairngorm (year 1)	10	221,000	22,100
Site 3	Cairngorm (year 2)	18	431,000	23,940
Site 4	Northern (year 1)	6	118,000	19,700
Site 4	Northern (year 2)	13	327,000	25,150

1 Expected number of assessments – 631,000.
2 Work sampling indicated – 31,000 per head possible.
3 Increase recommended from 15 to 26 staff.

of staff increase (from 30.5 to 26 employees). Table 10.3 shows the calculation of these cost savings.

Productivity measures are also useful in an organization to appraise management performance. It is in this area that financial measures have been particularly prevalent. Sales management might be appraised on the value of sales, managing directors on the rate of return on capital employed. In recent years added value statements have begun to become popular at the back of company reports. The reason for this is that added value is believed to give a clearer, less emotive picture of company performance to the workforce and the general public than profit. By using some measure of productivity as a yardstick for assessing management performance, the management team is being judged by its impact on organizational performance. Problems of comparison are often significant in this context, and care should be taken not to make unfair or unrealistic comparisons. Where like cannot be compared with like (in terms of a similar department or organization elsewhere) it is useful to monitor progress over time, and look for productivity improvements as compared to previous years (taking care, where

Table 10.3

Comparison of costs for alternative staffing levels

Grade	Mean salary £	Current Staff Number	Cost £	Original Request Number	Cost £	O & M Plan Number	Cost £
8	5412	0.5	2706	0.5	2706	1	5412
7	4830	1	4830	2	9660	1	4830
6	4311	—	—	—	—	3	12,933
5	3846	3	11,538	7	26,922	1	3846
4	3435	—	—	—	—	3	10,305
3	2958	3	8874	7	20,706	1	2958
2	2544	3	7632	7	17,808	8	20,352
1	1800	3	5400	7	12,600	8	14,400
TOTAL		13.5	£40,980	30.5	£90,402	26	£75,036

Plus overheads @ 33 1/3%:
Total: £54,640   £120,536   £100,048

appropriate, to allow for major capital investment and trade cycles).

Some form of productivity measurement is useful when considering investment decisions. This not only applies to investment externally where various financial ratios might be considered to identify growth industries and/or good rates of return, but also to advise on investment decisions internally. For an example of this Table 10.4 shows the calculation of the relative advantage of one plain paper copying machine over another. Choice 1 shows a company one machine rented and operated under supervision, the total monthly cost coming to £492. Choice 2, at first sight seems less attractive because of the utilization of two machines. But comparison of costs showed it could be operated for £100 less per month, with the advantages of far more flexibility of operation should volumes increase or equipment fail. To enable this comparison to be made, detailed information of past usage,

Table 10.4

Investment decisions—reprographics

Alternative 1: Cost of Company-One machine operated under supervision per month.

		£
Rental of machine		77.00
Cost of 25,000 copies Standard Tariff 5	215.00	
Cost of full-time operator	200.00	
		415.00
	Total cost	£492.00

Alternative 2: Offset duplicating machine plus Company-One smaller machine per month, purchased over 72 months

	£	
Offset duplicating machine	32.00	
1,400 runs @ 5p	70.00	
Consumables @ 10p per 1000	4.00	
Maintenance less mileage	15.00	
		£121.00
Plus Plate Maker		
Reduction Copier (£900 over 60 months)	15.00	
Consumables @ 0.5p per 1400 copies	7.00	
Maintenance	5.00	
		£27.00

Small Company-One machine monthly for 16,500 copies

Rental	33.00	
10,000 copies @ 1.42p	142.00	
6,500 copies @ 1.08p	70.00	
		£245.00
		£393.00

projected future usage, and run lengths needed to be collected.

The other main use of productivity measurement apart from comparisons of organizational effectiveness between time periods, between companies and between countries, is to improve the organization of work. Again, the data needed to be collected for this aim to be realized is often underestimated. Too often the closed approach of work study determines that man hours per unit of output be the sole factor examined and the importance of other inputs and variables are underestimated or misunderstood. In the Pay and Rewards Research Centre study it was found that very few companies who were making changes in their organization spent time on a thorough diagnosis of their organization to provide information about what productivity might in fact be contingent upon. Also few managers realised the significance of many of the variables in their organization that would either affect motivation or productivity. One explanation for this was that incentive schemes were being introduced by managers who did not fully appreciate the importance of contingency theory. Indeed, it emerged from field interviews that few managers had even heard of the concept and were often sceptical of academics and their jargon. There is an argument (Parris, 1979) and some evidence from Strathclyde research to suggest that even managers who do appreciate the need for a comprehensive assessment of the variables within a concern have neither the skills, training nor often the position to influence decisions. With specific regard to incentive schemes designed to increase individual performance it was found that many companies introducing schemes missed the potential for using alternative motivators at this crucial diagnosis and design stage.

An adequate assessment of the key factors contributing to improved organizational performance, and therefore to productivity, would enable management to plan changes aimed at appropriate aspects of the organization.

Total Productivity Measures

To return to the central theme of the argument, evidence suggests that if productivity measurement is to be accurate, realistic and comparable, many measures need to be made in the organization. Figure 10.2 shows diagrammatically the many means by which company performance can be improved, and therefore the many practices within the organization which *could* be measured to monitor productivity changes. There is no adequate universal measure that will indicate an organization's performance either over time with itself or with its competitors unless a range of factors are measured and their potential for generating outputs determined. At the Pay and Rewards Research Centre, attempts were

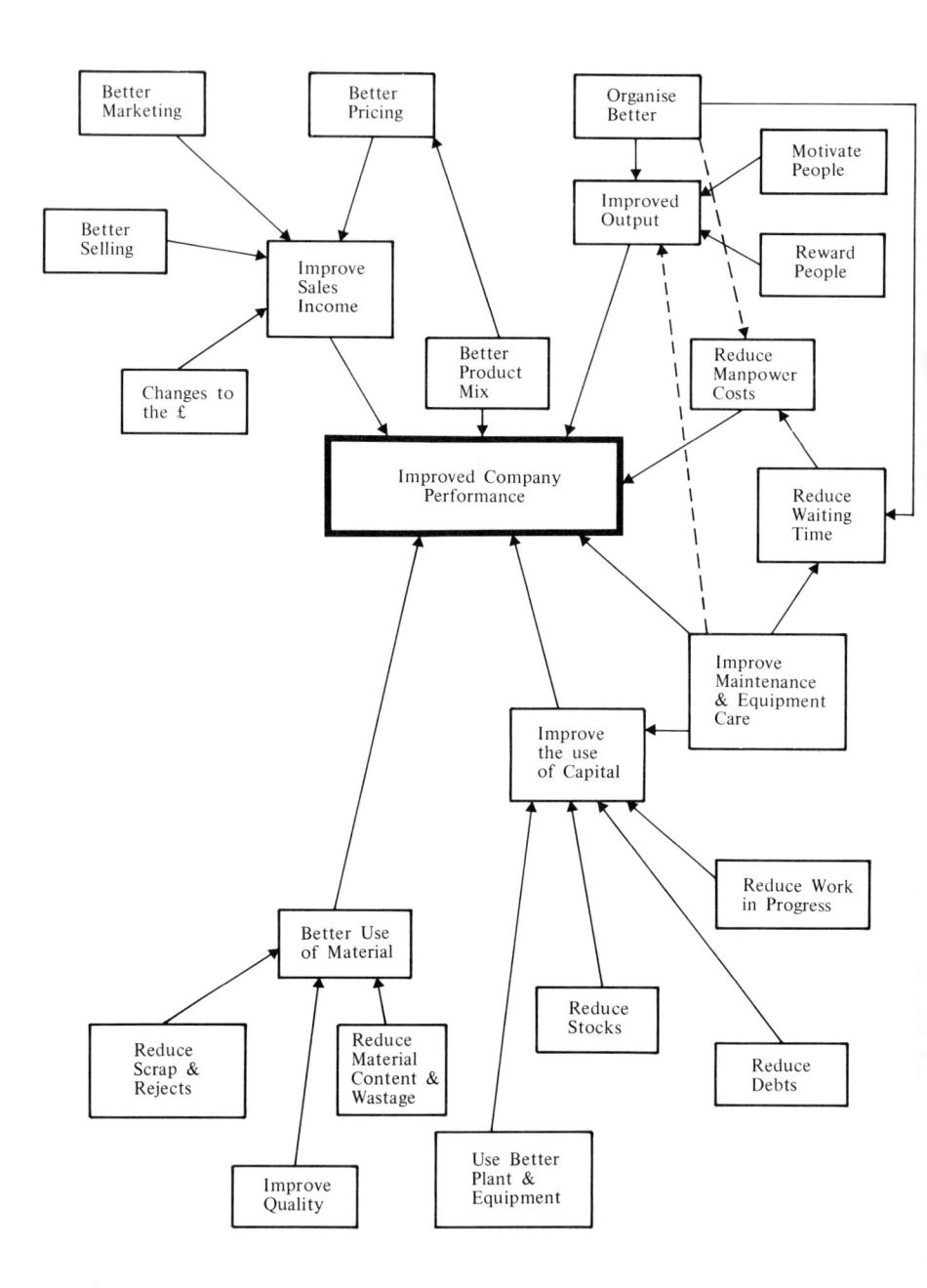

Figure 10.2 Areas of activity which could contribute to improved company performance

A
Causal Influences
e.g. Incentive Scheme
Management Effort
Consultant's Schemes
(e.g. Hay MSL, job evaluation, centralised maintenance, etc.)

B
Changes in Productivity

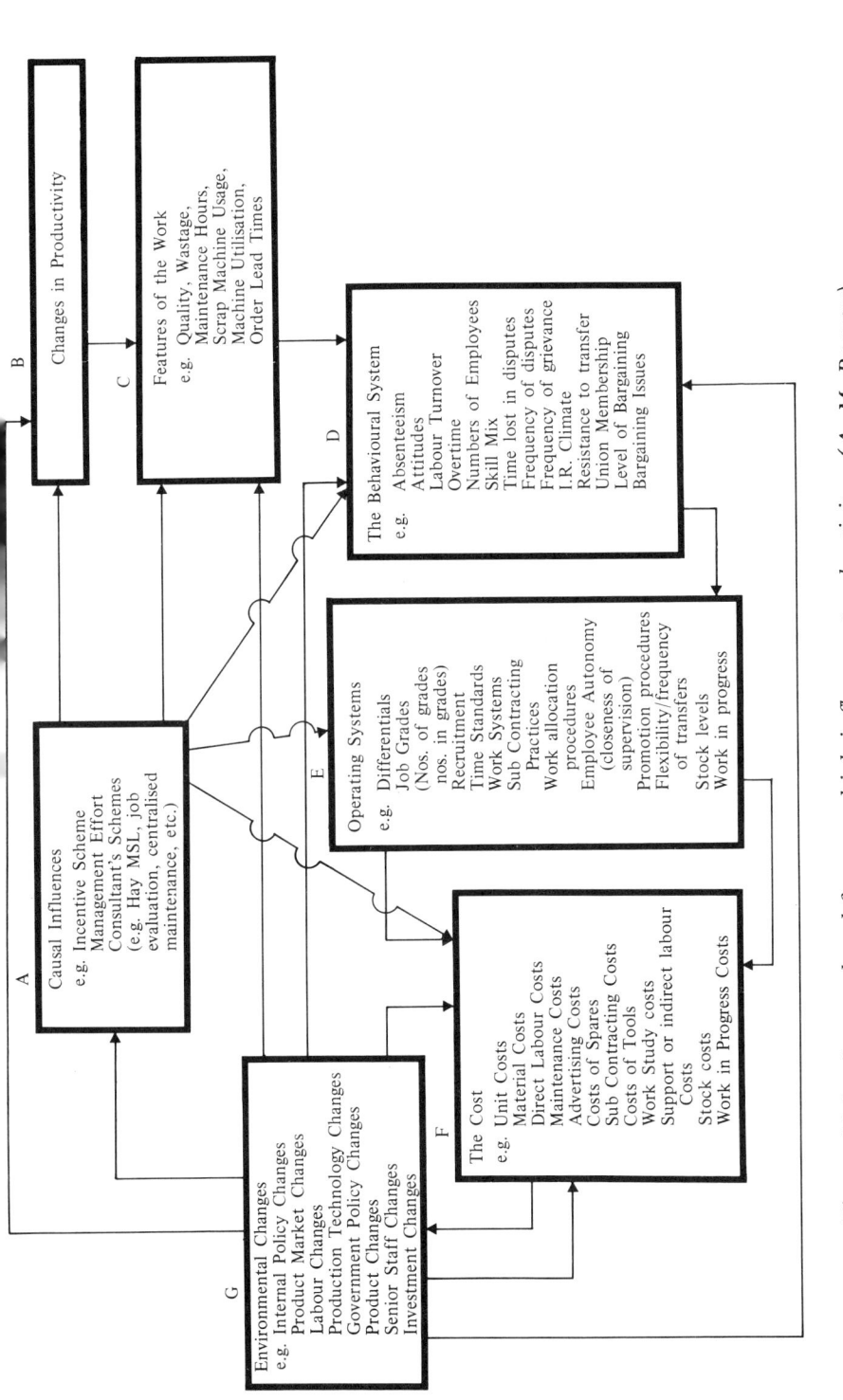

C
Features of the Work
e.g. Quality, Wastage, Maintenance Hours, Scrap Machine Usage, Machine Utilisation, Order Lead Times

D
The Behavioural System
e.g. Absenteeism
Attitudes
Labour Turnover
Overtime
Numbers of Employees
Skill Mix
Time lost in disputes
Frequency of disputes
Frequency of grievance
I.R. Climate
Resistance to transfer
Union Membership
Level of Bargaining
Bargaining Issues

E
Operating Systems
e.g. Differentials
Job Grades (Nos. of grades nos. in grades)
Recruitment
Time Standards
Work Systems
Sub Contracting Practices
Work allocation procedures
Employee Autonomy (closeness of supervision)
Promotion procedures
Flexibility/frequency of transfers
Stock levels
Work in progress

F
The Cost
e.g. Unit Costs
Material Costs
Direct Labour Costs
Maintenance Costs
Advertising Costs
Costs of Spares
Sub Contracting Costs
Costs of Tools
Work Study costs
Support or indirect labour Costs
Stock costs
Work in Progress Costs

G
Environmental Changes
e.g. Internal Policy Changes
Product Market Changes
Labour Changes
Production Technology Changes
Government Policy Changes
Product Changes
Senior Staff Changes
Investment Changes

Figure 10.3 Inter-related factors which influence productivity (A. M. Bowey)

made to monitor changes in productivity by means of a set of indices. Figure 10.3 illustrates the inter-relationship of factors influencing productivity levels drawn up at the Centre. Many of these factors can be viewed as inputs in productivity terms and providing they are in the control of the company, could be measured as such.

Consider for example a company introducing a directly work measured incentive scheme. The scheme, a directly work measured, work studied scheme, would appear in Box A. This would affect in the short run, productivity, Box B. Hopefully this would rise and be measured as an increase of units produced relative to resources used. If the only input measure was unit labour cost (as is sometimes the case), an observer could conclude that the scheme was a success. Consider further whether this view would be endorsed if the scheme had led to one or more of the following consequences, because of increased working and increased bonus earnings on the factory floor. Faster working may have meant quality deterioration, the number of rejects increased, and dissatisfied customers. Faster working may increase machine usage but also the cost of maintenance and repairs. Faster working may lead to dissatisfaction at work, conflict between workgroups, an increase in stoppages with a deteriorating industrial relations climate. The increased volume of production might not be saleable, due to lack of demand or an inappropriate product mix. This would represent additional company money tied up in stocks, with no corresponding increase in income. And the balance of work loads in different sections of the company and/or materials or component supply problems could lead to compensating bonus being paid for waiting time and increased labour costs out of proportion to the increased production. Bonus earnings enjoyed by direct workers, may have eroded the differentials previously established between manual workers and staff, with consequent staff discontent. If external factors such as incomes policy prevent management adjusting the differentials, then the introduction of the scheme could lead to serious difficulties in this area. All these problems assume there has been a real increase in production. But several studies have shown that it is possible for an incentive bonus scheme to lead to no improvement, or even to a deterioration, in productivity.

If this example appears a little far-fetched, it may be useful to illustrate the point with the example of a company studied in 1977, which introduced a productivity bonus scheme with the primary intention of raising the performance level of manual workers. This large national public company experienced many of the problems described above and with the resultant deterioration in industrial relations recorded enormous losses for the years 1977 and 1978, causing concern amongst its institutional share holders.

This illustrates the case for some total measure which would cover the whole system and include all important inputs and outputs so representing an adequate measure of organizational effectiveness. A package of multiple measures carefully chosen together with an overall measure would enable evaluation of the system, and changes in effectiveness or potential in any area could be highlighted.

Partial approaches to the measurement of productivity can be seen as part of a composite or integrated productivity model. Such a model incorporating productivity measurements from various perspectives was developed by Norman and Bahiri (1976) but their model had the disadvantage that all inputs and outputs were measured in financial units. Another attempt at a total productivity measure is the concept of added value. Added value as a means of measuring, informing and encouraging improvements in company performance has enjoyed recent popularity. It is based on the calculation of net output determined by subtracting from sales value all bought-out goods and services. This calculation equates with the value added to inputs by the processes carried out within the organization in order to produce the output of goods or services. Table 10.5 shows a typical form used by a company to calculate added value for bonus purposes. The concept is discussed further in Chapter 22, where alternative methods of calculation are explained and the advantages and disadvantages of added value discussed.

Significance of the Market Position

As discussed above, productivity does not necessarily equate with efficiency in the long term. It is useful to consider two extreme types of company in this context.

Organizations with a mature market, where it is important for people to 'perform known tricks faster' and so reduce unit costs and offer a cheaper product in a market with many competitors, and others where it is more important that people perform in a flexible way and it is the ability to improvise as well as to search for and secure new markets, that is of paramount importance. This consideration highlights the flaw in many of the indices used in productivity measurement today, which is exacerbated if wage payment systems are attached. Because if an organization at the new end of the product cycle tries to encourage people to perform their existing tasks in a faster way this can be totally the wrong answer for the company's long term interests. A high index of personal productivity may be recorded which is, however, not achieving the company's objectives. At the other end of the scale, an organization which tries to buy or encourage flexibility where flexibility is no longer required because the industry and the technology are stable, can achieve only marginal improvements from disruptive and

Table 10.5

Typical added value calculation

		£	%	Comments
1	Net Sales			
2	*Less*: Materials used Service and Supply Costs Process Materials Outside Processes Misc. Purchases Misc. Issues Power Maintenance Materials Jig Materials Transport			
	TOTAL			
3	Added Value (AV): (1−2)			
4	Employee Share at X% (3 × X%)			
5	*Less*: Participating Payroll a) Factory Wages b) Holiday Pay Account			
	TOTAL PAYROLL (5a + 5b)			
6	Employee Gain/Loss: (4−5)			
7	Productivity Index (3 ÷ 5) (AV ÷ total payroll)			
8	Distribution a) Gain/Loss b) Reserve Account c) Cash Payout (8a−8b)			

costly effort. It follows therefore that a further complication in productivity measurement is the difficulty of measuring the stage the company is at, so as to identify appropriate criteria for assessing productivity.

In addition we have seen that inputs to productivity have many components and each is often viewed, monitored and measured by different individuals within an organization. It is of prime importance to decide which resources in the form of inputs should be subjected to measure. Interminable arguments rage over which resources are the most important in any enterprise—most protagonists agree that differentiation between labour and capital is a problem. Some argue that capital is not worth measuring because if the labour force will not work for any reason there will be no productivity, no profits and no output. Others argue that there would be no output at all without the machines, especially in capital intensive industries, and therefore the productivity of the machines is more important. But with the increased emphasis on change in the economy, it is becoming more important in an increasing proportion of organizations, for productivity to be viewed in terms of flexibility and cooperation, rather than narrowly confined to improved performance of specified tasks.

Significance of Organizational Location

It should be remembered that resources not only means manual skills but also brain power, access to markets, access to other peoples' know-how, the use and development of materials, design skill etc.. The relevance of all these factors including the labour and capital has to be assessed together with the company's market position in order that the correct emphasis can be placed on the constituent factors in efficiency and productivity. The most appropriate measure for senior management looking at the company as a whole, over the mid and long term, would be some total measure indicating the effective use of all the inputs into the organizational system. It is for this reason that added value bonus schemes have become popular as a means of providing incentives for managers to raise their performance. It is usually at this level that coordination of the work done in areas of marketing, purchasing, design, sales, pricing, production, motivation, the use and improvement of capital equipment and capital itself takes place. These people therefore need information from productivity measurements, which will assist in their decisions. From their point of view if all the various inputs and outputs can be presented in the same units, or even as one index, they will be perceived as appropriate to the tasks in hand. Here again comes support for the added value index.

Going down the organizational hierarchy, concern for productivity becomes more immediate and partial measures begin to replace global ones. For the supervisor, output per man hour in his department might be a useful performance indicator. He may have little time or inclination to concern himself with whether goods he produces are saleable. Likewise, for the machine mechanic, machine down-time may measure his performance; and for the shop floor worker his daily performance is related to a time standard. As one descends the hierarchy therefore, concern for productivity not only narrows from considering multiple inputs to a single input but also contracts from a long term perspective on productivity at senior management level to a medium term perspective at middle management level and to a very short term perspective on productivity at the shop floor level, where weekly or even daily performance is measured in terms of a single input and a single output.

If, in addition, the workers' pay is related to the calculation of productivity at this very elementary level, it is small wonder his concern for increased organizational effectiveness does not go beyond the very narrow constraints of his own work situation. Other aspects of productivity in wealth creation go unheeded.

Wild (1980) noted three dimensions of productivity, namely that of machines, labour and materials. He suggested that in each case, the achievement of high productivity can be considered in terms of maximizing the resource utilization or minimizing the loss or wastage. (see Table 10.6)

A common problem with the use of partial measurements is that they have frequently been developed for other purposes and not adequately modified to ensure that they measure and project the correct information. The main offenders are financial measures which rely on the calculation of profit as an output measure where the inputs to the profit calculation have been controlled and adjusted for other purposes than appraising internal performance; and financial measures which rely on capital employed as the input measure, where again the figures were produced for different purposes and do not entirely correspond to the costs of resources employed. Labour productivity measures are equally prone to this problem. Work study performance measures used to calculate bonus schemes often include factors not relating to productivity at all such as assigning the average performance figure for time spent waiting, for holidays, etc, or the manipulation of performance figures in response to protests from the workforce, or in an attempt to make the bonus scheme pay what management feels is correct. These problems of incentive schemes and productivity measurements are documented elsewhere (Bowey, 1978). Figures which have been produced for other purposes and incorporate allowances or adjustments to take account of the uses for which the figures were intended, should not then be incorporated into productivity calculations.

A company in New Zealand manufacturing and selling forest products, recognized the limitations of a partial measure of productivity and decided to introduce a system of total productivity measure-

Table 10.6

Resource productivity and measurement

Resource	Productivity objectives	Productivity measures
Machines	e.g. *Maximize*	
i.e. all physical items, e.g. equipment, tools, buildings, space, etc., directly and indirectly used by the system.	Output/distance/through-put per machine hour Proportion of total available time utilized Effectiveness of utilization (e.g. capacity utilized) Occupancy/space utilization	Output/distance/through-put/machine hour Time(s) used or % Capacity used or % Occupancy/space utilization or %
	Minimize Idle time and downtime Under-utilized unoccupied space Machine cost content	Idle time and/or downtime or % % Utilized occupied space Machine cost content or %
Labour	e.g. *Maximize*	
i.e. those persons who directly or indirectly necessarily provide or contribute to the operation of the system, e.g. manual labour, supervision, etc.	Output/distance/through-put per man hour Proportion of total available time utilized Effectiveness of utilization (e.g. capacity utilized	Output/distance/through-put man hours Time(s) used or % Capacity used or %
	Minimize Idle and ineffective time Labour cost content	Idle and/or ineffective time or % Labour cost content or %
Materials	e.g. *Maximize*	
i.e. those physical items directly or indirectly consumed or converted by the system.	Yield (i.e. output/distance/through-put) per unit weight/volume, etc.	Yield quantity, weight, etc.
	Minimize Wastage, losses or scrap Material cost content	Wastage, losses or scrap quantity or % Rework/rectification quantity or % Material cost content or %

Source: Wild (1980)

ment. The company had experienced problems with its past method of assessing the work content of employees' jobs by direct study. This had resulted in a deteriorating industrial relations climate as dispute followed dispute over the times allowed for the various tasks and an ever increasing staff resource was needed to maintain the whole system of direct performance measurement. The new system relied on a total productivity measure (TPM) calculated simply as follows:

$$\text{Total Productivity measure} = \frac{\text{money value of output}}{\text{costs of labour, capital and materials}}$$

Costs of labour, capital and materials were calculated on an annual basis and men were encouraged to take action and contribute ideas to reduce the input costs in each of the three areas as well as attempting to increase output through harder or more effective working. Participation was recorded as a key factor and found to be crucial in the success of the scheme. A bonus committee was formed to administer the scheme. In New Zealand Forest Products' experience TPM was found to be good for managerial control, good as a measure of organizational effectiveness and as a way of rewarding the workforce for their contribution to increased performance. They had the advantage that small numbers of people were included in the scheme. Further discussion of schemes of this kind are to be found in Chapter 22.

Productivity Planning

Productivity is inextricably linked to change and it is the successful timing of a recognition of change and a timely response by adaptation of the resources used in the productive system that is crucial to improving or maintaining productivity. Productivity then, is closely associated with business planning and involves a planned approach to change and a planned response. This process can be demonstrated diagrammatically as in Figure 10.4. Long range plans as shown in the diagram are largely the response of senior members of management who use broad multiple measures to audit the strengths and weaknesses of the company and assess the long range market forecasts. This data enables the company to establish its long term objectives and to express these objectives in terms of some output measures that take account of all the inputs. Once objectives have been established more detailed plans for profit, for marketing and development can be established and their success monitored. This model takes account of where the company is in the product life cycle. If the company is producing an ageing product or is in a declining industry emphasis may well be placed on cost reduction or resource improvement plans. Productivity measures will then have to be used that relate to these, and simple indices such as volume of work, completed per man hour or work-measured performance figures may well be appropriate. However, if the company is in a growing or new industry, and feedback from its marketing plan, established from company objectives, is favourable it may well be that organizational resources are diverted into diversification plans, increased sales plans and changing production plans. In this context concern for flexibility and cooperation are more important than fast output; and appropriate productivity measures will relate to overall company objectives, such as fast and flexible responses to new opportunities; speed of adaptation to new procedures; initiative in resolving difficulties.

To an increasing extent productivity improvements are brought about by capital investment. In the Pay and Rewards Research Centre study of 63 companies it was found that improvements in productivity came not from raising employee performance but from cooperation with technical or organizational change. Even when incentive schemes were designed and introduced to raise performance and succeeded in doing so, it was often the redeployment of resources or new working methods, installed as an integral part of the exercise that produced the greatest proportion of the increased productivity.

Industrial Relations

Although a good industrial relations climate or increased job satisfaction does not in itself constitute a resource input in productivity terms, they do create an essential environment in which concern for productivity can be fostered. Turning again to the Strathclyde research, it was found that consultation was a significant determinant of the effects of incentive schemes designed to increase productivity. One dimension of consultation is that of participation. When studying this in more detail it was found that companies introducing productivity incentive schemes were more successful if consultation took place prior to the introduction of the scheme as well as following. Other researchers (Vroom and Yetton, 1973) found that participation and cooperation in design of payment systems lead to a greater understanding of their workings and of the need for their introduction. Consultation leads to increased commitment by the workforce on the introduction of change. Not enough time is devoted in many companies to developing programmes to enable this participatory process to take place. The very act of preparing an organizational diagnosis to determine the areas that may have potential for productivity increases, is in itself participatory as there will be employee involvement at the data collection stage.

Further, with the use of a wide spectrum of talent and experience

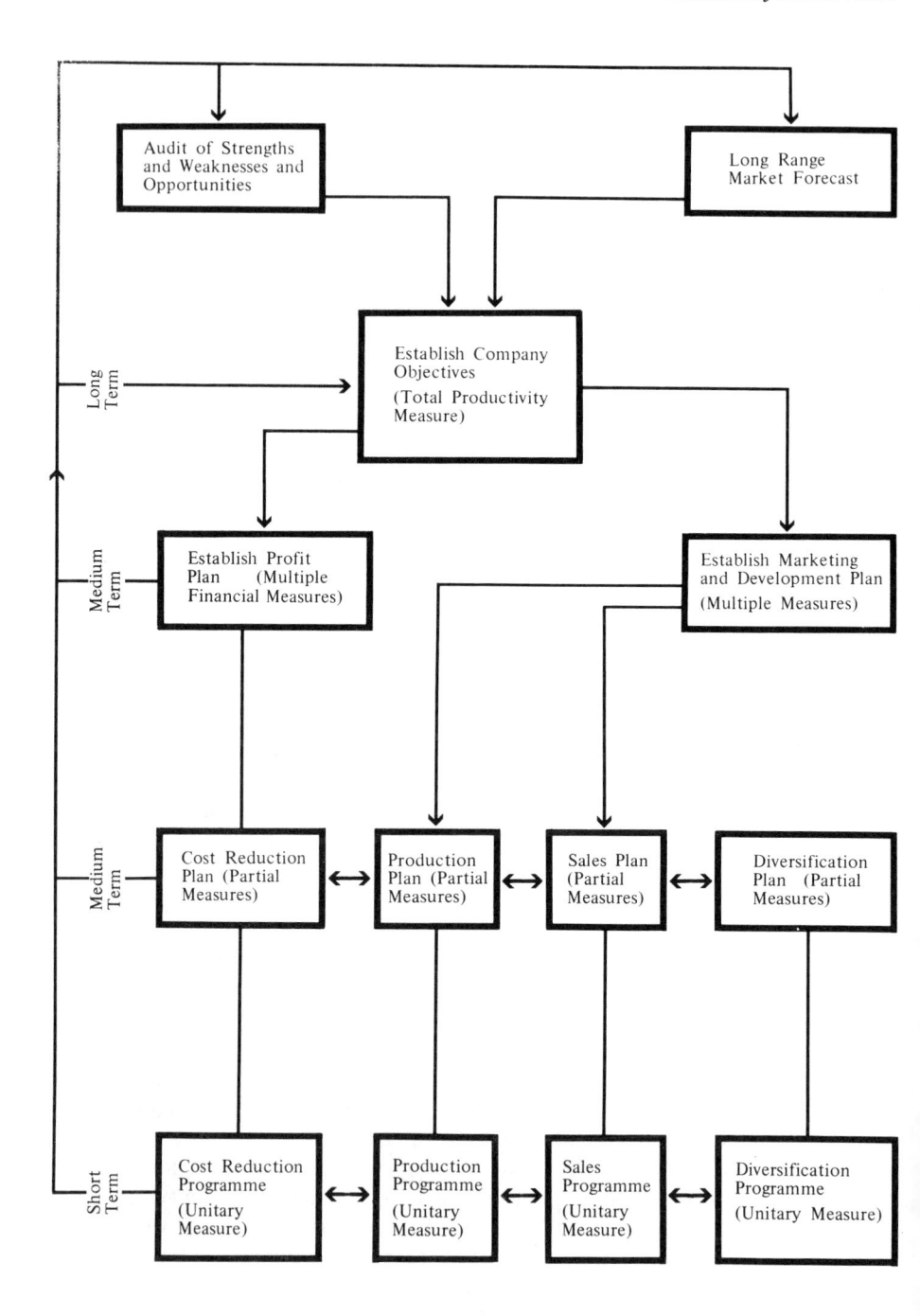

Figure 10.4 Organizing a company for productivity improvement

in an organization there will be as a consequence a higher quality of decision and debate that will in turn improve the plans for change and a degree of understanding of these plans within the organization. Work conducted in the USA at the Institute of Social Research, Michigan, has indicated that it is not sufficient to consult and explain—participation appears to be desirable if not essential for maximum success.

Also associated with consultation and good industrial relations is the degree of cooperation with change. The extent to which this will happen will also depend on national and local attitudes to the implications of productivity improvements. Attention given to a whole range of ancillary factors within the organization in an attempt to carry people along and maintain commitment and morale at a high level is important.

Conclusions

This chapter has focused attention on some of the less quantitative aspects of productivity and highlighted the importance of people in making improvements to the productivity of other resources. A case has been made for multiple measures at senior levels within organizations taking account of social as well as economic factors both external and internal to the organization.

As one descends the hierarchy measures become out of necessity, partial and direct, and the problems this brings have been highlighted. To counter individuals losing sight of the constituents of productivity and losing perspective of the organization's productivity requirements, the need for consultation and the positive benefits this brings has been brought out. In turn the very process of consultation will assist in facilitating change or maintaining morale at times when the organization needs to adapt to new technologies and markets. The need for different forms of productivity measurement in organizations at different stages of development was also stressed.

References and Further Reading

British Institute of Management. 'What is Productivity?' *Management Information Sheet no. 54*, 1976.
Bowey, A.M., 'Productivity, Motivation and Reward'. *Human Resource Management*. Australia. Autumn, 1978.
Currie, R.M., *Work Study*. Pitman Paperbacks, 1972.
Gold, B., *Productivity, technology, and capital: economic analysis, managerial strategies and government policies*, Lexington, 1979.
Gray, S.J. and Maunders, K.T., *Value Added Reporting: Uses and*

Measurement, Association of Certified Accountants, 1980.
Hirsch, F., *The Social Limits of Growth*, Routledge, 1977.
James, G., 'Total Productivity Measurement'. *Management Services*. Volume 24, no. 12, December 1980.
Lawler, E.E. III and Bullock R.J., 'Pay and Organisational Change'. *Personnel Administrator*. Volume 23, no. 5, page 32—6, 1978.
Lipsey, R.G., *An Introduction to Positive Economics*. Weindenfield and Nicholson. Fifth Edition, 1979.
Marchington, M., 'Worker Participation and Plant Wide Incentive Schemes', *Personnel Review*. Volume 16, no. 3, Summer, 1977.
McCormick, B.J., 'Methods of Wage Payment, Wages Structures and the Influence of Factor and Product Markets'. *British Journal of Industrial Relations*. Volume 15, no. 2, July 1977.
Norman, R.G. and Bahiri, S., *Productivity Measurement and Incentives*. Butterworth. London, 1972.
Novit, M.S., *Essentials of Personnel Management*. Prentice Hall, 1976.
Parris, J., 'Diagnosing Your Organisation's Problems'. *Management Services*. September, 1979.
Roy, D., 'Quota Restriction and Gold Bricking in a Machine Shop'. *American Journal of Sociology*. Volume 57, no. 2. March 1952.
Schumacher, E.F., *Small is beautiful: a study of economics as if people mattered*. Bland and Briggs, 1973.
Vroom, V.H. and Yetton, P.W., *Leadership and Decision Making*. University of Pittsburgh Press, 1973.
Wild, R., *Essentials of Production and Operations Management*. Holt, Reinhart and Winston, 1980.
Wild, R., *Production and Operations Management, Principles and Techniques*. Holt, Reinhart and Winston, 1980.

Part Three

Establishing the Rate for the Job

Editor's Introduction

The rate of pay for a job will depend on some or all of: the evaluation it has received from job evaluation procedures; the effort level at which the operative works as compared to the norm set by work study activities; the decisions made about how pay for this job should compare with pay in other organizations; and the outcome of collective bargaining procedures. The three chapters in this section are concerned with the mechanisms by which each of these activities affects pay.

There are conceptual and analytical difficulties which frequently occur because the four activities are pursued independently, and no one procedure determines the actual payments received by employees.

For manual staff the basic rate, and sometimes the rules which govern the job evaluation procedure and work study activities, are normally settled by collective bargaining. The management's case and the bounds within which they wish to reach a settlement are often determined by consideration of comparative rates in other organizations, product market position and the consequent need for production, and the company's ability to pay. To some extent the union argument in collective bargaining is also based on their assessment of these three factors, and of their own strength in the situation. And once the collective bargaining is completed, the operation of a job evaluation procedure determines each individual's basic rate; and his effort is translated via the mechanisms of any incentive schemes which are operating, into a variable increment in addition to the basic pay.

For these reasons there can be no easy answer to the question, how is the rate for a job determined? The explanation lies in the inter-relationships between the activities described in the next three chapters.

11

Relating Wages to Job Evaluation and to Work Measurement

Jack Butterworth

Subjectivity of Job Evaluation and Work Measurement

Job evaluation and work measurement are two subjective areas, which are of crucial importance to the operative and the manager as they radically affect the pay packet and/or the quality and quantity of work required in a period of time. The fact of this subjectivity does not invalidate the techniques—it merely means that we must be careful not to overstate the precision of the tools, and that we must use whatever safeguards we can to ensure that the results are accurate and fair.

If we could forget all our preconceived notions and were given a factory with a workforce of moonmen, would it not only seem reasonable—but essential—that we should determine 'how long' these creatures would take to manufacture the products we were selling. The measurement may not be precise, but faced with our unknown immigrant workforce even a crude measure would be better than none at all. Similarly, as we contemplate rewarding our new workers, we are forced to consider the worth of the various jobs that have to be done. If we avoid the issue and give equal rations to everyone, who do we designate to carry out the most onerous tasks—and on what basis do we make this choice?

It would appear, therefore, whether we like it or not, that managements have to make some decisions about the amount of work that is done, and about the worth or level of the work (relative to the other work in the organization). This is necessary irrespective of the payment method employed; linking payment to the quantity or level of work merely exacerbates an already difficult problem.

Many people might agree, but feel that it is worthless if we make personal assessments in the measurement and evaluation of work. But this is not so; if we take these first steps as honestly as we can and then use them as the basis for discussion or negotiation, the final outcome is likely to be better than if the negotiations had been carried out in complete ignorance. Many human activities are assessed subjectively, because we have no other method of quantification: the jury has no way of knowing whether the defendant is telling the truth; the audience has no accurate measuring device to assess the ballerina's performance; nor the critic to evaluate the artist's talent.

If money was not involved, job evaluation and work measurement would be less contentious though there would still be problems of status and output. However, when one evaluates jobs the corollary is that the more demanding tasks are given bigger rewards—so that basic rates are set in accordance with some defined criteria. Similarly, when one measures work, and consequently output per period of time, there is a strong inclination to link payment to output. It must be stressed, however, that work measurement is quite independent of payment by results schemes as such, although it is a necessary step in the formulation of a payment by results scheme, ie payment by result schemes depend on work measurement, but work measurement is not necessarily followed by a payment policy linking output and wages. Even if the employer and employees wished to use a flat-rate payment system, the employer has a need to know about the amount of output he can plan for in a given period of time. In this respect Wilfred Brown's book title, *Piecework abandoned*, often misleads. It does not mean that work measurement should be abandoned—only the direct linking of payment and output. For instance, in a hospital, it may be decided that piece rates were inappropriate in the physiotherapy department, but without work measurement the management would be incapable of deciding how many physiotherapists to employ, or how many patients per clinic could receive attention.

Job Evaluation

Rationally, one would start with job evaluation when presented with a large number of jobs. Using one or more of the techniques described in Chapter 7 the jobs will be arrayed according to their relative worth or contribution to the organization. Points rating schemes account for approximately half of all applications and so will be considered first. The problems to be answered are how many different pay grades are to be established, and what are to be the new basic rates. Ideally, every minute variation in contribution (ie in our evaluation) should be rewarded—but this has obvious drawbacks. First, we are 'evaluating' and some of the small differences between jobs may be difficult to defend if an appeal is lodged, and, secondly, labour mobility would be impeded or at best would involve an enormous amount of clerical work as an operator moved from job to job, each one with its different basic pay rate. From the practical point therefore as few grades as possible may be desirable, commensurate with providing adequate recognition for the job requirements in the particular situation under discussion. To establish the size of the problem the first step is to draw up a scattergram, which shows the relationship between present rates of basic pay and job scores (see Figure 11.1).

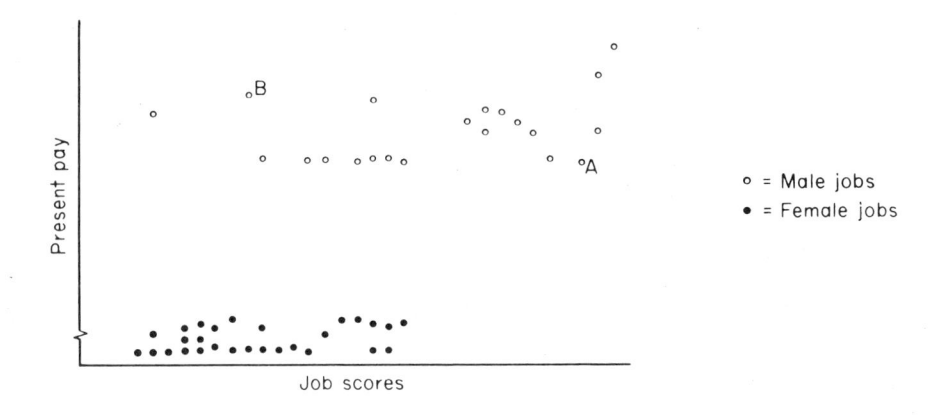

Figure 11.1   Scattergram to show relationship between present rates of basic pay and job scores

From the scattergram it is possible to see the anomalies that exist—jobs with high evaluations but carrying low pay and conversely, high pay jobs that seem to have no justification (see A and B on Figure 11.1). By drawing a line of best fit through the points a wage curve can be plotted which will give rise to the minimum of adjustment (see Figure 11.2).

However, in practice this is likely to be of little more than academic interest. Job A's rate can certainly be brought up to the line, but bringing down B is a different matter. The next step therefore is to draw in a higher pay curve which is pitched above the majority of the present pay rates. Only the jobs which are badly out of line now present a problem, and the cost of the scheme can be worked out by assuming that the new rates wil' fall on the proposed pay curve. This is bound to cost the company money and one of the criticisms of job evaluation at the present time is that it is inflationary. However, once the company knows the likely cost it can decide whether the benefits

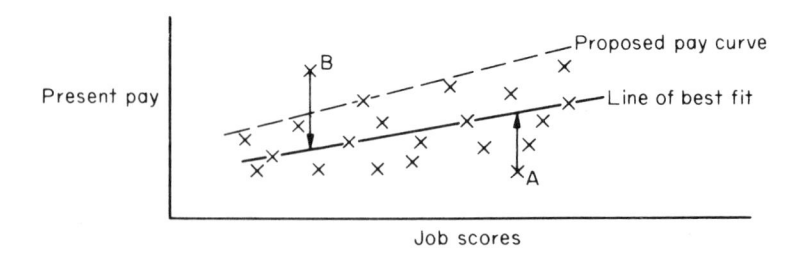

Figure 11.2 Line of best fit applied to scattergram

accruing from a more rational pay structure are worth it. At this stage the personnel department should be offering advice about the likely savings (reduction in disputes), about the possibility of obtaining better work practices (as part of an overall 'deal'), and about the rates of pay in the area and/or industry, which are in competition for the labour employed. It may be that an economic assessment of the situation determines that no more money, in total, can be paid out as wages. In that case all that can be hoped for is that the line of best fit can be used as the pay curve, and that a redistribution of the present wage bill can be achieved. This, however, is unlikely to be acceptable to the employees, although they may accept a compromise whereby those employees paid above the line receive no further pay increases until their pay is back in line. This too has drawbacks, and in particular may adversely affect motivation.

The distribution of the points on the scattergram allows us to consider the number of pay grades, and where the possible dividing lines might be. Ideally, one will choose intergrade boundaries so that there are as few jobs as possible immediately below that evaluation (see Figure 11.3). Obviously it is easier to defend AA than BB, as jobs in the lower class will have to move considerably further, on an appeal for upgrading, if they are to move into the higher pay grade.

Even if the distribution curve is favourable however, so that boundaries are easy to draw, problems still exist if jobs which have previously been equal find themselves in different pay grades. It is essential therefore that an appeals procedure should be set up to deal with all claims for upgrading, and that this procedure should be seen to be fair.

The next step is to determine the amount of money to be paid to each pay grade. The economic and market factors will determine how high and low the job rates could go (ie the accountant could state what the firm could afford as a total wage bill and the personnel manager indicate what is the lowest rate that is likely to attract and hold labour for jobs at the bottom of the evaluation scale).

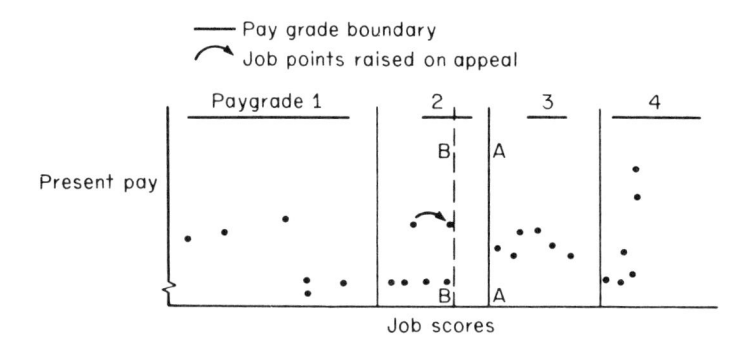

Relating Wages to Job Evaluation and to Work Measurement 151

```
                   ——— Pay grade boundary
                   ⌒  Job points raised on appeal
                 Paygrade 1      2        3       4
                                 B│ A                 •
   Present pay                    │
                          •       │       • •        •
                      •  •        ⌒      •
                             • • •│
                          •       B│ A           •• •
                                Job scores
```

Figure 11.3 Pay grade boundaries on scattergram

Within these limits it is possible to distribute the total money available in a variety of ways, but usually a basic rate is agreed, above which each succeeding grade receives a similar increase, so that with five pay grades the basic rates may be £60/£70/£80/£90/£100.

Alternatively, with a points rating scheme, one may decide to reward jobs on a 'payment for points' basis, rather than create pay grades (see Figure 11.4). In Figure 11.4 assume that job E is unlikely to find takers for less than £30 per week. Knowing the number of jobs at each points level and the total wage bill that management are prepared to pay out it is now possible to calculate the cash value of each point. Assuming that this works out at 60p then job A will receive £30 + (41 × 60p) = £54.60 and job D £30 + (12 × 60p) = £37.20.

Job	Points	Pay (£)
A	61	54.60
B	53	49.80
C	47	46.20
D	32	37.20
E	20	30.00

Figure 11.4 Payment for points scheme

Of course there is no reason why points should be rewarded equally throughout the scale. It may be decided that between 20 and 40, points will be worth 40p and that points between 41 and 50 are worth 60p each whilst points over 51 are worth £1.50 each. However, there should be some rational basis for differential rates as otherwise a further subjective factor is introduced.

The next most important job evaluation methods are grading and ranking. Both give jobs in order of contribution, but there is no way of determining the relative distances between jobs. Consequently the division into pay grades and the allocation of money to the pay grades may appear to be more arbitrary. The total amount of available money, the minimum and maximum rates and the construction of a scattergram can be done in exactly the same way as described above, but this is a situation where there is no sensitivity scale on which to base the remuneration and the allocation may therefore be much more open to dispute. Figure 11.5 shows equal distance between job ranks, but this does not necessarily reflect the perceived differences between the grades.

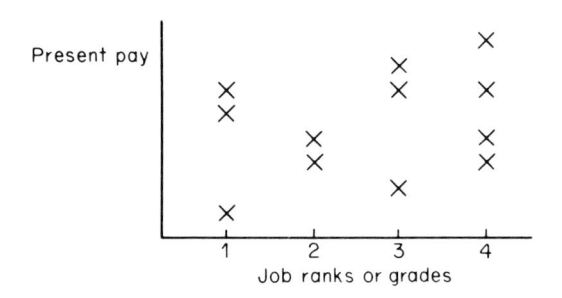

Figure 11.5 Scattergram showing the relationship between job ranks and present pay

Time-span of discretion, decision bands and guide-chart profiles are three other methods which are described in other chapters. Professor Jacques devised the time-span of discretion method, ie that within any job there is a prescribed content of work over which an individual has authorized choice, and a discretionary content which the individual chooses to do as he wishes (see Chapter 7). Using this discretionary element to measure the size and quality of a job lends itself to quantification in terms of the maximum length of time during which discretion has to be continuously exercised before the quality of the discretionary work becomes assessable. The concept of equitable payment is also used. Individuals were asked what payment was 'felt to be fair' for jobs at different stages in a career. By plotting time-span against felt fair pay Jacques maintains that a family of curves is produced which can be used to allocate a wage for an individual, in a particular job, taking account of his age and experience.

The decision band method of job evaluation (Chapter 7) is a system for grading jobs into six grades according to the nature of the decision made in each job. Each grade is then assigned a payment level which is a fixed percentage increase over the grade below.

The guide-chart profile method is used by HAY-MSL Ltd for managerial posts and sets out to determine the level of know-how, problem-solving and accountability necessary for each job (see Chapter 16). Each factor is split into subfactors to measure the depth, and degrees to measure the breadth of performance. There are, therefore, three matrices and scores are obtained from each matrix, aggregated and the total compared with the consultant's copyrighted pay curves which indicate high, medium or low remuneration firms. This sophisticated method of evaluation allows for the financial gearing to be in tune with other firms.

Work Measurement

Turning to work measurement let us first assume that a payment by results scheme is in operation. Despite much talk about firms moving away from payment by results schemes they are, in fact, still enormously popular with both management and men, and about 40% of the working population in Britain are affected by such payment schemes.

Chapter 6 has indicated how an observed time is corrected by applying a rating factor, and then further modified to allow for fatigue, contingencies, interference, etc, until finally a time for a task is calculated which can be used for planning and control purposes. This value (in BSI terminology) is termed the 'standard time', and is the time in which the job—over a large number of cycles—should be completed if the operator works at a standard performance. As a 'standard performance' is defined as the rate at which a qualified worker will work, provided he is adequately motivated (ie recompensed), the standard time implies that a rate of pay in excess of basic pay is available to the operative.

Unfortunately, a myth has grown up that if one supplements a basic rate with a payment by results scheme (or more commonly—and erroneously as the linking of earnings and output does not necessarily motivate but may merely frustrate—an 'incentive' scheme) the rate of working, of the average operator, will increase by one-third. This leads to the assumption that the standard time is not appropriate if the operator is not on a suitably designed payment by results scheme—and that only three-quarters of the standard performance will be achieved if the operative is on basic pay.

Even if the higher tempo of work associated with a payment by results scheme is achieved, there will be some variation around the mean. What happens to the wages of those employees who fall below the standard output? To avoid too many such situations, and to cater for the person not on a payment by results scheme an 'allowed time' for the job is usually used, which is calculated as 1 1/3 of standard time (ie assuming that the performance of the operator will be at three-quarters of the standard performance). This subterfuge has the effect of giving most people on a payment by results scheme, an increment on top of their basic pay—as the bonus is calculated in relation to the allowed time, but it obviously suffers in the sense that standard time and allowed time can all too easily be confused.

Figure 11.6 indicates the distribution of work performance and relates them to earnings. It can readily be appreciated that using 'allowed times' (derived from 'allowed performance' for want of a better title) most operatives are likely to receive an increment to their basic pay.

If, however, the basic pay level had been set for a standard output achievement, then a considerable number of staff would have a deducttion from their wage, or they would create a problem for the firm, because they had not achieved the output norm associated with the rate of pay.

We thus have allowed times calculated which conventionally are at a 75 BSI performance. These give the times for a task which would be reasonable if the operator were on a day-rate pay system. These allowed times also serve as the basis for bonus calculation (if payment by results is in operation), as it is a very simple matter to summate all the 'allowed times' for the total work done in a week. According to the type of payment by results scheme in operation (see Chapter 19) these minutes can then be given a cash value. A simple illustration would be as follows:

Basic wage is £48 per week (or 2p per minute for 40 hours per week) and the allowed time for the task is 20 minutes, so that in a week 120 jobs should be completed at 75 BSI performance. If standard times are issued then either an appropriately higher rate per minute can be used, or the standard time can be converted into an allowed time. However, if the operator worked at a 100 BSI performance he would complete the task in 15 minutes and do 160 jobs per week. His pay would be calculated by adding up all 'allowed times'—ie 20 mins × 160 = 3200— and rewarding them at the agreed rate of 2p per minute—£64. Similarly, an 80 BSI performance would result in £51.20 (£48 × 80/75) and a 110 BSI performance in £70.40.

Measured daywork attempts to avoid some of the problems inferred above. There are many quite different arrangements which are covered by this term, but in essence they all seek to avoid constant piecerate haggling. They require management to trust workers to give a fair day's work without specific short term incentives. The worker for his part gains security and is required to maintain an agreed performance to secure a stable wage.

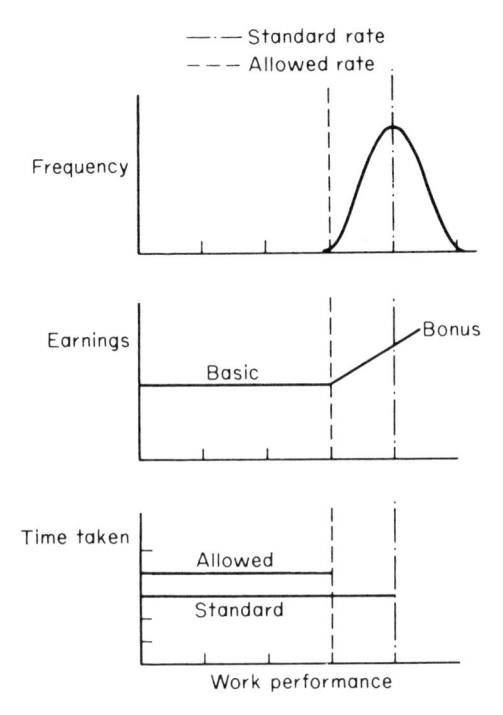

Figure 11.6 Distribution of work performance related to earnings

Once work has been measured, management would like to know the workers' work performance so that they can plan their production. Operatives now have the chance to indicate the level of performance that suits them, and many firms have contracted with their employees for a specified wage/performance relationship (see Figure 11.7).

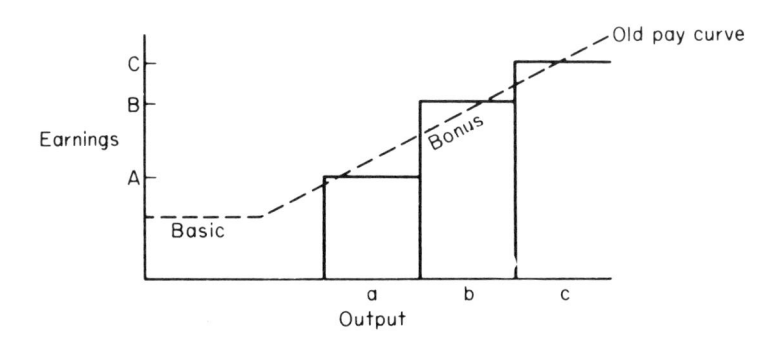

Figure 11.7 Graph showing specified wage/performance relationship

Thus instead of the old basic wage and bonus, the employees choose an output level that seems attainable for them, and the firm agree to pay the appropriate wage (A for a; B for b; C for c). This avoids constant short-term measurement of each operator's output, but obviously raises questions for management when performance dips below the agreed level (see Chapter 20). It is essential to remember, however, that measured daywork depends upon work measurement, as otherwise the performance levels to which are related the pay levels, are meaningless.

One of the difficulties encountered, in paying for work, occurs when different operators are forced to stand idle for different lengths of time. In the past 'process time' or 'unoccupied time' was paid mainly in the

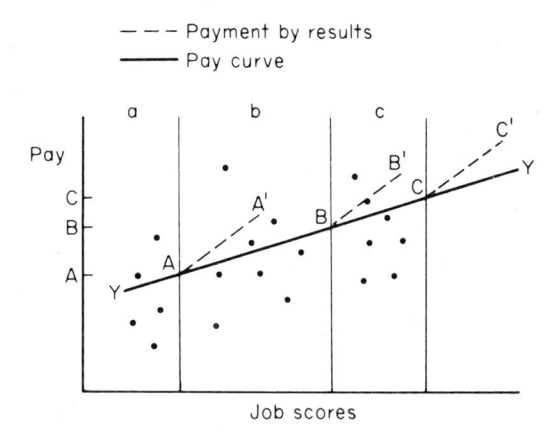

Figure 11.8   Rationalized pay structure

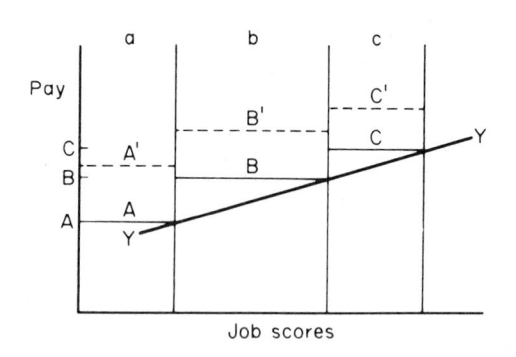

Figure 11.9   Rates of pay following introduction of measured daywork

Engineering Industry, but with increasing automation the problem is becoming much more general, and has caused difficulties in companies operating payment by results schemes and measured daywork schemes.

Summary of Effect of Job Evaluation and Work Measurement

One of our most satisfactory research projects involving job evaluation and work measurement was in a 'craft' industry, where 'measurement' was thought to be impossible. Due to the pay anomalies that had developed over the years there was growing frustration, and eventually the union asked management to bring in advisers from the university. We suggested that the three parties should form two work-groups—one to carry out job evaluation and the other to tackle work measurement.

Management was somewhat hesitant about handing over the decision-making to the men—but we pointed out that we were there to guide and to ensure fairness. Also the final schemes would have to be acceptable to both management and men if they were to work.

Over a period of six months each job was evaluated and measured by the workgroups. An appeals procedure had been laid down for the job evaluation, but only 2% of the evaluations were contested. The work measurement group startled everyone by laying down 'standards' which involved increases in output of over 20%.

The final outcome was most gratifying; productivity rose by over 25%, most men got a bigger pay packet, the pay structure was felt to be fair by the men—and, despite the increased output, quality was higher than it had previously been. The case study indicated the possibility for, and desirability of, participation in these subjective areas by both management and men.

Finally, then how can we summarize the effects of job evaluation and work measurement on the pay packet. Figure 11.8 shows the haphazard pay structure rationalized by the pay curve YY and the creation of 3 pay grades (a, b, c) with their respective new rates of remuneration (A, B, C). These basic rates of pay may now be supplemented by bonus earnings if a payment by results scheme is in operation, as shown by A—A', B—B' and C—C'.

On the other hand if job evaluation is followed by the introduction of measured daywork then Figure 11.9 shows the rates of pay for each pay grade (a, b, c) and the subsequent lifting of those rates to A', B' and C'.

References and Further Reading

ACAS, *Advisory Booklet no. 1: Job Evaluation*, Advisory, Conciliation and Arbitration Service, London, 197

Horn, C.A. and Horn, P.L.R., 'Wages Systems reconsidered', *Management Services*, volume 25, no. 4, May 1980.

Lee, T.A., *Income and Value Measurement*, Nelson, 1980.

Livy, B., *Job Evaluation: a critical review*, Allen and Unwin, 1975.

Naylor, Rachel, and Torrington, Derek (Eds.), *Administration of Personnel Policies*, Gower, 1974.

Thomason, G.F., *Job Evaluation: Objectives and Methods*, IPM, London, 1980.

12

Comparability

Angela M Bowey

Over the past twenty years in Britain comparing the pay of employees in one organization with those in another has become an increasingly important element in pay settlements, in spite of periodic attempts by politicians to move away from it.

In addition to ad hoc committees set up from time to time, there have been five major statutory bodies concerned recently with such comparisons, namely the Standing Commission for Pay Comparisons (Clegg), the Civil Service Pay Research Unit (CSPRU), and the three review bodies responsible respectively for the doctors and dentists, top salaries and the armed forces. The Clegg Commission was disbanded in 1980/81 and the operation of the other four brought under review. All five were concerned with the public sector, where comparability has been developed as a means of determining pay largely to compensate for the lack of other mechanisms. Public sector organizations tend to operate in monopoly markets and are often virtually monopoly employers of particular skills or professions. Economic factors which might regulate pay in the private sector (such as skill shortages or over-supply, ability to pay and profit levels) are not effective; and comparability is an alternative which can in the right circumstances ensure fair levels of pay to employees without over paying them relative to those in other parts of the economy. But it is important to consider the methods adopted by these bodies, and the effects of their work both on the groups whose pay they review and on the rest of the economy.

Comparability has also played an important part in pay settlements in the private sector. The Prices and Incomes Board made comparisons of jobs and pay when reaching some of its conclusions on both private and public sector pay (although on the whole it preferred to focus on rewarding for improved productivity or performance). In 1975 schedule 11 of the Employment Protection Act made provisions for employees' terms and conditions of employment to be brought into line with the 'recognized' or the 'general' level in their industry and district; and the Equal Pay Act 1970 decreed that women doing comparable jobs to men be paid equal earnings with those men. Both of these pieces of legislation resulted in the development and application by statutory bodies of formal procedures for comparing the jobs and the pay of private sector employees.

For many years comparisons with the pay of other groups have been part of the wage negotiation procedures of both trade unions and management in private sector companies. The tendency for statutory bodies to employ comparability procedures has reinforced the tendency to rely on comparability arguments to justify or validate a particular level of pay. Comparison procedures undertaken under 'schedule 11' legislation had a major impact on the credibility and familiarity with comparability within the private sector.

Quite apart from government initiatives which imposed some elements of comparability on private sector pay settlements, it has been shown that negotiators themselves often rely on comparisons, usually concerning traditional relationships to particular reference groups, when arriving at their claim or offer. Acceptance of a set of mutually agreed comparators can enable negotiators to achieve a smoother transition to the agreement stage and also to justify the settlement to interested parties not directly involved in the negotiations (Brown and Sisson, 1975).

Statutory and Informal Usage of Comparability

Both Clegg and the CSPRU in their 1979 reports spelled out the procedures they used, and the first and ninth Clegg reports discussed in some detail the main alternatives and their advantages and disadvantages. Essentially anyone making pay comparisons is attempting to assess how much one group should be paid relative to other workers. The key issues concern how to select the 'other workers' to compare them with; how to judge relative pay; how to take account of non-financial rewards such as job security, working hours, company cars and pension rights; and how to take into consideration other objectives which pay might serve such as productivity, recruitment or retention, responding to bargaining pressure and reflecting what the organization can afford to pay.

Judging relative pay is easy in theory, since one only has to make the decision to compare like with like; on the surface it may appear that the way to do this is to compare basic pay for a standard week. In practice it is more complex, because the length of the standard week varies between groups, bonus schemes exist in a multitude of shapes and sizes, shift working arrangements vary and carry differing premium rates, and average amounts of overtime pay vary considerably. Deciding to ignore all financial rewards except basic pay or compiling these additional earnings into an overall index involves complex subjective judgements about their importance. Most statutory bodies have compared basic pay for a standard week and ignored other payments; but in private industry practices vary, and the opportunity to earn overtime pay or an incentive bonus can be an important consideration in an employee's assessment of his pay relative to other groups.

The view expressed in the Clegg Commission's first report was that trying to include these elements of pay in the comparisons would have confused rather than clarified the picture. This may be so; but it then becomes important to exclude those jobs which have grossly different shift, bonus or overtime pay arrangements from the reference group.

Taking account of conditions of service such as pension rights, holidays, sick pay entitlement etc is a complex matter. The Civil Service spelled out its agreed procedure in an annex to the national pay agreement. This set out precisely how a whole range of benefits including pensions, hours of work, company cars, subsidised meals and discounts on purchases were to be taken into account in making comparisons. Even this left aside some of the most difficult considerations, such as how to take account of job security.

The Clegg Commission in producing its first report had only five months to complete its work, and consequently had to rely on existing data and procedures collected by the CSPRU and the consultants working for the Review Body on Pay of the Armed Forces. Although the former had data on benefits and conditions of service relating to the jobs in its relevant previous surveys and a procedure for handling that data, the consultants did not; so these factors were excluded from the calculations. However, in later references the Commission did take account of the estimated value of payments in kind and fringe benefits.

Pensions were the one key factor on which, even for the first reference, Clegg considered the public sector reference jobs fared significantly better than the comparator jobs, and the Commission used government actuaries to make a set of calculations to adjust pay before the comparisons were made. Increases of between 1.1% and 4.5% were added to the pay of the public sector jobs to allow for their better pension provisions.

It should be pointed out that one major disadvantage of some review bodies, ad hoc royal commissions and committees of inquiry into pay, is that they have not formalized and published the procedures they used for taking account of benefits and conditions. The review body for doctors' and dentists' pay has been strongly criticized, for example, for making imprecise references to 'morale' as a condition to be taken into account in comparing pay.

Methods of Making Comparisons

The most important question regarding comparability, however, is the issue of how the comparisons are to be made. There are three well-known methods: indexation, job-for-job, and the analysis of factor job descriptions.

Indexation

Indexation was used by the Pay Board in 1974 in relation to mineworkers' pay, it has been used by other review bodies although rejected by Clegg, and is likely to continue to be part of the review procedures for groups such as firemen whose pay has been linked to the upper quartile of the earnings of adult male manual workers, and police for whom the Edmund Davies Committee recommended increases in line with the general earnings index.

In principle indexation involves establishing and preserving a relationship between the pay of the reference group and an agreed index which may be average earnings in the society or the retail price index, or some similar index. But there are several arguments against it.

Clegg rejected the procedure although the unions involved in his first reference had put forward a claim that the lowest grade of the reference groups should have their pay linked to two thirds of average male manual earnings. His three objections were all specific to the particular reference. First, to compare basic pay with an index of total earnings is not comparing like with like, since the latter includes additional payments for bonus work, overtime, and shifts, whilst these would still be added to the former. Secondly, comparing the pay of these employees, many of whom were female workers in jobs such as cleaning and catering, with an index of male earnings would result in higher pay for them than for those in comparable jobs elsewhere, since women's average earnings are still lower than men's. This, however, is not a commendable argument from the point of view of equality of treatment for women. And thirdly, any comparison to average earnings assumes that the distribution of employees between unskilled, semi-skilled and skilled jobs is the same in the group under review as it is in the wider economy. This was not the case for local authority and university manual workers (Clegg's first review group), where there is a much greater preponderance of unskilled workers than in the economy.

However, these reasons would not necessarily apply to other groups, and at that stage Clegg indicated that he would not rule out indexation as a means of comparing pay in other situations. His report number 9, a year later, rejected indexation more totally, on the grounds that any link which could be established at any one time between a reference job and some index could only be expected to last for a short time because jobs and conditions of service change.

The general problem here is that linking pay to an index such as average male manual earnings assumes that, at the base point from which the calculations start the 'correct' relationship is held between the two rates; and also that there have not been significant changes in either the reference jobs or the population of jobs making up the average which would invalidate the comparison. If on the whole the structure of society was changing to a greater proportion of skilled jobs, then average earnings would be increasing to reflect this changing composition; jobs which had not changed in skill level but had their pay tied to the average index would push up the average even further.

Indexation has the advantage of being quick, cheap and easy to apply, requiring no detailed analysis of jobs or survey work. But because job changes alter the relationship between the reference job and the jobs in the index, it can only be appropriate for a few years; and would suit stable jobs better than changing ones.

Job-For-Job

The second method of comparing jobs has been termed job-for-job comparisons. This technique involves studying the reference job as a 'whole job' and then seeking comparator jobs which are as similar as possible to it. Clearly there are considerable subjective judgements involved, but the aim is to find jobs which are intuitively similar to the reference job, which the employees themselves and other interested parties are therefore likely to accept as being broadly comparable. The basis of the comparisons, although rarely examined in component terms, can be adapted to emphasize the important features of the reference jobs.

Job-for-job comparisons are only possible where there are many similar jobs in organizations outside the reference group. This is not true for a large proportion of public sector jobs, such as train drivers, ambulancemen, firemen, teachers and nurses.

The CSPRU uses job-for-job comparisons, but only for selected benchmark jobs which have many similar jobs outside it. They have built up a data bank covering jobs in about 300 organizations which are accepted as 'broadly comparable' to the benchmark civil service jobs, and they monitor the pay of these. Other jobs in the civil service, including any for which outside comparators are not easy to find, are then linked to the benchmarks by a set of internal relationships. The procedure seems to work effectively in this situation, where traditional comparators have come to be accepted and where many jobs do have similarities with work commonly found in other organizations.

The way the CSPRU operates is that each year it is assigned a programme from its steering committee, which usually involves deciding whether any changes are needed in the regular annual surveys of the major groups of civil service staff. When reviewing a particular grade, the unit's staff examine a representative sample of the current work of that grade, visit locations where the bulk of these employees work, and then interview job holders and collect supplementary information. From this they prepare job descriptions, and then visit outside organizations which employ staff in similar jobs in order to assess whether they are sufficiently similar to be included in the sample.

Information about pay, bonuses, fringe benefits and conditions of service in the comparator jobs are then provided in a report to the parties to the pay negotiations, and it is left to them to make the decisions about adjustments to pay. The CSPRU does not make recommendations about suggested levels of increase; and this is the modus operandi which the Clegg Commission preferred, rather than being required to make firm recommendations about increases to which both parties were committed in advance to accept, as the commission had been for several of its early references.

Since its establishment in 1955, the CSPRU has been suspended twice (in 1972 and 1975) and at the time of writing, is probably about to be suspended again (see Table 12.1). During suspension it operated with a skeleton staff servicing minimal administrative functions.

The Clegg Commission favoured job-for-job comparisons, and indeed employed the CSPRU to carry out such comparisons for those jobs in its reference for which this was possible. The CSPRU was able to use its data banks of information on jobs comparable to civil service grades collected in other surveys.

Factor Job Comparisons

In the public sector in particular there are jobs such as ambulancemen and refuse collectors for which no similar jobs are to be found elsewhere and those like gardeners who are so predominantly in the employ of public sector organizations that payment levels in outside organizations merely reflected the reference group pay levels. Job-for-job comparison are not possible here, and a third method of making comparisons, factor job descriptions, is required.

Factor methods of making comparisons as commonly applied are similar to job evaluation by points rating: a set of factors is chosen to reflect the important components of the work, and scales of measure-

Table 12.1

Key events in comparability

Date	Review Bodies	Reports
1955	Civil Service Pay Research Unit (CSPRU) established.	*Priestley on Civil Service.
1956	Standing Advisory Committee on Top Salaries established.	[·] Cameron on Railwaymen.
1958	Standing Committee on Pay of Armed Forces established.	
1960		[·] Guilleband on Railways. *Pilkington on Doctors and Dentists. *Willink on Police.
1961	Review Body on Pay of Doctors and Dentists established.	
1963		[·] Phelps Brown on London bus drivers and conductors.
1965	National Board for Prices and Incomes (PIB) established.	
1967		**170 Reports produced by PIB including 107 which considered pay and 89 specifically about pay for particular groups.
1970	Review Body on Doctors and Dentists (Kindersley) resigned when recommendations rejected by government. Equal Opportunities Commission established.	
1971	Review Body on Doctors and Dentists reconstituted under Halsbury. Review Body on Top Salaries replaced Standing Advisory Committee. PIB disbanded.	[·] Wilberforce-electrical supply. [·] Wilberforce-mineworkers.
1972	Review Body on Armed Services Pay replaced Standing Committee. CSPRU suspended.	
1973	Pay Board established.	**Pay Board-anomalies.
1974	Review Body on Doctors and Dentists resigned. CSPRU re-established in modified form.	**Pay Board-relativities. [·] Houghton-non-university teachers. **Pay Board-Civil Service science. **Pay Board-mineworkers. 74-75 Spate of ad hoc enquiries.
1975	CSPRU suspended due to incomes policy.	
1978		[·] Davies-police.
1979	Standing Commission on Pay Comparability established under Clegg. CSPRU re-established with new structure.	
1980	Clegg retired. Standing Commission on Pay Comparability disbanded on completion of current references. New Chairman—Wood. CSPRU report blocked by government.	**Clegg-11 reports on groups of public sector employees.
1981	Government review of all comparability bodies. CSPRU suspended?	**Wood-New Town Staff.

Key to types of reports

*	Royal Commissions
[·]	Courts or Committees of Inquiry
**	Statutory Bodies

ment chosen for each factor such that all jobs to be compared can be given a points score for each factor. The total points which can be scored for each factor are weighted in order to reflect the importance of that factor as an element in the work. Total points are then compared with total points for comparator jobs to find jobs of equivalent 'worth'. The method is similar to that described in Chapter 7 as points rating.

There are two main difficulties with factor methods of comparability, both of which result in totally unlikely and dissimilar jobs being pronounced comparable. The first is that one set of 'weighted' factors tends to be selected and then applied to a range of different reference jobs and comparators. This may result in totally unsuitable factors or weightings of factors being applied because no account has been taken of the important characteristics of a particular job. To find comparators which are genuinely similar requires that the key features of the reference job are reflected in factors which are heavily weighted in the system used. In this way jobs which share these key features, and are therefore more likely to be intuitively similar, will be more likely to have similar scores. Their similar scores on the heavily weighted factors will outweigh less important dissimilarities on other factors.

The second difficulty is that on the whole factor comparison methods use conventional job evaluation techniques of converting the many facets of a job into a currency called 'points' thereby enabling the evaluator to add up the differing components to get a 'value' for the job. This is crucial if one is comparing jobs within an organization in order to rank dissimilar jobs into a hierarchy. It is possible to see comparability as an extension of job evaluation, in which the same procedures apply and job features are converted into points which are added up and the various totals compared. Jobs with the same points, however intuitively different they may look, can be said to have the same value. But it is not very convincing to the parties concerned to tell them, for instance, that a lighthouse keeper is equivalent to a mid-Surrey constable without boot allowance. Evaluation for comparability purposes can, and should, be treated in a different way, in order to produce jobs which are intuitively similar, rather than jobs which are different but carry the same points value.

Comparability can be achieved by using the weighted factor scores which measure how much of each factor the job has and, instead of adding up to get an overall value, comparing them factor by factor to the reference job scores, and adding up the difference between the factor scores of the two jobs. The bigger the difference, the less similar the jobs; and if the factors are weighted to take account of their relative importance in the reference job, then the bigger the total difference score, the less useful that comparator is to the process of finding comparable jobs. This technique is explained further in Bowey and Lupton (1973).

Comparing Pay

After comparable jobs have been identified comes the task of comparing their pay and deciding how great an increase is justified by the results. The first step is to convert the various components of benefits and pay into a single figure. As discussed above, some review bodies such as CSPRU have standard procedures for this. Other review bodies and ad hoc committees are very vague about how they go about this conversion; and the Clegg Commission had little time to produce a standard procedure. The aim of such a procedure is to decide how much each benefit is worth in equivalent wages. This usually involves estimating the extent to which that benefit is drawn upon by the average employee (using statistical or actuarial techniques) as in the case of the government calculations of the value of pension rights for the Clegg Commission's first report. There is a case for arguing that the distribution to take-up of such items as overtime pay or discounts on purchases should be taken into account as well as the median. Once this has been done the composite pay figure for the reference job can then be compared to the set of composite pay figures for the comparator jobs. In the case of the CSPRU and most of the later Clegg references, it was at this stage that the unit handed over the material to the employer and union negotiators, making clear where the median of the comparator jobs lay. It was then left to the parties to negotiate the pay settlement.

The first half dozen Clegg Commission references and the other standing review bodies, on the other hand, required recommendations on the amount of increase justified by the figures. The simplest way to do this is to take the difference between the reference job and the median of the comparator jobs, and recommend that figure. Where only one grade of a hierarchy has been reviewed, this is a straightforward enough procedure. Existing internal differentials can be maintained by applying the same percentage increase to all grades. But an interesting feature of the Clegg Commission's first reference was that comparisons were sought for jobs in most grades of the work under review: seven grades of local authority manual jobs, eighteen grades of National Health Services ancillaries, three grades of ambulancemen, and seven grades of university manual jobs. And the percentage increases which would have resulted from applying the median of the comparator jobs varied considerably between these grades, from minus 5.4 for university domestic assistants to plus 55.6 for NHS kitchen superintendents. Applying these figures would have produced chaotic changes to the structure of internal differentials.

The procedure adopted therefore, was equivalent to drawing a graph of the grades and the percentage difference between their pay and the median pay of comparator jobs, and then using statistical regression techniques to produce a trend line through these scores, and reading off the percentage increases suggested by the line. The trend line was adjusted to allow for better pension rights in the reference group, and further adjustments were made in order to maintain the traditionally close links between pay of local authority manuals and the first seven groups of National Health Service auxiliaries. These procedures, taken together, had the advantage of causing as little disruption as possible to internal differentials and traditional links.

This kind of detailed information about the figures and methods of calculation are not available for the other statutory review bodies, and are not usually provided by ad hoc review committees and commissions. Clegg was widely praised at the time for laying out the figures for all to examine and explaining the procedures and methodology. By doing this the commission laid the ground for a more rigorous approach to the issues in the future.

Problematical Implications

Having considered how comparability reviews are carried out, we can look at the wider problems associated with these methods, and consider some of the advantages. The problems which have been linked with comparability include:

1 The extent to which the procedures are credible and acceptable to the parties involved.
2 Whether this method of reaching pay settlements hinders change in the structure of jobs in the society and therefore restricts development of the economy.
3 Whether it is an inflationary way of settling pay.
4 Whether it is fair to other groups whose pay is not reviewed in this way.
5 How one takes account of other influences on pay, such as the labour market, bargaining strength, ability to pay and increased productivity.

Taking each of these issues in turn, the credibility and acceptability to the parties concerned seem on the whole to be increasing as familiarity with the procedures increases. This is helped if the people responsible for these reviews publish details of what they did and why, and develop well-established methods and stable samples of comparator jobs. Technical problems with the procedures, which still exist and were discussed above, should be resolved in time, and the acceptability consequently increased. It does seem that there is a strong case for replacing the ad hoc procedures of the past by a permanent review body so that these developments can take place. Major errors, like the miscalculation which resulted in the Clegg Commission paying teachers approximately 4% too much in April 1980, do not help. Nor does the rejection of the principle of comparability by the government of the day. But these may yet prove to be temporary setbacks.

The second problem, whether comparability procedures hinder change, would depend on how they were applied. Certainly any attempt to rigidly maintain traditional differentials and relativities in the face of changing priorities in society would be a costly mistake, as it would divert people away from jobs in which they were needed. Comparing job contents and paying due account to the importance of facets of the work to the employing organization is one way of avoiding this problem. But the problem is there and should not be underplayed.

Comparability has been criticized as an inflationary practice, but again this depends upon the way in which it is applied. If it is simply a means for the public sector, the civil service, and some private sector jobs to be kept in line with changes in pay levels in comparable parts of the rest of the economy, then it should not be inflationary. But if it is used to restore some historically more favourable relativities or establish new rates above the comparable medians then it would be inflationary. If, for example, it was used to restore to its former relative position the pay of some public sector group which had been held back during a long period of statutory incomes restraint, and if that resulted in pay increases considerably higher than those currently being negotiated elsewhere, then it is likely that the publication of these figures would raise the level of expectation of wage increases in the rest of the economy. This would probably contribute to wage inflation. Equally, if some review body were to take an especially sympathetic approach to judging the comparative pay situation of a group referred for review, and award them a high increase out of line with current rates of increase elsewhere, then again this figure might be taken as a new yardstick by which other unions judged their own claims, and it could well be inflationary.

In relation to the inflationary effects of comparability, one of the problems with ad hoc review committees or commissions and the three standing review bodies referred to earlier is that they have a special relationship to one particular sector of the economy. Their boards and committees have representatives from that sector of the economy; and unlike the Clegg Commission and to a lesser extent the CSPRU, they are not reviewing a range of groups from different industrial and occupational sectors. There is therefore the danger that they lean more favourably towards the sector they are reviewing, and have little or no responsibility for considering how the methods they use will subsequently affect other groups. Comparability is only fair to other groups whose pay is not reviewed in this way provided it is used to keep the reviewed groups in line; not if used to push them ahead.

The final problem with comparability is to what extent and in what ways it can cope with labour market supply and demand problems, power bargaining tactics, abiliity to pay (including the constraints of 'cash limits'), and the desire to reward high productivity better than low.

Taking these in turn, Beenstock and Immanuel (1979) strongly criticized the work of the Clegg Commission on the grounds that it undermined the processes of wage adjustment in response to pressures from the supply and demand for labour. For jobs where the review group forms a small proportion of the total population of people doing that kind of work there is no problem. Market pressures in so far as they *do* operated to adjust wages to the supply and demand position, would result in the appropriate rates being prevalent in the wider society and so would be reflected in the median pay of comparable jobs. But where the review group comprises a high proportion of the people employed in these jobs, there is a real danger that supply shortages or surpluses will not be reflected in the pay levels arrived at by comparison methods. In these situations it may well be desirable for the review body to take some account of shortages or surpluses via an adjustment to the figures arrived at by comparability methods.

The potential for power bargaining tactics to disrupt the outcome of a comparability exercise is obvious, but the principle of taking pay to a review body relies on the good faith of both parties to accept the recommendations which come out of the procedure. In the case of the first several references to Clegg both parties had agreed in advance to abide by the recommendations. But the commission expressed the view that it would be preferable for the decision about level of increases to be made by the parties in negotiation, and this was how the later references were conducted. In this way there is much less scope for conflict with the review body's findings: and the comparability facts as presented to the negotiators can smooth the way for an agreement without application of overt 'power' by either side.

By emphasizing consistency, equity, and rationality in the procedures it has used, comparability can give the parties to a negotiation some sense of a fair settlement at the end of the day.

Another important consideration is the link between comparability and ability to pay. If the review body concerned actually makes recommendations about pay increases, then either the ability of the employer to pay is taken for granted or it has to be taken into account by the reviewers. In the latter case, this could mean paying less than was justified by the comparisons, on the grounds that the employer could not afford more. Apart from any potential benefits from adjustments to internal differentials resulting from the external comparisons, there is in this situation little point in the comparability exercise. One might just as well have started with the figure the employer could afford and worked back from that. It follows therefore, that a credible comparability procedure requires that the employer commits himself in advance to paying the figure awarded by the review body; or alternatively that the review body does not actually make a recommendation, but submits figures to the employer on the basis of which, and other relevant factors such as ability to pay or the prevailing cash limit, the employer then makes his offer and negotiates.

Finally there is the question of how differences in productivity can be taken into account when comparability is applied. Many employers and politicians hold the view that if an organization has low performance levels then its employees should earn less than those in organizations with high productivity. This is a difficult principle to use for comparing pay because of the difficulty of measuring the productivity of one organization vis-à-vis another (see Chapter 10). It also assumes that paying extra money to those who perform well in a high productivity organization will encourage others to perform better than they do. But doing a good job in a successful organization is reward in itself. Our studies of productivity and incentive schemes have shown that it is not lack of willingness or motivation which leads to low productivity; it is poor organization, poor communications and cooperation, bad planning and inadequate preparation—all things which most managers and employers would avoid if they knew how to, without a cash reward. It is therefore questionable whether incorporating an assessment of productivity into comparability procedures would achieve very much, even were it feasible. Nevertheless, there is an element of equity in the concept of paying more to efficient employees, if the technical problems could be resolved.

In conclusion, it is clear that comparability is a procedure which still has problems associated with it, but many of these can be resolved. It has the advantage of offering a mechanism for settling pay issues in situations where other methods have not worked.

References and Further Reading

Beenstock, M. and Immanuel, H., 'The Market Approach to Pay Comparability'. *National Westminster Bank Quarterly Review*, November 1979.

Bowey, A. and Lupton, T., *Job and Pay Comparisons*, Gower Press, 1973.

Brown, W. and Sisson, K., 'The Use of Comparisons in Workplace Wage Determination', *British Journal of Industrial Relations*, March 1975.

Report of the Civil Service Pay Research Unit Board and the Civil Services Pay Research Unit 1979, Shepherd Report, HMSO.

Standing Commission on Pay Comparability. *Report no. 1, Local Authority and University Manual Workers; NHS Ancillary Staffs; and Ambulancemen.* HMSO, August 1979.

Standing Commission on Pay Comparability. *Report no. 9, General Report.* HMSO, August 1980.

13

The Strategy and Tactics of Bargaining

Andrew Gottschalk

Objectives of Bargaining

This chapter will deal with the problems which managers must resolve before and during their negotiations with trade unions. It could equally well be applied, of course, to trade union preparations for negotiations with management. From the start we must make a number of critical assumptions. The first is that the philosophy held by those concerned with the conduct of the negotiations is fairly positive in that they perceive that the negotiating process can facilitate organizational change and growth and that the conclusion of the process will result in an improvement in the relationships between the parties both inside and outside the organization. The second assumption that should be made is that we are dealing with the behaviour of representatives of two parties who come together explicitly in search of an agreement about an issue or series of issues about which they have different aims which must be reconciled within a relatively limited period of time. The final assumption which will be made is that a formally convened meeting is about to take place at which the two parties, management and trade unions, are seeking to resolve a series of substantive and procedural issues which, when satisfactorily concluded, will govern the future conduct of their relationship for a specific period of time. This chapter will therefore be divided into two parts, the first will review the process by which management may develop its strategic options, the second will identify the range of tactics which are available and how these can be selected to facilitate the attainment of a jointly acceptable agreement.

Developing a Negotiating Strategy

Most managers are familiar with the language of conflict and cooperation. These two terms are used easily by both participants and observers of the collective bargaining process. Unfortunately the value judgements implicit in both terms has tended to direct our attention away from practical to almost philosophical issues. A strategy of conflict or cooperation must be judged by its results within the relationship between the two parties. It should also be evaluated within the negotiating process. To ignore the negotiating process and the immediate context does not help us secure organizational adaptation and change. For example, a strategy of conflict adopted by one or both parties may be a factor in reduced manpower productivity in an industry but it is only one of a number of factors. Others may easily outweigh its impact, for example raw material and distribution costs.

In developing a negotiating strategy it is advisable to think of conflict and cooperation as a continuum. What has to be avoided are too rapid shifts between one end of the continuum and the other. In Figure 13.1 a continuum is represented and the intervals mark different levels of

Strategy of conflict						Strategy of cooperation
very high/ public	clear/ firm	low/ cautious		low/ cautious	clear/ firm	very high/ public

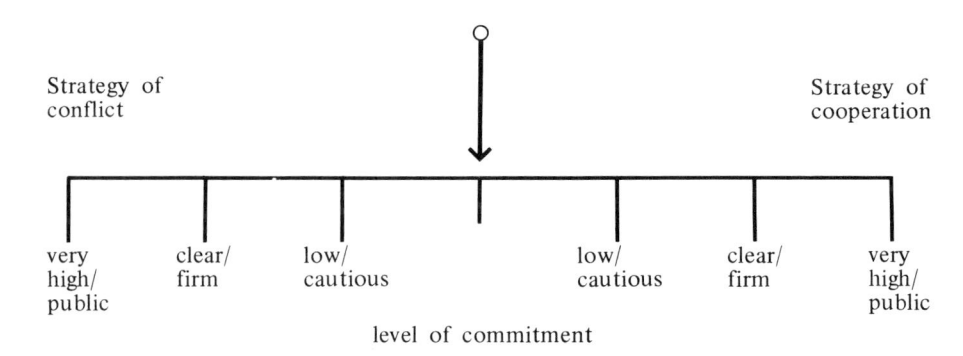

level of commitment

Figure 13.1 Continuum of strategies for bargaining

commitment to the particular strategy which can be identified. For each of the three points it is relatively easy to identify what the consequences of a commitment might be both within the negotiating process and outside for the parties themselves. To illustrate the various points on the continuum, a real example will be used, of a highly capital intensive UK company operating a continuous 12-hour shift system with a fully unionized workforce.

The six levels of commitment would imply the following actions:

1. *Conflict very high/public* A communicated willingness to take a strike or even initiate a lockout and layoffs in response to any form of industrial action. Previous communication with customers to arrange alternative servicing of orders. The clear formulation of a counter offer presented early in the negotiations or even a 'final offer first' which allows no room for meaningful negotiation. A commitment to any action aimed at reducing the power of the other party.
2. *Conflict clear/firm* An acceptance of protracted negotiations in which threats would be made and the costs of a failure to reach an agreement would be clearly spelt out. An emphasis on communicating the strength of the management and the costs to the other party of trying to secure any further concessions.
3. *Conflict low/cautious* A recognition that the costs of industrial relations conflict might be very high and that only minimum counter demands should be made in order not to provoke the union. A willingness to enter lengthy negotiations with a low opening offer or respond to the union's claim which indicates that over time a settlement can be reached. In some instances with the help of a third party.
4. *Cooperation low/cautious* A willingness to table a relatively long agenda of items for negotiation and to potentially risk a more expensive initial settlement which may only yield a benefit to the company in the second half of the collective bargaining year. A reluctance to disclose large amounts of information because of uncertainty as to their use and interpretation by the trade unions.
5. *Cooperation clear/firm* The identification of major areas of joint gain to both parties and the quantification and presentation of the potential benefits to both parties. For example, reduced absenteeism and savings on supplementary payments which are largely conceded to the union. Management gains being less easy to calculate but significant in terms of increased machine running times, simplified administrative procedures etc.
6. *Cooperation very high/public* The establishment of working parties to identify areas of potential benefit to both sides. A willingness to release information well in advance of the negotiations themselves at all levels in the organization—'an open book policy' building on the assumption that both parties recognize certain constraints ie no redundancies, no doubling of take-home pay.

It is both relatively easy and essential that prior to the negotiations the management negotiating team together with the company's senior management should sit down and agree what the three stages on either side mean within their plant. No more than three points/stages should be identified in order to avoid confusion. If the stages are not clearly differentiated in the minds of the negotiators they will not subsequently be able to communicate them effectively in the negotiations themselves. Senior management involvement in discussions about the overall strategic objective may also help to reduce some of the pressures which negotiators are subjected to by the critics who start with the phrase 'If only you had . . .'

The selection and implementation of a negotiating strategy requires more than a fairly simple choice between conflict and cooperation. We constantly hear references to attitudes and expectations of the two parties and the complex web of organizational pressures which develop in the collective bargaining relationship over a period of time. For this reason Figure 13.2 shows a diagram which can be completed prior to the negotiations in particular by those managers involved in the face to face meetings with the unions.

```
                    High emphasis
                    on attitudes and
                    relationships
                          |
                          |
                          |
  Low emphasis            |            High emphasis
  on internal             |            on internal
  organizational ─────────┼─────────── organizational
  issues                  |            issues
                          |
                          |
                          |
                    Low emphasis
                    on attitudes and
                    relationships
```

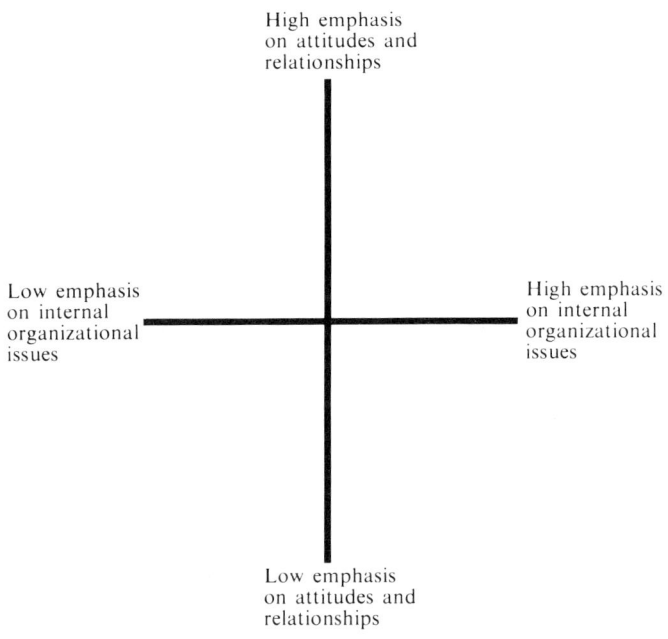

Figure 13.2   Emphases for a negotiating strategy

The objectives of this procedure are the following. Having made the initial choice of strategy in terms of conflict or cooperation the negotiators must take into account some if not all of the contextual complexity in which the negotiations are conducted. The dimension concerned with attitudes and relationships refers to values and expectations which the management bring to their relationship with the trade unions with whom they negotiate. For example, a high emphasis may involve either not presenting certain demands or counter demands if these are known to be highly sensitive to the trade union side; for instance, the rate of introduction of micro technology based on natural wastage; or if management recognizes that a future capital investment decision may be strongly influenced by a public statement of interdependence made by trade union negotiators and an expressed willingness to negotiate manning levels prior to the commissioning of the new plant. A low emphasis on attitudes and relationships can best be characterized as a 'couldn't care less approach'. For example, the company may be indifferent to the effect of announcing a redundancy amongst recently unionized white collar employees whilst engaged in negotiations with unions representing production staff in the belief that they have to live with the latter but that white collar unionization is a temporary phenomena.

The other dimension concerned with internal organizational issues seeks to recognize some of the problems which negotiators may need to recognize in the relationship between those actually at the table and their audiences. The audience consists of those groups and interests which must be considered by the negotiator in his attempt to secure an agreement which can be implemented. In the company used as an example earlier these might on the management side include the view of the corporate production and personnel staff, the demands of the local senior production manager, the four shift superintendents, the factory engineer, the safety officer and the plant personnel team. For the trade union side the following audiences can be identified for this particular company:—their members in the production area, the maintenance engineers (both mechanical and electrical), the instrument technicians, the shop stewards not included in the joint negotiating committee, the members of the Health and Safety Committee, the powerful local shop stewards committee operating in the port and local haulage industry whose support was obtained in industrial action two years previously, the full time official, the local branch organization. Each party should take into account during their planning for the negotiations and whilst the talks are taking place both the existence of these groups and their reactions to certain demands and proposals. The senior negotiator in his representational role must seek to balance the potentially optimistic demands with the reality of the situation. For example, a senior steward or convenor who leads the union side must recognize that the company's enhanced offer which carries the counter demand of the transfer of engineers mates or trade assistance to production duties whilst supported by his members might be vetoed by the local official of the electricians' union because of local rivalries with one of his own union's senior officers. He might also be aware of the conflict which exists between the plant superintendent and the personnel department. He must decide whether his short or long term interests are best served by exploiting these tensions or by ignoring them. On the management side negotiators are often aware of the 'political difficulties' faced by the convenor or an individual shop steward who have to work with a relatively small group of union activists whose opinions and values they must communicate in order to remain in their elected office. This situation is frequently described with the words 'better to deal with the devil we know'.

The matrix which has been shown in Figure 13.2 should be used to make the contextual dynamics of the negotiations far more explicit. During the planning phase it should allow the negotiating team to answer the 'what if' question and place it within the overall objectives of the negotiations. For example, if the management knows that its financial performance is critical over the next six months it might decide that it still wishes to place a high emphasis on attitudes and relationships and a low emphasis on internal organizational issues because it takes the view 'otherwise there won't be a business here at all, yet we depend on the people to do the job'. Negotiators have a choice to make between four alternative and mutually exclusive substrategies. Although these are not as important as the first decision they made between conflict and cooperation, they crucially determine the process itself and the format of any agreement which may be reached.

Having undertaken the conceptual analysis there now remains a number of practical considerations which must be resolved. The first concerns the ownership and use of the analysis. It was suggested that senior management be involved in the identification of the overall strategic choice between conflict and cooperation for a particular set of negotiations. The subsequent analysis of the relationship dimension and the internal organizational issues is much more likely to be of concern and interest to a smaller number of managers actually involved in the negotiations. As long as an effective degree of privacy can be guaranteed it is suggested that this smaller group of managers actually meet and 'brain storm' in order to determine the direction of the second set of strategic options. The benefit is twofold. First, it will facilitate communication of both the short and long term implications of the negotiations in this politically sensitive area between the negotiating team and their immediate management colleagues. Secondly, it will make the assumptions of the management team much more explicit and therefore help to avoid the 'hidden agenda' trap. Finally, it is a useful method of team building and stress reduction. The physical and psychological stress involved in the negotiating process is considerable enough without being compounded by behaviour which threatens the cohesiveness of the negotiating team.

During the actual negotiations the two stage analysis should be placed in the custody of the member of the negotiating team who has primarily been charged with the task of observing and analysing the meetings himself (herself). Of the four tasks which can be identified in a negotiating team (chairman, spokesman, recorder and observer) observing is not a junior or lower level activity. It requires considerable local knowledge of the company, the union and the people and personalities involved. 'Listening to the music and not the notes', this key task can often be given to a senior operations manager who otherwise might feel himself only marginally involved in the negotiating process itself. His report back to the negotiating team should take place at the end of each session and in particular during adjournments which might have been called under some pressure. Adjournment meetings of the negotiating team which do not begin with feedback about the overall strategic objectives often end up with bad, short term and retroactive decisions. If the negotiating team have a 'guardian' of their strategic objectives, who may not have been involved to the same extent in the verbal exchanges with the trade unions, they have an opportunity to constantly keep in mind the distinctions between strategy and tactics. The manager who takes on the role of observer/analyzer is not involved in a marginal activity. He is the navigator for the management team.

Analyzing and Selecting Negotiating Tactics

Once they have determined their overall strategic objective for the negotiations the management team must turn its attention to the complex issue of negotiating tactics. The first task is to correctly analyze the broad array of tactics which appear to be available. Some managers might argue, incorrectly, that tactics fall into two clear groups; those that work and those that fail. A more detailed analysis requires that we increase the number of categories. Negotiators select tactics with which they feel comfortable from four broad headings. There may appear to be hundreds of individual tactics, because of the differences introduced by persons engaged in the process itself, but a closer analysis will result in perceiving and choosing from amongst the following: tactics concerned with pace, information, people and pressure.

The pace tactics are those concerned with the rate of progress made or not made during a meeting. For example, the delaying tactics of repeating detailed statements, raising side issues etc. are well known.

The information tactics deal with the use of data during the negotiating process. Are detailed manpower costs presented before the negotiations as part of the first reply to a union claim or only released gradually in response to specific requests? The use of such tactics may be influenced by the existence of codes of practice and other consultative arrangements.

The people tactics refer to any attempt to make a distinction between the negotiator in his role as a representative and the role occupant himself. For example, questions about personal integrity or the inability of the senior negotiator to coordinate and manage the internal problems of his own team.

The pressure tactics are those which aim to persuade the other party of the costs associated with pursuing a particular aspect of his claim or resistance to a demand of the management side. To the outside observer pressure tactics are synonymous with strikes and threats of industrial action. Most experienced negotiators recognize that a more subtle range of tactics exist in particular in the use of time deadlines and reference back of an offer which, if rejected, might result in membership demands for industrial action.

It must be remembered that once the two parties have begun the actual negotiating meetings the tactics are perceived primarily in verbal terms. It is possible to interpret certain aspects of non-verbal behaviour but in most cases it is advisable to focus on the explicit public verbal exchanges. It should also be remembered that in some instances it is not the tactics which are chosen and deployed which become critical but those which are not utilized. In many instances it may be essential for the management negotiating team to explicitly recognize which tactics they do *not* want to use. In particular as the exclusion of the use of certain categories may provoke comment from managers who are not involved in the process. This is the 'why didn't you do this' observation.

During the final stages of the planning process before the negotiations actually begin, the management team must ensure that their two phase analysis of their strategic options and their proposed tactics can be seen to support one another. Even a fairly brief review may show up certain inconsistencies. For example, if the company wishes to adopt a cautious cooperative approach with a high emphasis on attitudes and relations but little concern for internal organizational issues it may wish to avoid using pace tactics which seek to overstate the areas of agreement or too frequent summaries of the management line. Instead they may wish to emphasize the use of questions. In Figure 13.3 a schema for tactics analysis has been included which has been used in a wide range of negotiating planning sessions both in the United Kingdom and overseas.

Preparing for Bargaining

If the management team are prepared to undertake such an analysis of their proposed negotiating tactics a number of results will follow. Initially there may be the subjective feeling of having potentially stilted the actual meeting but subsequently the members of the team may feel more relaxed and under less stress from the trade union side. By

The Strategy and Tactics of Bargaining

Conflict ← - → Cooperation			
Attitudes & relations	High ☐		Low ☐
Internal issues	High ☐		Low ☐

		Frequency	
	Often	Sometimes	Avoid
Pace	☐	☐	☐
Information	☐	☐	☐
People	☐	☐	☐
Pressure	☐	☐	☐

Figure 13.3   Scheme for analyzing tactics

creating a common analytical framework, communication and decision making during the negotiations will be facilitated. The manager acting as observer can also provide more meaningful feedback about the team's progress in securing their strategic objectives.

Before the negotiations begin the management team should undertake a number of simple tasks which will heighten their awareness of the tactical nature of the conference itself. Each individual member of the negotiating team should be asked to describe to the other members of the group three tactics which he or she like to use because they have proved to be effective in the past. Subsequently this process should be repeated focusing on three tactics which the manager dislikes or has found difficulty in coping with during previous negotiations with the trade union side. The group, as a group, should then develop and discuss counters to each tactic. As a result the negotiating team has acquired a shared repertoire of tactics and will be more sensitive to the requirement to support individual members during the negotiations. This discussion can be recorded on the matrix shown in Figure 13.4 which should become the property of the negotiating team but should for the period of the negotiations be lodged in the custody of the observer.

Many negotiators feel that they make concessions with considerable difficulty and a reluctance that is real because their presentation has not been sufficiently well rehearsed before the meeting. In order to

Tactics liked	Counter
Tactics disliked	Counter

Figure 13.4 Matrix for discussing tactics

facilitate this process it is important to accept that making concessions is an integral part of the collective bargaining process. What must not be forgotten is that making clear counter demands plays an equally important role. The formulation and timing of counter demands requires equal preparation and should be undertaken alongside the formulation and exploration of the concession range. The diagram in Figure 13.5 may facilitate this process.

Concessions management will make	Concessions management will seek from the trade unions
Concessions management must avoid making	Concessions from trade unions if obtained which cause surprise

Figure 13.5 Scheme for considering concessions

The dividing line between the top and bottom halves of the matrix has a particular purpose in practice. If the senior negotiator wishes to 'cross the line' he should be prepared to call an adjournment before making the concession. If not he runs the risk of damaging his credibility and the value of the preparations undertaken. If the company obtains many concessions that cause surprise they might again be advised to pause and review both their overall strategy and the value of their previous planning.

The purpose of this chapter has been to identify some of the problems associated with selecting a negotiating strategy and the tactics which should be used in their realization. From the standpoint of the manager involved in negotiations on a relatively infrequent basis what has been proposed may appear to be unnecessarily complex and detailed. The justification is both simple and essentially crude. In many situations the negotiating process appears to work despite the participants; perhaps we should seek to move to a situation where the outcomes are achieved because of the actors.

References and Further Reading

Atkinson, G.G.M., *The Effective Negotiator*. Quest, 1977.
Coker, E. and Stuttard, G., *The Bargaining Context*. Arrow Books, 1976.
Gottschalk, A., 'Behaviour Analysis of Bargaining' in Warner, M. (Ed.), *The Sociology of the Work Place*. Allen and Unwin, 1973. Chapter 2.
Morley, I.E. and Stephenson, G.M., *The Social Psychology of Bargaining*. Allen and Unwin, 1977.
Strauss, A., *Negotiations*. Jossey Bass, 1978.
Towers, B., Whittingham, T.G. and Gottschalk, A., *Bargaining for Change*. Allen and Unwin, 1972.
Walton, R.E. and McKersie, R., *A Behavioural Theory of Labour Negotiations*. McGraw-Hill, 1965.

Part Four

Salary Systems

Editor's Introduction

When salary systems are designed, it is usual to include definitions of salary bands, through which an individual progresses with his experience in the job; salary progression curves, or guide-lines for the rate at which individuals shall progress through those bands; and salary review procedures, whereby increases in salary are determined, usually on an annual basis. Each of these is dealt with in Chapter 14 of this section.

Chapter 15 is concerned with employee appraisal. Most manual workers' trade unions in Britain object to employee appraisal for their members, as it implies subjective judgements being made by managers which the union leaders believe places the employee in a beholden position in relation to management, and weakens the bargaining power of the union.

Appraisal procedures are common amongst managerial professional and technical employees in companies. It is often argued that appraisal should be as much in the interests of the employee as of the employer, and for this reason emphasis is laid on the identification of personal development and training needs. If the employee's major concern is with promotion, then this coincidence of interests will frequently exist, provided that the appraisal procedure does in fact operate as an aid to personal development.

Management by Objectives is a particular brand of appraisal system which became popular in the early 1970s. In some organizations which introduced MBO, much managerial time was wasted in preparing a good end of year case for why the targets had been unattainable. More recently, MBO has been modified to make it more suitable for a wider range of applications. In appropriate situations, shorter time horizons, variable time horizons or group targets have been applied.

Salary earners are frequently concerned about a range of monetary and non-monetary rewards which they receive in addition to their salaries. These may include such items as job interest and challenge, promotion prospects, share capital, security, status and fringe benefits. But recent studies of manager's interests and concerns indicate that these are not uniform across all specialisms, age groups and achievement levels, and if rewards for managers are to act as motivators and sources of satisfaction, these variations in interests need to be taken into account in the design of salary systems.

Inclusive schemes for managers are particularly sensitive to these variations in motivation, and in the design of such schemes the salary administrator may need to make his own studies of the particular patterns of motivations amongst the managers concerned, as research in this area has so far been of fairly limited scope. Chapters 17 and 18 cover these topics.

The Hay Guide-chart Profile system of salary payment is included in this section because in addition to producing a ranking of salaried jobs, the Hay Consultancy Company provides its clients with the means of determining absolute levels of salary payment, by comparison with other companies using the Hay Scheme. It is a fairly widely used procedure in British industry, and for this reason the editors thought it desirable to devote a chapter to it, Chapter 16.

14

Salary Bands and Salary Progression Curves

Lawson K Savery

Ask most people why they work and they will answer 'for money'. This basic need for money is important and decisions concerning:

1. The width of the salary band for each job.
2. The number of increments within each band.
3. If there is going to be a salary band for each individual job or for a cluster of jobs.
4. How a person progresses up the increment scale.

These are all critical to the success of an enterprise. Salaries have to be high enough to attract staff, but not so large as to make the firm's labour costs too high when compared with its competitors in the industry and/or locality. This chapter is concerned with how these decisions are made.

Wage Surveys

Before any decision on wages and salaries policy can be made, it is necessary to carry out a wage/salary survey to obtain standards of pay paid by other organizations. Wage and salary surveys are aimed to achieve external consistency (ie between the organization's wage and salary level and that of other firms with which the organization wishes to be compared). For this purpose wages or salaries paid to people with the same classification eg maintenance and installation fitters, can be obtained from the government published statistics (for example, the New Earnings Survey 1979). However, these statistics may not be appropriate because:

1. The firm may be in an area of:
   (a) Over-employment where the wages and salaries paid may be higher than the national average to retain and/or attract staff.
   (b) A depressed area where the wages and salaries paid may be lower than the national average.
2. The firm may want to compare people in its employ with like people in similar firms. To get comparability however, job descriptions are essential and one should never rely on job titles alone, since these may be misleading.
3. The firm may wish to obtain a survey of firms in the same industry in its own locality, taking care that the survey is statistically valid by including the whole population or an adequate sample (Income Data Service, 1970 p.3).

The decision as to what firms and areas are surveyed becomes more complex if the firm has several offices or plants in different parts of the country. Does the organization have only one rate of pay or several rates of pay for each type of job, depending on the economic environment in the different areas and the job being done? Executive rates of pay are frequently compared nationally whilst others tend to be more local to the plant, irrespective of whether the firm is a unit or multi-plant operation. Chapter 29 describes the various available sources of information on pay in other organizations, and Chapter 12 considers various methods of making the comparisons.

The results of wage and salary surveys must be interpreted with care because rates of pay are influenced by such things as amounts of fringe benefits, bonus payments, and job security. However, surveys do produce benchmarks to enable an organization to compare its present wage and salary scales of well defined jobs and to ascertain if any adjustment is necessary to comply with the overall wage and salary policy.

This policy may be to pay more, the same, or less than the average or median wage for the job, as determined by the survey. There is a difference between median and average wage, as can be seen in Table 14.1, the median wage being the central point of the pay range. The modal wage (ie the one which is most frequently paid) is not used as often as it should be in designing pay scales, as it is useful to compare the organization's modal score with that of the survey.

Table 14.1

Analysis of 452 salaries

Mean (average) salary	£6185 p.a.
Median salary (mid-point of range)	£5800 p.a.
Modal salary (most common)	£5000 p.a.

There are two main benefits from using survey data:

1 It is almost inevitable from time to time, that a firm will have a supervisor who will argue that the firm's pay rates for his subordinates are too low, and he is losing his best people to competitors for much higher pay. To respond to this argument it is necessary to have sufficient reliable survey data.
2 Particularly in periods of high wage demands it is necessary to keep in close contact with the amounts of wages and salaries paid in other firms.

Internal Consistency

Internal consistency can be obtained by using a job evaluation system. Here all the jobs within the organization are considered and the relative worth of each job for the enterprise is measured. A hierarchy of jobs is formed with those jobs of low worth being at the bottom and those of high worth at the top. There are several techniques available for achieving this classification such as factor comparison and point schemes, and these are considered in detail in Chapters 7 and 8.

Designing Salary Bands

Once the data is obtained from external pay surveys and job evaluation, salary bands can be designed. Suppose that it is decided to take the median pay rate from the survey as the mid-point of the salary range for a particular job, then the decision has to be made as to the range between the minimum and maximum pay for this job. Usually the limits are set at between ± 15% and 20% about the mid-point, (see Figure 14.1) bearing in mind that minimum rates of wages in many jobs and industries have been fixed by collective bargaining between trade unions and employer organizations or set by statutory orders under the Wages Councils Acts or the Agricultural Wages Acts (New Earnings Survey 1979, p.A13). The horizontal axis can be points obtained from a job evaluation scheme. This graph is then superimposed over the scattergram of the actual earnings of the people in the employ of the firm.

The visual analysis of the scattergram identifies those jobs which appear to be under or overpaid according to their evaluation. Care should be taken to investigate why these jobs appear to be wrongly paid. Is the problem due to faulty job evaluation or an historical mistake, which may have been made before formal job evaluation was used? This means the jobs have been consistently under or overrated. If after a check of the evaluation process the jobs are found to be correctly evaluated, then the firm has a decision to make. It can

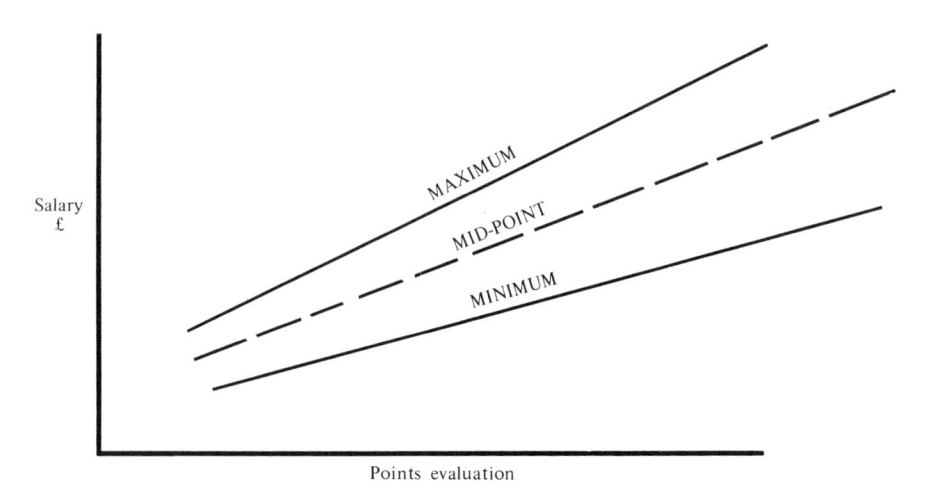

Figure 14.1 Pay scales: decision where to set mid-point, maximum, and minimum lines

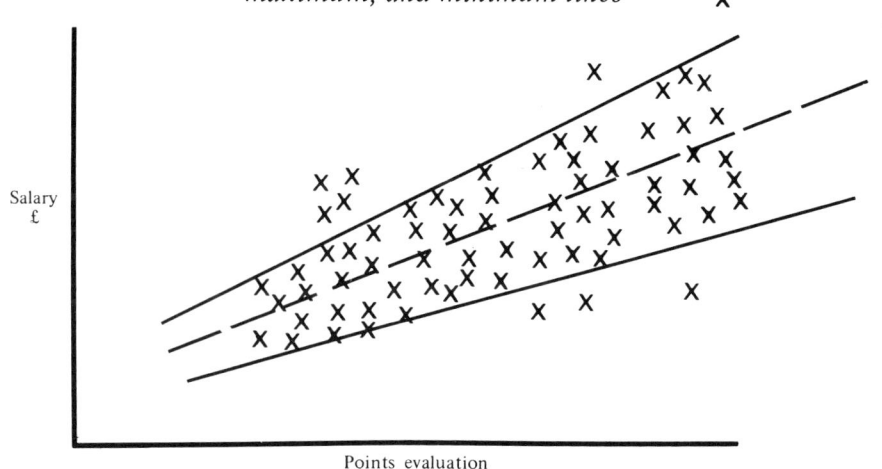

Figure 14.2 Pay scales superimposed over the scattergram of actual earnings

increase the differential between the top and bottom to say 50% ie ± 25% about the mid-point of the scale. This increase in the range of the pay scales will thus mean more jobs are encompassed within the boundaries of the pay scales. This method should remove some, if not all, of jobs which originally fell outside the boundaries. But it can raise problems where people in lower grades earn substantially more than those senior to them. It can also raise the ceiling for other employees in each grade, and so increase the employee costs. If this method is not acceptable or there are jobs which cannot be brought within the boundaries unless the salary range is so large to be unacceptable then other methods have to be used. The firm can:

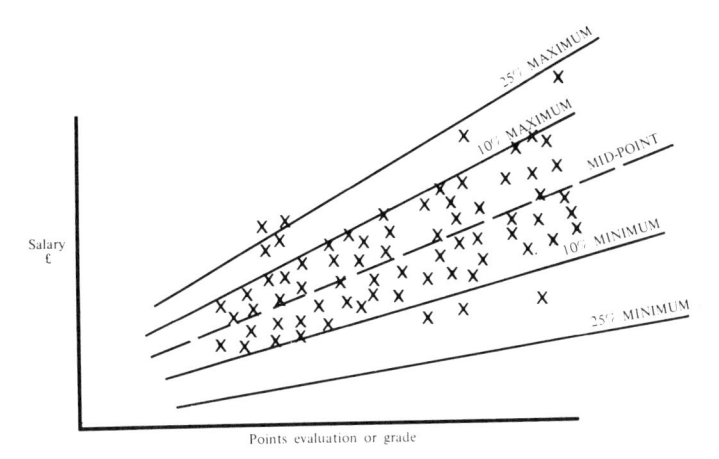

Figure 14.3 Enlarged pay scales superimposed over scattergram of actual earnings to try and encompass all jobs within the boundaries of the pay scales

1 Give the underrated jobs a pay increase to bring the underpaid qualified persons up to their correct pay level.

or

2 Give more frequent and/or larger increases than normal to rapidly bring the underpaid people up to their correct level.

The overpaid can be:

1 Moved, if qualified, to higher rated jobs where their rates of pay would suggest they should be.
2 Kept at a constant income until pay increases to everyone else brings them down to their correct level.
3 Given smaller and/or less frequent increases until they are in the correct pay range.
4 It can be recognized that the firm has a group of people who are overpaid and accept this.

Thus, the wage would consist of the new rate of pay plus an ex gratia payment equal to the difference between the new rate and the individual's old rate of pay. This ex gratia payment is sometimes only paid to present employees doing the job; new employees being paid the new rate. This latter method can cause internal conflict and should only be considered after discussion and acceptance by employees and their trade union representatives.

Grades

The above section described how to obtain a band of salaries for each job within the enterprise. Since the number of jobs can be very large it is often simpler to cluster jobs into grades and determine wage and salary bands for these grades. To do this, the wage and salary grades should fit the actual job clusters, ie the dividing line between one job cluster and the next should pass between them never through them.

Relationship between Bands

Once it is decided to use a graded structure then a decision has to be made concerning the relationship that is to exist between the minimum and maximum of one grade and minimum and maximum of the next grade. These relationship values can be obtained in several ways:

1 By past experience in this organization, on the principle that what works best is correct.
2 Taking the clusters and drawing a vertical line through the mid-point of the cluster (illustrated in Figure 14.4) and where this line cuts the maximum (X) and minimum (Y) lines gives the limits of the salary band. Draw horizontal lines through the points X and Y until they intersect the dividing lines between the clusters and hence one has wage/salary band for each grade.

Obtain Mid-point of Cluster

'Double-grade overlap' should be avoided wherever possible; that is, where the minimum of one grade is very near the mid-point of two grades below. This can be achieved by making the mid-point of each grade one-third to one-half more than the mid-point of the preceding

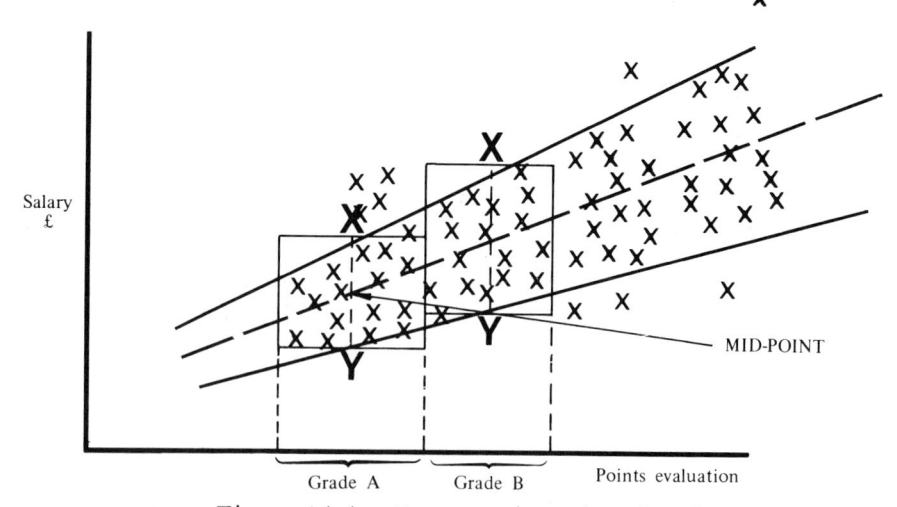

Figure 14.4   Constructing salary bands

grade. Note that the mid-point of the range for a grade need not have the same number of jobs above as below it. Also the difference between adjoining grades should be large enough to allow for promotion, if promotion normally occurs from one grade to the next.

Methods of Salary Progression

Once the maximum and minimum values are established it is then necessary to divide this range into progression levels or increments. The increase in pay as the person moves through the band can be either linear (equal increments at each stage of progression) or curvilinear or a combination of these depending upon the requirements of the firm.

Figure 14.5a
Linear increments
Annual increments
0 — 7 years

Figure 14.5b
Curvilinear increments
Annual increments
0 — 8 years

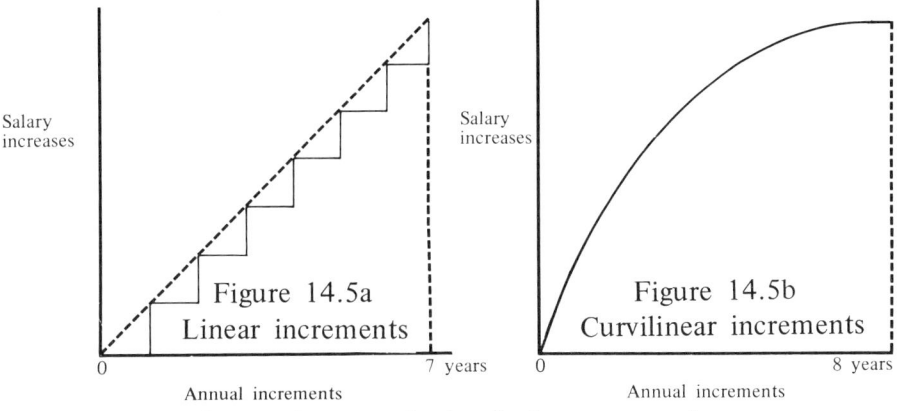

Figure 14.5   Methods of salary progression

In the first case (Figure 14.5a) each incremental step is rewarded by the same amount. These divisions can be obtained by dividing the difference between the minimum and maximum by the number of increments it is believed are necessary, remembering that the increase has to be large enough to be perceived as a worthwhile reward for increased responsibilities. The second graph (Figure 14.5b) illustrates the situation where most learning occurs in the earlier years, or the firm wishes to reward people more in the early part of their career to improve motivation for promotion. There are other curves which can give similar results, such as Figure 14.6; although the two halves of this curve are linear, the rates of increase of pay for the two halves are different. Thus, the design of the progression curve will depend upon the firm's requirements.

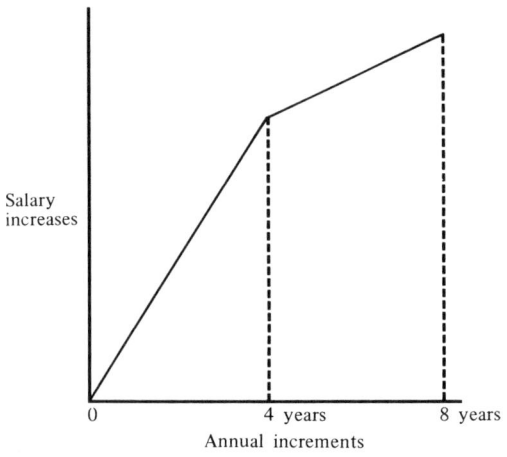

Figure 14.6 Another form of linear increments

Relationship to performance

In some organizations people progress through the pay band automatically every year, getting one incremental increase annually, until they reach either the top of their band, or a merit bar somewhere in the top half. This means that irrespective of ability and quality, people automatically progress up the pay scale. This process undermines the principle of the mid-point of the scale being set as the competitive rate and thus the salary which most people should earn, with only those of above average ability and performance earning the higher rates, see Figure 14.7. (See Chapter 15 on Performance Appraisal).

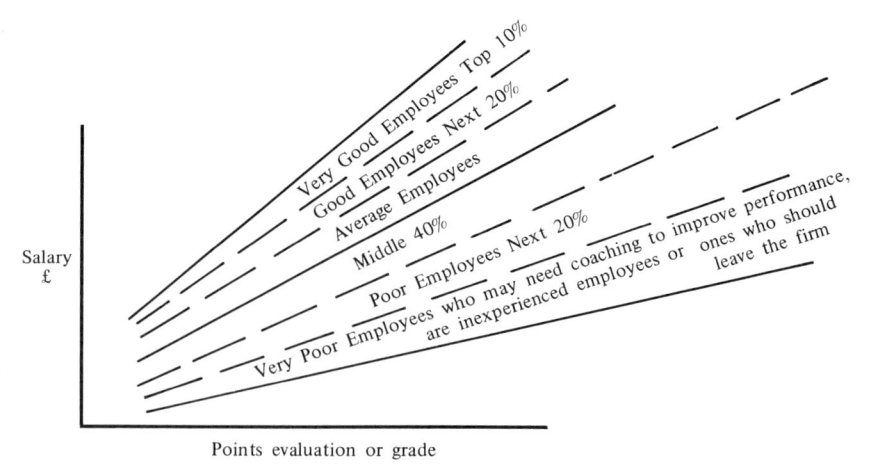

Figure 14.7 Salary band graded according to performance

Salary Bands and Salary Progression Curves 195

Progression Curves

Where length of service is used as a means of progression through the salary band then bars are often placed in the scale, and progression beyond that point can only be achieved by passing some test or satisfying superiors of ability, confidence and competence above a certain level. The problem of automatic increase for everyone leading to undeserved high pay for poor performers can be solved by using another basic principle for progression curves, multi-progressive curves. This method is applied in conjunction with an appraisal system. The idea is that since there are a number of progression lines a choice can be made as to which one is to be used, depending upon the performance appraisal, standard data collected on the person's work, and the individual's estimated potential. Two alternative schemes exist, involving linear or curvilinear progression, as illustrated in Figures 14.8a and b. As can be seen from Figure 14.8 in both situations a person on the 1st curve reaches the maximum fairly quickly whilst in the 4th and 5th the individual progresses more slowly and never reaches the maximum.

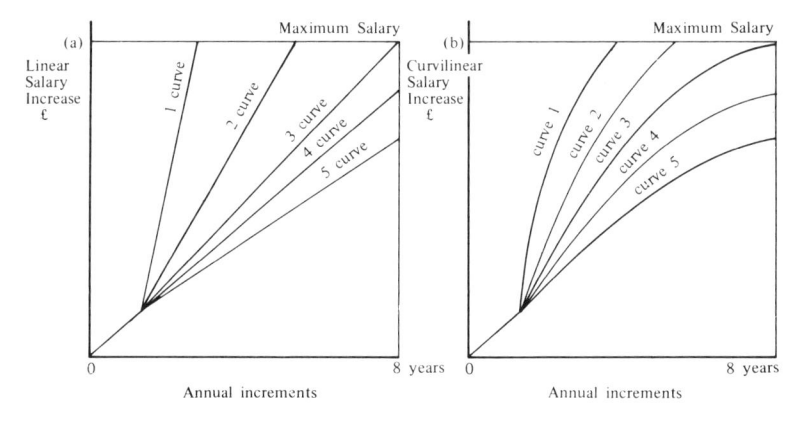

Figure 14.8   Increments graded according to performance

It is better to start the multi-progression curves at the 1st or 2nd increment thus allowing all people to receive at least two assessments before a decision is made on which curve the person will be placed since it often proves difficult to drop a person from a higher to a lower scale. In order to ensure that the full range of scales are adequately used a forced distribution may be required. Thus, if there are five curves a superior or an appraisal committee can be required to rate subordinates by forced distribution with, for example, the top 10% placed on curve 1, the next 20% placed on curve 2, next 40% on curve 3, next 20% on curve 4 and the lowest rated 10% of subordinates on curve 5.

It is also important to remember that in higher grades, the individual increments in each band are normally larger, in order to ensure that the increase is perceived as worthwhile in relation to basic pay. Normally the increments are expressed as a percentage of the rate, and the percentage tends to be similar across the grades, thus giving rise to the larger increments.

New Employees

It is generally argued by managers that one starts new employees at the minimum rate for the job, but this is not always easy, due to the qualifications held by the new employee or the experience of the new employee.

However, if a new employee starts above the minimum care should be taken to fit them in carefully in relation to existing employees, and if possible leave at least two increments before the maximum of the band so that performance appraisals may be carried out before a decision needs to be made about promotion to the next band; and to leave room for improvement where such a promotion is not considered likely. The decision about which progression curve the new employee is to be placed upon should be delayed until their first, or preferably their second, annual review.

Clearly performance and potential appraisal, the topics of the next chapter, are vital contributions to any organization's policy on salary bands and progression curves.

References and Further Reading

Department of Employment, New Earnings Survey 1979, HMSO, Publication of Government Statistical Service 1979-80.
Incomes Data—Guide to Salary Surveys, Incomes Data Services Ltd., London, June 1970.
Ingham, H.E. and Taylor Harrington, L., *Interfirm Comparison: The Latest Techniques for Comparing Business Performance*, Heinemann, London, 1980.
Jaques, E., 'Taking time seriously in evaluating jobs', *Harvard Business Review*, volume 57, no. 5, September/October 1979.
Rock, M.L. (Ed.), *Handbook of Wage and Salary Administration*, McGraw-Hill, New York, 1972.

15

Performance Appraisal and Review

David Cameron

Performance appraisal and review is a process in which 'bosses' evaluate and report on the performance, attainments, abilities, potential for future development and other qualities of their organizational subordinates. Randell *et al* (1974) point out its developmental aspects as: 'any procedures which help the collecting, checking, sharing, giving and using of information collected from and about people at work for the purpose of adding to their performance at work'. Not surprisingly, therefore, performance appraisal and review can be a controversial subject, since how well or how badly it is done and the use which is made by higher management of the results, invariably affect the employee's morale and motivation to work and also his prospects of career advancement.

The use of performance appraisal and review has gained wide acceptance and few well managed institutions, especially the larger ones, do not employ some variation of the technique, however informal. It has been commonplace in the public sector for a long time, having been introduced into the British civil service before World War I in an effort to improve individual performance, and contemporary public and private sector managers are no less interested in achieving this long sought goal today.

Informed opinion among practising managers as to the validity of the techniques employed and the value of the results achieved is as variable as their individual experiences, and certainly research has put beyond all reasonable doubt the fact that even the best of appraisal schemes are fraught with difficulty. Nevertheless, the continued and increasing use of such schemes and the now substantial literature on the subject powerfully reinforce the argument that some form of appraisal is central to improving individual and corporate performance, and there is no let up in the search for better and more acceptable methods.

Anderson (1980) goes to the heart of the matter when he states that 'performance appraisal is undoubtedly important to management development, since if an employee's strengths and weaknesses are not known, it would be only accidental that development efforts would be aimed in the right direction'.

Two penetrating surveys conducted in the United Kingdom by the Institute of Personnel Management indicate substantial growth in the use of systematic appraisal schemes. Reported in depth by Gill, Ungerson and Thakur (1973) the first was a survey of 360 British companies (this represented a 55.4% response from 649 organizations selected at random from the *Times 1000* and the Dun and Bradstreet 'Guide to Key British Enterprises') which showed that 59% of the respondents had introduced their current performance appraisal schemes between 1968 and 1973 and, even more significantly, 77% had set up their first systematic appraisal schemes of any kind during the same period.

Four of the main conclusions drawn from the survey data were:

1   The three main purposes of appraisal as seen by the respondents were: to assess future potential (94%), to assess training and development needs (93.6%), and to assess past performance (92.2%). Thus, the emphasis was on development, both organizational and personal.
2   Appraisal schemes were provided mainly for managerial grades and were not frequently extended to levels below foremen and the first line supervisors.
3   A more participative and objective approach to appraisals was reflected in the trend to show subordinates their appraisal reports, either in full or in part, although in the majority of schemes it was usually the section of the report dealing with current performance which was open to view.
4   The future for performance appraisal and review appeared to be reasonably healthy with increasing numbers of firms moving to appraisal based on achievement of measurable objectives. Assessment of potential was the area which seemed in most need of attention, and while there were indications of developments in this difficult aspect of appraisal, less than 4% of the respondents were using multiple assessment techniques such as assessment centres, although here, too, there appeared to be some signs of growing interest.

A second survey was undertaken towards the end of 1976, the results of which were published by Gill (1977). Of the 288 participant organizations, 82% had appraisal programmes while 18% had not (as over and against 74.2% and 25.8% respectively in 1973), the main findings concluding that (a) despite criticism in the literature and elsewhere of the ways in which performance appraisal schemes are operated, they show no signs of decline; indeed, the reverse seems to be the case. And (b) most appraisal schemes are still applied to managers, with secretarial and clerical staff included in only 45% of the schemes surveyed, a mere 2% of which covered shop floor employees.

Parallel investigations in the United States show similar results. Fournies (1973) estimated that 85% of American firms had appraisal schemes, a view reinforced by Locher and Teal (1977) who found that 89% of 216 respondent organizations in Southern California operated them.

Objectives of Performance Appraisal and Review

The objectives of performance appraisal and review are:

1 *Administrative* To provide an orderly way of determining promotions transfers, salary increases, etc.
2 *Informative* To supply data to management on the performance of subordinates and to the individual on his strengths and weaknesses.
3 *Motivational* To create a learning experience for subordinates that motivates them to improve.

Looking at performance appraisal in the context of management coaching, Singer (1974) states that:

> many of the problems connected with performance appraisal stem from lack of clarity in determining what it is intended to achieve, and then an attempt to do too many things at once. Normally these include:
> Letting the manager know how he is getting on in the opinion of his superior.
> Spotting talent so that good promotion prospects are not overlooked.
> Forming part of the input into salary review discussions.
> Identifying the training needs of the managers.
> Standing back and reviewing progress in the job.

There is general agreement as to the goals of performance appraisal and review, and the goals themselves do not appear to have changed much over time. What has changed, in Britain at least, is the degree of importance attached to particular goals. Asked to rank the three main purposes of their schemes, respondents to the 1973 IPM survey replied:

Purpose	Percentage companies
To assess future potential/promotability	96.0
To assess training and development needs	94.5
To assess past performance	91.3

while respondents to the 1977 survey considered the three main purposes to be:

To assess training and development needs	74.0
To help improve current performance	73.0
To assess future potential/promotability	52.0

This was indeed a sign of the times. By the mid 1970s the business performance of many companies was static or even declining in response to mounting economic pressures, hence it would appear that one casual factor of the change in perceived purposes was probably the concomitant reduction in opportunities for promotion. In 1973, 54.6% of respondents regarded assessment of increases or new levels in salary as a major goal of appraisal. By 1977, this had dropped to 39.0%, probably a reflection of the effects of Government pay policies in controlling wage and salary increases.

Looking at the purposes of assessment, Torrington and Chapman (1979) identify two areas of personnel work in which the technique is used. The first is 'in employment, placement and training where there is a need to assess current capabilities, motivation and personality in order to predict future potential for job performance'. The second is in performance appraisal where, as they put it, 'instead of prediction there is assessment of the current level of job performance'. They justify this approach when they add:

> Our reason for integrating the two areas of assessment here is that the essential features of understanding and practice are the same; only specific methods and techniques vary in response to different circumstances. Performance appraisal is frequently concerned, implicitly or explicitly, with future potential. Similarly employment decision-making applications would be simpler if it were possible to assess current performance directly. Some applications such as promotion decisions and management development involve both current performance and future potential.

In line with this approach, three additional goals of performance appraisal can be listed:

1 To aid selection of personnel for special assignments.
2 To act as a yardstick for measuring the effectiveness of personnel recruitment procedures.
3 To provide data without which it would be difficult, if not imposs-

ible, to undertake effective appraisal interviewing, counselling and coaching of staff.

Procedures for Appraisal and Review

In discussing specific procedures for appraisal and review it is useful to do three things. First, examine some of the methods which have been used over the years and critically assess their major defects; secondly, consider whether there might not be better, more accurate and more acceptable methods, and thirdly, speculate on the way ahead. In other words, where has appraisal and review been, where is it now, and where is it likely to be going in the future? Schick (1980) has pointed out that: 'Every company has a performance evaluation monitoring system (PEMS) to measure individual performance against company standards. It may not be recognized, formalized or documented, but the need to evaluate performance is present in all business environments'.

In small concerns with few employees, the owner or manager knows all his people personally, often working closely with them, and therefore can easily assess their performance informally at first hand. However, in larger organizations with several, perhaps many, hierarchical levels, first line and middle managers are often quite remote from their top management superiors, thus necessitating the introduction of formal procedures for appraisal and review as an aid to making similar decisions. There are certainly plenty of well-known methods to choose from, a dozen of which were listed in the 1973 IPM survey report:

1 *Alphabetical/numerical rating*: In this method, the rater is provided with a pro forma which lists a number of factors such as cooperation, job knowledge, versatility, analytical ability, quality and quantity of work, etc., and required to assess the performance of individual subordinates in terms of these factors, by awarding letters or numerical marks from given scales of, eg, A–E or 1–5.
2 *Free written report*: Sometimes referred to as 'the blank sheet of paper approach', this method does not employ a pro forma, raters merely being asked to express in their own words their assessment of the performance and potential of each of their subordinates.
3 *Controlled written report*: An extension of the free written report, this method also avoids use of a full questionnaire by setting out a small number of headings as guidelines to the rater.
4 *Personality trait rating*: Here the rater is required to complete a form which calls for assessment of personal qualities such as drive, initiative, judgement, social acceptability, etc.
5 *Forced choice rating*: The most common form of forced choice rating is usually found in extensions of the alphabetical/numerical system. Against each factor there is a set of four or five phrases or

adjectives relating to proficiency or personal qualification (eg poor, fair, average, good, excellent), and the rater is required to indicate in respect of each factor which of these most nearly matches his opinion of the performance or personal qualities of the person being rated. This is usually done by ticking or by placing a cross in a box against each adjective or phrase.

6 *Forced distribution method*: The assumption implicit in this method is that the proficiency of members of a work group follows a statistically normal distribution. The rater is therefore required to allocate marks or points to each of his subordinates so that specified proportions fall into each category.

7 *Graphic rating scale*: In this approach, the rater is asked to assess the performance or characteristics of subordinates by placing a tick somewhere along an open scale between low performance and high performance, thus:

factor ┕_____✓_____┙

               low   high

8 *Ranking*: This is the simple arrangement of subordinates in order of preference from 'best' to 'worst'. All managers make mental ratings of this sort anyway.

9 *Paired comparison*: A rather simple development of Ranking, this system requires the rater to compare each individual with every other being ranked and state which of the two is preferred in a series of pairs, so arranging from 'best' to 'worst'.

10 *Critical incident method*: In this type of scheme the rater is required to give examples of various 'critical incidents' over the assessment period which indicate the subordinate's 'good' or 'bad' performance.

11 *Results-oriented schemes*: Often a part or variation of management by objectives, results-oriented performance appraisal and review schemes call for the assessment of employee performance against previously agreed goals or key results areas. While by no means perfect, this approach has much to commend it, hence will be dealt with separately later.

12 *Self rating*: Used in varying degrees, frequently in public sector enterprises, self rating gives the subordinate the opportunity of evaluating his own performance over the appraisal period and of indicating how he would like to see his job, and possibly also his career, developing in the future. Forms used in this approach usually contain a statement to the effect that while the subordinate's opinions and wishes will be considered, it does not follow that they will necessarily be acted upon. Interest in self rating appears to be increasing, but in general the method is not intended

as a substitute for appraisal by a superior, rather as an adjunct to it.

Interesting and important questions are to what extent these different methods of performance appraisal and review are used in practice and the way in which the popularity or otherwise of specific types of scheme has changed over time. Table 15.1 compares results obtained from a British Institute of Management Survey reported on in 1967 and those of the 1973 and 1977 Institute of Personnel Management surveys.

Table 15.1

Percentage usage of different types of performance appraisal and review schemes

Type of scheme	BIM 1967 survey (N=107)		IPM 1973 survey (N=156)		IPM 1977 survey (N=180)	
	No.	%	No.	%	No.	%
Results oriented	13	12.1	80	51.2	102	56.7
Alphabetical/numerical rating	89	83.1	56	35.9	19	10.6
Personality trait rating	73	68.2	28	17.9	61	33.9
Self rating*	–		12	7.6	51	28.3
Free written report	10	9.3	9	5.7	2	1.1
Controlled written report	36	33.6	7	4.5	10	5.6
Forced choice rating	1	0.9	–		–	
Forced distribution rating	2	1.8	–		–	
Graphic rating scale	4	3.7	–		–	
Ranking	–		–		–	
Paired comparison	–		–		–	
Critical incident technique	–		–		–	
Unclassifiable	–		29	18.6	24	13.3

* Use of employee-prepared interview forms.

Sources: BIM Information Summary 133, 1967
IPM Information Report 14, 1973
IPM Information Report 25, 1977

The steady growth in the use of results oriented schemes over the decade covered by the data is self-evident, as is the corresponding decline in popularity of alphabetical/numerical rating. However, against contemporary predictions, personality trait rating, following a substantial decline between 1967 and 1973, was showing a marked increase again by 1977—a movement which appears to be still continuing. The increase in the use of self rating methods commented on earlier is also clearly in evidence from Table 15.1. The use of free written reports shows a steady decline over the whole period to almost negligible proportions. And after a substantial drop, there is a slight upturn in the use of controlled written reports by 1977.

Over the years, detractors have been scathing—often with justification—in condemning both the alphabetical/numerical and personality trait rating methods of performance appraisal and review. The two are still in use, often together, with the former providing a scale against which the rater is required to assess the latter. The design and installation of such a system is far from easy, since decisions must be made about:

1. What aspects of individual performance and/or behaviour it is hoped to assess, ie what appraisal 'factors' are to be used?
2. How are these factors to be stated and defined?
3. Against what standards of performance are they to be measured and what form of measurement is to be used?
4. Will all the factors be regarded as equal in degree of relative importance or not, and how can this be done?

Factors must be chosen to avoid ambiguity and to avoid overlapping. The use of too many factors means that some will overlap and thus be difficult to evaluate; too few, and some vital aspect of performance or behaviour is likely to be missed.

In one scheme of this type, aside from timekeeping and attendance (monitored and evaluated separately as a matter of simple record keeping) five 'factors' are used for assessment purposes: aptitude, attitude, diligence, quantity of work, quality of work.

APTITUDE is defined as the employee's aptitude for the work he is doing with particular reference to his ability to adapt himself to new requirements and situations (eg how long does it take him to grasp a new method of doing something or to understand a new instruction?). Not everyone would necessarily agree that this is a good or even acceptable definition of 'aptitude'. What matters is that within the system and among the people working with and subject to it, it is clearly understood. To secure some degree of consistency between raters, each point on the numerical rating scale is illustrated with a statement, as shown in Figure 15.1 for the first factor, aptitude. Many similar schemes, especially those using only a few 'factors', make no attempt to differentiate between factors in terms of their relative importance to the job of the person reported upon. In the scheme illustrated, however, weights are applied to the five factors as shown in Table 15.2.

From this table it is easy to allocate to the performance appraisal of each employee a numerical value which reflects (a) the rating he has been given for each factor, and (b) the degree of relative importance attached to this factor in his particular job, the sum of the total points scored being the employee's overall rating (see Table 15.3).

Numerical values arrived at in this way are sometimes used in 'merit rating' schemes, the total points scored determining a monetary award. The problems likely to arise through linking performance appraisal and

APTITUDE   *This factor assesses the employee's aptitude for the work he is doing with particular reference to his ability to adapt himself to new requirements and situations (eg how long does it take him to grasp a new method of doing something or to understand a new instruction?)*

Slow to grasp new ideas—requires repeated instructions 1

Grasps new ideas or instructions fairly well but requires close supervision to ensure satisfactory work 2

Ability to understand and act upon instructions is average, requires normal supervision 3

Quick to grasp new ideas, requires less follow-up than most .. 4

Very quick to pick up new ideas, often makes useful suggestions, requires minimum supervision 5

Figure 15.1   Extract from a rating form

Table 15.2

Weights applied to factors

Factor	WT %	1 Poor	2 Fair	3 Average	4 Good	5 Excellent
Aptitude	10	2	4	6	8	10
Attitude	10	2	4	6	8	10
Diligence	20	4	8	12	16	20
Quantity of work	30	6	12	18	24	30
Quality of work	30	6	12	18	24	30
	100%	20	40	60	80	100

review with merit rating for reward distribution purposes are dealt with later in the section on Salary Review.

While suitably designed and well administered performance appraisal and review schemes of the personality trait and alphabetical/numerical types can and do work, there is ample evidence in the literature and elsewhere of growing dissatisfaction with them, especially when it comes to the difficult business of appraisal interviewing. These

Table 15.3

Example of employee's overall rating

Factor	Rater's assessment	Points scored
Aptitude	3 (average)	6
Attitude	3 (average)	6
Diligence	4 (good)	16
Quantity of work	2 (fair)	12
Quality of work	5 (excellent)	30
	Total points scored	70

criticisms cannot be ignored since they are partly responsible for the clearly identified shift in emphasis towards results-oriented appraisal schemes.

First, many of the factors used are highly subjective and are thus incapable of accurate measurement. Secondly, research has demonstrated very convincingly that superiors are often reluctant to make formal assessments of their subordinates, especially on these kinds of factors. Raters tend to bunch their assessments around the average, the so-called 'central tendency syndrome'. Also a 'halo effect' can appear, whereby an overall impression of an individual is allowed to colour the scores given to them on all factors.

To some extent, these faults can be minimized by careful training of the raters. A rater who continually assesses the performance of his subordinates as 'average' may well be asked what, if anything, he is doing about it, if his subordinates really are average. Alternatively, rating subordinates as average may be perceived as safe by the rater, in which case corrective action by higher management is necessary. This highlights the need for periodically monitoring the results being produced by the scheme.

The halo effect produces scores which are consistent with the general impression. If this is favourable, it tends to colour the rater's judgement of specific attributes, causing him to rate too highly on desirable attributes or traits and too low on undesirable ones. On the other hand, a generally unfavourable impression is likely to result in desirable characteristics being rated too low while undesirable ones are rated too high. We can never completely eliminate this subjectivity from our judgements of others, and therein lies a powerful argument in favour of using objective rather than subjective criteria in performance appraisal and review.

A fourth problem is that managers are frequently more reluctant to conduct appraisal interviews than they are to make the appraisals in the first instance. The appraisal interview is one of the most sensitive and difficult situations in the interface between superior and subordinate since, by definition, there is a continuing relationship between the two. It is extremely difficult for a superior to communicate an adverse evaluation to a subordinate without producing defensive reactions.

In view of these and other difficulties which will be dealt with later, the quest for better, more accurate and more acceptable methods of performance appraisal and review continues. Many different approaches have been tried, probably the best known being that suggested by the philosophy and techniques of Management by Objectives.

Management by Objectives

Effective managers in all spheres of human endeavour have long recognized the need for precise definition of their operational goals and clear specification of the means by which they should be achieved, a fact highlighted by Muczyk's (1979) view that Management by Objectives (MBO) 'appears to be the most persuasive management idea of the last decade, although its roots go back at least a quarter of a century'. The term 'Management by Objectives' (MBO) was coined by Drucker in 1954 for a concept which achieved an impressive level of international acclamation and acceptance in both public and private sector operations.

At a time when managers beset by mounting economic, technological, social and political pressures were desperately seeking better ways of running their enterprises, Drucker's concept, encapsulating both an attractive managerial philosophy and a viable, commonsense modus operandi of managing, was seized upon by those seeking the holy grail of the ultimate managerial panacea, only to find that it was just another idea, better than most perhaps, but no instant cure-all for the managerial problems of the naive or the lazy.

Partly because of such disappointments and partly as a result of close and detailed scrutiny of the reasons for the success or failure of MBO in different circumstances and situations, both of which have been over-generalized, it has become somewhat fashionable to denigrate the technique. To obtain a balanced perspective of the subject much depends upon how one regards MBO and what one thinks it really is and can do. As Reif and Bassford (1979) point out 'it is disconcerting to discover how many versions . . . there are of the concept'—a way of setting objectives; a method of performance appraisal and review; a scheme of management development; a technique for reward distribution, or even a form of manpower planning!

The total concept comprises both philosophy and methodology. The philosophy according to Bass and Ryterband (1979) 'is consistent with

Locke, McGregor and Maslow: what people want most from work is to succeed at clear and personally valued activities, so concentrate on getting employees to understand the objectives of their particular assignments'. MBO is thus a process founded on a philosophy of participation with personnel heavily involved in—and through involvement committed to—the determination of compatible institutional and personal goals. It is a process according to Steers and Porter (1979) 'by which employees of an organization, working together, identify common objectives . . . and co-ordinate their efforts towards goal attainment. The major focus in this process', they maintain, 'is on the future—where the organization wants to go—not in the past', objectives being established to facilitate planning and coordination of available resources to maximize the opportunities and minimize the threats in the institution's environment.

Every organization has a hierarchy of objectives, each level linked to the one above, ranging from the institution's continuing raison d'être—through strategic long-range goals which, in turn, are sub-divided into shorter range tactical ones, ultimately being broken down into specific objectives for functions, departments and individual managers. The latter, working closely with their superiors, are deeply involved in setting objectives which their groups must achieve in order to meet the institution's forward plans. Properly practised, the technique would be better entitled Management by *Shared* Objectives!

While a good deal of detail work is involved, the basic technique is simple enough. In respect of each individual manager's job some fundamental questions must be asked and answered:

1. What is the reason for the existence of the job and what contribution does it make to the overall results of the enterprise?
2. What are the key results areas of the job? The underlying premise here is that there is a relatively small number of activities absolutely essential to the job in which excellence of performance will make a substantial difference to the overall results achieved (the '80/20' rule).
3. What standards of performance are to be used? A performance standard is a statement of the conditions which will exist when the required end result is being achieved satisfactorily.
4. How is performance to be measured and controlled against standards and what units of measurement are to be used? It is imperative to use quantitative rather than qualitative units of measurement—output, quality, cost, return on investment, labour turnover, etc. Even in areas of work in which it is difficult to do so, quantitative criteria should be sought, questions such as how many? how well? how much? and how long? being the most likely to produce useful standards of performance.

5   What improvements in the job and the manner in which it is done should be sought and how can incumbents work towards them over a stated period of time?

Given this type of approach, it is possible to base performance appraisal and review on more realistic and acceptable lines with considerable advantages:

1   Knowing what their goals are, manager and subordinate can monitor progress towards their achievement on a continuing basis, dealing with problems as they arise. In these circumstances the manager who, in an appraisal interview, tells a subordinate something that comes as a surprise to him is less effective than he may think himself to be. Faults should be put right as they occur as part of the day-to-day superior/subordinate relationship and only referred to constructively by way of example during the appraisal interview.
2   Performance rather than personality becomes the salient issue on which to concentrate.
3   Participation is the key to the success of the MBO approach to performance appraisal and review, with superior and subordinate jointly involved in the setting and monitoring of mutually agreed performance goals.
4   Performance appraisal and review can be separated from the assessment of potential. Both are important and clearly interlinked, yet, as we shall see later, in assessing potential it is necessary to take more than performance into account.
5   Salary review can be separated from review of performance and potential. Inevitably the question of a possible increase in salary will be in a subordinate's mind during an appraisal interview, but if discussion of salary and performance are separated in time, the probable success of the latter will be enhanced. However, if the subordinate does raise the matter of salary during the appraisal interview, then the superior must be prepared to deal with it. The same applies to consideration of promotion prospects.
6   When achievement of performance is measured quantitatively rather than qualitatively, the exercise of value judgement or opinion by the rater is minimized. Changes in circumstances since the original goals were set can be taken into account when the degree to which they have been met is under consideration. Job improvement plans lead naturally and positively to manager development, and since the subordinate has been involved in setting his own goals the chances of his being committed to their achievement are considerably enhanced.

Despite the undoubted benefits of the MBO approach to performance appraisal and review in many circumstances, even its most committed devotees will conceed that it has had its failures. Muczyk, whose penetrating critique gives a detailed and valuable insight into the more important grounds for disquiet with the technique, holds that 'evidence is mounting that MBO has more clear failures than successes', going so far as to suggest that 'we may be approaching an era where more time is spent taking MBO out than putting it in'. Some of the more obvious drawbacks are:

1. The essence of MBO is that goals are shared, but this presents at least three major difficulties. First, before goals can be shared they must be operational and to make them so requires a great deal of accurate, detailed, painstaking work. Secondly, research suggests that superiors' value systems frequently cannot cope with the courage, trust and openness necessary to make the mutual exchange system work. Thirdly, it follows that the very real apprehension of many superiors often inhibits the development of a supportive organizational climate.
2. When objective rather than subjective criteria are used for performance appraisal and review the relative ease or difficulty involved in reaching particular targets should be taken into account.
3. Despite arguments to the contrary, some goals really are hard to quantify. Consider the schoolteacher doing remedial work with a below average pupil. To be sure, some parts of the work can be measured quantitatively, but there are substantial job components crucial to effective overall performance which simply cannot be dealt with in this way.
4. Struggling to attain the unattainable will only result in frustration. Even though being given an objective which he believes to be beyond him and then achieving it can be a powerful motivator for a subordinate, this stretching process will succeed only if the goal to be attempted is just marginally out of reach, is firmly believed by the superior to be attainable and is thus a calculated part of the individual's development.
5. By definition goal setting is concerned with the future and this means dealing with uncertainty which can upset the best laid plans. Unless changing circumstances are recognized and goals adjusted accordingly, the organization and its staff can become locked into plans which are no longer relevant to the situation, and spend excessive amounts of time explaining the failures. It is important to set the time scale for the targets to suit the rate of change prevailing.
6. The time dimension in forward planning is important. Rewards often go to managers for short-term successes which are incompatible with longer-term organizational needs. It is not uncommon for managers to be promoted before they have to live with the consequences of their own actions. Maintenance of a suitable balance

between short, medium and long-term goals is crucial and must be recognized in the reward distribution system.

Notwithstanding these and other difficulties, the management by objectives approach to performance appraisal and review still has much to commend it. Moreover, as noted earlier, there is evidence to suggest a revival of personality trait rating, often using some form of alphabetical/numerical scale against which the rater is required to assess the degree to which subordinates possess particular traits. Examination of contemporary performance appraisal and review schemes indicates that some organizations are, in fact, combining all three methods—results oriented, trait rating and the alphabetical/numerical approach—in their assessment forms, as the following examples demonstrate (see Figures 15.2, 15.3).

REVIEW OF PRESENT PERFORMANCE

1. Assess the employee's performance against agreed objectives. Please check appropriate box and give any qualifying comments below. For example, did circumstances affecting agreed goals change during the period under review.

    Outstanding performance ☐

    Performance above requirements ☐

    Meets performance requirements ☐

    Performance below requirements ☐

2. Assess the employee's main strengths
   (eg. ability to plan, organize, analyze situations, direct, motivate and develop subordinates, etc.)

3. Assess the employee's main weaknesses
   (eg. in planning, organizing, analyzing situations, directing, motivating and developing subordinates, etc.)

4. Specify what training/development you consider would help the employee to improve work performance.

Figure 15.2   Review of present performance

ASSESSMENT OF PRESENT PERFORMANCE	1	2	3	4	X
Operational effectiveness					
Success in meeting agreed work goals					
Knowledge of present duties					
Planning ability					
Skill in implementing work plans					
Decision-making ability					
Accuracy of work					
Ability to communicate orally					
Ability to communicate in writing					
Relationships with others					
Relationships with — superiors					
— peers					
— subordinates					
— clients					
— others					
Intellectual ability and skills					
Creativity and original thought					
Willingness to accept new ideas					
Problem solving ability					
Personal attributes					
Qualities of leadership					
Drive, diligence, enthusiasm					
Ability to work under pressure					
Level of Initiative					
Ability/willingness to delegate					

In this case 1 = outstanding; 2 = good; 3 = acceptable; 4 = below required standard, and X = unacceptable.

Figure 15.3   Assessment of present performance

In addition to the assessment of performance and particular attributes, many appraisal documents in current use also ask the rater to give some sort of overall appraisal, usually against a preset scale of values, the following being fairly typical examples of this requirement (see Figures 15.4 and 15.5).

OVERALL PERFORMANCE RATING

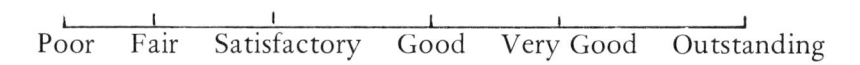

|⎯⎯⎯⎯|⎯⎯⎯⎯⎯⎯|⎯⎯⎯⎯⎯⎯⎯⎯|⎯⎯⎯⎯⎯⎯|⎯⎯⎯⎯⎯⎯⎯|
Poor Fair Satisfactory Good Very Good Outstanding

Rater's comments: (Including any other factors affecting overall performance.

Figure 15.4 Overall performance rating

OVERALL PERFORMANCE APPRAISAL AND RATER'S
GENERAL COMMENTS

Please check which

☐   Performance is outstanding

☐   Performance is highly satisfactory

☐   Performance is satisfactory

☐   Performance is adequate to requirements

☐   Performance is inadequate

Figure 15.5 Overall performance appraisal and rater's general comments

The Appraisal Interview

Inherent social skills can be enhanced by training and the techniques of appraisal interviewing can be taught, but the chances of success with the delicate task of appraisal interviewing are likely to be greatest when a climate is created in which superior and subordinate can discuss freely and frankly the extent to which current objectives have been met and new or modified goals are set for the future.

Success also depends heavily on the extent to which the superior is clear about the desired outcomes of the interview, ie what are *his* objectives in conducting it? Usually these will be some combination of:

1 Endeavouring to improve the subordinate's performance by setting mutually agreed goals and standards, the reasons for which are clearly understood by both parties.
2 Ensuring that the subordinate knows how well he is doing, building on his strengths rather than attacking his weaknesses.
3 Mutually agreeing plans for development of the individual's potential through training programmes, planned movement, special assignment and similar activities.
4 Creating a bond of strong personal relationships in a constructive, supportive organizational climate, thus unfreezing communication and reducing or eliminating tensions and anxiety.

Adequate pre-interview preparation is essential. The interviewee's job, work goals and performance should be considered in detail, as should all other available information about him—his past record, knowledge, experience, training, future potential and development needs. Lest questions of fact become issues during the interview, it is prudent for the interviewer to have the record handy for ease of reference if required.

In discussing the assessment, particular points the interviewer wants to make should always be backed up by specific examples. There is little value in criticizing, say, the quality of a subordinate's written communication, unless the interviewer can point out specific faults and, in a highly constructive way, discuss how he proposes to help the interviewee to overcome them. Moreover, in a first interview, the superior should be prepared for a variety of reactions ranging from anxiety and tension, through curiosity and suspicion, to downright hostility.

A critically important pre-interview decision is the extent to which the detailed assessment of the subordinate's performance and potential will be used. Is the situation to be completely 'open' with the interviewee being shown the rating forms and perhaps asked to sign them? Or is he to be given only selected information, maybe concerning his performance but not his potential?

Managers who favour a 'closed' system sometimes argue that it enables them to report more frankly and freely on the performance and potential of their subordinates than they could under an 'open' system, and that their reports are thus much more valuable aids to decision-making on pay and/or promotion. Quite apart from understandable (and undesirable) feelings of suspicion and resentment engendered by a situation in which employees know that they are being 'secretly' reported on with no opportunity of defending themselves, just how such managers can expect improvements in their subordinates' performance without some form of feedback it is difficult to imagine. Moreover, the fact that almost by definition open systems give subordinates a chance to express their own views and to appeal against assessments which they consider to be biased or unfair, puts pressure on their superiors to do their best to write accurate and constructive reports rather than necessarily favourable ones. The prospect of having to disclose an assessment to a subordinate and to discuss it with him may deter some faint-hearted managers from reporting what they really think, but as the movement towards greater openness in performance appraisal and review continues to gather momentum, they will be obliged to do the job properly even if they find the process somewhat painful at times.

Simple and obvious as it may seem, an essential and frequently neglected part of a manager's preparation for conducting an appraisal interview is to allocate sufficient time to cover the ground adequately and allow for meaningful discussion, thus creating—correctly—the impression that the meeting is of paramount importance to both parties.

The interviewee also needs time to prepare and should be given at least one week's notice of where and when the interview is to take place.

Many extant appraisal schemes, especially those based upon mutually agreed goal setting, attempt to assist the subordinate in this respect by supplying him with some type of interview preparation form aimed at helping him to clarify his opinion of his own performance during the period under review and his aspirations for the future.

These vary substantially from scheme to scheme but, generally speaking, cover at least the subordinate's assessment of:

1 How effectively he feels that he has performed in his key results areas.
2 What barriers to more effective performance arose during the period under review and how these were dealt with.
3 Areas of work in which he feels that he has done particularly well or especially badly.
4 How he feels about the job in general and, in particular, those parts of it which he likes and/or dislikes most, and why.
5 Any parts of the job about which he has feelings of uncertainty or ambivalence.
6 What help he feels he needs from his boss and/or the organization in order to improve his performance.
7 His ambitions for future career development and what steps he is taking to achieve these, also what help he would like from his boss and/or the organization in this respect.

Many such interview preparation forms try to avoid the pitfall of creating unfounded hopes of advancement by including a statement to the effect that while the employee's views are sought and will be given serious consideration, it does not necessarily follow that they can be acted on.

Appraisal interviews should be held in private and it is up to the interviewer to arrange things in advance so that rapport, once established, is not destroyed by interruptions such as telephone calls and visitors. Even if the interviewee has had previous appraisal interviews, it is always useful for the interviewer to begin by outlining the purpose and format of the meeting, and this is especially important in the case of a first interview. A reasonably relaxed, friendly and supportive atmosphere is highly desirable, therefore the interviewer should temporarily abandon the citadel of his structural authority and come out from behind his desk to meet the subordinate more informally or even on neutral ground in another room.

Once the preliminaries of opening the interview have been completed, it is useful for the interviewer to get discussion started by encouraging the subordinate to talk about his job, his performance and himself. This is where the use of an interview preparation form can be of substantial help in concentrating the interviewee's attention on key issues and, by asking him to refer to it, the 'boss' can demonstrate that he really does want to know what the interviewee thinks. By gentle prompting and the use of open rather than closed questions, the employee can be led on to evaluation of his own performance and if he can be encouraged to articulate his own shortcomings, so much the better. The interviewer's assessment can be introduced into the conversation naturally and easily by way of commentary on what the interviewee has said, and it is by no means uncommon for managers to find that their subordinates are inclined to judge themselves and their performance more harshly than they would. Sometimes, however, negative points may be glossed over by the interviewee, or he may try to steer the conversation away from them by skilful manipulation of the discussion, and it is up to the interviewer to bring them out and deal with them in a constructive way, highlighting areas in which improvement may be required and how he intends to help his subordinate achieve it.

Through genuine praise for good work and building on the employee's strengths, with periodic pauses to sum up the discussion so far to ensure mutual understanding and agreement on the points talked about, the interviewer can move towards getting the interviewee to discuss his aspirations for the future and thus lead on to consideration of action plans to meet his training and development needs.

Throughout the interview, the superior should demonstrate his willingness to listen and to try to understand his subordinate's point of view, especially as regards sensitive issues. He should make it clear that his assessment, while arrived at after the most careful consideration, is not necessarily unalterable, and that he is prepared to change it in the light of new information. On the other hand, if a point is in dispute and if he remains convinced that his view is the right one, the interviewer should maintain his position and try to win the interviewee over to it by convincing argument.

Sometimes immediate agreement cannot be achieved, in which case the point at issue is best left open for discussion at a subsequent meeting after both parties have reconsidered their points of view. It may take several meetings to get agreement and in some instances complete agreement cannot be attained at all.

To ensure that he does not forget them, the interviewer will wish to make notes of the more important points as they arise. However, excessive note taking is off-putting to both parties and is likely to destroy rapport by creating an atmosphere of unnecessary formality and artificiality. Experienced interviewers usually take some notes and with practice this can be done quite unobtrusively. It is useful for the interviewer to have an edited extract from the performance appraisal and review forms to hand so that he may note his observations under the various headings, these outline notes later serving as a basis for compiling his report on the interview.

In some respects, ending an appraisal interview is more difficult than starting it, and the time to stop is when the interviewer feels that he has achieved his goals—or as many of them as he is likely to—and has put across to the interviewee the various points he intended to communicate at the outset or which may have arisen during the discussion. Ideally, the interviewee should have accepted these and be resolved to follow whatever course of action has been mapped out for him.

A short concluding summary by the interviewer of the things which he has undertaken to do, such as arranging for the interviewee to attend a training course or undertake some special assignment, should be followed by getting the interviewee to summarize the actions he has agreed, especially those which call for an improvement effort on his part.

No appraisal interview will ever run completely smoothly or go exactly according to plan. There will be disagreements, uncomfortable moments, and important points glossed over or missed. But with careful preparation and goodwill on both sides, the result should be better mutual understanding of each other's problems, a strengthening of relationships and increased motivation to work together more effectively.

Who Does the Appraising and Reviewing?

It is implicit in much of what has been said that in the greatest proportion of extant schemes appraisal, review, and interview are carried out in the first instance by the employee's immediate superior—the 'primary rater'. However, it is very common for the superior's superior to review and approve the primary rater's evaluation and interview comments. Such 'countersigning' acts as a defence against carelessness, bias, inexperience or lack of commitment on the part of the primary rater. It also creates an opportunity for the boss's boss to add comments of his own, where appropriate, usually in connection with career development and assessment of the employee's potential for future development in the organization.

In a smaller number of cases, usually in the public sector, it is the more senior 'countersigning officer' who conducts the appraisal interview. While this practice gives the interviewee an opportunity to discuss his performance and his future with someone more senior than his immediate superior, and there can be advantages in this, badly handled it may lead to problems for the employee's boss. A fairly typical selection of countersigning arrangements is shown in the following examples:

Performance appraisal carried out by

Signature: Date:

Position:

Employee's signature: Date:

Appraisal Form completed and attached/not required
(Delete as appropriate)

This performance appraisal has been seen and is approved by the appraiser's superior with the following amendments and/or comments:

Signature: Date:

Position:

FORM PA1

Figure 15.6   Example of a form used in an 'open' scheme

Figure 15.6 shows a form used in an 'open' scheme, the employee whose performance has been assessed being required to sign the appraisal document after it has been shown to him and discussed during the appraisal interview. Provision is made for the employee to respond to or comment on any item in the appraisal if he so wishes and a separate form is provided for this purpose. In this organization another form, which is discussed with but not shown to the employee, is used for the assessment of potential and this also requires the signatures of both the assessor and his immediate superior.

Manager's brief summary of main points discussed at appraisal interview:

Objectives agreed upon:

Statement of training needs and how it is proposed that these should be met:

Manager's signature: Date:

Employee's signature: Date:

Approved by Manager's immediate superior

Signature: Date:

Figure 15.7 Concluding section of performance appraisal and review document

Figure 15.7 shows the concluding section of a large company's performance appraisal and review document. This covers performance, potential, and proposals for training and career development. The form includes a brief report of the main points discussed at the appraisal interview and a note of the three or four principal objectives towards which superior and subordinate have agreed that the latter will work over the next twelve months. As in Figure 15.6 except for the section on potential, the employee sees his appraisal report and is given an opportunity to respond in writing to anything with which he disagrees.

Assessing Employee Potential

A recent survey (Industrial Market Research, 1980) of 335 companies revealed that over 75% of the respondent organizations fill their managerial vacancies from internal sources, a finding reinforced by an IPM report on executive redundancy (IPM, 1980).

In the current economic climate, increasingly fierce competition and accelerating technological advances are producing massive changes in the structure and balance of Britain's labour force. Redundancies, early retirement plans, staff rundown and non-replacement policies have become commonplace, with the progress of individuals in organizations severely restricted by available job opportunities. Manpower planning and managerial career planning have thus become more difficult and more necessary. More difficult in that the further into the future one attempts to forecast labour requirements the more unreliable the results are likely to be. As Bennison rightly points out:

> Who is to say that policies . . . developed now and thought to be appropriate to getting young inexperienced people into the management stream will still be appropriate in the conditions of 20 years from now [Bennison, 1979].

However glad employees may be to hold on to their jobs, understandable frustration at lack of advancement can limit creativity and productivity just when these qualities are most needed to combat competition in the marketplace. Realistic career planning and counselling is needed to convince staff that the organization still has plans for their future, although perhaps over a longer time scale than either they or their employers would wish.

Despite the continuing movement towards basing performance appraisal and review on objective criteria, the subjective opinions of employees' bosses still carry considerable weight when their potential is under consideration. Moreover, the way in which potential is often assessed is far from reassuring, especially since the managers required to make judgements which will vitally affect the future of both the individual and the organization may know little about the demands of jobs several grades above them in the hierarchy.

Analysis of a sample of typical appraisal documents from both private and public sector organizations show that they tend to ask raters to do one of three things:

1 *Answer general questions on potential such as:*
   (a) Comment on the individual's potential, highlighting significant strengths and weaknesses.

Performance Appraisal and Review 221

    (b) What are this employee's outstanding attributes? Are they fully utilized in the employee's present job? Has the employee any special attributes not previously mentioned?
    (c) What are the employee's most valuable and outstanding qualities (eg special talents, abilities, skills, ambitions)?

2 *Check boxes against 'degrees' of potential:*
    (a) Has the employee potential above his present job?
        Yes ☐
        Possibly ☐
        No ☐
    (b) Estimate the potential of the individual and give recommendations of any course of action for realizing this potential.
        Outstanding potential ☐
        Good potential ☐
        Some potential beyond present position ☐
        No apparent potential beyond present position ☐
        Undetermined ☐

3 *Check boxes against degree of potential but in relation to a number of specified criteria:*
    (a) His performance in the higher post is likely to be (check which)
        Very good ☐
        Fully acceptable ☐
        Not quite good enough ☐
        Unsatisfactory ☐
    (b) in that he would
        ☐ Be able to grasp the more complex problem and identify salient factors.
        ☐ Exercise sound judgement in weighing facts and deciding action.
        ☐ Readily accept personal responsibility within his own sphere both for making decisions and for implementing them.
        ☐ Bring a constructive approach to the work.
        ☐ Be capable of introducing new ideas.
        ☐ Have the ability to communicate competently in writing.
        ☐ Intelligently employ and interpret statistics and figures.
        ☐ Develop satisfactory relationships with his staff and colleagues and with other departments.
        ☐ Be resilient, equable and efficient when hard pressed.
        ☐ Control his staff efficiently and guide and develop them.
        ☐ Organize and coordinate the work of his group.
        ☐ Delegate work appropriately but remain in control.
        ☐ Represent his department with credit at meetings, conferences, etc.

This last example encourages the rater to think in terms of specific criteria, and is therefore preferable to the ones above it.

From a survey of the nation's top managers, Margerison (1979) reported that those who had reached the top attributed their success to the five factors shown in Figure 15.8, the high percentage response rates indicating their perceived importance.

	% response
An ability to work with a wide variety of people	78.5
Having a need to achieve results	75.0
Having early overall responsibility for important tasks	75.0
Having leadership experience early in one's career	74.0
Having a width of experience in many functions prior to the age of 35	68.0

Figure 15.8 *Factors for managerial success*

Source: Margerison [1979], p.27.

A major issue in the evaluation of potential is therefore *selecting the right people for advancement*, and the following examples of common current practice again show that a great deal of responsibility rests with the individual's immediate superior to make an accurate evaluation of his promotability. In almost all cases, these forms ask the rater to specify *when* employees should be promoted and in many instances also to indicate the type of promoted post thought to be most suitable.

1 Please state the type of jobs (regardless of availability) for which you believe the employee should be considered.

2 Please indicate timing by ticking as appropriate.
    Promotion — immediate   ☐
              — early   ☐
              — within three years   ☐

3 How suitable is he for promotion within the department or elsewhere? Tick the appropriate box even if you know of no obvious vacancy:

Overdue ☐
Ready now ☐
Not quite ready ☐
Far from ready ☐
Not promotable ☐

4   Does this employee have potential for further promotion:
    Yes ☐
    Not yet ☐
    Suitable in present position but should not be
    considered for further promotion ☐
    Not suitable in present position ☐

This last point raises the possibility of transfer to another job or, ultimately, of dismissal, and appears in a number of forms, eg:

5   Please indicate your view as to whether this employee:
    Should be considered for early promotion ☐
    Is recommended for promotion ☐
    Is not yet ready for promotion ☐
    Should not be promoted—has reached his ceiling ☐
    Is unsatisfactory in present rank ☐

Some forms look at the employee's qualifications for promotion, viz.

6   Please indicate your view as to whether this employee is:
    Highly qualified and would be expected to qualify
    for further promotion ☐
    Fully qualified ☐
    Has some qualifications for the higher duties but
    not qualified in all respects ☐
    Shows potential but needs further development to
    acquire necessary qualifications ☐
    Not at present qualified ☐

and others attempt to consider promotion from the point of view of the duties involved in a higher post:

7   Is now capable of performing the duties of the next higher post:
    (check which)
    Satisfactorily ☐
    Very well ☐
    Exceptionally well ☐

8   Is not at present capable of performing the duties of the next higher
    post but is: (check which)
    Likely to qualify in time ☐
    Unlikely to qualify ☐

In all of these examples except one, the assessment of potential and promotability is made on the same form and by the same rater(s) as appraisal of performance, therefore to some extent at least, the latter must influence the rater's judgement when dealing with potential and promotability. However, it is now widely accepted that while appraisal of performance against previously agreed goals does produce useful assessments of how well, or otherwise, an employee is doing in his *present* job, it has much less relevance when it comes to attempting to predict how he will behave in a *future* promoted post.

Over the years a number of well-known (and in some instances well-validated) techniques have been devised or developed in continuing attempts to solve the problems of assessing potential, yet all the evidence points to the fact that these are little used in British organizations. Thus Gill (1977) reported the results shown in Figure 15.9

Method	% response
Assessment centres	4
Psychological assessment by external consultants	4
Psychological assessment by internal specialists	7
None of the above	83

Figure 15.9   Methods used in the identification of management potential (N=236)

Source: Gill (1977).

adding: 'It is clear from the table that use of relatively more "scientific" methods of assessing managerial potential is very limited. In particular, it is interesting to note that assessment centres do not appear to have gained in popularity since our 1973 study when we found only 3.6% (of companies) which had experience of this particular technique'.

The Stewarts (1979) commented in similar vein that 'so few British organizations treat the problems of assessing potential with the serious effort they deserve', adding that 'small efforts in the right direction may be rewarded with great improvements in job performance'. From the statistics provided by Gill and others it would appear that the most important and promising 'small efforts in the right direction' are likely to include psychological testing and variations on the assessment centre theme.

Somewhat more encouraging (albeit earlier) data on the use of psychological testing is provided by Sneath, Thakur and Medjuck (1976) who report on the extent and level of test usage as shown in Figure 15.10. They also report that further analysis of the phrase 'any other purposes' shows that the tests are used mainly for assessing the training needs of individuals and for internal transfer of employees.

	Yes, all the time %	Yes sometimes %	No %
For initial selection of applicants	7	62	31
For promotion	4	28	67
For any other purpose	11	25	64

Figure 15.10 Use of psychological tests (Sample size=281)

Source: Sneath, Thakur and Medjuck (1976).

There are a large number of psychological instruments designed to test for such human attributes as intelligence, aptitudes, abilities, attitudes and even personality. Properly used by competent practitioners who are skilled in selecting the appropriate tests for particular purposes and, above all, in interpreting the results—usually in conjunction with additional data from other tests, personal interviews and individual histories—well validated psychological tests are useful aids to decision-making on potential. The statistical probability of the accuracy of the findings is also usually stated, although these must be interpreted with caution.

In commercial practice, the results of psychological tests are most commonly used to establish a 'cut-off point' below which the performance of an individual being considered for a particular post is regarded as unacceptable, rather than as an accurate predictor of success. The idea of fitting measured personality profiles to identified job requirements is far from being in general use.

Few organizations employ full-time skilled testers, although some 'buy in' the necessary expertise from universities and elsewhere as required. Testing is time-consuming and expensive, although a reasonable success rate, or even the avoidance of some costly mistakes, may well justify the expenditure of both time and money.

However, if test performance is used as a criterion for promotion, it should not preclude some consideration of successful current job performance, even though the reliability of the latter as an accurate predictor of future success is limited. Otherwise, people may feel that interviewing skills and doing well in tests are more important to their future development than hard, effective work in their present jobs. While talents and abilities which are unsuspected or even overlooked can be brought to the attention of higher management as a result of using well chosen, well administered tests, it is important to note that the results provide only *one* source of evidence for determining future career patterns.

Assessment Centres

The first industrial assessment centres, notably those set up by the American Telephone and Telegraph Company in the 1950s were off the job locations in which programmes designed to identify managerial potential through the simultaneous evaluation of several individuals by a number of trained observers were carried out.

Neither the concept nor many of the techniques involved are new, having originated during the second World War when British, American and German psychologists first started using multiple assessment methods in an effort to improve success rate in the selection of candidates for commissioned rank. After the war, the civil service adapted the method for its selection board (CSSB), the main instrument for selecting officers capable of rising to the highest levels in the service. With few exceptions, however, British industry displayed little interest, and it fell to AT & T, IBM, Sears Roebuck, General Electric and a number of other American corporations to develop their own variations on this theme. While a few leading British companies introduced programmes which they had developed themselves from the AT & T model, or imported an American Management Association 'package' marketed through Management Centre Europe, real interest in this country has never been very great.

Today, the term *management assessment programme* is more accurate, since the so-called assessment centre is, in fact, a *process* which uses a variety of evaluative techniques such as simulation exercises, psychological tests, management games, group discussions, individual and group interviews, and feedback sessions aimed at improving the selection and development of managers. As such it may or may not be conducted off the job. It is the procedure and not the location in which it is carried out that is important.

In general, the techniques and exercises employed can be divided into two main categories—group and individual—and are likely to include at least some of the following:

1 *Group exercises*
 Leaderless group discussions in which each of the half dozen or so participants is required to attempt to convince the others to accept his ideas on how to solve a problem, often one related to the work situation. A participant is considered to have failed if he cannot get his ideas accepted by the group, while the group will fail if they cannot agree among themselves on one solution.
 Multi-disciplinary task force exercises. Here the participants are allocated roles as members of a multi-disciplinary top management committee (each member of which has a vested functional interest in the outcome) charged with choosing between several conflicting courses of action to solve a difficult company problem. They must agree on a common solution and present the case for it to the 'managing director'.
 A negotiating exercise in which some members take the part of the firm's management and others act as full-time trade union officers and shop stewards. This can be made very realistic and calls for the deployment of considerable social and negotiating skills on the part of participants.
 Preparation of a strategic plan. Working in sub-groups representing different parts of an organization, or sometimes separate organizations within a group, participants are required to prepare a long-range strategic plan for their own activities based on financial and other information supplied to them. The sub-groups then meet in plenary session to agree the overall corporate plan for the organization as a whole.

2 *Individual exercises*
 An in-basket exercise in which participants, working under strict time constraints, must deal individually and unaided with a score or more of items (ranging from routine matters to emergency situations) from a top manager's in-tray, deciding action, allocating priorities, delegating tasks to subordinates, etc.
 An exercise in oral expression. Participants are required to prepare and deliver a short talk either on a subject of their own choice or on one allocated to them by the organizers of the programme. Performance is judged by effectiveness of delivery, quality of content, level of interest created, organization of material, and ability to persuade others to their points of view.
 An individual written exercise. Not only is this used to judge the participant's ability to express himself in writing, but also it is often used as a vehicle for a statement of career and life goals. In the latter case, participants are asked to describe their career to date,

indicating achievements and the extent to which these resulted from deliberate planning and execution of a personal career programme. They are also asked to state future goals and the means by which they hope to achieve them.

The range, purpose and degree of relevance of the various exercises and other techniques which may be used in a management assessment programme are well illustrated in Bell's comprehensive grid which is reproduced in Figure 15.11 (Bell, 1977).

Dimension	In-Tray	Interview	Mngt. Game	Leaderless Group	Fact Finding and Decision Making	Autobiography	Personality Questionnaire	Self Assessment	Leadership Exercise	Personal Talk
Oral Expression	1	1	1	1	2				2	1
Written Expression	2					1		1	3	
Numeracy	3		1		1		2		3	
Impact		1	1	2	2	1		1	1	1
Stress Tolerance	2	2	2	2	1				1	
Sensitivity		2	2	2		3	1	2	2	3
Initiative		3	1	2			1		1	2
Planning	1	3	2		1				2	3
Delegation	1		3						1	
Decisiveness	1	2		2	1		1		2	
Tenacity		2	1	2		2	2		2	3
Tolerance			1	2		2	1		3	

The key indicates those exercises which usually generate behavioural information relevant to a particular dimension.
1 = Very high relevance. 2 = High relevance. 3 = Some relevance.

Figure 15.11   Bell's grid for results of assessment tests

Source: Bell (1977).

Most programmes of the type described take from two to four days to complete depending on content and administrative arrangements. There are usually up to about 12 participants on each programme, some of whom may be self-selected to the extent that their firms invite them to apply without guaranteeing acceptance, while others are chosen as a result of regular performance appraisal and review.

Assessors, often in the ratio of 1 : 2 or 3 participants, are normally line managers from positions several grades higher in the organization than the participants. They have intimate knowledge of the jobs for which participants are likely to be considered in future and receive special training in assessment and counselling techniques at the beginning of the programme, undergoing some of the tests and exercises themselves as part of the learning process. In this way an organization operating regular assessment programmes can soon build up a panel of competent assessors to draw upon. The assessors are coached and supported throughout the programme by skilled company organizers who specialize in the management of the scheme, often assisted by a professional consultant from outside the organization.

The time available is frequently divided about equally between assessing participants as they work through the various tests and exercises, and giving them feedback in counselling sessions with the assessors and members of the core staff, the aim being to ensure that each participant receives an evaluation of his performance and skilled practical assistance in drawing up a plan for his own future development. As far as the individual is concerned, the accent is on development, while the performance data accumulated will become part of the information upon which future promotion decisions will be based.

Hart and Thompson (1979), argue that for companies in a 'stable' (ie very little or no growth) situation, career development has become a much more pressing issue than the selection of managers. They also claim that there is increasing evidence that, used for selection purposes, some assessment centres are creating serious problems for the organizations concerned, mainly because of excessive and unfounded reliance on results and faulty methods of selecting people to attend. However, as research and experiment combine to overcome the problems involved, it is likely that organizations looking for managerial talent will come to view the cost in time, effort and money well spent, and that the process will be more widely used, particularly in view of the crude subjectivity clearly apparent in other methods of evaluating employee potential.

Management Development

Despite current lack of promotional opportunities, it is important to ensure positive follow-up after appraisal and appraisal interviewing to create development programmes for staff.

In many typical appraisal forms, assessors are asked not only to comment on their subordinates' potential, but also to recommend positive development action plans chosen from a wide range of existing conventional techniques and processes. These include personal coaching by the superior in defined aspects of the subordinate's job; giving the employee extended experience in his present job; creating opportunities for him to 'act up' by deputizing for his superior; undertaking project work; reading and private study under supervision; broadening his experience through membership of committees, working parties or task forces, or secondment to another department, plant, associated company, technical college or university.

Nor should the employee's own views on his personal development be ignored. Many extant schemes of performance appraisal and review include interview preparation forms on which the individual is encouraged to state jobs for which he would like to be considered, his preferences and/or reservations regarding mobility and the timing of any future transfer, and whether he is actively seeking a change of function or location.

Every day in the course of their normal duties managers are, in fact, being developed and trained; sometimes consciously by their superiors, much more often without even being aware of it simply as part of doing their regular jobs. Effective management development goes far beyond merely putting staff through some of the types of activity noted above or sending them away on courses. It requires an approach in which manpower planning, performance appraisal and review, assessment of potential, appraisal interviewing, management development and organizational development are all integrated in a cohesive, well-planned programme through which suitably motivated managers can be helped to develop themselves.

Salary Review

Chapter 14 dealt in depth with the various issues involved in establishing salary bands and methods of progression through them, including the relationship to performance. While consideration of appraising and reviewing performance would be incomplete without some reference to salary review, only a few salient points need to be outlined here.

In the United States, performance appraisal and review has always been closely linked with salary review. Thus, in 1974, a survey by the Bureau of National Affairs indicated that 85% of respondents used performance appraisal as a basis for decisions on salary, and by 1977 Locher and Teel confirmed that this was still its most widespread purpose. While the position in America—and in many American owned concerns elsewhere in the world—is much the same today, British opinion and practice is very different. According to the IPM survey quoted earlier, by 1977 the use of performance appraisal and review to assess increases or new levels in salary came last in the list of purposes reported by respondents, only 39% including it as compared with 54.6% in 1973, when it was the penultimate item in the list.

Nevertheless, there are cases which, because they appear to be somewhat exceptional, are extremely interesting. Gill reports that of ten organizations visited as part of the 1977 IPM survey, only one, a company with over 20,000 employees, was using appraisal mainly for determining salary increments. Annual review determined progression on incremental scales, increments being withheld or doubled as considered appropriate in the light of performance reports. Having been in operation for over 22 years, the system, an open one in which appraisees can record any disagreement in writing, has become almost traditional in this highly unionized situation.

For a variety of reasons, including trade union opposition, many contemporary British managers are either unwilling or unable to use remuneration linked with performance appraisal as a means of rewarding or controlling subordinates. First, over the years, especially in the public sector, the mere passage of time (ie service) rather than merit has become established as a main criterion for upward progression on negotiated incremental salary scales. This practice, has become so entrenched that, far from being able to award an increase in pay for good work, some managers now find themselves having to prove inadequate performance—in itself no easy task—before they can withhold one.

A second factor is the effect of successive government pay policies, aimed at curbing inflation, under which wage and salary increases are restricted to cost of living awards hammered out between employers and unions at national level during the ritual annual pay round. Under the last Labour administration, merit increases beyond this level were only acceptable as part of self-financing productivity agreements, an arrangement not infrequently abused by the use of bogus schemes designed to circumvent the regulations.

Thirdly, these considerations aside, leading British opinion is that performance and potential review should be kept separate from salary review, and there is much evidence to show that such separation is widely practised. Thus, reporting on civil service study, Anstey, Fletcher and Walker contend: 'The appraisal scheme should not be linked too closely with merit ratings for pay purposes. If trade unions suspect that the appraisal scheme is an indirect means of assessing the pay that various staff merit, they are likely to oppose the scheme'. (Anstey et.al. 1976).

Such opposition is linked with the long-held trade union view that individuals doing the same kind of work should receive the same remuneration.

Fourthly, in addition to practical considerations such as the possibility of trade union opposition and the effects of government pay policies, linking performance and potential review with salary review is likely to prove counter productive when attempting to communicate an evaluation and an improvement or development action plan to an employee during an appraisal interview.

As pointed out at the beginning of this chapter, personnel know very well that their chances of career advancement, and possibly also their salaries, will be influenced by how they are assessed by their superiors. Dealing with performance and potential review at one point in time and salary review at another—intervals vary, but three to six months would appear to be the norm—will not prevent the employee from drawing his own conclusions regarding the correlation between them. Nevertheless, if performance, potential and salary review are all dealt with at the same interview, there is a strong probability, especially in the current economic climate, that the employee's attention will be dominated by the latter. There will be a sense of relief, perhaps elation, if a salary increase is forthcoming, and of disappointment, probably resentment, if it is withheld. Either way, the psychological effect will be much the same, unwillingness or inability on the part of the employee to listen to and accept whatever is said concerning his performance and potential, thus defeating the whole object of the exercise which is to help the individual improve his performance, realize his full potential and enhance his value to the organization.

References and Further Reading

Anderson, G.C., *Performance Appraisal in Theory and Practice*, Glasgow, Strathclyde Business School Working Paper no. 8002. October, 1980.

Anstey, E., Fletcher, C.A. and Walker, J., *Staff Appraisal and Development*, London, Allen and Unwin, 1976.

Bass, B.M. and Ryterband, E.C., *Organizational Psychology (Second Edition)*, Boston, Mass., Allyn and Bacon, 1979.

Bennison, M., 'A New Approach to Career Management', *Personnel Management*, Volume 11, no. 9. September, 1979.

Bureau of National Affairs Inc., *Management Performance Appraisal Programs*, Washington D.C., Bureau of National Affairs, 1974.

Fournies, F.F., *Management Performance Appraisal: A National Study*, Somerville N.J.: F.F. Fournies Associates, 1973.

Gill, D., *Appraising Performance*, London, Institute of Personnel Management Information Report 25, 1977.

Gill, D., Ungerson, B. and Thakur, M., *Performance Appraisal in Perspective*, London, Institute of Personnel Management Information Report 14, 1973.

Hart, G.L. and Thompson, P.H., 'Assessment Centres: for Selection or Development?', *Organization Dynamics*, Volume 7, no. 4, Spring, 1979.

Industrial Market Research Ltd., *Selecting Managers—How British Industry Recruits*, BIM Management Survey Report 49, London, BIM and IPM, 1980.

IPM. *Executive Redundancy*, London, Institute of Personnel Management Information Report 30, 1980.

Locher, A.H. and Teel, K.S., 'Performance Appraisal—A Survey of Current Practices', *Personnel Journal*, Volume 56, no. 5. May, 1977.

Margerison, C., 'Highway to Managerial Success', *Personnel Management*, Volume 11, no. 8. August, 1979.

Muczyk, J.P., 'Dynamics and Hazards of Management by Objectives Applications', in Golembewski, R.T., *Approaches to Planned Change—Part 2*, New York, Marcel Dekker, 1979.

Randell, G.A., Packard, P.M.A., Shaw, R.L. and Slater, A.J., *Staff Appraisal*. (Revised Edition), London, Institute of Personnel Management, 1974.

Reif, W.E. and Bassford, G., 'What MBO Really Is: Results Require a Complete Programme', in Huseman, R.C. and Carroll, A.B., *Readings in Organizational Behaviour: Dimensions of Management Actions*. Boston, Mass., Allyn and Bacon, 1979.

Schick, M.E., 'The Refined Performance Evaluation Monitoring System: Best of Both Worlds', *Personnel Journal*, Volume 59, no. 1. January, 1980.

Singer, E.J., *Effective Management Coaching*, London, Institute of Personnel Management, 1974.

Sneath, F., Thakur, M. and Medjuck, B., *Testing People at Work*, London, Institute of Personnel Management Information Report 24, 1976.

Steers, R.M. and Porter, L.W., *Motivation and Work Behaviour (Second Edition)*, New York, McGraw-Hill, 1979.

Stewart, V. and Stewart, A., 'How to Spot the High Flyers', *Personnel Management*, Volume 11, no. 9. September, 1979.

Torrington, D. and Chapman, J., *Personnel Management*. London, Prentice-Hall International, 1979.

16

The Hay Guide-chart Profile Method

W F Younger

Meeting the Needs of Employers and Employees

Wages and salaries have two aspects. To the wage and salary earners they are a receipt or income. To the employing organization wages and salaries are cost items from which an effective return should be obtained. In order to match the needs of both employer and employee a wage and salary structure must satisfy two main requirements. It must provide pay at levels which allow the employing concern to attract and to retain the number and quality of people it needs and also provide for pay differentials which reflect the differences in relative importance of jobs to the employer and which are acceptable to the employees. The structure and the method of payment should also encourage employees to develop their capacities and their performance in ways which will be of benefit to themselves and to the employing organization.

These requirements are met when the pay structure is based on:

1. Internal logic. There must be a means of establishing the relative worth of jobs which is relevant and understandable and pay must reflect that relativity.
2. External competitiveness. Pay for jobs in the structure must bear a sensible relationship to the payments made for jobs of similar content and size in other organizations.

The Hay system of salary and wage management establishes internal logic through use of the Hay guide-chart and profile method of job evaluation. It establishes market relationships by comparing the remuneration paid for jobs of similar content and evaluated size in different employing organizations.

Development of the Hay Guide-chart Profile Method

The guide-chart profile method has evolved over a period of about 40 years. First based on a simple factor rating system created by Edward N. Hay of Philadelphia it has been refined and developed as a result of experiment and experience by Edward N. Hay Associates in whom the copyright is vested, and in the UK by HAY-MSL.

The factor rating system was built on three main elements:

1 Know-how. The total of the knowledge, skills and experience, however they may have been acquired, which are necessary for satisfactory job performance.
2 Problem-solving. The type and the degree of thinking required in a job for analyzing, evaluating, creating, reasoning and arriving at conclusions.
3 Accountability. The answerability in a job for action and for the consequences of those actions.

These three main elements of know-how, problem-solving and accountability have been subdivided, in the light of experience gained in employing the method in various types of organization.

Know-how has three subelements:

1 Technical, professional, manual, theoretical and scientific know-how.
2 Managerial know-how—the requirement for planning, organizing, monitoring and controlling resources and the degree to which this involves coordination of competing and divergent objectives or strategies.
3 Human relations know-how.

Problem-solving has two subelements:

1 The environment in which the thinking takes place, ranging from routine to completely unstructured.
2 The challenge presented by the thinking to be done; ranging from repetitive to 'blue sky' creativity.

Accountability has three subelements:

1 The degree of discretion or freedom to act
2 The value of the areas affected by the job
3 The directness of the impact of the job.

In the early stages of development of the system each job being examined was ranked under each factor with the other jobs with which it was being compared. Rating of relative values was introduced by use of a four-step scale. One step difference was considered to exist in know-how if after careful consideration the assessors sensed a just discernible difference in this factor between two jobs which they were examining.

Two steps were said to exist where a clear difference was sensed. Three steps or more existed where there was an obvious difference even without detailed study. No measurable difference existed and the know-how requirement was considered to be the same in two jobs where first one job seemed to have a greater requirement and then the other.

The step system of measurement was later converted to a geometric scale of numbers, with a ratio of approximately 15% between each step in the scale. A geometric scale was used because a characteristic of measurement by human judgement is that 'in comparing objects we perceive not the actual difference between them but the ratio of this difference to the magnitude of the two objects compared', ie Weber's law of psychometric perception (Garrett, 1930). Thus in comparing jobs the difference we perceive is related to the size of the jobs themselves. This aspect of perception is also generally recognized in salary practice when an individual is considering the amount of money he expects for promotion to a job of higher responsibility. A difference of £600 might attract the £4 000-a-year job holder, it would not attract the £20 000-a-year salary earner but £3 000 might; in each case a difference of 15%.

Hay units geometric scale	Step value	Percentage increase
200	1	+15
230	2	+15
264	3	+15
304	4	+15
350	5	+15
400	6	+15

Figure 16.1 Relationship between numbering pattern, step value and percentage increase (copyright HAY-MSL 1974)

The concepts of step differences and a geometric scale were brought together by assigning a number arbitrarily to the lowest step in the scale and building up in 15% steps from that number. Thus if the smallest know-how content in a series of job was assigned the number 200 then jobs with increasing know-how steps value 1:2:3:4 and so on would have know-how measurements of 230:264:304:350: etc, each number being a 15% increase above the previous one (see Figure 16.1). Problem-solving and accountability factors were ranked and rated in a similar way; the measured size of each job being the sum of its know-how, problem-solving and accountability scores.

Guide-chart construction was the next step in the development of the Hay system. After several thousand jobs had been evaluated on the factor comparison method it was seen that similar semantic definitions could be applied to groups of steps in the scale of each job content factor. This made it possible to establish a visual representation of evaluation results on a grid system or guide-chart. A separate guide-chart was developed for each factor: know-how, problem-solving and accountability. Skeletons of these are shown in Figures 16.2, 16.3 and 16.4, with step values inserted in the first know-how cells for illustrative purposes, and the measurement scales given below.

The size and range of a guide-chart is obviously determined by the size, complexity and structure of the organization in which jobs are being measured, but ever since the introduction of the first guide-charts, evaluators using them have in effect been evaluating jobs relative to all jobs which have been evaluated in the past. The guide-charts also have the advantage of providing visual guidelines and a semantic framework which help evaluators in their judgements about jobs. In practice the guide-charts have also proved to be helpful in considering the design of individual jobs and the interrelationship between jobs in an organization. For example, there should be some realistic balance between the know-how requirement built into a job and the degree of accountability it carries, otherwise we have power exercised from ignorance, or deep know-how frustrated through lack of authority (accountability) to get things done.

The profiling aspect of the Hay guide-chart profile system refers to the relationship between know-how, problem-solving and accountability requirements in a job. The profiling assessment is made as a separate practical judgement of the proportion of know-how, problem-solving and accountability which make up the total job, expressed as percentages. This profile assessment is then compared with the measurements made on the guide-charts as a check on evaluation judgements. It is used as a check on the relativities between the know-how score and the problem-solving and accountability scores for the job. A number of jobs have fairly clear profiles, eg a sales manager's job is likely to be heavily weighted toward accountability and a basic research worker's job toward problem-solving. Many skilled craft jobs are most heavily know-how jobs. Although some jobs are not so clear-cut in their profiles, experience indicates that, when a team of evaluators understands a job, each of them have little difficulty in making a reliable profile judgement, consistent with other team members. Disagreement about a job profile usually means disagreement about the content of the job being measured or vagueness about job content.

Installing and Using the System in Practice

Their own wage or salary is a sensitive subject for most people; they will naturally resist arbitrary change and be suspicious of any arrangement which purports to put a value on their job. Explaining to people in advance what is contemplated is therefore a sensible, reasonable and necessary first step in introducing any change in a payment system. Involvement of people including employee representatives who are knowledgeable about the jobs being considered and who have the respect of the job holders is also highly desirable when jobs are being analyzed and evaluated.

After the initial communications a series of benchmark jobs is usually selected for measurement. These jobs should provide a good representative cross-section both horizontally and vertically through the organization.

Jobs can only be measured properly if they are understood; and jobs can only be understood if there is also an understanding of the environment in which they exist. Two jobs of apparently similar content will differ in terms of pressures and pace if they exist in different management climates with different management styles.

Job descriptions will normally be used to provide understanding about the benchmark jobs. Such descriptions will deal with the essence of the jobs; their purpose; why they exist; the tactical or strategical matters with which they must deal; their influence on the overall objects or policy of the organization, or department, or section within which they exist. These benchmark job descriptions are usually prepared by trained analysts after discussion with job holders. The descriptions are agreed by the job holders, verified by their immediate superiors and supplemented by the evaluation committee. The environmental climate is usually assessed by the evaluation committee and outside observers.

Job evaluation takes place after the job analysis has been completed and evaluation is best carried out by a committee whose members have knowledge of the organization, so that concensus judgement can be reached by knowledgeable individuals, together with an individual who has knowledge and experience of the guide-chart measuring instrument.

Each job is first profiled by members of the evaluation committee and profiles compared. Then each job is rated for know-how, problem-solving and accountability on the guide-charts. The derived profile from the guide-chart measurement is compared with the agreed initial profile as a check on judgements. After a number of jobs have been rated the results are compared to check for any real or apparent inconsistencies (or 'sore thumbs') which would indicate either false rating or significant departure from previous perceptions of relative job values.

The final result of the benchmark job evaluations will be a list of the

Definition: Know-How is the sum total of every kind of skill, however acquired, required for acceptable job performance. This sum total which comprises the over-all "savvy" has 3 dimensions—the requirements for:

* Practical procedures, specialized techniques, and scientific disciplines.
** Know-How of integrating and harmonizing the diversified functions involved in managerial situations occurring in operating, supporting, and administrative fields. The Know-How may be exercised consultatively (about management) as well as executively and involves in some combination the areas of organizing, planning, executing, controlling and evaluating.
*** Active, practising, face to face skills in the area of human relationships.

Illustrative
c
Hay Guide Chart
for Evaluating
KNOW-HOW

Hay-MSL Ltd. London

Measuring Know-How: Know-How has both scope (variety) and depth (thoroughness). Thus, a job may require some knowledge about a lot of things, or a lot of knowledge about a few things. The total Know-How is the combination of scope and depth. This concept makes practical the comparison and weighing of the total Know-How content of different jobs in terms of: "How much knowledge about how many things".

** Managerial Know-How

	I. None or Minimal			II. Related			III. Diverse			IV. Broad			V.		
*** Human Relations Skills →	1.	2.	3.	1.	2.	3.	1.	2.	3.	1.	2.	3.	1.	2.	3.
A. PRIMARY:	1	2	3	3	4	5										A
B. ELEMENTARY VOCATIONAL:	2	3	4	4	5	6										B
C. VOCATIONAL:	3	4	5	5	6	7										C
D. ADVANCED VOCATIONAL:	4	5	6													D
E. BASIC TECHNICAL-SPECIALIZED:	5	6	7													E
F. SEASONED TECHNICAL-SPECIALIZED:	6	7	8													F
G. TECHNICAL-SPECIALIZED MASTERY:	7	8	9													G
H. PROFESSIONAL MASTERY:																

Practical Procedures / Specialized Techniques / Scientific Disciplines

Human Relations Skills

1. Basic: Ordinary courtesy and effectiveness in dealing with others.
2. Important: Understanding, influencing, and/or serving people are important, but not critical considerations.
3. Critical: Alternative or combined skills in understanding, selecting, developing and motivating people are important in the highest degree.

Measurement Scales for Know-How

SKILL–EDUCATION–TRAINING

[Each of these degrees is sub-divided into three levels]

Jobs requiring:

A Education to post-primary level.
B Practised in standard work routines and/or use of simple equipment and machines.
C Procedural or systematic efficiency and use of specialized equipment.
D Specialized skill gained by on-the-job experience or through part professional qualification.
E Understanding of theoretical principles normally gained through professional qualification or through a detailed grasp of involved practices and procedures.
F Seasoned proficiency in a highly specialized field, gained through experience built on theories or a broad and deep understanding of complex practices.
G Mastery of principles, practices and theories gained through wide experience and/or special development.
H Unique command of principles, theories and practices.

BREADTH OF MANAGEMENT KNOW-HOW

I Non or minimal—performance or supervision of jobs which have closely specified objectives.
II Homogeneous—integration of operations which are homogeneous in nature and objective, and coordination with associated functions.
III Heterogeneous—integration or coordination of diverse functions or sub-functions in a company; or inter-company coordination of a tactical function.
IV Broad—integration of the major functions in an operating company; or group-wide coordination of a strategic function affecting policy formation.
V Total—the management of strategic functions and policy formation.

HUMAN RELATIONS

Each degree of management know-how is also subdivided into three according to required *Human relations skills*:

1 Basic—ordinary courtesy and effectiveness in dealing with others.
2 Important—understanding and influencing people, important but not over-riding considerations.
3 Over-riding—skills in developing and motivating people are over-riding considerations.

Figure 16.2 Hay guide-chart for evaluating know-how

Definition: Problem Solving is the original, "self-starting" thinking required by the job for analyzing, evaluating, creating, reasoning, arriving at and making conclusions. To the extent that thinking is circumscribed by standards, covered by precedents, or referred to others, Problem Solving is diminished, and the emphasis correspondingly is on Know-How. Problem Solving has two dimensions:
* The environment in which the thinking takes place.
** The challenge presented by the thinking to be done.

Illustrative
©
Hay Guide Chart
for Evaluating
PROBLEM SOLVING

Hay-MSL Ltd. London

Measuring Problem Solving: Problem Solving measures the intensity of the mental process which employs Know-How to: (1) identify, (2) define, and (3) resolve a problem. "You think with what you know". This is true of even the most creative work . . . The raw material of any thinking is knowledge of facts, principles and means; ideas are put together from something already there. Therefore, Problem Solving is treated as a percentage utilization of Know-How.

Thinking Environment

Thinking guided and circumscribed by:

	1. Repetitive	2. Patterned	3. Interpolative	4. Adaptive	5. Unchartered
A. STRICT ROUTINE:					A
B. ROUTINE:					B
C. SEMI-ROUTINE:					C
D. STANDARDIZED:					D
E. CLEARLY DEFINED:					E
F. BROADLY DEFINED:					F
G. GENERALLY DEFINED:					G
H. ABSTRACTLY DEFINED:					H

** Thinking Challenge

Problem Solving Measurement Scales

[Each of these degrees is divided into two sub-degrees]

THINKING ENVIRONMENT (8 DEGREES)

Thinking within:

A Detailed rules and/or rigid supervision.
B Standard instructions and/or continuous close supervision.
C Well-defined procedures, somewhat diversified and/or supervised.
D Substantially diversified established company procedures, and general supervision.
E Clearly defined company policies, principles and specific objectives under readily available direction.
F Broad policies and objectives, under general direction.
G General policies, principles and goals under guidance.
H Business philosophy and/or principles controlling human affairs.

THINKING CHALLENGE (5 DEGREES)

I Repetitive – identical situations requiring solution by simple choice of things learned.
II Patterned – similar situations requiring solution by discriminating choice of things learned.
III Variable – differing situations requiring searching, finding and selecting solutions within the area of things learned.
IV Adaptive – situations requiring analytical, interpretive and/or constructive thinking. Judgement is required.
V Creative – novel or non-recurring pathfinding situations requiring the development of new concepts and imaginative approaches.

Figure 16.3 Hay guide-chart for evaluating problem-solving

Definition: Accountability is the answerability for an action and for the consequences of that action. It is the measured effect of the job on end results. It has three dimensions in the following order of importance:
* Freedom to Act—the degree of personal or procedural control and guidance, as defined in the left-hand column below.
** Job Impact on End Results—as defined at upper right.
*** Magnitude—indicated by the general size (measured in £'s) most clearly or primarily affected by the job (on an annual basis).

Illustrative
©
Hay Guide Chart
for Evaluating
ACCOUNTABILITY

Hay-MSL Ltd. London

Impact of Job on End Results
Remote: Informational, recording, or incidental services for use by others in relation to some important end result.
Contributory: Interpretive, advisory, or facilitating services, for use by others in taking action.
Shared: Participating with others (except own subordinates and superiors), within or outside the organizational unit, in taking action.
Primary: Controlling impact on end results, where shared accountability of others is subordinate.

* Freedom to Act   *** Magnitude (annual basis)

** Impact →

	(1) Very Small or Indeterminate				(2) Small £				(3) Medium £				(4) Large £				(5) Very Large £			
	R	C	S	P	R	C	S	P	R	C	S	P	R	C	S	P	R	C	S	P
A. PRESCRIBED:																				
B. CONTROLLED:																				
C. STANDARDIZED:																				
D. GENERALLY REGULATED:																				
E. DIRECTED:																				
F. ORIENTED DIRECTION:																				
G. BROAD GUIDANCE:																				

A
B
C
D
E
F
G

Measurement Scales for Accountability

FREEDOM TO ACT

These jobs are subject to:

A Prescribed—direct and detailed instructions, and close supervision.
B Controlled—established work routines and close supervision.
C Standardized—standardized practices and procedures, general work instructions and supervision of progress and results.
D Generally regulated—practices and procedures which have clear precedents.
E Directed—broad practice and procedures covered by functional precedents and policies and managerial direction.
F Oriented direction—functional policies and goals, and general managerial direction.
G Senior guidance—inherently and primarily to direct top management guidance.
H Ownership guidance—only to ownership review and public recreation.

MAGNITUDE OF ACCOUNTABILITY

The 'dimension' *Magnitude* of Accountability is divided into four degrees *Very Small, Small, Medium* and *Large* to each of which is assigned a number representing a money value of that which is at risk or is affected by the decisions made in the jobs under Freedom to Act.

Each of these Magnitudes is divided into four sub-degrees according to the way in which the decision-maker plays a part in the doing of his job. In other words an expression of shared responsibility, thus:

1 REMOTE—giving information on other incidental services for use by others involved in the action.
2 CONTRIBUTORY—interpretory, advisory or facilitating services to those involved in the action.
3 SHARED—participating with others (except superiors and subordinates) in taking action.
4 PRIME—wholly responsible, with little or no shared responsibility.

Figure 16.4 Hay guide-chart for evaluating accountability

jobs in rank order with ratings against the know-how, problem-solving and accountability factors and a total 'score' for each job together with a profile. The remaining jobs in the organization can then be 'slotted in' relative to the evaluated size of each of the benchmark jobs.

With the jobs now evaluated the organization's existing pay levels can be plotted against the measured value of its jobs in the form of a scattergram to give a visual illustration of its existing pay structure (Figure 16.5). If a line is now drawn through the scatter of plottings the shape and degree of slope of the line will indicate the extent of 'logic' and 'equity' in the existing pay structure.

Although an evaluation exercise of this kind enables a consistent internal pay structure to be built, another step is necessary to provide comparability with the external market. This step is the comparison of one organization's pay structure with that of others so that pay for evaluated job content at any point can be compared.

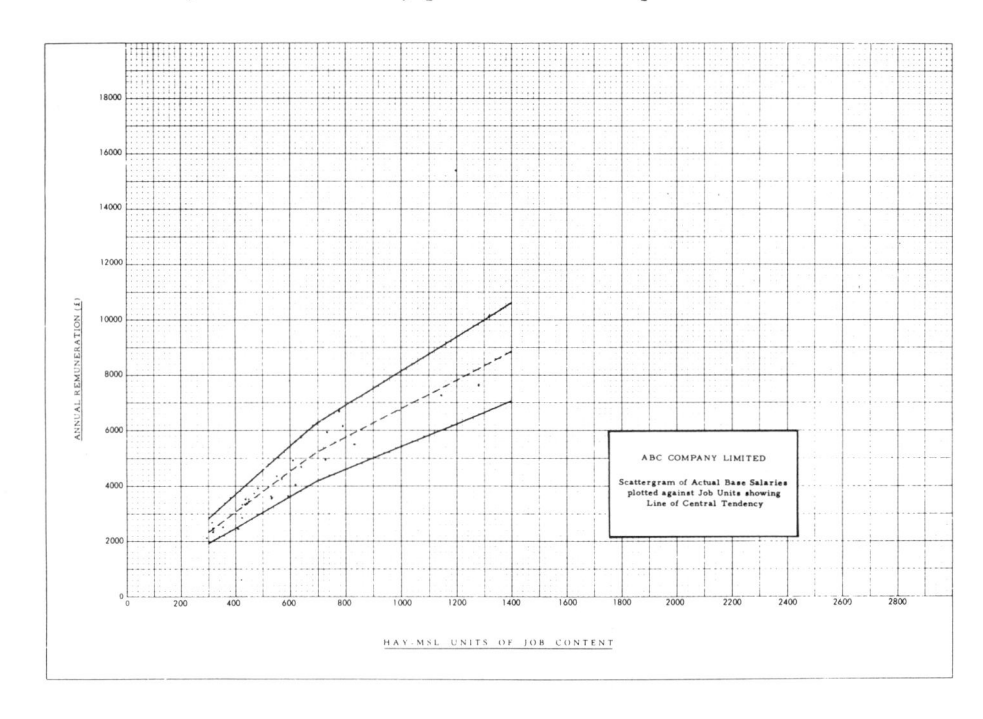

Figure 16.5   Scattergram of actual base salaries plotted against job units showing line of central tendency

Such a comparison could be made directly if all evaluation committees in all organizations used in the same guide-charts and made exactly the same judgements about the same values. In practice there are frequently different nuances and different values for the scales on the guide-charts may be used. It is therefore necessary to convert all measurements to a common scale by a process termed by Hay 'correlation'. The correlation process is carried out by experienced evaluators in order to adjust evaluations made in different environments to a common scale. After correlation adjustment has been completed the total pay structure for all the jobs calculated is compared with other total pay structures. The comparison of market rates through comparison of total pay structure lines has a number of advantages over that of individual job comparison. It enables pay attached to jobs of similar sized job content to be compared, rather than job title comparison which is often misleading. It avoids distortions which arise from exceptional payments made to specific jobs for historical, personal and other reasons. It highlights situations in which groups of jobs are paid out of line with the pay practice being applied to other jobs.

Management of a pay system is a dynamic matter, particularly in times of changing economic and social values. Pay levels and pay differentials which are appropriate today are unlikely to be so in one, two or five years time, and any pay system which is not kept up to date disintegrates, or worse still it becomes an impediment rather than an aid to efficient operations. The final stage in the Hay guide-chart profile system is therefore an annual audit of the market and updating of pay structures to keep them in line with changing external conditions and changing internal needs of organizations.

Summary of Objectives

The Hay guide-chart profile system of wage and salary management has been developed over a number of years to provide internal logic and external competitiveness in pay systems. Effective pay management involves the creation and maintenance of pay structures which allow employing organizations to recruit, retain, develop and motivate the numbers and calibre of people they need to achieve their objectives.

The Hay guide-chart profile system is designed to meet these objectives by:

1   Careful initial explanation and discussion with those affected.
2   Clarification of job understanding by analysis and description of the purpose and content of jobs.
3   Evaluation of jobs by a committee whose members understand the environment in which the job exists. Evaluation is by:
    (a) Hay guide-chart measurement
    (b) Job-profiling
    (c) Sore-thumbing.

4 Construction of scattergrams of job evaluations and pay to show existing pay structure.
5 Comparison of existing pay structures (scattergrams) with those of other organizations, after conversion of evaluation values to a common scale.
6 Establishment of desired pay policy and structure on the basis of evaluations and comparisons.
7 Regular auditing and updating of evaluations and market pay data.

References and Further Reading

Garrett, M.E., *Great Experiments in Psychology*, Century, New York, 1930.
Rock, M.L., *Handbook of Wage and Salary Administration*, McGraw-Hill, 1972.

17

Incentive Bonus Schemes for Managers

Michael White

Why have Incentive Schemes?

The basic idea of a management incentive scheme is that a part of remuneration is variable, rather than fixed, and the variation depends on some aspect of management performance. Introducing a management incentive scheme is always a top-level policy issue, and the first step is therefore to consider what are the main policy questions raised. Only when these questions have been defined and answered should the company press on to consider the methods and techniques available.

First, why does the company wish to provide an incentive scheme? Incentive schemes are sometimes seen primarily as a way of enabling managers to share in corporate prosperity. This might be justified either in terms of fair reward or perhaps as a way of building up loyalty. Alternatively, the incentives may be seen as a means of emphasizing and developing high standards of business performance, and of differentially rewarding those managers who make the biggest contribution. This, a pure policy question, will have a great influence on the subsequent design of the system.

This chapter assumes that, due to the competitive and financial pressures facing most companies in contemporary business conditions, the appropriate policy will in most cases be the latter—performance-related incentives. This choice leads to another policy issue, ie which aspect of business performance is it most important for the company to improve? In the long run, most commercial companies wish to improve rate of return on capital employed, or earnings per share. In the medium term, however, there are different paths to that common objective, and in any case, various members of the management team contribute towards it in special ways. Diversification, growth, market penetration, new product development, change in financial gearing, cost reduction—all of these may be relatively important or unimportant at particular stages. Naturally it is outside the scope of this chapter to review all these possibilities. But it is worth stressing that the incentive scheme is much more likely to be effective when it has grown out of a policy review of the company's business and financial situation, and of its strategic objectives and priorities.

The third and last main policy issue arises whatever the type of incentive: How much is the company prepared to earmark to fund the scheme? The *precise* figure cannot be decided without going into the design of the scheme, but to have a broad guideline or bracket is helpful before this detailed work begins. Experience suggests that unless a sum equivalent to at least 15% of the salaries of the group of executives concerned can be earmarked, it is not worth proceeding further. Some companies have run schemes at a much higher level of incentive than this—50%, 100%, or more. The company is likely to be influenced in its choice by its view of how much business improvement is possible. Hence again, the overall business review is an important preliminary in forming incentive policy.

Major Types of Management Incentive Schemes

There are innumerable fine variations on management incentive schemes. But it is possible to simplify the task of designing a scheme by focusing attention on four main choices that between them distinguish the major possibilities from one another. By systematically reviewing the differences between these main types of scheme, we can get a clearer understanding of the choices that have to be made.

The first way of distinguishing between types of incentive scheme is in terms of which managers the scheme relates to. Incentive schemes for top managers (board-level, or divisional chief executives, for instance) have different possibilities and pose different design problems than do schemes for middle management.

The second basic decision is whether to relate the incentive paid to the individual manager's performance—eg his achievement relative to budget—or to the performance of the group of managers, such as the profitability of a product division which is the responsibility of a particular management team. Another distinction, following closely on the previous one, concerns the type of performance measurement. Here the chief split is between schemes using quantitative measures of performance (eg percent return on capital employed) and those using qualitative measures such as ratings from an appraisal system. Although this choice may seem to be only a technical detail, it can have large consequences for the development of the scheme.

The fourth distinction is between schemes where the incentive payment is in the form of cash, and those where the payment is in the form of capital—shares or share rights. Cash bonuses are the traditional type, but capital schemes have become common in recent years.

To summarize the four main distinctions:

1   Who should be included? (top-management/middle-management?)
2   Whose performance to use as the basis? (individuals/groups?)
3   What kind of performance measurement? (quantitative/qualitative?)
4   What form of incentive payment? (cash/capital?)

Before going into the detailed analysis of these variations, it may be helpful to give illustrations of incentive schemes, to show how they can be described in terms of these distinctions. Here then are pen-pictures of four incentive schemes, drawn from the author's experience.

1   In this retailing group, top-management (executive directors) received individually negotiated bonus incentives. Though individually established, the bonus was calculated on group performance, ie pre-tax profits; what varied individually was the profit-sharing entitlement, though in all cases this was substantial. Obviously, the type of performance measurement was quantitative—each individual director's bonus was automatically fixed by the profits achieved. Finally, payment was in cash and was made annually.
2   This diversified engineering group concentrated its incentive scheme on the middle-management level. Although the average level of bonus was based on the company's overall profit achievement (ie group performance), the individual manager's bonus varied depending on his personal performance appraisal rating. So the main basis of the incentive, from his point of view, was individual performance, which was judged in a qualitative way. The payment was in cash and was calculated as a proportion of salary.
3   In a consumer products company, a strong emphasis was placed on management teamwork, and a group performance basis was accordingly used. Market penetration and overall sales growth—both quantitative factors—were measured to provide the basis of the incentive, and both top-level and middle-managers participated provided that they were involved in the product development and marketing team. Payment was in cash.
4   Here, in a service business, a top-management scheme was recently installed. Both individual targets and company performance (growth in share value) were used as the basis of incentive, which in both instances were measured quantitatively. The individual had to achieve his personal targets in order to share in the incentive

scheme, but no incentive could be earned unless the management team collectively had achieved a specified level of growth. The payment in this scheme was in the form of capital, a special category of incentive shares having been set up.

So, by using these four questions, we can quickly bring out the chief features of a scheme. Each of these distinctions helps to bring out a number of important factors involved in decisions concerning management incentives, and to provide the framework for a systematic review. The main factors to be considered, under each of the four main questions, are tabulated in Figures 17.1 to 17.4.

It can be seen from these figures that each choice has its possibilities and limitations, its strengths and weaknesses. For example, Figure 17.1 reminds us that when designing a top-management incentive scheme it is relatively more appropriate to take some aspect of long-term business performance as the basis of the scheme, since this is the prime area of responsibility of the senior executive. Conversely, a middle-management scheme would be more appropriately related to short-term or medium-term performance. Which of these would be a better focus of attention for the scheme would depend on the business situation of the organization concerned.

Other items in the figures can be used in the same way, as 'reminders' of important points to consider. A factor is only included if it has some bearing on the question, by bringing out a major difference between the main alternatives involved.

Key Questions

To discuss all the factors in the figures is not possible within the scope of this chapter. Hopefully many of the points are self-explanatory; fuller discussions can be found by using the further reading list on p.263-4. There are one or two key questions in each figure, which should be given priority before considering the other details. The following discussion focuses on these key questions.

In Figure 17.1 the main choice is between schemes for top-management only, and schemes for middle-management. The figure summarizes the main considerations to be reviewed in making this choice. The key question in the comparison is undoubtedly 'managerial contribution'. If the purpose of an incentive scheme is to stimulate improved company performance, then it will be most effective if it is directed towards those managers who make the largest contribution to performance. In general, individual top-management action must have a much greater bearing on company performance than individual middle-management action. Thus it is normally logical for a company to begin

Incentive Bonus Schemes for Managers

Aspect to be considered	Top-management schemes	Middle-management schemes
*Managerial contribution to company performance	(a) Top managers make relatively large contribution to business (b) Contribution relatively easy to identify, especially in long term	(a) Middle managers make relative small contribution to business (b) Contribution relatively difficult to identify
Time-scale of performance	Long-term performance more appropriate as basis of scheme	Short- or medium-term performance more appropriate
Flexibility of scheme	Scheme can be negotiated individually; or can be uniform	Scheme must be of a standardized type
Size of incentive for individual	Can be high relative to salary	Can only be moderate relative to salary
Deferred payment of incentive	Likely to be attractive to top-managers	Relatively less attractive to middle-managers
Cost	(a) Marginal cost of incentive may be high, due to taxation (b) Total cost relatively low, due to small numbers in scheme	(a) Marginal cost relatively low (b) Total cost relatively high if many managers in scheme
Administration	Administrative requirements relatively slight	Administrative requirements relatively great
Discrimination of performance	Relatively easy to achieve high discrimination between different levels of performance	Relatively hard to achieve high discrimination

*Key question

Figure 17.1   Who should be included in the scheme?

management incentives at the top level, extending them to middle-management levels only at a later stage. Any other approach would need to be specially justified, in view of the strength of this key point. It can also be seen from Figure 17.1 that the other factors generally suggest that top-management schemes are easier to build up in an effective way than are middle-management schemes.

Aspects to be considered	Schemes based on individual performance	Schemes based on group performance
*Managerial contribution to company performance	(a) Appropriate where individual's contribution is relatively independent (b) Appropriate where performance standards are relatively variable ie some managers at much higher standard than others	(a) Appropriate where individuals' contributions are relatively interdependent (b) Appropriate where performance standards are relatively uniform
Type of behaviour	Encourages entrepreneurial, self-reliant or creative types of behaviour	Encourages greater cooperation, coordination and team management
Flexibility of scheme	Scheme can be negotiated individually; or can be uniform	Scheme can be negotiated individually, but is more likely to be standard or uniform
Administration	Administrative requirements relatively great	Administrative requirements relatively slight
Discrimination	Relatively easy to achieve high discrimination between different levels of performance	Discrimination can be achieved between different groups or teams, but not so easily between individuals

*Key question

Figure 17.2 Whose performance to use as the basis?

The factor of managerial contribution also emerges as a key question in Figure 17.2, where we are considering whether to relate the scheme to individual or group performance. Here though, the question is not how big the individual's contribution is, but whether it is independent of or interdependent with the contribution of other managers. Where the individual manager works in a situation that makes him largely autonomous—eg in profit-centre organization, some kinds of project management or new ventures—an incentive scheme based solely on his own achievement makes sense. But where the company's emphasis is on the coordination of complex operations, with close-working between different management functions, then it is relatively more appropriate to base the incentive scheme on some measure of group performance.

Another way of looking at this is in terms of the kind of management behaviour encouraged, and under some circumstances this may also be considered a key question. Many large companies at the moment, for instance, are concerned to stimulate a spirit of entrepreneurism in the organization. Individually-related schemes are appropriate tools for doing this. In other companies the problem is to integrate ever-larger organizations, and to foster teamwork; here the group-performance bonus may be more suitable.

When we come to the choice of performance measurement (Figure 17.3), the key question is whether the type of measurement selected is able to distinguish between different levels of management performance. In Figure 17.3 this factor has been labelled 'discrimination', and it also appears (as a subsidiary question rather than a key one) in two of the other figures. If the system of measurement does not discriminate between good and mediocre performance then the incentive scheme stands little chance of encouraging higher standards of management. In principle quantitative measurement enables better discrimination than qualitative methods such as performance appraisal, and this would suggest that the former should be used wherever possible. On the other hand qualitative methods of appraisal are more versatile and flexible, and hence the question 'range of application' is also a key one to consider. If the intention is to develop an incentive scheme covering a wide range of different types of manager, working in a wide variety of situations, then the choice between the two possible approaches becomes more difficult. For this reason, schemes employing a mixture of the two types of measurement—bonus depending on a combination of both—are quite common.

Choice of cash or capital as the form of incentive payment (Figure 17.4) is primarily a matter of cost-effectiveness. So the question of 'cost factors' is selected as the key one. The essential differences between the two forms of payment are, first, that they are funded in different ways by the company, and second, that they are taxed in different ways for the individual recipient. Which form of funding is

Aspects to be considered	Qualitative measurement of performance	Quantative measurement of performance
*Range of application	(a) Equally applicable to all kinds of manager (b) Equally applicable to all types of managerial action	(a) Ease of application will vary, eg staff-type jobs tend to be less quantifiable (b) Easier to apply to some kinds of managerial action than others, eg development of subordinates hard to quantify
Reliability of effect	Reliability depends on high level of agreement among managers concerning standards of performance	Reliability depends on technical quality of measurement systems, eg budgetary accounting
Ease of introduction	Relatively easy to introduce (eg as extension of performance appraisal)	Relatively difficult to introduce, especially when measurement is complex
Cost, administration	Substantial effort required on continuing basis to ensure reliability of judgements, etc	Relatively less effort required, once scheme is established
*Discrimination	Relatively difficult to achieve high level of discrimination, due to tendency towards 'conservative' judgements	Relatively easy to achieve any desired degree of discrimination between levels of performance

*Key questions

Figure 17.3   What kind of performance measurement?

Aspects to be considered	Cash bonus scheme	Capital bonus scheme
Time-scale of performance	Applicable to management performance measured over any time-scale	Mainly applicable to relatively long-term management performance
Time-scale of reward	Either immediately upon performance, or deferred	Deferred reward only
*Predictability of value	Relatively easy to calculate and predict value of bonus	Relatively unpredictable, due to possible changes in tax law and in market value of shares
Acceptability to managers	Less prestigious—some associate with 'commission' schemes	More prestigious—associated with 'ownership'
Flexibility of scheme	Highly flexible—few constraints on altering terms of scheme	Relatively less flexible—eg need to obtain shareholders consent when terms are varied
Ease of introduction	Relatively simple to introduce	Relatively complex to introduce, due to legal and fiscal requirements
*Cost factors	(a) For company: Funded out of cash (b) For individual: Taxed as earned income	(a) Funded through share issues and capital reserves (b) Taxed as capital gain when share rights are exercised

*Key questions

Figure 17.4   What form of incentive payment?

preferable will depend on the company's financial position, and how seriously it regards calls upon cash as against dilution of equity capital. The taxation factor is one which is widely regarded as giving a decided advantage to capital schemes. It means that instead of an executive paying tax on his incentive earnings at progressive surtax rates, he will pay at some later date, when he exercises his rights under the scheme, and then at a fixed capital gains rate. Thus the company can achieve the same net-of-tax incentive with a smaller financial input. However, in the evaluation of cost-effectiveness, the reduced predictability of a deferred capital gain must be taken into account, and this has therefore also been picked out as a key point. Capital incentive schemes of former years (both in Britain and the USA) have had their effectiveness greatly reduced by changes in taxation law; and another difficulty is the chance of a general depression of share values, quite independent of the individual company's performance. These risks, however, will often be thought acceptable.

We have now briefly covered the key questions under each of the four main design choices. When evaluating an existing scheme, or choosing one's approach to the design of a new one, it is recommended that the systematic point-by-point approach provided by Figures 17.1–17.4 should be followed, first considering the 'key questions', and then reviewing the subsidiary ones as well.

This has two advantages. First, it may identify situations where little-used types of incentive scheme could usefully be applied. For instance, where a company has already established a strong system of management by objectives (MBO), there may be a good opportunity for installing a scheme based on individual, quantitatively measured performance down to middle-management level. This is a possibility which is at present very little exploited. Again, while capital based schemes are particularly suitable for long-term performance incentives, it will also be noted from Figure 17.4 that cash schemes can be linked to *any* time-period of performance. If for some other reason a capital based scheme is ruled out, then the possibility of a cash bonus scheme, related to long-term business performance, or perhaps the completion of personal long-term project assignments, should be seriously considered. This is a type of cash incentive scheme little used in Britain but quite familiar in many American companies.

The second advantage of the systematic, point-by-point review is that it can reveal situations when *no* incentive scheme is suitable—where, in other words, it is better to do without one. If, for instance, it is not possible to introduce a top-management scheme, can a middle-management scheme really be justified? This is a simple point to make, but it is one which many companies have avoided. A complicated set of difficulties can often become apparent when trying to decide the basis for the scheme (individual or group) and the type of performance measurement. Perhaps the company's need is to develop the individualistic entrepreneurial type of performance. But perhaps the only kind of performance measurement available for the individual managers is a qualitative appraisal scheme giving only a weak power of discrimination between different levels of performance. The logical decision, then, is to set aside all ideas of an incentive scheme until the basis of performance measurement has been strengthened.

Finally, there are a number of general considerations, to do with the company's general business situation and its type of staffing, which may affect the amount of emphasis given to incentive schemes within the total remuneration plan. These considerations are reviewed fully in Chapter 18.

Technical Problems in Management Incentives

So far this chapter has presented the main types of management incentive schemes, and pointed out the factors involved in developing each of these variations. In addition, there are a number of technical problems which crop up with *all* kinds of management incentives. Because of poor techniques, numerous incentive schemes have in the past been unsuccessful. The main shortcomings have been of five types:

1. Poor definition of performance standards for managers.
2. Poor measurement of actual performance of managers.
3. Poor method of calculating the bonus amount.
4. Lack of monitoring of the effectiveness of incentives.
5. Lack of flexibility in the schemes to cope with changing circumstances.

The first two of these problem areas—performance standards and performance measurement—have formed a large part of the discussion in Chapter 15 of this handbook. They are topics which have to be taken extremely seriously in the design of management incentives. If performance standards are too easy, it is likely that actual performance will decline. If the standards are too tough, however, the decline may be even more severe. Even if the standards are pitched at just the right level to achieve performance improvement, inaccurate or unreliable measurement of actual performance will cast doubt on the entire incentive scheme. Appropriate techniques for these areas, as described in Chapter 15, must therefore be used as an integral part of the incentive scheme design.

Bonus formulae

Once the company has set up methods for defining these two aspects, it must next decide how the incentive payment is going to be related to actual performance. This question really has two parts to it. First, which aspects of managerial performance are to be selected as the basis for the incentive? (These we will call the 'performance criteria'). Second, what will be the actual arithmetical relationship between the performance criteria and the incentive paid?

Many schemes go wrong because inadequate thought is given to the first part of this problem. A frequent mistake is to select a performance criterion which is too general for most of the managers in the scheme. 'Return on capital employed', a commonly-used performance criterion, is appropriate in most cases for the managing director but not usually for the marketing director and still less for the production manager. Unless the individual manager can see how his own actions are reflected in the performance criterion, the incentive will be ineffectual from his point of view.

A common mistake at the other extreme is to select a performance criterion which is too narrow—one which does not adequately reflect the range of the manager's activities. A familiar example is sales turnover as a criterion for the sales director or sales manager—one which may encourage neglect of, for instance, margins or service levels. Less obvious, but perhaps far more widespread and dangerous, are incentives stressing short-term criteria and completely neglecting the long-term.

These observations point to the need to base incentives on a combination of several performance criteria. It will usually be necessary to choose these sets of performance criteria separately for each manager, or for each closely-related group of managers.

Having done so, it is quite straightforward to establish the relationship between performance and reward by the use of arithmetical formulae. No problem is posed by wanting to use at the same time several different performance criteria. These can be combined in the formulae, if necessary by attaching weights to the individual criteria to reflect their relative importance to the company. An example, in this case for a hypothetical production manager, may help to clarify the principles:

bonus % of salary =

$$20 \times \frac{actual\ output}{budgeted\ output} \times \frac{budgeted\ average\ unit\ cost}{actual\ average\ unit\ cost}$$

$$+ 10 \times \frac{actual\ manpower\ saving}{planned\ manpower\ saving}$$

This type of formula expresses, in rather a succinct way, a fairly sophisticated kind of incentive with the following main features:

1 Three separate performance criteria have been used—production

output, unit production cost and manpower reduction.
2 Each of these criteria have been expressed relative to some budgeted standard or target.
3 Because the 'output' and 'cost' parts of the formula are multiplied together, the manager cannot gain by pushing up one aspect at the expense of the other. For instance, if output were pushed up through increased subcontracting at higher rates, actual cost would also go up and this might more than cancel out the incentive gain.
4 The 'output' and 'cost' criteria are considered crucial, and rewarded at a rate of 20% of salary for standard achievement; manpower savings are given a lower importance rating, and reward at only a 10% rate. On the other hand, if manpower actually increased, the manager would start to lose some of the bonus he had earned through output and cost performance.

With a little practice, formulae such as these can readily be constructed in accordance with objectives and priorities for the incentive scheme. The discipline of expressing the scheme in this way can play a useful part in clarifying and quantifying the objectives and priorities themselves.

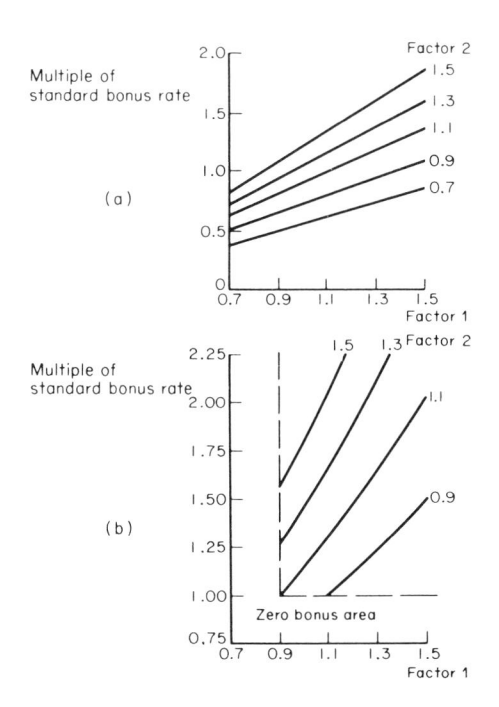

Figure 17.5 Using graphs to show incentive relationships

An alternative way of summarizing bonus formulae is by means of graphs. Figure 17.5 shows two such graphs. The first (a) represents the kind of straightforward multiplicative arrangement which has just been presented in the example. The second (b) shows a different kind of bonus situation, where there is no bonus until the performance standard is achieved, but above that bonus rises in a steeply accelerating curve. If three factors were used, it might be necessary to construct two graphs to show the incentive relationship. By preparing such graphs and distributing them to the managers participating in the scheme, one can leave them in no doubt about what the scheme means to them personally.

Monitoring effectiveness

The next technical problem concerns checking up on the effectiveness of the incentive scheme. It is rather extraordinary that this is so seldom done; only the costs, not the effects, of incentives are usually analyzed. There are however some rough but useful indications of effectiveness which can be collected without too much difficulty:

1. Comparing actual effect with predicted effect (the latter might be, for instance, the predicted retention of senior executives; or the predicted increase in incentive earnings as a proportion of salary over a period of years).
2. Changes in performance criteria set and achieved, graphed period-by-period or as moving averages.
3. This year's performance relative to standard, as a proportion of last year's performance relative to standard, for each incentive-paid manager.
4. Numbers of managers failing to achieve standards or 'make bonus', period-by-period.
5. Numbers of managers failing to 'make bonus' for two or more periods running.

These figures will not in themselves prove whether the scheme is working well or not, but they will provide the basis for reasonable discussion of what can, otherwise, be rather an emotional topic.

Provisions for flexibility

Finally is the problem of achieving flexibility in the incentive system. Partly, this is a question of thinking through the terms of the scheme and anticipating its full range of outcomes. For instance, by drawing up the incentive payment graphs in full, one will be able to see just how much money the scheme will mean to a recipient in either an extremely successful year or an extremely bad one. Are these outcomes really part of the scheme's intentions? If not, then some additional 'stopping rules' will have to be written into it.

The deeper problem, however, is that of being able to vary the actual terms of the scheme under different circumstances. If a company's business position is quite suddenly changed (for better or worse) by government intervention, does it make sense to stick to the terms of the old incentive scheme? If the company does, then it may well be a deathblow to the scheme's motivational effectiveness. On the other hand, sudden arbitrary changes in the terms may also weaken the scheme, since the managers involved will no longer know where they stand.

Part of the solution will come when companies use the more sophisticated approaches to budgetary planning or target-setting which are now being advocated. These include the use of flexible budgets which will automatically smooth out some of the unpredictable or uncontrollable influences which might otherwise make the incentive system calculations meaningless.

To cope with the problem in a general way, however, some companies have found it helpful to set up an incentives review committee as part of the system. This committee (usually a top-level one) has the responsibility for altering the total amount of incentive payment, or the performance criteria on which payment is to be based, in the light of changing circumstances. It is important, if this committee is not to be seen as 'fixing' the incentive scheme, that the circumstances under which it can intervene are defined in advance. These should include, in view of current business conditions:

1. Government action seriously affecting the growth or profitability of the business.
2. International or national crises having a similar effect.
3. Worldwide changes, beyond a predetermined ratio, in the price of specified key raw materials or supplies.
4. Changes, beyond a predetermined ratio, in the stock market value of the company's business sector.
5. Industrial relations disputes affecting the company's industry sector, beyond the control of the company itself.

It is particularly important that the rules of the incentive scheme, including those rules concerned with giving it flexibility, should be made known to all the participating managers. This will give the scheme the best chance of retaining flexibility without losing face.

References and Further Reading

Burdon, S.W.R., *Share Incentive Schemes for Executives*, British Institute of Management, London, 1971.

Copeman, G. and Rumble, T., *Capital as an Incentive*, Leviathan House, Epsom, 1972.
Cox, B., *Value Added*, Heinemann, 1979.
Crystal, G.S., *Financial Motivation for Executives*, American Management Association, New York, 1970.
White, M., *Motivating Managers Financially*, Institute of Personnel Management, London, 1973.

18

Selecting a Salary System

Michael White

Need for Systematic Approach

Previous chapters have shown that there is a wide range of options available to an organization in designing a remuneration system for its salaried staff. These options are partly to do with the balance of the remuneration 'package'—ie the combination of salary, benefits and incentives—and partly with the financial structure of the remuneration system, eg gradings, pay levels and relativities. Also involved are the support systems for remuneration, eg performance appraisal. What then can guide an organization in making its choice from this wide and complex range of options as it develops a salary system suitable for its circumstances?

In the present state of knowledge one cannot answer this question precisely, or arrive at a strictly optimum choice. The design of remuneration systems is still a matter for judgement. But in making such judgements, it is preferable to adopt a systematic approach which ensures that the main factors have been considered. One can also bring to bear an increasing body of research evidence concerning remuneration systems.

In this chapter, a systematic approach to the problem of choosing a salaried staff remuneration system is proposed, using two overlapping types of review method:

1 A review of the appropriateness of remuneration options for the recruitment, retention and motivation of staff.
2 A review of the potential effectiveness of options in relation to costs and to use of the organization's resources or strengths.

The Appropriateness of a System

An appropriate remuneration system is one which 'fits in' well with the situation in the organization and provides for its main requirements. It is by no means uncommon to find remuneration systems that are grossly inappropriate. The consequences of this appear in difficulties of recruitment, loss of valuable and experienced staff, and widespread dissatisfaction. These acute problems may even occur in organizations or occupations where the salary levels are high relative to comparable organizations or occupations—for reasons discussed below.

Which are the crucial factors in determining whether a remuneration system is or is not appropriate? As a first stage in answering this question, it is helpful to think of remuneration systems design as involving five main choices of emphasis. (These five factors have been selected because they concisely reveal the major differences between actual remuneration systems, both in the author's personal experience and researches, and in published case studies).

1. A choice between linking the system to external comparisons, or making it relatively independent of external comparisons.
2. A choice between emphasizing internal comparability (ie a system which is highly integrated and uniform across, say, departments or subsidiaries) or emphasizing 'de-coupled' structures (where the different departments may have quite separate remuneration provisions).
3. A choice between systems that are based on universal rules (rules which apply to all equally—as in job grading, perhaps) or those where many salary decisions are made on a personal case-by-case basis.
4. A choice between systems that are based on fixed increments, or systems that are not based on increments but on some variable review method.
5. A choice between systems that include a major incentive element, ie a part of remuneration varies with performance—and those which include little or no incentive element.

In practice, these choices are not between two simple extremes, but more a matter of finding a suitable balance between the extremes. For instance, most salary systems currently include incremental aspects and variable review aspects. Nevertheless, there is a considerable difference of emphasis among various companies, so it is reasonable to think in terms of some kind of choice taking place.

These distinctions cut across salary, fringe benefits and incentive bonus schemes. Fixed increments, for instance, may apply to salary scales and to entitlement for certain kinds of fringe benefits. Incentives can be supplied partly through salary increases, if these are genuinely

1	*Emphasis on external comparability*	*No emphasis on external comparability*
	Competitive job market Mobile staff Standard jobs interchangeable between firms Formal qualifications required	Geographical remoteness of firm Jobs and skills special to firm
2	*Emphasis on internal comparability*	*Emphasis on separate or 'de-coupled' treatment of staff groups*
	Internal mobility and interchangeability of staff High contact and communication between staff groups	Highly specialized staff groups with important role in firm
3	*Emphasis on universal rules*	*Emphasis on 'particularism' or personal case-by-case treatment*
	Size of organization large	Size of organization small Family-managed or entrepreneurial type of business Fluid, rapidly changing situation
4	*Emphasis on fixed increments*	*Emphasis on variable review methods*
	Long-term career commitment of staff to organization High stability of staff in their jobs Size of organization large (tendency to bureaucracy) Inflationary pressure	Mobile staff Rapid career progression Financial instability of business
5	*Emphasis on incentives*	*No use of incentives*
	High degree of performance measurement for salaried staff	Not possible to measure performance of salaried staff

Figure 18.1 Key choices for salaried staff remuneration schemes

related to performance, as well as through bonus schemes. External and internal comparability apply to all aspects of the remuneration package.

The first step in evaluating these choices of emphasis is essentially commonsense—to consider the internal structure of the organization, its staffing requirements and the job market on which it has to draw, and to ask of each of the remuneration policies available whether it is appropriate to such circumstances. This may seem a tall order, but fortunately in practice there tends to be a fairly small number of key factors in the situation which need to be singled out for attention. A summary of the most common key factors is presented in Figure 18.1. Five key choices of emphasis (numbered 1—5) in the design of a salaried staff remuneration scheme are shown. Below each choice to be made, are the main factors which make a particular emphasis more appropriate.

External comparability

The importance of emphasizing external comparability primarily depends on the organization's relations with its job market. If it has to obtain its staff in a competitive job market, and if the type of staff it requires are mobile and easily able to market their skills, then to base remuneration on external comparisons will be highly appropriate. Most large organizations have experienced many years of competition for staff in job markets, so external comparability has indeed become one of the main pillars of their salary systems. The main methods used are periodic job market surveys; a continuing interchange of salary information between organizations recruiting in the same markets; or simply a willingness to move salaries swiftly upwards whenever they seem to be causing difficulties in recruitment or retention of staff.

Two other factors tend to underlie the competitiveness of job markets. For a long time the idiosyncratic methods of administration which many organizations used have been giving way to more standardized methods. This helps to create job mobility and fosters an active job market. Another factor is that many more jobs now require occupational qualifications rather than knowledge of a particular organization.

There are numerous cases where these factors do not apply and where, accordingly, it is appropriate to de-emphasize external comparisons. When an organization is geographically remote from its job market, for instance, staff mobility is likely to be lower than usual. When it offers very special types of training and work experience to its staff, then again external salary comparisons may not be too helpful. A better strategy for organizations in this position is to develop special kinds of remuneration provision which are rather out of the ordinary range provided by other companies. The best opportunities for doing this are generally in fringe benefits provisions.

Internal comparability

Internal comparability is not a direct alternative to external comparability; an organization may choose to have either of the two, or both, although in practice being responsive to the external situation is likely to put some strains on maintaining internal comparability.

The biggest factor which favours an emphasis on internal comparability is the internal mobility of staff. This tends to matter most at the management level, where the organization may require men to move from one department, division or subsidiary to another. Unless the pay for these jobs has been aligned, such moves will throw up anomalies and cause dissatisfactions. A second factor is the amount of contact and communication required between different groups of staff. The more closely they work together, the more pressure there is likely to be for a system of internal comparability. There is now a trend towards greater personal frankness about salaries and people who in the past might have worked for years together without knowing of a disparity in their salaries are now far less likely to remain in ignorance. Most companies now place considerable emphasis on internal comparability, through such methods as job evaluation and job grading.

The situations in which the opposite policy—what I have called 'de-coupled' salary systems—is appropriate, seem to be less well understood. This occurs, particularly, when an organization has a vital group of staff who are highly specialized and seek their career purely within their field of specialism. Examples of this might be buyers in a department store or fashion retailing organization, or R & D staff in a science-based industry such as pharmaceuticals. Aligning these staffs' salaries with other groups inside the company is likely to be quite inappropriate. The company will do well to set up separate salary scales and conditions of employment, to meet their special requirements.

Universal rules

All organizations operate some kind of compromise between completely impersonal universal rules in their remuneration systems, and completely personal case-by-case, 'particularist' treatment. The personal approach—represented by such customs as knocking on the boss's door for an increase, or *ex gratia* pension awards—was the traditional one. It has gradually tended to be pushed out by the more standardized impersonal approach.

The major factor pushing in the direction of universal rules is the increasing size of organizations. Control over salary costs in large organizations is facilitated by a strict system of rules, governing what can or cannot be offered to new staff, and when and how salary reviews are to be conducted. Such networks of rules are often accompanied by job evaluation and grading schemes, formal appraisal methods, etc, but there are companies with strict central control over all salary matters yet without using these more sophisticated techniques.

However there is plenty of evidence that white-collar staff often still prefer the personal touch and regret its demise. So it is worth considering the factors which can help to preserve it as an appropriate approach.

First, there is the ownership factor. Family businesses generally find that it is quite acceptable to staff to control salaries on a personal basis. Companies which have passed into wider shareholding, but have retained a strong entrepreneurial outlook, can often be successful in keeping salaries on this strongly personal basis. Another quite different factor favouring particular rather than universal treatment is when a company is in a highly fluid, rapidly changing business situation demanding a continuous state of adaptability and flexibility. Under these circumstances a case-by-case approach to salaries will seem quite reasonable, while any detailed set of impersonal rules is likely to be unworkable in practice, due to the continuous pressures of change.

Fixed increments

One might imagine that fixed-increment salary systems are just an extreme example of basing remuneration on impersonalized, standard rules. But curiously, in practice some commercial companies have combined fixed increments with a considerable degree of 'particularist' treatment of staff. This has been achieved, for instance, by having incremental scales, but allowing individuals to progress up the scales on an *ex gratia* basis. Systems in which fixed increments are given as of right have been mainly confined to jobs in the public service.

One of the main factors to be considered here is the career attitude of staff. Where staff think of their employment as a long-term career committed to one organization, an incremental approach would be more appropriate. The same applies when there is a tendency for staff to remain for long periods in the same job, since the incremental scale provides a sense of progression within the job.

On the other hand, where staff are highly mobile, or where career progression tends to be rapid, incremental schemes lose much of their point. Another factor is whether the business is or is not in a financially stable situation. Fixed increments represent a financial commitment that not all companies can assume with confidence.

At present certain forces seem to be pushing companies, particularly large ones, willy-nilly towards an incremental approach. One such force is administrative inflexibility and bureaucracy. Another is the pressure of inflation, which gives the incremental system a new role even though it robs it of much of its traditional advantages.

Incentive element

Whether or not an organization incorporates a performance-related incentive element in its remuneration scheme is much less dependent on outside circumstances than any of the other choices. This is probably because incentives can serve so many different purposes and be of so many different types (see Chapter 17).

The main constraint is whether it is possible and meaningful to measure performance in the type of job (or group) of jobs being considered. Incentives are inappropriate when one can see no direct link between what the individual does and how the organization fares. In this case, introducing an incentive element, based on some spurious measure or evaluation of performance, is only likely to divert attention from individuals' real work. In many instances, such as government services, the performance of the organization itself is very hard to measure, let alone apply this at the level of the individual.

On the other hand, developments in measuring performance and defining white-collar tasks enlarge the scope for incentives. Such developments are, at the management or specialist level, management by objectives (MBO) and budgetary planning methods; and at the clerical level, the introduction of computerized administrative systems and clerical work measurement.

However, perhaps an even more important consideration in introducing incentives is the attitude of management and staff towards performance improvement, and their willingness to accept the challenge of an incentive system. This question can only be fully answered by introducing another general approach (discussed below) to reviewing the appropriateness of remuneration systems.

Matching Remuneration to Motivation

So far the appropriateness of various broad aspects of remuneration systems has been discussed in a purely commonsense way, without introducing any general explanation of what constitutes appropriateness. To go a step further, whenever we talk of the appropriateness of salary systems, we are mainly concerned with matters of motivation. Thinking about motivation will prove helpful in grasping the nature of the choices in designing a remuneration system. It will also lead to some techniques for defining the requirements for remuneration in further detail.

Perhaps this will become clearer if we consider a specific example. It was previously noted that when an organization has to compete on a job market for highly mobile staff, then it does well to be sensitive to external salary comparisons. This is not because of any abstract principle of justice, but because in these circumstances staff will be well-informed about jobs and salary levels elsewhere, and will use this information to judge whether or not they themselves are being fairly paid. So external comparability in this situation merely reflects the comparison which is natural to the staff themselves, and on which they base their feelings of satisfaction or dissatisfaction.

In general terms, the remuneration system designer should try to understand the factors which the staff themselves will be aware of. This applies first and foremost to the 'equity' or 'felt fairness' of the remuneration system. An appropriate salary system is one which is likely to be judged equitable by the staff themselves. The various key factors which have been stressed so far, can be thought of as pointers to the staff's likely feelings of what is relevant and fair.

This approach can be pushed further to help solve problems of remuneration system design. The desire for a fair and equitable system is only one, albeit an extremely important one, of the motives which remuneration may satisfy. It is reasonable, therefore, to propose the following principle of remuneration system design:

> There should be a correspondence between the characteristics of the remuneration system and the motives and preferences of those staff whom the organization wishes to recruit, retain and encourage.

This can only be applied in practice if the organization knows what are the motives and preferences of its staff. Do staff, for instance, regard money as the means to short-term material enjoyment, or to long-term security? Are they eager for the social status of being a well-paid salaried man, or are they more concerned that monetary reward should be a positive recognition for personal achievement? Recent research (particularly in the field of management remuneration and motivation) has shown that money has all these meanings, and more, to various people. A study within a large British company (McDougall, 1973) suggested that its managers could be divided into six distinct groups, each with its own pattern of motives and remuneration preferences. It was also apparent that some of these groups' motives were much worse catered for by the existing remuneration scheme in their company than were others.

These differences in motives reflect directly on specific details of the remuneration system, eg the acceptability of job evaluation and grading, the preference for straight salary or fringe benefits or the willingness to participate in incentive schemes. Consider the differences between two contrasting groups of managers, from the study just referred to. One group attached a very high importance to having a job with opportunities for promotion and advancement, to having money for spending, and for opportunities to accumulate capital. They were strongly in favour of performance-related individual rewards, some scope for individual choice in the remuneration package and more use of tax-advantageous fringe benefits. The contrasting group primarily wanted a job which satisfied their intellectual and vocational interests, and were less motivated by money. They would have preferred a remuneration scheme that was simple and easy to administer, they did not approve of individually-related incentives to nearly the extent of the former group, and would like all their remuneration in salary rather than fringe benefits. Clearly, no single uniform remuneration system would be appropriate for the needs of both these groups. On the other hand, knowledge of their motives and preferences should greatly improve a company's chances of designing an appropriate system for either. The guidance provided by information of this kind goes beyond the broad characteristics of the remuneration scheme (ie the five 'choice of emphasis' questions) and down into the finer details.

Unfortunately, at present it is not possible to give general guidelines about what are likely to be the prevailing motives and remuneration preferences of different types of staff. The only practical approach is to investigate each situation in its own right. The same techniques which have produced the research findings mentioned above can be applied to analyzing the situation within any particular organization, and giving it an improved basis of information on which to develop or revise its remuneration system. As these techniques are not yet widely known, it may be helpful to give a description of them.

The essential tool used is a confidential questionnaire to be completed by the managers or staff concerned in the remuneration system review. The questionnaire will generally be in three parts, and the relationships between these parts and their subsequent analysis and use are shown in Figure 18.2. The most obvious section of the questionnaire is that which obtains the individuals' preferences, by means of a standard rating scale, for a variety of aspects of remuneration, including both the components of the package and the underlying principles. Exactly what questions should be included in this section will naturally depend on the range of options which the organization thinks are realistically available. Care should be taken, though, to ensure that the various possibilities mentioned in the questionnaire are fully understood by the individuals answering it.

While the first section of the questionnaire tells *what* the staff's preferences are, it does not explain *why* those preferences exist. The second section of the questionnaire helps in this direction. It covers a much wider range of topics, not just remuneration but such things as security, status and job satisfaction, and asks the individual to express how important he feels each of these aspects is to him in his working life. The answers build up a broad picture of his motives. It is then possible to see the way in which the answers to the remuneration questions tie up with these broader motives. This can be extremely important from a policy viewpoint. For instance, staff may want an increased emphasis on fringe benefits because they believe that it will bring them tax advantages in the short run. Or they may want them because they are seen as status symbols which show the prestige of their jobs—much more of a long-term motive. Without knowledge of the background motives, the company could misinterpret the need quite seriously.

```
                        Questionnaire
        ┌───────────────────┼───────────────────┐
        ▼                   ▼                   ▼
Ratings of types of   Ratings of types of   Factual information
remuneration and      values or motives     about individual
of remuneration       that might be         (age, salary level,
principles.           satisfied through work department, etc)
        │                   │                   │
        ▼                   ▼                   ▼
Information about     Information about the  Groupings of staff by
staff's               importance of          type of job,
remuneration          various motives to     seniority level,
preferences           be satisfied at work   career progress, etc
        │                                       │
        ▼                                       ▼
    Interpretation of remuneration        Comparisons between the
    preferences in terms  ──────────────▶ preferences and
    of the                                motives of different
    underlying motives                    groupings of staff
                    │               │
                    ▼               ▼
            Design of remuneration systems, keyed to
            the preferences and motives of staff
            as a whole, or of particular groups of
            staff having common preferences
```

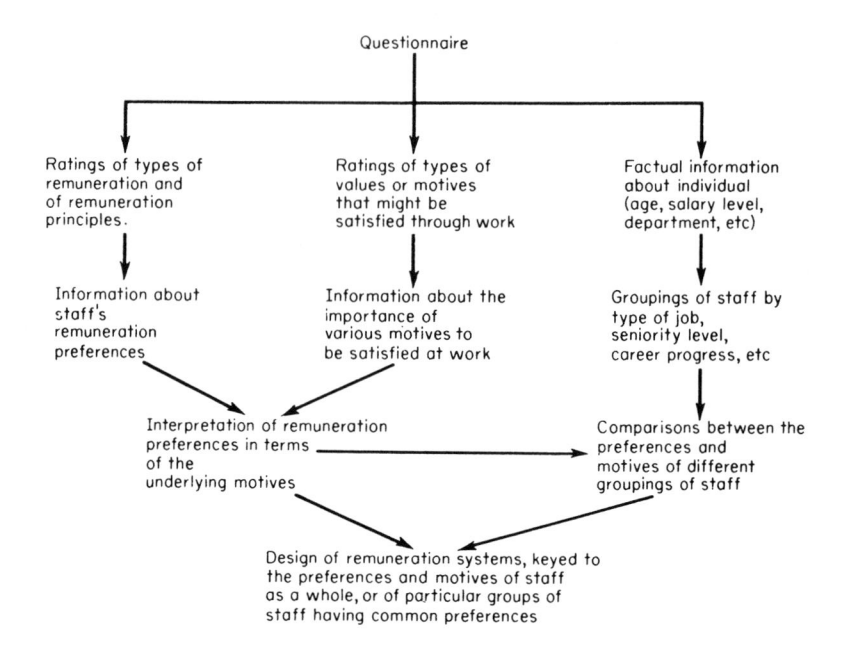

Figure 18.2   Build-up of remuneration preference analysis

The third step is to try to group the individuals who share common motives and preferences in a way which will be of practical use to the organization, eg whether the different departments or specialist groups express different remuneration needs. If not, the task of designing the remuneration system is considerably simpler, but if there are differences, it is important to know how serious these are and to make provision for them. Therefore the third section of the questionnaire obtains classifying information which enables the individuals to be grouped in this way.

Other information from the third section concerns the age and career progression of the individual. The motives and preferences of different age-groups in the organization, or of slow-progressing and rapidly-progressing groups, are likely to vary. Information about these differences may often shed light on weaknesses or stresses in the existing situation. For instance, if large numbers of older staff feel that there is no more incentive or opportunity for them in the company, then an atmosphere of frustration and apathy might build up. If those members of the company who are making the most rapid career progress and have the highest ambitions, are also finding the greatest disparity between the existing remuneration system and the kind of system they would like, then there is a strong chance that the company will be losing some of the men it most wants to retain. These may be problems to which the company wants to give priority attention in redesigning its remuneration system.

One difficulty which may be experienced in designing a remuneration system to match the motives and preferences of staff, is that some factors which would contribute greatly to the motivation of those employees are not within the control of the organization in the short term. For example, promotion aspirations in a company offering poor prospects, or stock options in a family-owned firm. The problem is then one of determining how much scope there is for providing the desired rewards, and devizing alternatives where this is very limited.

One final consideration when looking at remuneration systems in terms of their appropriateness is whether the staff's motives and preferences fit the requirements of the organization? One may well find a company facing a period of great external pressure and need for imaginative change, yet equipped with managers whose motives and preferences are oriented towards security and comfort. The appropriate remuneration system in this case may be one which does not satisfy the majority of present staff, but does fit in with the kind of staff the company wishes to recruit for its future needs. Instead of changing the system to fit in with present motivation, we may wish to change the system to change the motivation.

Cost-effectiveness in Remuneration Systems

So far we have concentrated on how to make the remuneration system motivationally appropriate. Salary administrators who are unfamiliar with that approach may think it is idealistic. After all, no organization can afford to be wholly philanthropic to its staff; it is essential to take account of costs.

In fact, given a slightly different emphasis, all the preceding points can be shown to be highly relevant to the cost of the remuneration system. Whether or not the system is motivationally appropriate is a question which overlaps with whether it is cost-effective. The two questions are opposite sides of the same coin.

Consider again one of the 'choice of emphasis' questions previously discussed, ie the degree of external comparability required in the system. In terms of appropriateness, we need to consider whether the staff are likely to feel that there is sufficient emphasis placed on these external comparisons; and if it is felt to be insufficient, we know we can expect some resulting dissatisfaction. In terms of cost, we need to consider whether we are placing too much emphasis on the external comparisons, and if so whether this carries a cost penalty. For instance, keeping abreast of external salary levels is unduly expensive if the organization is able to function with staff of relatively low levels of ability or qualifications, and if the staff themselves are uninterested in making outside comparisons. This is certainly the case with some types of retailing, and certain types of hotel business. In these circumstances, a minimal emphasis on external comparisons may be acceptable to the staff themselves while economical from the organization's viewpoint.

In this way, the remuneration designer can systematically review the five 'choice of emphasis' factors from the point of view of cost-effectiveness, asking each time what the minimum effective emphasis is going to be.

Emphasis on internal comparability, where this is not strictly necessary, is perhaps one of the most widespread types of inefficiency in remuneration systems. Employers often overrate the tendency of their staff to make such comparisons; once a system of internal relativities has been set up, however, such comparisons are invited and stimulated. Any requirement to increase the quality of staff in one area of the company by raising recruitment salaries then may be hindered by the inflexible salary structure, or if achieved may be followed by pressure from other groups to have their salaries adjusted as well.

Similarly, incremental salary systems are not only inappropriate when there is a situation of high mobility through the organization and upward within it, they are also wasteful. This is because they will be giving many increments to men who are likely to leave the organization, and also to those whose financial aspirations will in any case soon be satisfied by internal promotions.

The analysis of individuals' motives and preferences (see p. 272) is also relevant to questions of cost-effectiveness. One might perhaps have expected that when staff were asked to express their opinions on topics such as pay and benefits, their response would be simply 'let's have more of everything'. In practice this does not happen, and staff state clear priorities among different types of remuneration, making realistic assumptions about the total size of the cake. From this, it is possible to identify specific types of provision which are, or would be, cost-effective. For instance, a company providing expensive fringe benefits appealing to long-term security or to the motive of social status and prestige, is in fact wasting its money if these benefits are going to men who want job interest, achievement or capital accumulation. What an organization spends on its staff is not necessarily equivalent to the value the staff place on it. On the contrary, investigations repeatedly reveal mismatches, with underprovision and overprovision by the company relative to the staff's preferences. Careful attention to these subjective factors can therefore considerably reduce the cost of remuneration without reducing staff satisfaction.

A recent innovation in the design of remuneration systems has partly been shaped by thoughts such as these. This is what has been called the 'cafeteria system' (Chapter 24). The idea is to allow the individual a certain amount of selection in making up his own remuneration package, from a range of options or 'menu' specified by the employer. Thus the individual might prefer to take nearly all his remuneration in salary, and forego most of his benefits. The next man, however, might prefer to take a large proportion of his total remuneration in the form of benefits, provided that these benefits fitted in with his personal circumstances and motives. And so on. There are of course administrative costs involved in this approach, as well as many technical difficulties which are still being resolved. However, it does illustrate the principle of trying to increase the effectiveness and favourable impact of remuneration for a given cost. Naturally, the company must still decide on the cost structure of the system, and ensure that the various options offered are equivalent in cost terms.

Using the organization's resources effectively

Another way of approaching the cost-effectiveness question is to ask whether the organization is making the most of those resources which cost it relatively little to use in remuneration and motivation. These are resources which are built-in to the company's situation—but in many cases it may so much take them for granted that it does not use them fully.

Obvious examples of such special resources are the long-term security and orderly career progression of executive and administrative grades in the Civil Service, or the job interest and vocational satisfaction provided by medical or nursing work in the hospital service. One might argue, in these cases, that the organizations concerned were only too well aware of their special motivational resources, and tended if anything to over-play them. The general point holds, though, that when organizations have some special advantage of this kind to offer their staff, they can often simplify their remuneration provisions and in the process make them more economical.

There are some quite important instances where companies have started to use a resource, which previously had existed for a long period but had not been appreciated. The rising value of equity capital has of course been one of the major advantages for companies in post-war years (in spite of a set-back at the time of writing this chapter). But it was only in the late 1960s that British companies began to appreciate that this resource could provide the basis for a highly cost-effective form of incentive—the capital or share incentive scheme for senior managers (see also Chapter 17). Another example concerns company house purchase loan schemes. These have been provided by some banks and financial institutions for their staff for many years, at extremely advantageous interest rates. But it is only relatively recently that some large industrial companies have appreciated that, as they too have large financing resources, they can provide a similar staff benefit. While this is an expensive provision, it is quite likely to have a far greater effect on retention of staff than any other form of expenditure of equal size.

One of the most crucial resources for any organization, in relation to staff remuneration and motivation, is the promotion opportunities it offers. For most types of white-collar staff, and particularly for managers, promotion opportunities in the organization are extremely important. An organization in which the rate of promotion tends to be high can in many instances go for a very simple type of remuneration system. It may need to pay less attention to external comparisons, it should be able to reduce the incremental aspects of the system, and it may well also feel that performance-related incentives are superfluous. Although simple, its remuneration scheme is likely to be flexible and effective. On the other hand, a company with a low rate of promotion will need to apply considerable ingenuity if it is going to recruit, retain and motivate able staff and managers.

Unfortunately, it is not particularly easy for a company to assess objectively how strong its position is in terms of the promotion opportunities it is providing. Misleading claims about the prospects available abound in recruitment literature and job advertisements. While interfirm comparisons of salary levels are quite readily obtainable, promotion indices are completely lacking. Even if a company goes to the trouble of checking the historical rate of promotion in its own company, it will find it very hard to get anything with which to compare this. In any case, past rates of promotion may not be at all a good indicator of future promotion prospects; in some cases, it will be the reverse, since a spate of promotions for younger men will be followed by a longish period of low opportunity. For all these reasons, it is not uncommon to find organizations with unrealistic views about the opportunities they will be able to offer. This in turn probably means that they are not developing the right kind of salary policies to fit in with their true situation.

Recently, however, a valuable practical aid to analyzing this resource has been developed. Based on detailed research in a variety of industries, Lupton and Bowey (1974) have selected a list of eleven situational factors which influence the rate of promotions in organizations. They have also provided a key for assessing the individual organization's position on each of these factors. This is shown in Figure 18.3.

The first factor in Figure 18.3 concerns the labour turnover of the particular group of managers in the industry—previously called job mobility. The higher the labour turnover in the industry, the greater the

Labour turnover of these managers compared to other employers of similar jobs	*very low* say half of the average	*low* three-quarters of the average	*moderate* the same as the average	*high* one-and-a-half times average	*very high* say double the average
Labour stability compared to other employers	*very high* double the average	*high* one-and-a-half times average	*moderate* average	*low* three-quarter times the average	*very low* half the average
Number of employers in the labour market with jobs requiring the same experience and recognizing the same promotional criteria (ie transferable jobs)	*very few* less than 10	*few* 10 to 50	*moderate* 50 to 100	*many* 100 to 500	*very many* over 500
Rate of increase in the whole labour market of the numbers of transferable jobs	*static* not increasing; even decreasing	*slow* increasing by about 1% per annum	*moderate* increasing by 2% to 5% per annum	*fast* increasing by 5% to 10% per annum	*very fast* increasing by 10% and over per annum
Rate of expansion of the employer's managerial labourforce	*static*	*slow* 1% to 2% per annum	*moderate* 2% to 5% per annum	*fast* 5% to 10% per annum	*very fast* 10% per annum or over
Size of managerial labourforce	*very small* less than 10	*small* 10 to 50	*medium* 50 to 100	*Large* 100 to 500	*very large* over 500
Average age of managerial labourforce	no scores here	*young* 20s and 30s	*average* 40s	*old* 50s	no scores here
Centralization/ decentralization of the company	*totally centralized*	*much centralization*	*centralized to about the 50–50 extent*	*much decentralization %*	*totally decentralized %*
Extent of geographical dispersion of the company's plants and offices, as compared with other companies	*very little*	*little*	*average*	*much*	*very much*
Product diversity	*only one product or line*	*few* 2 to 10 lines	*average* 10 to 50 lines	*many* 50 to 100 products	*very many* more than 100 products
Degree of segmentation	*none*	*few* 2 to 5 segments	*average* 5 to 10 segments	*many* 10 to 50 segments	*very many* over 50 segments

Figure 18.3   Factors affecting the promotion resources available

chances (other things being equal) that someone will leave the company for a post elsewhere, thereby creating an internal opportunity for someone else. Again, halfway down the list in Figure 18.3 is a reference to the size of the managerial labourforce. The more management posts there are, the greater the chance of one or another of them becoming vacant. Of course, there will also be greater competition for such vacancies as they do occur, but from an individual's viewpoint it is still generally preferable to a situation where there are very few vacancies at all. In the same way, for each row entry in the table, promotion prospects tend to become more favourable as the situation changes from what is described at the left of the scoring key to what is at the right.

So, by assessing the company's position on each of the factors in turn, and then looking at the overall picture or profile which results from this analysis, an organization can evaluate the importance of promotion opportunities to itself as a motivational resource. In fact (in the reference already mentioned) the approach is taken a stage further, by identifying a number of the most commonly occurring combinations of circumstances which influence promotion possibilities (Figure 18.4).

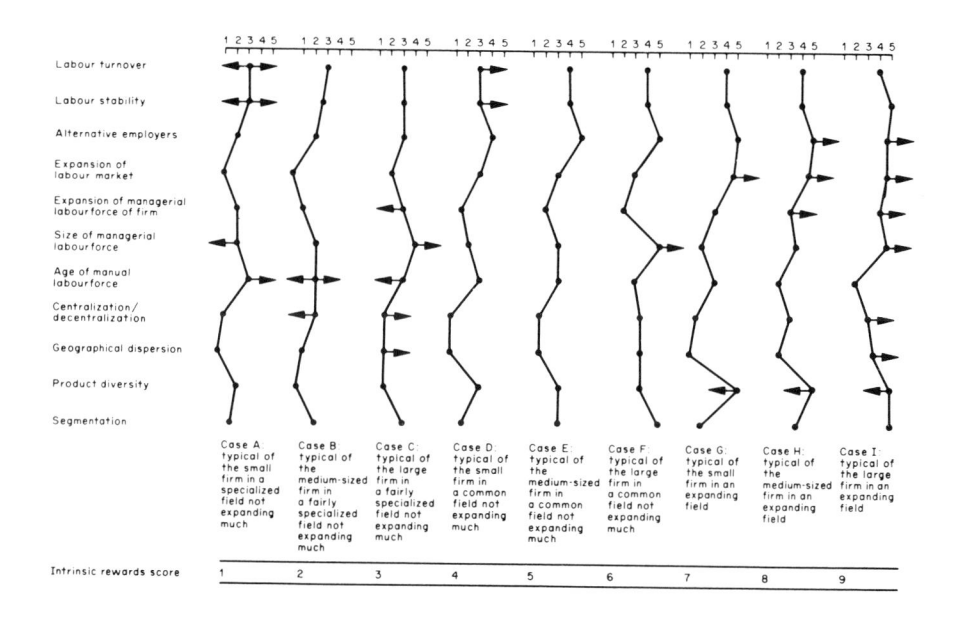

Figure 18.4 Commonly occurring promotion situation

It will be seen that these common patterns depend on three factors, in various combinations: the size of the company, its degree of specialization and its rate of expansion. If the company is a small one in a specialized field without much expansion taking place (case A in Figure 18.4), then promotion opportunities are likely to be particularly few and far between. At the other extreme, any large company in an expanding field is likely to provide high promotion potential. Most companies should therefore be able to identify themselves quite rapidly with one or another of the profiles shown in Figure 18.4. Having done so, a company can compare itself in more detail with the typical profile shown (the arrows in the figure indicate the most likely points for variations from the standard picture). It can also use the more detailed explanations given in Figure 18.3 where necessary. Having located itself within the range of profiles given, it can then realistically assess how strong it is relative to other organizations, in terms of the promotion opportunities it can reasonably offer.

But what practical steps can be taken once this analysis has been taken? In very broad terms, if it has strong promotion potential, it may be able to ease back on some of the other provisions in its system and look for methods of simplifying it. If however it is relatively weak in promotion potential, then it must search more widely among the possible remuneration options for some that will help to strengthen its position in other respects. Consider the smaller firm in a situation without much possibility of expansion. To recruit ambitious men into the company, with direct promises of future advancement, is going to lead only to frustration and cynicism. Equally, a benevolent incremental salary policy to keep loyal staff contented, will probably result in stagnation and a steady escalation of salary costs. However, a selective incentive scheme, rewarding either cost reduction achievements or the opening up of new business opportunities, could help to get a company in this situation moving. Until this has happened, the company must face up to the severe limitations on what it can offer its staff.

References and Further Reading

Armstrong, M. and Murliss, H., *A Handbook of Salary Administration*, Kogan Page, 1980.
Lupton, T. and Bowey, A., *Wages and Salaries*, Revised Edition, Gower, 1982 (forthcoming).
McBeath, G. and Rands, N., *Salary Administration*, Business Books, 3rd Edition, London, 1976.
McDougall, C., 'How well do you reward your managers?', *Personnel Management*, March, 1973.
Vernon-Harcourt, T., *Rewarding Management 1982*, Gower, 1982.
White, M., *Motivating Managers Financially*, IPM, London, 1973.

Part Five

Wage Systems

Editor's Introduction

In Britain and the United States there are a small number of fairly clearly defined types of wage payment system, and each of these is discussed in a separate chapter in this section.

Payment-by-results schemes of various kinds have been common in industry for the past 70 years or more, but during that period their popularity varied considerably. Originally conceived as the rational way to motivate workers to produce more work, they fell into some disrepute in the 1940s, 1950s and 1960s as a result of experience and research which indicated that in some circumstances they led to restriction of output and the proliferation of non-productive activities on the shop floor. However, in recent years in Britain there has been a revival of interest in payment-by-results, which can be explained at least partly in terms of the greater autonomy afforded to both workers and their immediate managers with such schemes and the desire for autonomy which has developed, and partly as a result of direct encouragement under some stages of incomes policy.

The major alternatives to payment-by-result schemes are payment-by-time schemes, where the wage level is determined by the hours worked rather than by variations in amounts of work done. Prominent amongst such schemes are the various types of measured daywork, although the link with rate of working is not broken entirely in a measured daywork scheme. Rather the worker is required to work at a fixed effort rating, the level of which he may have selected himself at some earlier stage.

With this kind of scheme total labour costs are not variable, and not prone to wage drift to the same extent as PBR; and the total production is a fairly predictable item. There is often resistance from shop floor workers, to the introduction of measured daywork schemes, due to the perceived ceiling on earnings and the greater management control and supervision which they imply. They have become less popular recently than they were in the 1960s.

A third type of payment system for manual workers is the company wide bonus scheme, of the Scanlon, Added Value and other kinds. In such schemes an annual bonus is paid on the performance of the entire factory based on a suitable index such as productivity improvement or cost reduction. In circumstances where favourable results are assured and the effort of the various departments appears equitable and the employees are satisfied with the management's accounting procedures, these schemes have been successful. But there have been failures due to low bonus payments, dissatisfaction with the contribution made by various departments, distortion of the management's figures and other causes.

Another factor in rewards which is often overlooked in the design of payment systems, is the significance of status as a reward. This topic is considered in Chapter 21; while Chapter 23 considers the problem of selecting a suitable wage payment system for a particular situation.

19

Payment by Results Systems

G H Webb

Straight Piecework and Flat Day Rate

The wages system which has imparted most of the classic nomenclature into discussions on the subject of wages systems is that known as payment-by-results (PBR). It springs from a basic philosophy, ie that a simple relationship can be established between effort and reward. In its primitive form it can be simply expressed as in Figure 19.1.

PBR presumes that if money can be used to induce effort, then more money will result in more effort. In its simplest form it still exists wherever, for example, outworkers or casual labour are employed on simple tasks. In essence the result of the effort must be clearly seen. The method of setting the standard of output is usually settled by a simple piecework bargain.

On the other hand, due to social, economic and political pressures the assumptions underlying such schemes are largely unacceptable in today's industrial climate. There is a contrary view, ie that a flat day rate is necessary to ensure that the worker is guaranteed a minimum or basic rate which should be sufficient to meet the social requirements and rising expectations of the workforce (Figure 19.2). This is the basis of the day rate systems and presumes that the employer, having struck the wage bargain, can secure a work output which is commensurate with the rate which is reflected in the wage bargain.

Alternatively, it is presumed that in negotiating the wage rate, the trade union, by implication, is admitting that there is an agreed amount of work that corresponds to the rate negotiated on behalf of their members.

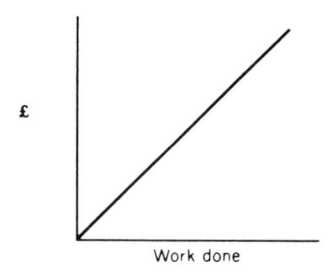

Figure 19.1   Simplest form of PBR—straight piecework

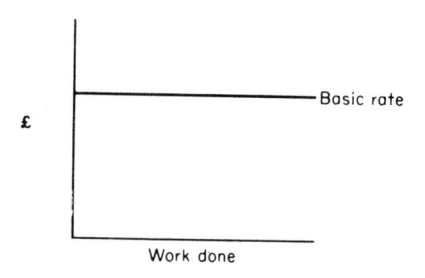

Figure 19.2   Flat day rate

The essential and underlying philosophy is that there is a fair day's work which corresponds to a fair rate of pay. In so far as the only finite part of the bargain is the wage rate, the only realistic assumption is that the rate of work is what one could expect from an unmotivated employee, who otherwise was working conscientiously. Thus as a wage system it is redolent with abstract conceptions like fairness, and consequently it is just as open to argument as straight piecework.

Philosophically, both systems are in conflict and most PBR schemes seek to resolve the difference by the superimposition of the systems (see Figure 19.3). The point at which the curves intersect in Figure 19.3 is the point at which a fair day's work is presumed to be given for a fair day's rate of pay. From the conventions established in the early days of work study (by Bedaux and his associates) the point of intersection is presumed to be that at which in one hour, 60 minutes of work were carried out by a competent and conscientious worker who was not motivated by a bonus incentive.

Payment of a Bonus Reward

How much extra work can be obtained from the payment of a bonus reward? Although in absolute terms there is little evidence to support the proposition, empirical data and observation tends to support the view that in favourable circumstances a financially motivated worker can produce about a third as much extra work as a financially unmotivated worker. The basic Bedaux nomenclature is shown in Figure 19.4.

For a variety of reasons, usually stemming from the need to rapidly compute bonus calculations in the wages office the 60/80 convention was abandoned, and replaced by the British Standard effort rating points of 75 and 100. Thus the basic discipline that is presumed to underlie PBR systems is that one-third extra effort should result in one-third extra payment. Where this simple linear relationship between

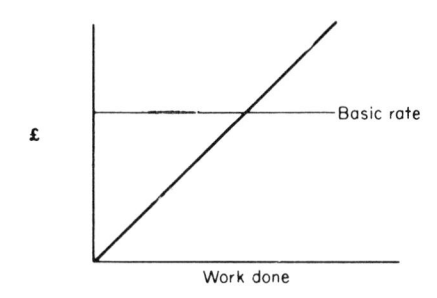

Figure 19.3 Superimposition of straight piecework and flat day rate curves to find fair day's rate of pay

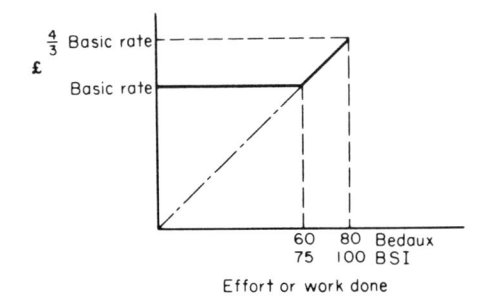

Figure 19.4 Effort rating scales

effort and reward is effected the resultant bonus scheme is called a straight proportional PBR scheme. Detailed consideration of effort rating scales is contained in Chapter 9.

There are more far-reaching, if less explicit, assumptions. In the first instance there is the presumption that in setting a standard bonus reward (at 4/3 base rate) the work study engineer has correctly defined the range of motor abilities and perceptual skills inherent in the job, whilst simultaneously the personnel selection procedures have correctly matched up to these and produced a workforce which has a distribution of these skills about the norm.

Thus the form of bargain, translated into personal abilities and bonus opportunity, is presumed to be of the form shown in Figure 19.5. The statistical assumption of the normal distribution of worker abilities and the evenly matched psychological response to the financial incentive presumes that for every worker exerting a 125 performance (with a related reward of 5/3 of the base rate) there is an employee only

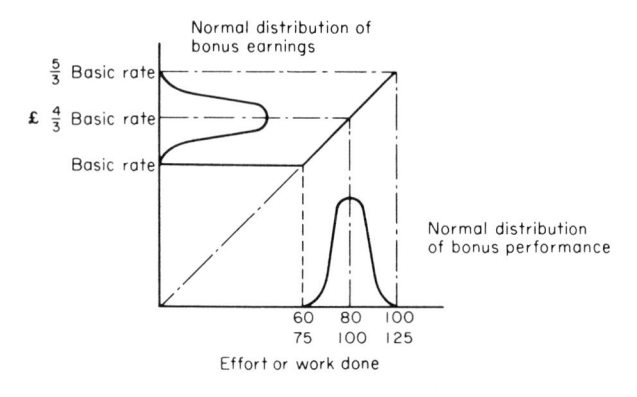

Figure 19.5   The form of bargain in terms of personal abilities and bonus opportunity

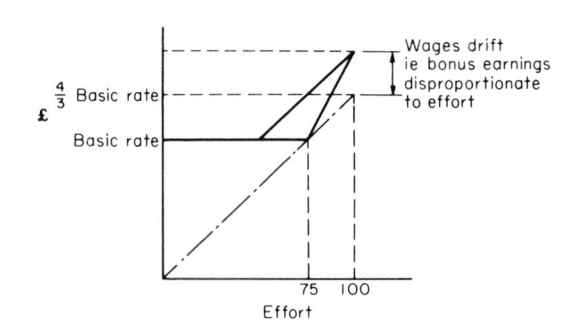

Figure 19.6   Distortion of presumed relationship between effort and reward—ie wages drift

capable of achieving a 75 performance and is thus only receiving the basic rate.

This makes further presumptions about the social group, namely that the social group is prepared to tolerate a spread of bonus earnings about a physiological and psychological norm established by a work study engineer. Clearly, bargaining activity will quickly result in the distortion of the relationship between effort and wages, which is the classic definition of wages drift! (Figure 19.6).

Historically, PBR schemes were introduced and applied to individual workers who were directly employed on the productive process. Notoriously this produced distorted earnings patterns between those directly employed on the production process and those who, like toolmakers, were only indirectly employed. Hence group PBR schemes evolved. Because of this, whilst there are many group PBR schemes, the underlying assumptions of individual PBR schemes should be examined and tested for their applicability to both individual and group schemes.

The underlying assumptions and consequently the necessary preconditions for successful operation of a PBR scheme are:

1. Left to himself a worker has a particular speed and tempo of work which he will intuitively select and employ during the course of his day's work.
2. A significant number of operations can be accurately measured.
3. The proportion of indirect to direct operations is relatively low and that these can be adequately covered by a 'reflected' bonus.
4. Properly motivated, an employee can make an additional effort of about 30% over and above his natural pace, for which he should receive more money.

The latter proposition has far-reaching implications. In order that the limitations of these schemes can be assessed and the efficacy of alternatives be appraised, these implications are explicitly stated as that:

1. There is a direct and demonstrable link between individual effort and the results obtained.
2. The cause of defective work can be precisely determined and responsibility for this be accurately apportioned and rectified by the person(s) responsible for the defective work.
3. The method of production is directly under the control of the operator (or those affected by the bonus opportunity).
4. The type of operation permits objective work standards to be set, which are attainable and can be enforced.
5. Variations in output (due to individual variations in performance) can be tolerated by the production control system, ie sufficient back-up stocks are available to meet fluctuating demands and variations in output can also be tolerated.

6 Costs resulting from the attainment of these standards can be carried and can be incorporated in the estimating procedure.
7 The employees will tolerate variations both in their individual earnings and between each other.
8 Cooperation will be forthcoming from those employees who are not able to participate directly in the bonus schemes.
9 High bonus earnings of one individual, or group of employees, will not stimulate pressures from other individuals for parity.
10 When high bonus earnings are obtained, these can be restricted to relatively small numbers of individuals in isolated groups even if they are not attainable by other sizeable groups of employees.

On balance the foregoing conditions apply to simple repetitive operations of short-time cycle where manual operations predominate. Where these conditions obtain a PBR wages system offers a satisfactory prescription.

If the total earnings, say in a week, derive from a number of jobs being performed (eg in a jobbing engineering plant) then it is the mix of standards (with all their tendencies to vary, one against another) that must also approximate in aggregate to the 'fair' standard designed to produce the desired bonus opportunity. The examination of the socio-economic method of production has been examined in detail by Lupton and Gowler (1969). However, the earnings accruing in a jobbing engineering plant from PBR systems invariably stem from not one job but a series of jobs carried out during the working week. As each of these jobs may have different time standards it follows that it is the aggregate of the time values, as expressed in the bonus earnings, which constitute a fair week's wage. Furthermore since the relative 'slackness' or 'tightness' of the mix of standards may vary there is a real tendency for the operator to select those jobs which give the best financial return and hence, in jobbing situations, PBR systems demand a high standard of production control.

The difficulty is reduced to one of work study. Assuming the method of manufacture has been properly determined by method study (the techniques which derive from methods time measurement (MTM) or other methods of predetermined method time study (PMTS) are discussed in Chapter 9), then traditionally the basic problem is to establish the time standard by time study.

The basic steps required to set up a labour standard by time study are:

1 Obtain and record all the information about the job, the operator and other factors likely to affect the job.
2 Record a complete description of the method and analyse it into its constituent elements.
3 Measure and record (usually with a stopwatch) the time taken by

the operator to perform each element of the process being timed—ie record the observed times.
4   Assess the effective speed of the operator—ie establish the rating relative to the accepted normal speed.
5   Convert the observed times to normal times by applying the rating factor (see below).
6   Apportion the allowances necessary for personal needs, fatigue and other factors.
7   Express the foregoing steps as an agreed standard time for the job.

The methods of timing (continuous, flyback, etc) are outside the scope of this chapter, but it is important to ensure that sufficient readings of each operation are carried out so that the number of observations of each part of the job are statistically valid. The tests applied are the normal statistical checks to ensure that a representative sample has been employed.

It is important to ensure that each operation is rated, ie an assessment is made of effort level that is employed, when each element is time studied. A representative number of operators must be time studied to diminish the possibility of the results being 'skewed' by basing the sample observations on an unrepresentative operator.

Granted that the rating is the same, a good practical check on the accuracy of the timing procedure is to reject any times which are outside a tolerance band of ± 2%. Since the purpose of rating is concerned with ensuring that different operators, performing identical tasks, are given parity of treatment, the basic philosophy of rating is established as:

$$\text{observed time} \times \text{rating} = \text{constant}$$

Since the object of rating is to establish a time for the operation which is fair between various operatives who at the time of observation were working at different rates and hence taking different times it follows from the basic equation above that a normalized time for the operation can be established from:

$$\text{observed time} \times \frac{\text{rating}}{\text{normal rating}} = \text{normalized time}$$

Thus, if we have two operatives doing the same job and one is rated at 125 taking 0.16 minutes while the other, rated at 80 takes 0.20 minutes and assuming the BS scale (75/100) was being employed, then:

Normalized time of first operative = $0.16 \times \frac{125}{100}$ = a standard time of 0.20 minutes

Normalized time of second operative = $0.25 \times \frac{80}{100}$ = a standard time of 0.20 minutes

Since the critical element is the rating, and rating which is subjective may be carried out by different time study engineers, it is important for the head of the work study department to perform rating checks at regular intervals, ie not exceeding one month. Essentially rating checks embody a simple idea, that all personnel involved in rating observed jobs should be conditioned to assess rates of work against predetermined subjective standards. In practice all the time study observers are called upon to observe the same jobs and to assess the rate of working. These are then compared with each other and the predetermined rate of the normalized test. By a series of successive approximations it is normally relatively easy to ensure that the effort ratings employed are consistent between the observers and lie within a tolerance band of ± 2% of the predetermined standard.

It is essential to insist that the consistency of rating is more important than the absolute value assigned. This is because inconsistent ratings are a fertile source of dispute and conflict.

Before the time studies can be reliably employed ensure that the operative is allowed time for relaxation or personal needs. The latter proposition is self-evident and by convention 5% (men) and 7% (women) of the standard time is allowed.

Subsequently according to the operation, and the circumstances in which it is performed, it will be necessary to allow pauses in the productive cycle to overcome the effects of:

1 Sustained physical exertion.
2 Prolonged concentration.
3 Cramped posture.
4 Adverse environmental conditions.
5 Inconvenience due to the need to wear protective clothing.
6 Monotony.

There is a substantial library of evidence related to the ergonomic characteristics of various categorized types of work and the appropriate allowances can be assessed from them. When the 'standard' is finally determined the remaining question is the 'learning curve effect'. It has been determined that, after the initial difficulties in achieving a standard operation, individual performance readily improves. Thus every standard has within it an element of inbuilt 'slack' which derives from increasing operator facility.

Accordingly, in some industries provision is made for reducing the initial standard over the passage of time. This, conventionally, is in accord with the empirically observed characteristic of improved performance over a period of time.

To summarize, a straight proportional individual PBR scheme is presumed to reflect the relationship between work and the final reward. The determination of the work is the key issue which characteristically follows the algorithm set out in Figure 19.7.

Payment by Results Systems 293

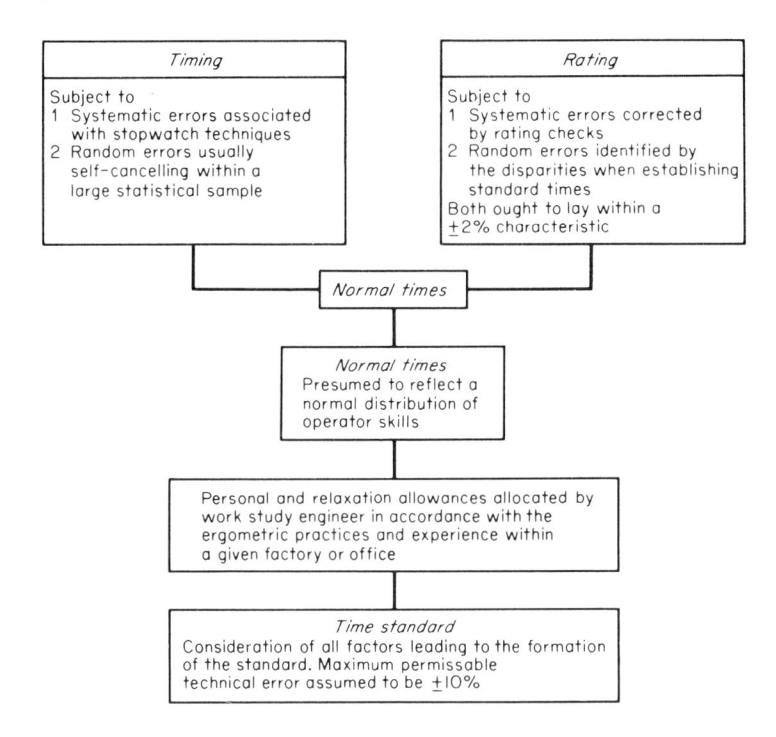

```
┌─────────────────────────────────┐      ┌──────────────────────────────────┐
│           Timing                │      │            Rating                │
│ Subject to                      │      │ Subject to                       │
│ 1 Systematic errors associated  │      │ 1 Systematic errors corrected    │
│   with stopwatch techniques     │      │   by rating checks               │
│ 2 Random errors usually         │      │ 2 Random errors identified by    │
│   self-cancelling within a      │      │   the disparities when establishing│
│   large statistical sample      │      │   standard times                 │
│                                 │      │ Both ought to lay within a       │
│                                 │      │ ±2% characteristic               │
└─────────────────────────────────┘      └──────────────────────────────────┘
                        │                         │
                        └───────┬─────────────────┘
                                ▼
                        ┌───────────────┐
                        │ Normal times  │
                        └───────────────┘
                                │
                                ▼
                ┌─────────────────────────────┐
                │        Normal times         │
                │ Presumed to reflect a       │
                │ normal distribution of      │
                │ operator skills             │
                └─────────────────────────────┘
                                │
                                ▼
        ┌──────────────────────────────────────────────────┐
        │ Personal and relaxation allowances allocated by  │
        │ work study engineer in accordance with the       │
        │ ergometric practices and experience within       │
        │ a given factory or office                        │
        └──────────────────────────────────────────────────┘
                                │
                                ▼
        ┌──────────────────────────────────────────────────┐
        │                 Time standard                    │
        │ Consideration of all factors leading to the formation│
        │ of the standard. Maximum permissible             │
        │ technical error assumed to be ±10%               │
        └──────────────────────────────────────────────────┘
```

Figure 19.7   Basic steps in establishing a time study standard

Geared Schemes

It is not always possible for each operation to be accurately measured nor for tests of statistical confidence to be applied to work study values. Even if these conditions are met, inherent variations in the material may cause the accuracy of rating on time study to be suspect.

Despite the technical limitations on accurate work study and to enable the operative to begin to earn a bonus, a well-tested device in such cases is to allow the operative to start earning a bonus at an effort that is less than that expected from an operative on a straight proportional scheme. Unless this was controlled, a form of wages drift would be present, by design. Hence, to stop the bonus earnings running away, the slope of the bonus curve is depressed. With such a scheme, although it is relatively easy to earn a bonus at the lower effort rating, the bonus at the higher levels is reduced (Figure 19.8).

The Economics of PBR Schemes

The economic attractions of PBR schemes derive from the fact that a given volume of production can, in turn, be expressed in terms of its unit labour costs. The practice is to equate a desired unit labour cost, referred to as the standard cost, to a 75 effort performance.

The attainment of a 75 effort performance means that the production director is achieving the norms of his standard costing system. Thus, by inducing the operative to increase his or her performance beyond a 75 effort performance, not only is the standard cost being attained but improved recovery of the fixed overhead burden is also achieved.

Beyond a 75 effort performance, however, the effect of bonus payments is to increase the labour cost, but this should be offset by the aforementioned improved overhead recovery. It is the attraction of relating the unit cost structure to the recovery of the overhead burden that has led to the widespread adoption of PBR schemes (see Figure 19.9). At a zero effort rating in Figure 19.9 the unit labour costs are ∞ (infinity) and the labour costs fall dramatically as one approaches the 75 effort performance or standard labour cost.

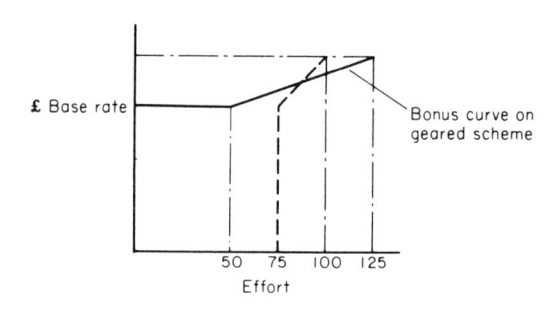

Figure 19.8   Geared bonus system

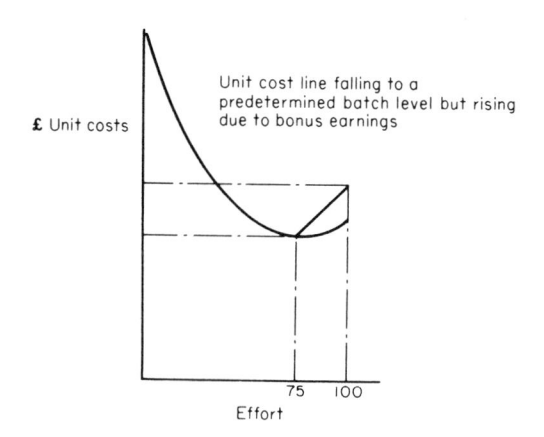

Figure 19.9   Unit cost curves

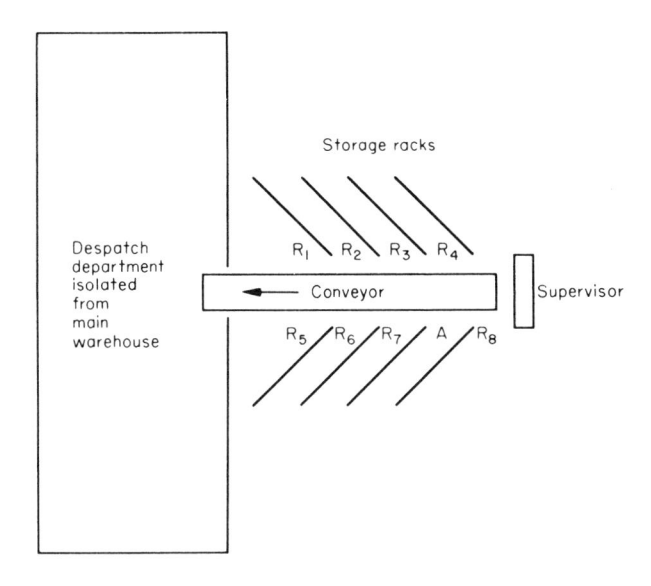

Figure 19.10   Example of a layout of a successful PBR scheme

Practical Illustration of a Successful PBR Scheme

The workplace comprises a large warehouse whose products are called off from a 'mail order' type of catalogue. Each operative is free to pick up from the supervisor the individual customer's order which details the products to be picked from the storage racks and packed for despatch. Each item of the customer's order has a work study value dependent upon its physical characteristics, ie weight, bulk, ease of handling, etc and its position on the storage rack and distance from the operative's work station.

The most important aspects of the system are:

1   That an adequate back up stock is always available on the storage racks.
2   The variable output of the individual operatives can be absorbed by the despatch department and this does not cause any consequential production problems.

In essence, the workplace is laid out as shown in Figure 19.10. An operative at station A, for example, picks up the work cards from the supervisor. Dependent upon the order slip the operator may be called to visit one (or more) of the racks R_1, R_2, R_3, R_4, R_5, R_6, R_7, R_8. The goods required are packed at the operative's station A and then conveyed mechanically to the despatch bay.

The despatchers are trained to record the shipping characteristics (including the code number of the packer) and the bonus department is able to translate the recorded characteristics of the packed items into the financial reward earned by the operatives.

It can be seen that by accurate work study the values of each item to be picked from the racks and packed can be used to express the work done by each individual operative.

Furthermore, since each operative can work at his (or her) own pace and by retaining a control sheet assess his (or her) daily output the application fulfills the classic criteria for successful PBR schemes.

References and Further Reading

ACAS, *Introduction to Payment Systems*. Advisory Conciliation and Arbitration Service, London, 1980. Advisory Booklet, no. 2.
British Standard Institution, *Glossary of Terms in Work Study*. BS 3138, British Standard Institution, London, 1979.
Brown, W., *Piecework Bargaining*, Heinemann, 1973.
International Labour Office, *Introduction to Work Study*. International Labour Office, Geneva, 1979.
Karger, D.W. and Bayha, F.H., *Engineered Work Measurement*. Industrial Press Incorporated, New York, 1979.
Lupton, T. and Bowey, A., *Wages and Salaries*. 2nd Edition, Gower, 1982 (forthcoming).
Wood, A., *A Theory of Pay*. Cambridge University Press, London, 1978.
Woodmansey, M., *Added Value: an Introduction to Productivity Schemes*. British Institute of Management, 1978.
Yetton, P., 'The efficiency of a piecework incentive payment system', *Journal of Management Studies*, Volume 16, no. 3, October, 1979.

20

Payment by Time Systems

Anne G Shaw and D Shaw Pirie

Introduction

Just as there is a range of payment by results (PBR) schemes from the most direct piecework to payment only very tenuously linked with real results, there is a range of schemes within the payment by time group. Some of these are concerned with results as well as time in that they define the workload or performance required in return for bonus or enhanced rates of pay.

Definitions

Figure 20.1 shows some of the main types of PBR and payment by time schemes set out in relation to one another. But the precise line between the two is difficult to draw. In this table stepped measured daywork is placed as the last in the PBR group rather than the first of the payment by time schemes, while measured daywork in its simple form is on the time side of the line. To demonstrate why we draw a distinction here it is necessary to define measured daywork as it was originally conceived and as in our organization it has been applied. The best definition of measured daywork in its purest form is:

> Measured daywork is a system of payment in which an additional fixed sum or bonus is paid on top of the basic rate for the job. This bonus does not vary with the amount produced. It is paid in return for maintaining a prescribed level of performance in terms of 'effort' or other composite measurement or assessment. If this level cannot be achieved for reasons for which management is responsible (not

enough work for example, machine breakdown, planning mistakes, etc) bonus is still paid. If the failure however is the fault of the operators there is an agreement that after due investigation and warning it is ultimately possible to withdraw bonus until they have returned to the agreed performance level. The bonus is therefore a reward for maintaining a standard performance (interpreted in the broadest sense). It is a guaranteed payment provided that the operators are available for work and ready and able to meet the standards required of them.

Payment by results—variable individual or group bonus payments

> Piecework—negotiated prices or time per unit.
>
> Work study based variable bonus schemes relating time to output as 'performance'.
>
> PPP—Philips premium payment plan—stabilizing the variable bonus into steps.
>
> 'Stepped measured daywork'—usually still broader steps and less frequent changes.

Payment by time schemes—fixed hourly or weekly payments with or without a bonus element

> Measured daywork—one fixed bonus guaranteed to workers ready and willing to meet an agreed common standard.
>
> High day rate—high level of hourly pay for unspecified high performance.
>
> Staff status or salary—a similar arrangement but on a weekly basis and with no performance implications.

Figure 20.1 Main types of payment by results and payment by time studies

The various kinds of stepped fixed bonus systems often called stepped measured daywork differ in important respects and on the whole belong more to the PBR group than to payment by time. The dividing line is drawn by classing as essential types of PBR schemes where the operators work to a target of their own choice rather than to a management-planned target.

On the other side of management-controlled measured daywork and firmly in the payment by time group are 'high day rate' type fixed-rate schemes where no declared relationship exists between pay and standard of performance. The term 'measured daywork' is frequently used for these schemes too, perhaps to recognize that they often contain a bargain to work at management-controlled speeds. Some 'high wage high task' schemes approach measured daywork very closely but the connection between task and payment is not usually as definite as in typical measured daywork. There is also a significant practical difference in that as there is no separate bonus element overtime and shift premiums are paid on the full enhanced hourly sum.

The concept of high day rate needs little further explanation (though many existing schemes have variants accounted for by the circumstances of the work and the industrial relations climate). The principle of staff status and of weekly and monthly salaries is also well known (though here again there are many local rules).

Measured daywork

The definition of measured daywork on p. 297 allows a wide variety of interpretations, designed to suit local circumstances and agreements. The 'additional fixed sum . . .' may be added to an existing basic rate or to some two- or even three-part payment structure allowing for job grading or occasionally for merit rating where this is feasible or acceptable. It may be expressed as a sum of money (£4 for 40 hours for example) or it may be negotiated as a percentage of the basic rate. It may be the same for all operators or the same percentage for all operators.

The 'prescribed level of performance' may be expressed in conventional work measurement terms as for example a performance of 95 or 100 on the BSI0–100 scale, or it may relate to some composite measure of machine or process efficiency or level of service or material utilization where such measurement more nearly meets management objectives.

In the case of failure to meet targets, action may vary between the extremes of a daily calculation with bonus withdrawn after two or more successive days of failure and not restored until the same number of days of success have been achieved, to setting up thorough investigation procedures and giving repeated warnings at the end of each weekly period and making a special re-taining effort to restore performance before accepting final failure. Much depends on operating needs and the nature of the work and skill required of the operators. It is also true that it is less easy in some types of work to be sure that the operator is solely to blame for failure. On the whole under measured daywork failure is most often met by investigation and remedial action rather than threats or actual withdrawal of bonus. Where measured daywork has been chosen as the appropriate incentive, getting the work done within the time allowed for it is usually much more important than penalising slack performance.

Within the definition, 'bonus' may or may not be paid for holidays, absence or sickness, depending on agreements, but it is usually withheld for casual absence. It should not be subject to any overtime or shiftwork premium.

Philosophy of Time-based Systems

A management that believes that motivation to exert maximum individual effort and achieve maximum output is the most important objective for a pay scheme, chooses some type of PBR.

The payment by time idea is consistent with other objectives and a different philosophy. Within this philosophy schemes of the measured daywork type offer management the opportunity to obtain a close control over output, performance or work allocation, making sure of a consistent steady optimum result rather than looking for occasional maximum individual effort or results. Such schemes can provide a strong framework within which employees can cooperate with each other and management without fear of losing financial advantage. Where control over throughput is provided by the nature of the plant or process, simpler schemes of the high day rate type may well be sufficient.

But in deciding how much control is needed there is another aspect to be taken into account. There is a great difference between firms (and trades) where no PBR has ever existed and those trades, managements, supervisors and employees who have been conditioned by the stresses and strains of any kind of PBR system (whether or not this is work-study based).

If it is desired, for whatever reason, to institute a time-based system where there is a history of PBR, we find that some interim measures are very often needed to allow a change in attitudes and that here measured daywork is one possible interim measure available on the way from PBR to high day rate or salary conditions.

Similarly where there is no history of PBR but where performance is very low, some inducement may be needed at first to raise it to desired levels. In this case measured daywork can be very useful as a step towards the later application of some kind of high day rate/salary agreement, meanwhile allowing closer control to develop over the relationship between hours and output.

Payment by time in all its forms is consistent with the idea that payment systems should be designed to encourage cooperation between work-people and management to achieve optimum results of whatever type may be required. Such schemes recognize the desirability of a regular, and as far as possible unchanging, pay packet for the average man or woman who has the need for a steady income to meet such weekly payments as mortgages and hire purchase as well as normal housekeeping expenses.

This was often the strongest argument for preferring it to PBR but the idea is perhaps less attractive under conditions of rapid inflation.

Why Choose a Time-based System?

Where a really effective PBR system has been in operation, recognizing and paying for wide and real differences in individual skill and effort (eg in some sections of the garment-making industries) the time for change may not necessarily have arrived. (Though this type of work is declining rapidly and is increasingly confined to a part only of the workforce even in these industries).

Replacing a degenerate PBR scheme

But there are many more situations where PBR (however otherwise suitable) is a disruptive force and a danger to good industrial relations, or where it has deteriorated as an incentive or is out of control. For these there is a strong case for abandoning it, though it is unrealistic to expect that this will immediately change attitudes or restore 'performance'. Positive action must also be taken to agree the alternative with union representatives and set up the revised management and supervisory controls that the change will require.

There must also be positive action to open new channels of communication between shopfloor and management with encouragement to discuss methods, manning and standards, and to aim at reconciling management and shopfloor objectives. Taking out a PBR scheme will remove a major source of conflict but it leaves a gap in communications by also removing the main reason for shop stewards and management to meet.

Where there has been no previous incentive scheme

The choice is easier where attitudes are not conditioned by previous experience of PBR. In these circumstances there is a strong argument for choosing a time-based system rather than PBR where:

1   Consistent output from everyone is required rather than maximum output from a few.
2   The rate of output is controlled more by machines or processes than by operators.
3   One operation is closely linked with others.
4   Optimum utilization of material is required.
5   It is important to maintain the standard of quality.
6   Management wishes to control production flow.

But the measured daywork type of scheme can also be successful in obtaining control and achieving a satisfactory performance in conditions quite different and almost the direct opposite of the conditions set out above, where frequent change in specifications, product or materials is necessary and, work is variable and difficult to measure (engineering or building maintenance for example, or other kinds of service work).

In these circumstances PBR is almost always ineffective because of measurement difficulties which also make it excessively expensive. Measured daywork can be an effective incentive and achieve control on a basis of much less precise measurement.

Advantages of time-based systems

Time-based systems have certain advantages over PBR. These include:

1 Simplicity of operation
2 Stable pay structure (no leapfrogging)
3 Unchanging weekly pay packet
4 Overall labour cost control
5 Minimum strain on industrial relations
6 No bar to the mobility and flexibility of labour
7 Readier acceptance of change
8 Economy in installation and administration
9 An encouragement to cooperation between workers
10 A positive incentive to improve training.

Selecting the most appropriate type

In deciding the particular type of time-based system the difference between measured daywork and high day rate, staff status or salary is often more a matter of priority and emphasis than of total difference of objectives.

Within the time-based group measured daywork offers the greatest control over overtime working since it requires a prescribed level of performance, and extra time taken causes failure to meet target. The fact that premium is not paid on bonus for overtime hours also has some significance. Again measured daywork is usually the most positive incentive to improve operator training since it requires a consistent output from everyone. In the same way, applied to groups, it is a strong incentive to cooperation within the group. Where these are not important considerations or where there is some non-financial incentive or control to take the place of the financial incentive, high day rate and even salary may be equally appropriate and simpler still to operate. The choice of high day rate in chemical and other plants where hours are controlled and much of the work is of an attendance kind where 'effort' is of little relevance, is obviously appropriate. At the opposite extreme a case can be made out for high day rate for car assemblers where speed of work is set and controlled by the pace of the assembly line, though measured daywork would be equally appropriate (and indeed it seems that the distinction between the two in the car industry is frequently not very clear—except that there is no distinct bonus element in the schemes as published). Staff status or salary on the other hand offers no direct control over either hours or performance.

It is often suggested that a company cannot afford a time-based system where work is seasonal or intermittent. In fact where such a system is adopted (for other overriding reasons) in these circumstances it is a very powerful incentive to management to forecast and plan the use of manpower resources economically. Measured daywork and high day rate firms can afford to spend a little more on matching their manpower to their work since they pay less to calculate bonus earnings.

Operational Points

The purely payment aspects of even the most elaborate time-based scheme of the measured daywork type are essentially easy to administer since the basic control over the pay packet is simply that bonus is paid on the same basis as hourly pay—varying only with variations in the number of hours worked. Any change is exceptional and after warning. This is no more difficult for the wages department than day rate or salary.

On the shopfloor the checking of bonus entitlement again goes on the exception principle. For bonus purposes it is not necessary to calculate how much anyone has exceeded target (though this may be needed for planning purposes). The only requirement connected with pay is to examine all the details of those who may possibly have failed. Most other aspects of administration are also simpler but there are some exceptions and variations.

Work study requirements

The least demand for work study support is made in those already controlled situations, eg machine controlled and process work of all kinds where the requirement is to man the area or plant to a certain measured level and from then on merely to make sure that the agreed manning produces the required programme or quality of work. Very often for this type of work no very fine measurement is involved since most decisions are of a type involving choice between say 3 men or 4, a large difference as a percentage. Work study responsibility for standards, beyond the first manning study, is therefore minimal and is confined to periodical checks which can be planned in advance.

In more complex situations, for example production lines, variable work such as repair maintenance, repetitive individual or group production with a degree of operator control and many kinds of packing, there is a need for continued monitoring of performance against target. Work of this kind needs measurement, or assessment for measured daywork very like PBR but a higher proportion of assessment to measurement is acceptable, and because operators do not gain or lose by mistakes, less immediate work study attention is needed. It is possible to run for considerable periods on assessed time standards, since changes made later do not affect the pay packet.

Management information

Management information may need special attention under a time-based system. Quite often less detailed records are needed for payment than are needed for management control of a wider kind, and it may therefore be necessary to require additional special shopfloor records to be kept for use, for example, for estimating and costing.

Raising performance levels

It is possible to ask for performance at any level between BSI 75 and 100. It depends very much what the work requires and what is possible to negotiate.

If before introducing a scheme of the measured daywork type there has been no incentive scheme and performance is (as is often the case) below BSI 75 it may be necessary to use two or three steps to reach maximum performance (if this is to be in the BSI 75—100 range). Bonus levels can be adjusted to these steps and in due course the top level will be reached. This is a legitimate way to allow time to achieve maximum results but it must be a one-way ladder and the steps should be taken by whole departments at the same time or the measured daywork principles of regular equal earnings and steady performance are lost.

Group working

Wherever possible when changing from PBR to measured daywork the fixed bonus should be paid to groups not individuals. It may sometimes be advisable to make an interim change from individual to group PBR before moving one step further to measured daywork or beyond to high day rate. Any group, even quite a small group, provides some averaging effect and this encourages cooperation within the group and makes it easier to meet high average performance targets. If it is also less easy to withdraw bonus from a group this in our opinion is a good feature since the whole objective of time-based schemes is to achieve steady performance. Penalizing bad performance does not get the work done. Helping operators to raise it does.

Some Implications of Adopting a Time-based System

Where a time-based system is adopted and particularly where it replaces PBR there are certain effects upon the role of staff and workers representatives at shopfloor level that need to be given some consideration.

Shop stewards

Having accepted either measured daywork or high day rate, a shop steward is committed to equality of earnings. The shop stewards as a group lose the opportunity to use the differences between departments to achieve a leapfrogging effect by negotiating policy allowances on the time standards set in less successful areas or obtaining other concessions to raise earnings. There is no doubt that some union opinion is reluctant to agree to change from PBR to a time-based system for these and similar reasons.

But further experience suggests a new and better role for the shop steward. Free from the divisive effect of PBR it is possible to develop real workplace participation in the development of all kinds of improvement in methods of work and working conditions which will benefit both workpeople and management.

Supervisors

There is nothing in a time-based system, even in one of the measured daywork type, that alters the basic job specification of a supervisor, but there is quite a lot that alters the bias and the detail of his work if he has previously operated within a PBR scheme.

The main change is towards helping operators to meet targets instead of leaving them to choose their own level of performance. This involves analyzing their difficulties (mainly of method or understanding) and applying the relevant correction. Alternatively it means analyzing the work itself and identifying what is holding operators back (for example machine stoppages, material and component shortages or faults and so on).

The second major change is that instead of being under pressure to share out 'good' and 'bad' jobs between all operators, a supervisor under any time-based scheme can and should give out the work where it will be done best and most easily.

PBR schemes are known where supervisors (and work study staff) spend a considerable part of each morning sorting out bonus anomalies from the previous day. Instead of this, with a time-based scheme the supervisor keeps a daily watch on the minority who may be falling behind and warns and helps them in time to pull up and is left at the end of the week (or, in some cases, day) with only a very small number of apparent failures to investigate. These will usually be reduced to a still smaller number to be officially warned and marked down for further intensive help during the warning period. If this help is effectively given there should be no offenders at the end of the next period.

As well as watching for and helping those who are in danger of falling behind through their own inadequacy, a supervisor has a positive role to play in anticipating problems and preventing holdups generally. For example, instead of, as under PBR, the operators complaining about material shortages, it is now the supervisor's job to take action in advance. The same applies in cases of machine breakdown. He has the entire responsibility for seeing that the interruption is as short as possible.

It has been suggested that time-based systems need more supervision. This is because there is a belief that under PBR workpeople are motivated to keep working with minimum supervision. This has not been our experience. If in fact any large number of workpeople have been left without direct supervision under PBR there is a very good chance that all kinds of irregularities will have built up and then of course when the PBR incentive is removed the supervisory problems will be exposed and require extra appointments.

Other staff concerned with production

It may be that under PBR shopfloor supervision, planning, work study (including clerical assistants) and even the personnel department have taken over some of the normal supervisory duties. Some of these duties can be returned to the line supervisor under a time-based system which may increase the number of line supervisors but only in proportion as the other specialists are reduced. Certainly there is likely to be a reduction in the work study establishment. But this is felt only at the lower levels. The senior well-qualified work study staff have a wider role under a time-based system and much more opportunity to concentrate, for example, on method improvement and planning techniques.

Summary

It is perhaps useful to sum up what can be expected from instituting a time-based scheme or substituting such a scheme for PBR.

Effect on performance and labour cost

Where no incentive has existed previously and 'performance' is at a daywork level, it takes time and a deliberate re-training exercise to bring it up to the full potential but even if it is necessary to create a series of upward steps performance can be raised in due course and this achieves a net cost reduction provided that manpower planning and control is exercised at the same time. If the labour available is not balanced to the workload then of course the cost of idleness has increased. But as soon as the numbers are in balance with the quantity of work at a higher level of performance the same output costs no more in wages than under non-incentive daywork conditions and there is a saving in social security and other labour on-costs. This is true even where work is seasonal. It costs rather less to have the same percentage of higher paid people idle than the equivalent larger number of lower paid.

Cost of changing schemes

Where there has been a PBR scheme the cost of the changeover is usually greater and in theory it can result in a net additional cost. It may be necessary to compensate above average earners and it is usually not possible to negotiate the new hourly pay or bonus at a strict average of previous earnings. It may also be necessary to alter a whole pay structure to bring bonus back to a smaller proportion of total pay and this will have other costs of adjustment. It is not necessarily difficult to maintain average performance because although in theory, and sometimes in practice, the highest PBR earners may hold back for a time after a change to a time-based scheme, the lower performers have a much stronger incentive to pull up, particularly if the new scheme is of the simple measured daywork type. The same re-training suggested above for the daywork situation is effective for below-average performers previously on PBR and by bringing them up nearer to average offsets any falling back by exceptional performers.

Because most PBR schemes have not in fact maintained the ideal position where all work is well measured and all operators are equally motivated to do their best, the real effect of a changeover from PBR to measured daywork can be a substantial net saving and a rise in productivity in spite of requiring an above average bonus payment.

Long-term effects

The long-term effect on productivity depends entirely on the quality of management control. Experience shows that where the measurement (and manpower planning and control) has continued as originally set up, productivity actually increases in the long term. Where this control is allowed to lapse productivity does not continue to increase and may even drop back.

References and Further Reading

Brown, Wilfred, *Piecework Abandoned*, Heinemann Educational, London, 1962.

Jaques, Elliott, *Equitable Payment*, Heinemann Educational, London, 1967.

Office of Manpower Economics, *Measured Daywork*, HMSO, London, 1973.

Shaw, Anne G., 'Measured daywork—a step towards a salaried workforce', *The Manager*, January 1964.

Wilson, C.H., Shaw, Anne G., and Greenhow, Arthur, 'How to make productivity pacts', *Management Today*, August 1967.

There have been very few publications on the topic of measured daywork since 1973.

21

Status, Effort and Reward

Dan Gowler and Karen Legge

The relationship between status and reward is one about which most managers hold implicit assumptions, but which few examine systematically. Most would argue that a 'high status job' should be more highly rewarded than a 'low status' one and that differential rewards for jobs of different status are not only inevitable but, subject to debate about what is the appropriate status of each job, right and proper. Yet few would consider it necessary to make explicit exactly what they meant by status or by reward. However, these definitional issues cannot be ignored by those involved in the design of wage payment and salary systems, for what may appear to the layman to be mere quibbles over semantic niceties can in fact involve serious practical difficulties. Ambiguities of definition that are not resolved in the design of payment systems may reappear as problems in their administration.

Our first intention was to examine the definitional and practical problems inherent in the relationship between status and reward. Yet, in doing so, we were confronted by another issue. In Lupton and Gowler (1969), a salary or wage payment system was defined as 'a number of rules and procedures which relate effort and/or status to reward'. What this statement implicitly ignores is a consideration of the relationship between status and effort. Any examination of the relationship between status and reward is incomplete if it ignores the question of effort. This chapter considers what the characteristic relationships between status, effort and reward are, or, to put it more precisely, how different definitions of these concepts reveal different patterns of relationships, which have important consequences for decision-making about such problems.

What is Status?

The term 'status' is confusing, as it may be used in two distinct but related ways. It may mean simply a social position which is defined and identified by the cluster of rights and obligations attached to it. Alternatively, it may be used to refer to how a social position is ranked relative to other positions. This confusing dual usage arises because it is generally how society evaluates the cluster of rights and obligations that comprises a social position that determines its rank. Thus, the position of manager is a status, but the term may equally be used to indicate the level of prestige attached to that position (eg a 'high' status job). Although many managers explicitly equate status with prestige, they often implicitly equate it with social position, ie with certain rights and obligations. Job evaluation provides a case in point. The first step in this technique is a careful study of all the jobs within a given area, in which they are described and assessed in relation to certain dimensions, eg responsibility, skill, difficulty, physical demands. The second step is that the jobs are ranked in order of their score on each of the variously weighted dimensions. Sometimes these rankings are then directly related to a system of reward. Thus, in terms of the definition of status, the first step constitutes an examination of what the job comprises, ie the job as a social position (status as rights and duties), while the second step involves an evaluative process which identifies the job's rank relative to other jobs (status as rank and prestige). Whereas managers generally recognize that the concept of status is involved in the second step, they are not often aware that, in another sense, it also underlies the first.

Thus, status, in terms of social position, is identified by the cluster of rights and obligations that are attached to it. It is now necessary to add that these rights and obligations arise either from what the person occupying the status is perceived to be, or from what he is perceived to do.

Hence, it is possible to classify status as either ascribed or achieved. An ascribed status refers to those positions that an individual inherits, eg those that arise from such characteristics as age, sex, kinship, relation, birth into a particular class, caste or ethnic group. In other words, positions he acquires by virtue of what he is, rather than through what he does. An achieved status refers to those positions that result from the personal attainment of goals set by society, ie positions that an individual acquires as a result of what he does rather than what he is. A clear example of the difference between ascribed and achieved status is provided by women in employment. Prior to the Equal Pay Act (and, many would say, despite it), there still existed categories of jobs either formally or informally classified as 'women's' or 'men's' work, irrespective of the actual abilities required to do the job. Or, put differently, there will be (and still are) some statuses closed to individuals on the grounds of their sex (what they are) rather than through any inability to exercise the rights and obligations attached to the status (what they can do). However, a woman, say, might be ascribed to only certain classes of work but, within this constraint, she may still have the opportunity to achieve certain statuses, eg, that of supervisor over other female workers.

It is necessary to indicate this distinction here, because in the examination below of the relationships between status, effort and reward, whether status is ascribed or achieved has totally different effects on the type of effort the individual provides, and, ultimately, on the choice of an appropriate reward system.

Effort and Reward

As with status, neither 'effort' nor 'reward' are unitary concepts, and this causes confusion in their use. For example, when we speak of the 'effort' a job entails, we may be talking about any one of three different, if overlapping, requirements. As classified in Lupton and Gowler (1969), 'effort' may be considered as involving behaviours along three different dimensions, viz. time, energy and competence. Briefly, in the performance of his job, an employee may be called upon to expend in various degrees one or all three of these resources: he may be expected to devote a certain number of hours over a given period to his job (time), and/or to achieve a certain rate of working, as measured by the quantity and quality of his output (energy), and/or to provide and utilize the skills and experience he has acquired in the past (competence). Clearly, these dimensions are not discrete: to achieve a required rate of working (energy), skills and experience (competence) may need to be utilized. Further, the skills an individual brings to his job and his rate of working are likely to influence the number of hours he is either required, or is willing, to provide (time). However, we believe these distinctions provide a useful point of departure for our analysis.

It must also be remembered that this is really an observer's classification of effort. Different individuals and groups within an organization may wish to interpret or use such a classification in different ways. For example, while an individual might recognize that his job demands the exercise of certain skills and competences (ie a type of effort in the observer's eyes) he may classify this opportunity in terms of reward rather than effort, if he believes that his use of his skills contributes to his development and provides him with a great deal of job satisfaction. Alternatively, a group of individuals may agree that these dimensions constitute the 'effort' involved in their job, but may disagree with their superiors as to the weighting and remuneration of the various types of effort involved. For example, it is well known that employees often consider that all the skills they bring to the job should be rewarded on a continuous basis, even if they are utilized only intermittently, while management may only recognize and reward these skills when they are directly used in the performance of tasks.

The point being made is that, while we may define and classify a concept like 'effort' on the basis of what we observe individuals to find relevant, different individuals may choose which of the several meanings they impute to it, and the meaning(s) which is (are) chosen will determine the perceived relationship with other concepts (such as status and reward).

The same point might be made about the concept of reward. As with 'effort', this concept is multi-dimensional, but again without the dimensions being fully discrete. 'Reward' may refer to either tangible (ie material) rewards, eg in an organizational context, wage packet, salary, fringe benefits, or intangible (ie non-material) rewards, eg job satisfaction, prestige, influence. However, some forms of reward contain both tangible and intangible aspects. In the case of promotion, the movement to a higher ranked job not only brings with it increased prestige and, say, influence over the allocation of scarce resources, but also an increased salary and fringe benefits. But different individuals may not only interpret these 'rewards' in different ways, but place different values and priorities on them. Thus, while most employees would regard promotion as a reward, a minority would undoubtedly regard it with anxiety, fearing their abilities to cope with the demands of the 'larger' job. In such cases, employees often prefer to do without the increased material reward, regarding, as a higher priority, the more intangible reward of a job with which they are reasonably comfortable. Similarly, an employee may directly substitute one form of reward for another, as when he chooses to do a 'good job' and so enjoy job satisfaction at the risk of a loss of earnings, when working under an incentive system which puts a higher priority on quantity rather than quality of output.

Status as Rank

Clearly the terms status, effort and reward can have several meanings both to the individual who is using them, and to the individuals and groups in reference to whom the terms are being used. Hence, there is no single pattern of relationship between status, effort and reward, but many permutations. This section discusses some of the most characteristic.

First, if we take 'status' to imply some form of ranking, then high status may be a reward in itself and low status a form of deprivation. Thus, the prestige attached to positions such as 'member of the board' or 'professor' may give rise to as much gratification in the holder as the accompanying material rewards. Recognizing this, organizations frequently seek to reward employees by the provision of symbols to make visible the 'high' status of their jobs, eg the attainment of a certain managerial grade may be marked by the privilege of a company car, the use of exclusive dining and washroom facilities, extra holiday entitlement, etc. Even between manual and white-collar workers the differences in rank are still marked by such symbols as the different 'clocking-on' procedures, although between these groups other differentials, eg pay, have been greatly eroded. However, the extensive use of status symbols is partially self-defeating. Because they are often highly prized, as much for their symbolic as well as material content, there is a tendency for their use to permeate down the managerial hierarchy. Yet, if this occurs their symbolic content (and value) is largely debased (as today with 'executive' dining rooms and use of company car) as they cease to be associated exclusively with 'high status' jobs, this process often being accompanied by their recipients assuming a more calculative attitude to their material value. Finally, there is the well known fact that such symbols may create envy and resentment in those who do not have them.

In most organizations, it is recognized that the level of material reward attached to a status (social position) should be consistent with its rank. Thus, the 'higher' the status within an organization, the higher the salary, and fringe benefits and, conversely, the lower the status, the lower the associated material rewards. This practice, of course, serves to reinforce the rank ascribed to any status. But what is less readily recognized is that the mode in which the material rewards are packaged may accentuate the differences in status. Thus, the man in a high status job not only can command higher earnings than the man in a low status job but, because they generally come to him as a stable salary rather than as a variable wage, he can raise credit, eg a mortgage, on the basis of this stability. However, this process also has its limits. Although the achievement of high material rewards, directly or indirectly, is consistent with high job status, a blatant calculative materialism is not. Furthermore, many people in our society claim high occupational status partly on the grounds that they have to sacrifice material rewards to preserve and maintain certain values, eg to serve the 'best interests of the client', to protect 'the pursuit of excellence', 'professional integrity', etc. The satisfaction obtained from pursuing these values, an intangible reward, is often argued to compensate for any sacrifice of material reward.

Status as Ascribed Social Position

Turning now to status as a social position, the relationship between ascribed and achieved status and reward raises several interesting issues. Generally speaking, in companies, and in our society as a whole, there is a belief that individuals should be rewarded for what they do (achievement) rather than for what they are (ascription). For example, charges of nepotism are likely to be made if a managing director's son is believed to receive promotion to a high status job because of his kinship position rather than through the demonstration of competence. However, in one instance, it is common to reward on the basis of ascriptive status. This is when we reward individuals on the basis of age, as with 'juvenile' and 'adult' rates or, more commonly, in white-collar and managerial jobs, with annual 'birthday' increments, or the placing of a new employee at a certain point in the salary bands on the grounds of what is appropriate to his age, as well as to his experience. One reason for this is that many people believe that there is a relationship between age (ascribed status) and experience (achieved status), which is often expressed in such aphorisms as 'experience comes with age'. In other words, the achievement of certain competences is often thought to be a function of age and maturity. For example, in the armed services, promotion up to a certain level is more or less automatic upon the achievement of a certain age (with an implied length of service and assumed experience).

It is in the area of promotion that the relationship between age and reward is most apparent. Even in organizations where there is a genuine commitment to promotion on merit, there is often reluctance to promote employees to senior jobs until they have achieved a certain age, on the grounds that young men, irrespective of ability, may lack the appropriate experience and 'maturity'. Equally, there may be reluctance to promote a younger, if more capable, employee over the head of an older, if less able, one. Nevertheless, we consider that the relationship between age and promotion is, and will continue, to weaken. With the rate of change in market and technical environments progressively increasing, the value of such experience as is slowly acquired over the years, may be diminished, as much of it may simply not be relevant. It is likely that in place of the 'experience of age', the ability to absorb, analyze and evaluate new information quickly and effectively and adapt rapidly to change will be necessary for promotion.

It is however unlikely that age, as an ascribed status, will disappear entirely from consideration in the allocation of rewards, for two reasons. An employee's age will largely reflect what statuses he occupies in the developmental cycle of his family, as husband, father, grandfather, etc, and reflect the likely nature of his domestic financial obligations. Any organization has to bear these in mind when attempting to attract and retain labour, whether it is a question of providing overtime for the married manual worker with children and a mortgage, or establishing a competitive salary structure. Indeed, one of the most tenacious survivals of rewards based on ascribed status, ie the practice of paying men and women different rates for performing the same job, was for long justified on the grounds of the heavier domestic financial commitments that male workers were assumed to have. Furthermore, there is the practical problem that as employees now live longer following retirement, as the practice of 'early retirement' develops, and as the rate of inflation increases, generous pensions, as a form of reward, become more necessary and more desirable. Again, as with other age-related payments, this can be argued to reflect achieved as well as ascribed status. For the size of the pension is usually related to the size of the final salary that the employee receives, ie it reflects the promotions he has had and the position he has achieved in the company.

Given all this, are material rewards for ascribed status on the decline? We would argue that in a rationalistic, means-ends oriented society there exists a strong value that reward should be received for endeavour and achievement, and not for any ascribed characteristic. Furthermore, it is also difficult to establish a rational relationship between ascribed characteristics and effort, ie there is a tendency for the relationship between ascribed status and effort to be very tenuous. Organizations therefore find it difficult to justify the allocation of any material rewards on ascribed characteristics alone, especially if the reward, as in the case of increments to salary, is on a regular and continuing basis. It is interesting that in one example of a reversal of this trend away from rewarding on the basis of ascribed status, ie compensation paid to the redundant employee, not only was the practice instituted by the state, but the payment is in terms of a lump sum, and on a once-and-for-all basis. Generally speaking, though, reward on the basis of ascribed status, is increasingly likely to be of a non-material, intangible nature— eg the respect and deference given to the oldest employee in the department.

An apparent example of the reverse trend, ie from reward for achieved status to reward for ascribed status, is provided by the move towards 'staff status'. But note that we use the term 'apparent' since we hold the view that this is not the case. For the introduction of staff status may, in the short term, sever the relationship between achievement and reward, in the sense that the employees concerned are then rewarded for what they are rather than for what they do. However, in the longer term, the relationship between achievement and reward tends to be re-established through appraisal schemes, tighter managerial control, etc, where employees are then rewarded for what they do rather than for what they are.

Furthermore, the change to staff status, with progression from reward for achievement to reward for ascription and then back to reward for achievement, is accompanied by changes in the definition of achievement or effort. What happens here is that, at the outset, employees are generally rewarded for combinations of time, energy and competence effort. Then, following the transitional period of reward for achievement, employees tend to be evaluated in terms of competence effort alone. Thus there is a change from traditional payment systems based on output (energy effort) and hours worked (time effort) to salary schemes based on assessments of skills and qualifications (competence effort).

These comments on the change to staff status provides a striking example of the main theme of this chapter, ie that changes in the type of status also change the type of and relationship between effort and reward.

Status as Achieved Social Position

The relationship between achieved status, effort and reward raises different issues. By definition, as individual's achieved status reflects what he actually does (his effort) rather than what he is. Yet it is quite clear that the different types of effort an individual may expend are allocated different forms of tangible and intangible rewards. In our society, competence effort tends to be more highly rewarded, whether in terms of prestige or material rewards, than energy or time effort, eg a surgeon is more highly rewarded than a hospital porter. The reasons for this are not hard to determine; they range from the 'scarce resource' argument (brains are harder to come by and less easy to replace than brawn) to the 'investment argument' (the time and costs incurred in the acquisition of the skills and competences concerned). However, although these distinctions between types of effort and their relationship with types of reward look reasonable enough, they warrant further discussion.

Firstly, the different components of effort, as commented earlier, are not fully discrete. Second, individuals and groups may evaluate types of effort in different ways. Thus management may place a higher value on the level of output their craftsmen achieve than on their level of skill, and this view may be reflected in the introduction of a reward system, comprised of a relatively low basic rate supplemented by a highly geared incentive scheme. The craftsmen, in contrast, may consider that it is their level of skill and investment in training that should be rewarded (by, say, a high basic rate) as it is this that gives them their identity, whilst also encouraging them to maintain a satisfactory level of output. Similarly, disputes about earnings levels often occur around the recognition and evaluation of the types of effort a job involves—as in differentials disputes, or during job evaluation exercises. In other words, the value attributed to the different types of effort a job involves directly influences not only the level of material reward but the method by which it is paid. This is important, because it is now well-known that the type of reward system influences the level and stability of earnings that may be achieved. It is not surprising then that the different values attributed by individuals and groups within an organization to the types of effort they claim to provide are a potential source of conflict and an area where intelligent organizational design is crucial.

Secondly, there is another important difference between ascribed and achieved status, which involves their relationship with reward. In the case of ascribed status, its relationship with reward cannot be reciprocal—a term used to describe the fact that certain systems of reward, eg payment by results, explicitly incorporate the principle of the incentive, ie that effort and reward are reciprocally related. (In other words, extra effort results in extra reward and extra reward encourages extra effort). This is because extra reward cannot encourage more of an inherent characteristic, eg age, sex. (In practice, though, when an ascribed characteristic is rewarded, individuals often try to present themselves as having 'more' of that characteristic in an attempt to manipulate the reward system. Thus, when 'juvenile' and 'adult' rates exist for a job, young adults may lie about their age in an attempt to secure the higher rate, thereby introducing and operating an illicit form of the reciprocal principle). As such the relationship between these characteristics and effort is, to say the least, ambiguous. In contrast, the relationship between reward and achieved status is frequently based on the reciprocal or incentive principle, since rewards are intended to elicit more of the time, energy or competence effort, which are the basis of the individual's achieved status. An example of this reciprocal relationship between achieved status and reward may be seen in such practices as the deliberate linking of performance appraisal systems to salary systems, such as in the well-known Hay—MSL packages. The importance of this reciprocity is that it acts both to recognize and reinforce the close relationship between effort and achieved status.

The closeness of this relationship is underlined by another aspect of the relationship between achieved status and types of reward. For the skills involved in the performance of an achieved status are often themselves regarded as an intangible reward in themselves. Note that we say 'skills', for it is generally, but by no means exclusively (see Baldamus, 1961 and Turner and Michette, 1962), the level of competence effort (rather than energy or time effort) that is perceived to provide the intrinsic rewards of a job. Hence, there exists the situation where, with some notable exceptions, the most intrinsically rewarding jobs are generally those with both the highest prestige and financial remuneration. (Note, however, the caveats as to the possible inconsistencies between the observer's and actor's frame of reference discussed above).

However, this positive correlation between intrinsic and other rewards is not always the case. For example, individuals may place more emphasis on the intangible intrinsic rewards to the detriment of their tangible material rewards. Thus there is the example quoted by Lupton (1963) of '45-percent Wilf', a craftsman who placed a higher value on turning out a perfect job than earning even average bonus; or there is the example of the manager who values the satisfactions of his present job, to the extent of sacrificing promotion to a more materially rewarding, if less personally satisfying job. Moreover, this type of personal choice may cut both ways. While it may be an advantage to an organization to have a craftsman who is prepared to forego earnings to produce high quality work or a manager who is fully committed to his job 'for its own sake', the disadvantages are only too apparent, eg uneconomic workers and immobile managers. When an individual identifies his effort as a significant part of his reward, the organization's formal (material) reward systems may cease to motivate and control to the extent they were designed to do. In other words, they become less capable of controlling the type of effort which the organization requires, because satisfaction in matters of task content and style of performance are more valuable to the individual than the rewards offered in return for the acceptance of organizational control. This caveat should be borne in mind when an organization seeks to design 'more satisfying' jobs as a form of rewards for its employees. For the question is, not only will the redesigned job 'improve' motivation, but will it also motivate the individual to behave in a manner that is congruent with those behaviours elicited by other organizational control systems? (Legge, 1978).

Conclusions

At first sight, status-based payment systems may appear to be a relatively trivial aspect—the mere gilt on the gingerbread—of an organization's total reward structure. In the authors' view, such impressions rest on a misunderstanding of the meaning and importance of concept of status. Allport (1968) not only defines it as the *sine qua non* of existence, but adds:

> To have one's virtues acknowledged, and one's self-love thus vindicated, is to experience *status*. Such elation has survival-value, for it indicates to the person that he is, for the time being at least,

secure and successful—not only in his dealings with the physical world, but what is harder to achieve, in his dealings with the social world where other egos, too, are clamoring for recognition. Egoism in human nature, is, then, a *sine qua non* of existence. Its social manifestation is the *need for status.*

In this general sense, it could indeed be said that all reward systems are status-based.

References and Further Reading

Allport, G.W., *The nature of Prejudice*, Doubleday Anchor, New York, 1968.
Baldamus, W., *Efficiency and Effort*, Tavistock, London, 1961.
Legge, K., 'Work in Prison: The Process of Inversion', *British Journal of Criminology*, Volume 18, no. 1, 1978.
Lupton, T., *On the Shopfloor*, Pergamon, Oxford, 1963.
Lupton, T. and Bowey, A., *Wages and Salaries*, Harmondsworth, Penguin, 1974.
Lupton, T. and Gowler, D., *Selecting a Wage Payment System*, Research Paper number 3, Engineering Employers' Federation, London, 1969.
Lupton, T. and Gowler, D., 'Wage Payment Systems: a review of current thinking'. *Personnel Management*, November, 1972.
Turner, A.N. and Michette, A.L., 'Sources of satisfaction in repetitive work', *Occupational Psychology*, volume 36, 1962.

22

Bonuses Based on Company Performance

Fiona Wilson, Sally Haslam
and Angela M Bowey

Principal Objectives of Company-wide Bonus Schemes

This chapter concentrates on those types of bonus scheme that can be applied to all employees within a company. The principal objective of such schemes is to foster cooperation between all parts of the organization so that corporate objectives may be better achieved. It is usual, though by no means essential, to base the bonus payments on a single measure of labour productivity, eg labour cost per unit output, output per man hour or labour cost per unit of added value. The bonus payments themselves are then based on the calculated labour-cost savings which are distributed according to an agreed system to all employees. In theory, any measure of company productivity which can be influenced by labour could be used in a company-wide bonus scheme. The most obvious examples of this are profit-sharing schemes, where annual bonuses are paid as some proportion of company profits. The main weakness of such schemes lies in the tenuous relationship between employee efficiency and the productivity measure used, resulting in probable failure of the scheme when bonuses drop due to the effect of outside factors.

Company-wide bonus schemes lie at the opposite end of the spectrum to individual incentive schemes. Their motivational appeal is to the socially integrative rather than the self-assertive tendencies in human behaviour. Koestler (1967) gives a penetrating analysis of the role these tendencies play in the behaviour in all organizations. Corresponding to the motivational spectrum we also have a scale relating to the degree of directness or indirectness of the productivity measures used, since the more we attempt to cover the different types of work done in a company the less will it be possible to apply direct work measurement techniques.

The principal features of company-wide bonus schemes may be summarized as:

1. The motivational appeal is for group cooperation in achieving one or more corporate objectives. The appeal is to the integrative as opposed to the self-assertive tendencies in human behaviour.
2. The achievement of corporate objectives is defined through the use of one or more company-wide productivity measures.
3. These measures are necessarily indirect, ie they are subject to the influence of factors outside the direct control of the workforce. The implication of this is that the scheme must take account of these outside factors if it is not to fall into disrepute. Since management are responsible for dealing with these outside factors, it follows that the successful operation of a scheme must involve regular discussions between management and employees. Inevitably, then, a well designed company-wide bonus scheme leads not only to increased cooperation within the workforce but also to increased participation by the workforce in the management of the company.

The main requirements for the successful introduction of any type of incentive scheme are:

1. The industrial relations climate must be satisfactory.
2. There must be commitment to the scheme by management.
3. The scheme in all its details and implications must be adequately explained to and agreed by employees.
4. The scheme itself must be properly designed in terms of:
    (a) The relevance of the productivity measure to the work being done by employees.
    (b) The rewards offered.
    (c) The feedback of information to employees on performance levels achieved and performance levels required.
    (d) The scope for regular and meaningful discussions between management and employees on methods of increasing productivity.
    (e) The maintenance of the scheme as products, plant and methods of working change.

Types of Scheme

The Scanlon plan

This type of scheme was developed by Joseph Scanlon in the USA in the mid-1940s. It first achieved fame through an article in *Life Magazine* by Chamberlain in 1946. This was a case history of the Scanlon plan applied to a steel tank manufacturing company called the Adamson Company, where profits had increased by two-and-a-half times and the men had earned bonuses of up to 54% of a high basic wage.

The essentials of the Scanlon plan are its reliance on a productivity measure that is developed individually for each company, and the emphasis it places on management-worker cooperation. The productivity measure can be physical output, total production cost or even monthly operating profit, related to the total labour cost. A 'normal' unit labour cost is established and all workers receive a share of the calculated labour-cost savings each month. If, for example, the productivity measure was tons per £ of labour cost and the normal or standard value established for this was, say, 0.5, then the normal or standard labour cost in a month when production was 10 000 tons would be £20 000. If the actual labour cost in the month in question was £15 000, a saving of £5000 has been achieved and either the whole of this amount or some agreed fraction of it is available for bonus payments.

Management-worker cooperation in the Scanlon plan is effected through productivity committees consisting of representatives of both management and unions, whose function is to consider and agree suggestions for improving productivity. This is, perhaps, the key feature of the Scanlon plan that has led to so much of its success, since the productivity committees enable the workforce to genuinely participate in the management of their jobs. The discussions that take place in these committees inevitably involve almost all aspects of the business such as sales, competitors, production control, quality, spoilage, raw material supplies, etc.

A very readable account of the Scanlon plan and its application to an engineering company in the United States is given by Russell W. Davenport in Lupton, (1972). At the end of this chapter is an account of one British company's experience with a Scanlon plan.

Added Value or Rucker plan

In this type of scheme the method of generating increases in productivity is not specified. The term refers to the type of productivity measure used, which is the ratio of added value to labour cost, where added value is the value of sales less the costs of raw materials and production purchases (power, consumable stores, etc). Added value is thus the sum of labour costs plus overhead costs plus profits. The Engineering Employers' Federation (1972) produced a useful booklet on added value bonus schemes.

The basis of the approach is its assumption that there is a normal or standard value for the ratio of added value to labour cost for any particular company, and that the workforce is entitled to the fixed share of added value implied by this ratio. If, for example, the ratio was 2:1 and the added value in a given month was £100 000, then the workforce share would be £50 000. If now the actual labour cost in the month in question was £40 000, a 'saving' of £10 000 has been made, of which an agreed proportion can be distributed back to the labour-force.

Rucker devised this kind of scheme after analyzing the USA census of manufacturers for the years 1899 to 1954. He found that hourly paid labour consistently received 40% of the added value (sometimes called production value). Analyses carried out in the UK for various companies have shown that the ratio of labour cost to added value varied from 8 to 59% over a sample of firms studied (*The Times*, 30 September 1958).

Added value schemes became very popular in Britain in 1977-78, largely because of the publicity given to a small number of successful schemes, support from the CBI, and the government incomes policy which encouraged such schemes initially.

Other types of scheme

Although the Scanlon and Added value plans are the two most well-known types of scheme there are, in fact, many others. One of the earliest of these is Towne's gain-sharing scheme, reported in 1899, where a bonus of 25% of any saving in an agreed 'standard cost' of production was paid. This bonus was calculated monthly but paid annually, and was in addition to normal piecework earnings. The Priestman plan, introduced in 1917, rewarded each 1% increase in production over an agreed standard with a 1% increase in pay.

The modern approach to designing company-wide bonus schemes is based more on individually tailored schemes, taking account of the wishes of both management and employees and embodying the best features of all schemes. It is not even essential to base a scheme on just one single productivity measure. Where material costs are significant, for example, and the workforce are able to influence material usage, an index of material utilization could be used. In this case the normal or standard ratio of material spoilage to material throughput would have to be established. In most companies this would have to be calculated in terms of standard costs because of the wide variety of materials used. The bonus would then be based on the difference between the actual spoilage value and the standard value calculated from the established spoilage ratio and the material throughput.

Advantages and Disadvantages

The relative merits of any type of payment system can be discussed under the four main headings:
1. Effect on total costs.
2. Effect on industrial relations.
3. The costs and effort of administration of the system.
4. Effect on other corporate objectives embodied in sales, production or financial policies.

The principal aim of individual incentive schemes is to reduce the labour cost and by implication, the total cost, per unit of output. Historically at least, the possible effects of such schemes on industrial relations and other corporate objectives have either been ignored or assumed to be of little significance. Some companies, however, have found serious problems with such schemes due to the continual bargaining over work values that takes place. This can lead to excessive costs and effort in the administration of the schemes and bad industrial relations. This in turn can lead to labour and total costs being increased, rather than reduced, through disputes and stoppages of work. In order to overcome these problems some companies, of which British Leyland is perhaps the most noteworthy example in recent years, turned to measured daywork systems. The emphasis in these systems is placed more on the control of labour rather than the achievement of savings, the assumption being that a more or less guaranteed level of earnings will lead to fewer disputes over individual work standards.

Another important disadvantage of individual incentive schemes, where such schemes are based on work measurement, lies in the difficulty in establishing work standards for indirect labour. Such labour can comprise perhaps 70 or 80% of the total workforce in a factory. The application of incentives to the remaining 20 or 30% can lead at best to only a partial saving in labour and total costs and at worst to the establishment of an elite of production workers and poor relationships between them and other workers in the maintenance and factory service areas.

Company-wide incentive schemes attempt to overcome the main disadvantages of individual incentives. Their advocates claim that such schemes involve greater cooperation between workers and between workers and management and lead, therefore, to greater savings in costs and better industrial relations. Also, because the productivity measure relates to a large group of workers, any individual work standard that may be used is of relatively minor significance, so that the risk of disputes over these is very much lessened. Further advantages are their relative simplicity and low cost of administration and the separation of payments from work study, facilitating continued improvements in methods of working, plant layout, etc. The disadvantages of such schemes lie in the indirectness of the productivity measures used and the relative weakness of the incentive for any individual worker. The next section shows how the effect of these disadvantages can be minimized. For more detailed discussions on the advantages and disadvantages the reader is referred to Lupton (1972).

How to Design and Implement a Scheme

The factors which must be considered in designing and implementing a scheme are:

1. The productivity measure or measures
2. The payment system
3. The method of implementation
4. The means of achieving results
5. The maintenance of the scheme.

The productivity measure or measures

The main considerations are:

1. The directness of each measure considered, ie its relevance to the work being done by employees and the extent to which it is likely to be influenced by external factors.
2. The degree of difficulty and the costs involved in constructing the measure and calculating it thereafter.
3. The frequency with which the measure is calculated. A higher frequency will in general have a greater incentive effect than a lower one.

Any productivity measure seeks to measure output in relation to input. The measure is usually expressed as the ratio output/input. Figure 22.1 below shows the more commonly encountered output and input measures in company-wide bonus schemes.

Each of the output measures could be associated with any one of the input measures to form a valid measure of productivity. However, the most commonly used measures are:

1. Work content of production/time worked by labour
2. Physical production/time worked by labour
3. Physical production/cost of labour
4. Added value/cost of labour
5. Materials cost of production/cost of materials input to production.

The first four of these ratios seek to measure labour productivity either in terms of output per man hour or output per unit labour cost. The

Output measure	Input measure
Physical sales Cost of sales Physical production Cost of production Work content of production Added value Materials cost of production Time that plant is usefully operating Manufacturing profit	Time worked by labour (man-hours, etc) Cost of labour Cost of materials input to production Time that plant is manned

Figure 22.1   Common output and input measures

last ratio measures material utilization. Figure 22.2 below shows the main features of these ratios under the headings of (a) directness of the measure, (b) difficulty of calculation and (c) frequency of calculation.

The choice of the most appropriate measure or measures to be used in any particular case will depend on the views of both management and the workforce as to the relative importance of the factors in Figure 22.2. However, the decision should never be taken without a full analysis showing the values of the measures considered, calculated over an earlier representative reference period. The reference period should be at least six months, but preferably twelve months or longer.

Methods of Calculation

Work-measured scheme   In the author's experience the productivity measure 'work content of production/time worked by labour' is the one most frequently used and this is therefore, described in detail. The main problem is usually that of establishing output measures for the indirect work areas of plant maintenance and factory services. This may be dealt with by allowing for such work either as a fixed proportion of the output calculated for direct work, for that part of the indirect work assessed as variable with production, or as a fixed daily or weekly number of hours, for that part of the indirect work assessed as fixed in relation to production. The calculation of these variable and fixed elements can be based on either labour budgets or an analysis of hours worked over a suitable reference period. Statistical regression analysis can sometimes be useful with the latter method. The resulting productivity measure is calculated as:

$$\frac{(1 + k) \times (direct\ hours\ earned) + F}{total\ actual\ hours\ worked}$$

Productivity measure	(a) Directness	(b) Difficulty	(c) Frequency
1 *Work content of production/* Time worked by labour	Most direct measure of labour performance	Requires complete work measurement system	Usually weekly
2 *Physical production/* Time worked by labour	Sensitive to changes in product mix	Usually easy	Usually weekly
3 *Physical production/* Cost of labour	Affected by product mix and changes in wage rates	Usually easy	Usually weekly
4 *Added value/* Cost of labour	Affected by product mix, finished stock variations, selling prices and wage rates	Usually easy	Usually quarterly, half-yearly or yearly. Can be done monthly, but then likely to be affected by stock fluctuations
5 *Materials cost of production/* Cost of materials input to production	Most direct measure of cost-effectiveness of material utilization	Usually easy with standard costing system. Can be difficult with fluctuating material usage and costs	Usually monthly

Figure 22.2 *Comparison of main productivity measures*

where k is the established ratio of variable indirect hours to direct hours worked, and F is the fixed hours of indirect work.

Whichever productivity measure is chosen it will be subject to the influence of factors outside the direct control of the workforce. The use of raw materials requiring less production operations or the introduction of new plant and machinery can clearly have an effect on both labour productivity and material utilization. Unless management and employees agree to accept this situation with its consequential effects on bonus earnings and labour costs, it will be necessary to modify the productivity measure when such changes take place. This may be done by calculating the effect of each individual change and allowing an agreed proportion of any benefits to be counted in the productivity measure.

Added Value Schemes

Added value is often calculated in the following way:

Added value = Sales value less:

raw materials
bought out components
sub-contracted processing
consumable stores purchases
loose tools purchases
repairs and maintenance
light, heat, power
transport
production services
other purchased services
commission, discounts and royalties

used in goods
sold or scrapped

plus:

any increase (or minus any decrease in value of work-in-progress and finished stock

The following expenditure is then left to be met from the added value earned:

profit before taxation
wages and salaries
depreciation
rent, rates, insurances
advertising
professional services
interest charges
other administrative and overhead expenses

Whilst this is a reasonably standard way of calculating 'added value', there is considerable variation in the methods of calculation used by different companies. Some deduct 'depreciation' from the sales value figure, and not from added value; some treat rent, rates and insurances in the same way; some regard advertising and professional services as part of the costs of earning the sales value, and so deduct them from sales value first.

Although some writers have implied that there is a logical or financial/economic distinction between the items which are deducted in order to arrive at the added value figure and those which are paid out of it, the wide range of current practices belie the claim. This wide range of options has the advantage of allowing companies to make the calculations in a way which is most appropriate for their particular industry. For example, some factor which was subject to wide variation due to matters outside the control of the employees and their managers could be included in such a way as to not affect the bonus payments based on the added value figure.

Another major source of variation between companies lies in the way in which the added value figure is converted into a financial reward for employees:

1. ICI designed a new share incentive scheme where the shares earned were related to the ratio between the ICI added value performance and the added value achieved by other major international chemical companies.
2. One large public sector corporation paid a productivity bonus based on the added value performance but subject to compliance with an agreement relating to restrictive practices. Since added value is not expected to fall below the bonus-earning level, variation in this case arises only if productivity payments are withdrawn from a particular group because of non-cooperation.
3. A Scottish engineering company paid a bonus to all its employees based on the percentage improvement in added value over the base period (just prior to the introduction of the scheme). This bonus is paid on top of existing payment by results and measured daywork schemes operating in various parts of the company.
4. A North Western vehicle company paid a fixed bonus to its manual employees giving them a high wage provided the company's added value figure did not fall below an agreed level.
5. A Midlands engineering company paid a monthly bonus to all employees and staff based on the ratio of payroll to added value.

Table 22.1 shows simple calculation of an added value bonus, in which the sales value per month in the reference period was on average £1000; costs of 'bought in' items per month were £500, and so added value was £500. The payroll bill in this reference period was £200 per month, which represented 40% of added value. This is then taken as the norm for comparing with performance in subsequent months. Suppose that in the first month of operation of the Added Value Scheme, sales value has increased to £1100, with no change in the value of stocks; but it has cost £510 for materials, services, and other 'bought in' items. Added value is then £590. If the 40% ratio is applied to this (from the reference period), the 'payroll share' of added value is £236. Comparing this to the actual payroll in this month, £206, we find a saving of £30, which is then made available for the bonus fund.

Table 22.1

Simple example of an added value bonus scheme calculation

Improvements in the value added to 'bought in' materials and services are distributed between employees and company.

Reference period
Output/Sales value normally = £1000
Cost of 'bought in' items = £ 500
∴ Normal added value = £ 500
Normal payroll cost = £ 200
 = 40% of added value

Subsequent periods
Suppose in period 1:
Sales value = £1100 (stock unchanged)
'Bought in' costs = £ 510
Added value = £ 590
Payroll share = £ 236 (40% of added value)
Actual payroll = £ 206
Sum for bonus fund = £ 30

£25 bonus paid out; £5 retained in bonus fund equalization.

Table 22.2 shows another method of calculating an added value bonus. The figures are exactly the same as the previous example, and the difference comes in the way the calculation is related to bonus. The payroll cost of £206 is 35% of the £590 added value, an improvement over the 40% norm which is converted to a bonus by reference to a graph relating these percentages to bonus payments.

There are in fact a wide variety of ways in which one added value bonus scheme may differ from another. The following list indicates the most common variations to be found in Britain in recent years:

1 The amount of the saving which goes into the bonus fund can differ (a BIM survey found the percentage of the payroll proportion of improvement in added value which was distributed varied from 17% to 85%).
2 The method of converting payroll/added value improvements into bonus may vary, as illustrated in Tables 22.1 and 22.2.
3 The method of calculating added value can differ (which items are deducted from sales value to get added value).

Table 22.2

An alternative added value bonus scheme calculation

The productivity bonus is based on improvements in the value added to 'bought in' materials and services.

Reference period
Sales value = £1000
Costs of 'bought in' items = £ 500 (materials, services)
Added value = £ 500 (for payroll, interest expenses profit, investment etc.)
Payroll cost = £ 200
Payroll as % of added value = 40%

Subsequent month
Sales value = £1100 (including stock changes)
'Bought in' costs = £ 510
Added value = £ 590
Payroll = £ 206

Payroll as % of added value = 35%

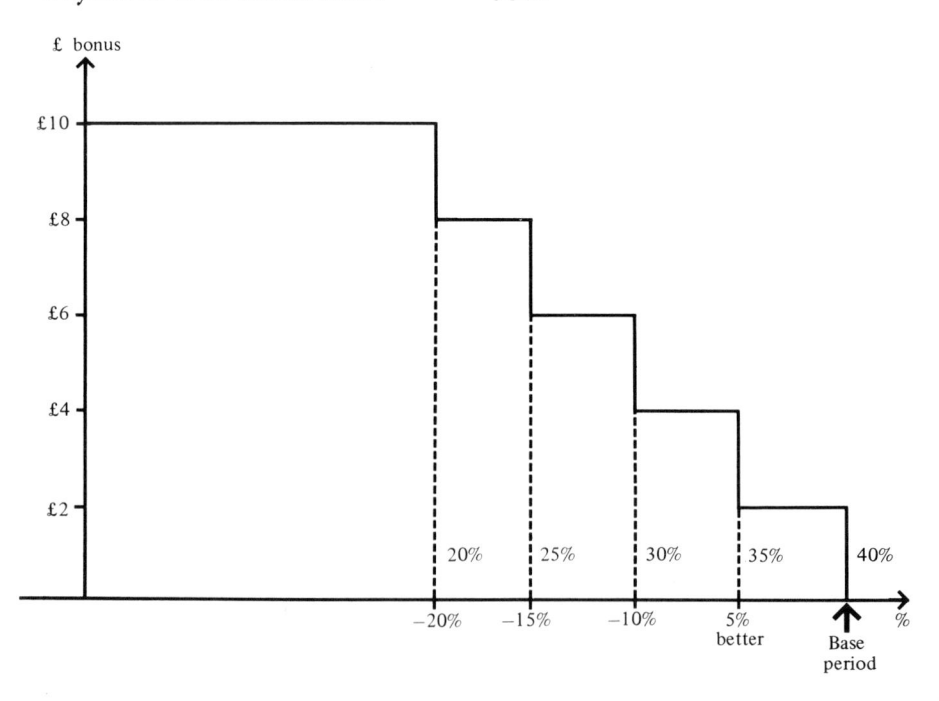

Table 22.3

Simple example of a Scanlon plan calculation

Improvements in labour costs relative to sales value are distributed between employees and the company.

Reference period
Sales value normally = £1000
Labour costs normally = £ 200 = 20% of sales value

Subsequent month
Sales value = £1200
Labour costs = £ 210
Standard labour cost = £ 240 = 20% of sales value
Improvement = £ 30 to be shared.

4 The method of relating added value to employment costs may be
   (a) Added value per £ employment cost.
   (b) Employment cost as a % of added value.
   (c) Added value per employee.
5 The bonus may be paid monthly (common recently); bi-monthly; 3-monthly; 6 monthly or annually.
6 The bonuses may be paid in cash or shares.
7 The bonus may be paid as a flat sum to all employees or as a percentage of wage/salary.
8 The bonus may be conditional, ie withheld under certain circumstances such as lateness; absence; industrial action; non-cooperation.

Many advantages are claimed for added value schemes, most especially that the added value figure does not go up when prices go up if costs have also increased, whereas other indices, such as the Scanlon plan, would not be insulated in this way.

Scanlon Plans

Table 22.3 shows a simple example of a Scanlon plan calculation which can usefully be compared with the added value calculation shown in Table 22.1. In this example, the average sales value per month in the reference period was £1000 and labour costs £200, ie 20% of sales value. In the first month of operation of the scheme, sales value had increased to £1200 and labour costs to £210. Standard labour costs at 20% of sales value would have been £240; so there has been an improvement of £30 to be put into the bonus fund.

A more detailed example of a Scanlon Plan is described and evaluated in the case study at the end of this chapter.

The Payment System

The decisions to be made in the payment system are concerned with the amounts of the bonus payments and how frequently they should be calculated and paid. In designing the payment system it is usual to calculate first the potential savings that can be achieved and then agree both the proportion of these that is to be distributed in bonus payments and the allocation to individual employees. Savings can arise through the improved utilization of labour, materials or capital facilities such as plant and machinery, and these should all be taken account of in the determination of bonus payments. Where labour productivity rather than material utilization is being measured it is usual to base the bonus payments on an agreed share of labour cost savings alone, the proportion being typically between 50% and 100%. The company will then receive any additional savings due to improved material or plant utilization.

The bonuses paid to individual employees can be based on either job gradings, basic or actual earnings levels, or simply be an equal hourly or weekly rate to each employee. Whichever method is chosen, one or more payment scales have to be devised.

In order to ensure stable bonus earnings, eg when the measure is being calculated weekly, the pay index may be computed as a 4-, 6-, or even 8-week moving average. This, of course, adds to the complexity of the scheme, and it would be necessary to clearly demonstrate to employees the effects of the calculations in order to allay any possible suspicions on their part. Equally, the actual cash payments need not be made at the same intervals as those at which the bonus earnings are calculated. It may be desirable, for example, where the bonuses are calculated weekly, to make the actual payments at 4-weekly intervals. This helps to retain the distinction between bonus and normal earnings.

Sometimes it may be useful to make the bonus payments in two ways, part of the bonuses being paid at weekly, monthly or quarterly intervals, and the remainder once a year. This may be done to keep normal bonus earnings within acceptable limits in relation to average earnings levels, the annual bonus earnings being pooled and used to increase basic wage rates. This two-tier system is also used sometimes where the bonus payments are based only on part of the total savings achieved. If, for example, the normal bonus payments are based only on savings in labour costs, any savings due to improved material or plant utilization could be taken account of in an annual review.

The final choice of the most suitable payment system should only be made after a thorough analysis over a representative reference period of its likely consequences on earnings throughout the company.

The method of implementation

The method of implementation includes the whole process of negotiating the scheme with employees, setting up the routine of scheme administration and determining any special conditions that should apply at the start of the scheme.

The aims in negotiating the scheme are to communicate its principles and to explain to everyone concerned how they can benefit from it and what they have to do to achieve that benefit. This is a tall order in firms of over, say, 500 employees, but it cannot be too highly stressed that this is of critical importance to the success of the scheme. The whole communication exercise is usually undertaken in stages with presentations to management and supervision preceding those to the shopfloor. It is often useful to prepare a short four- or five-page description of the scheme which can be distributed to all employees in advance of the presentations. The usual method of negotiating the scheme with employees is via a two-tier structure. The principles of the scheme are first discussed with a company-wide committee consisting of senior management and trade union representatives. Discussions are then held with individual departmental committees, consisting of representatives of management and employees, in which the details of the scheme, insofar as it affects the department concerned, are explained. Following these discussions, amendments to the scheme may have to be made, followed by further meetings to agree and confirm the final scheme. When this stage is reached it is advisable to produce the agreement in written form to be signed by management and employee representatives.

The routine of scheme administration is usually quite straightforward, providing sufficient attention to detail is paid. Routines need to be established for the collection of all necessary data, the calculation of the productivity measure and payment index, where this is different, and the calculation of bonus payments.

The means of achieving results

One of the main potential weaknesses of company-wide bonus schemes lies in the relatively low incentive they provide to individual employees. This problem can only be overcome by giving each employee the maximum encouragement and opportunity to contribute to the achievement of improvements. This is obtained through the working of the departmental committees. The function of these committees is to consider any suggestions at the departmental level for generating improvements, to recommend courses of action, and to monitor the effects of any suggestions already put into practice. Where the overall productivity measure allows the calculation of departmental performance, such measures can be used to monitor progress. Suggestions which go outside the terms of reference of a departmental committee are referred to the main company committee.

In companies that have established work measurement systems it is sometimes worthwhile to retain individual or sectional performance measurements. These can be useful in highlighting areas where action needs to be taken.

It is vital in the operation of the departmental committees that the principle of group cooperation underlying the use of the company-wide scheme is not overlooked. Satisfactory results will rarely be achieved through undue criticism or pressure. On the other hand a constructive approach based on careful analysis of the facts and problems in each area will lead to good industrial relations as well as higher productivity.

The maintenance of the scheme

One of the most common reasons for the failure of incentive payment schemes has been their inability to deal with the changes that take place within companies over comparatively short periods of time. Such changes mainly involve new products, new machinery or new working methods. Failure of the schemes is due to either insufficient attention being paid to the effects of changes or to disputes arising from employee's demands for a share of labour-cost savings even when the savings arise solely from capital investment or other action taken by management. The solution to these problems is to plan for them from the outset by making provision in the productivity agreement for:

1   An annual review of the complete scheme, including all parameters or work values used, savings achieved and bonuses paid.
2   A system whereby the productivity index is increased according to an agreed formula to reflect increases in productivity due to capital investment in new plant or machinery.
3   A system whereby the productivity index is adjusted to take account of the changes that are outside the direct control of the workforce and would otherwise adversely affect it.

The method in (1) is to calculate the labour-cost savings due to the introduction of the new plant or machinery and then return some agreed proportion to the workforce. This proportion is usually between 10% and 50%. In order to avoid an excessive number of calculations of this nature it is sometimes agreed that the system is only applied to capital projects costing more than a certain amount, say, £5000. The workforce would then automatically receive the normal scheme share of all labour-cost savings due to projects costing less than £5000.

The method in (2) is to calculate the effect of the change and make a corresponding compensatory change in the productivity index.

Thus, the main requirements for a successful company-wide bonus scheme are:

1. All concerned in the scheme must have a clear understanding of its objectives, the method of calculation, the influence of outside factors and the role that each individual or group can play in obtaining improvements.
2. There must be a clearly established and agreed relationship between improvements in productivity and improvements in pay.
3. The employees concerned must have the opportunity through regular meetings with management to discuss, analyze and recommend on all matters relevant to the productivity measures used.
4. The scheme must be so designed as to encourage the achievement of true corporate objectives and not individual or sectional objectives which may be in conflict with these.
5. There must be regular reviews of both the productivity measures used and the related payment scales. As a general rule these reviews should be at not more than annual intervals.

Case Study of a Scanlon Plan*

This Midlands engineering plant (a wholly-owned subsidiary of an American company) had experimented with two incentive schemes prior to the introduction of the Scanlon scheme. In 1968 a profit-sharing scheme had been introduced based on divisional results, but as an incentive towards increasing productivity the scheme was felt to have very little impact.

In the early 1970s the company also implemented an incentive scheme for production operators based on production targets. This scheme rapidly became hard to control and the bonus payment kept increasing. In 1972 the management took the decision to abandon these incentive schemes and pay a fixed hourly rate of pay. From this time the general philosophy was that the plants could be run without any form of incentive bonus. However, problems arose when the company was unable to encourage increased output when demand was high. In certain departments clear patterns began to emerge with production falling drastically before holidays and rising dramatically immediately afterwards. At the same time sales were expanding quite significantly and the company wanted to increase output. No agreement could be

* This case study is based on research conducted by its authors, Fiona Wilson and Sally Haslam.

reached. Incomes policy gave the company little room for manoeuvre. Changes in production could not be negotiated without an increase in wages so deadlock was reached. The management decided to move towards work measured incentive schemes, but the parent company expressed dissatisfaction with this approach and favoured a Scanlon type scheme.

The UK management approved of the principles of the Scanlon plan, and particularly the style of management advocated, but were daunted when they could find no examples of its successful operation in the UK. In the Spring of 1977 two senior managers visited the USA to see the scheme in operation and returned convinced that it could work in the British company. They had also learned that an enthusiastic and totally committed management team was essential if the scheme was to be successful, and that it was advisable to have an independent assessor during the design and implementation of the scheme who could also act as adjudicator if there were any difficulties. The consultants who were approached took the view that to introduce any gain sharing scheme successfully required a high level of mutual respect and trust between managers and workforce. With support from management and unions they began a survey to assess the attitudes of employees towards supervision, pay and differentials, motivation, communication, management/ union/worker relations, interest in work and the situation at work in general. A questionnaire was distributed to all employees, including managers. After discussions with management, who felt the results were an accurate reflection of feelings in the plant, the consultants presented the findings over a period of a few weeks to all of those groups who had completed the questionnaire. The findings and the interest they aroused during the group feedback sessions showed that manager/union/worker relationships were such as to augur well for a joint approach to the design of a plant-wide scheme. The workforce was stable, reasonably content, and skilfully represented by their shop stewards. It was therefore decided to go ahead.

The mechanics of the scheme

At the consultants' suggestion a joint union/management group was set up with the task of exploring possible bases for a Scanlon-type bonus scheme. They looked first at the possibility of a bonus scheme based on scrap reduction and then abandoned the idea because of the technical problems of controlling scrap and the meagre savings that would result.

The continuous dialogue with the parent company during this period revealed their preference for a scheme based on straight cost-savings. The consultants developed a scheme based upon an attack on the various elements that made up the unit cost given the market conditions then obtaining, and which looked like continuing. A decision was made to develop a scheme which rewarded both cost-saving and increases in the sales value of output.

For the rest of 1978 attention was devoted to drawing a final draft of the plan. Pros and cons of the scheme were discussed at the Joint Steering Committees, and in technical discussions between the consultants, managers and accountants from the company. Details of the working of the plan were circulated. Attention was then directed to the introduction of the plan, getting the details of the scheme and the structure of the committee worked out. From October the scheme began operating.

The basic principle of the scheme was that the percentage ratio between sales value of production and certain defined costs for a given period, was compared against an historical standard ratio between these items. The monetary difference between the actual achievement and the value of the standard ratio was contributed to a bonus pool, to be shared equally between the company and the employees. A reduction in defined costs, or an increase in the sales value of production, or both, would lead to a contribution to the bonus pool.

$$(\text{The standard ratio} \times \text{SVP}) - (\text{Actual ratio} \times \text{SVP})$$

The defined cost items were those which employees could affect:

1. Indirect, direct and maintenance wages (hourly paid) and fringe benefits.
2. Works salaries and fringe benefits.
3. Maintenance and repair of plant.
4. Scrap and rework.
5. General expenses and consumables.
6. Divisional selling, administration and general expenses.

Certain adjustments were necessary since changes in sales prices, wages and prices of certain defined costs could influence the operation of the scheme and affect the level of the bonus pool. The standard ratio was, therefore, subject to amendment every six months. Table 22.4 shows the calculation of the standard ratio, and Table 22.5 shows an example of an actual bonus calculation.

Clear guidelines had to be established to deal with the adjustments in standard ratio. Where sales prices rose, with no change in unit costs, then the standard ratio was proportionately adjusted downwards. If sales prices fell with no change in unit costs then the standard ratio was adjusted upwards. An increase in basic wages/salaries also lead to an adjustment based on applying the exact increase to the wages or salary element of defined costs. Increases in payments resulting from the productivity bonus scheme did not result in changes in the standard ratio. If within any six-month period basic wages/salaries or sales prices changed, the previous levels were used in calculating actual results until

Table 22.4

Scanlon plan standard ratio—basic calculation fiscal 1978

	£
Total sales division	5,623,130
Less Opening stock finished cord	306,118
Add Closing stock finished cord	603,900
= Sales value of production	5,920,912
Defined costs	
Wages hourly paid	1,307,285
Fringe benefits hourly paid	355,123
Works salaries including fringe benefits	246,462
Consumables	74,667
MRP	381,180
Small tools	22,523
General expenses	80,833
Canteen	22,728
Dies	17,726
Personnel & welfare	11,598
Training expenses	4,066
First aid and safety	11,187
Scrap/Rework	851,844
SAG	
Salaries & fringe benefits	94,807
Personnel & training	1,605
Stationery	12,522
Telephone & telex	4,953
General office expenses	40,897
Travel/Entertainment burden/SAG	8,530
Postage	909
	3,551,475

$$\text{Standard ratio} = \frac{\text{Sales value of production}}{\text{Defined costs}} = \frac{5920912}{3551475} = 59.98\%$$

the next scheduled change in the standard ratio. Increases or decreases in other defined costs were reviewed against the official wholesale price index for manufacturing industries. Finally, if, as a result of new investment or new products, the ratio changed causing a 10% or more change in the bonus pool, then the standard ratio would be adjusted to

Table 22.5

Calculations (October 1978–March 1979)

	Standard ratio amended	Actual performance
Sales value	5,804,440	3,388,078
Add closing stock—finished cord	608,868	638,185
Less opening stock—finished cord	327,236	608,868
= Sales value of production	6,086,072	3,417,395
Wages & fringe benefits	1,842,408	1,075,435
Salaries & fringe benefits	381,269	205,077
Other defined costs	1,633,444	879,476
Total defined costs	3,857,121	2,159,988
Standard ratio $\frac{3,857,121}{6,086,072}$ =	63.38	63.21
Bonus pool		£2,905

Notes on Adjustments to Standard Ratio

(i) Basic wage increase to value of £180,000 added.
(ii) Basic salary increase to value of £40,000 added.
(iii) Defined costs indexed $\frac{158.3}{150.0}$

take account of the new circumstances. No new plant, or new product was to be included in the scheme until it had been fully operating for one quarter.

The committee structure was designed to encourage everyone to participate in generating improvements. Departmental bonus committees consisted of elected representatives from work areas. Each work area also had a group responsible for receiving and assessing ideas for improvements. A sum of £12,000 pa was made available to the steering committee made up of representatives from all departmental bonus committees and chaired by the plant manager, for expenditure on productivity improvements involving equipment and plant. The departmental committee had the authority to implement ideas using its allocation from this budget if these changes would not affect any other sections. All other acceptable suggestions were forwarded to the factory steering committee for final approval and implementation. This committee also had the responsibility to consider the level of bonus likely to be paid each quarter; to review the operation of the plan; to forecast possible changes in the standard ratio; and to authorize any such changes. The consultants provided the departmental bonus committees with some guide-lines on the most fruitful areas on which to concentrate when assessing suggestions. Changes in some cost items, for instance scrap and rework, had a greater impact on total defined costs than others, and some cost savings were easier to achieve than others. Scores were established for the importance of each cost item and how easy it was to achieve a reduction in them, and the information used to help departmental committees establish their priorities. The bonus was paid as an equal share to all employees, irrespective of level of earnings, on a quarterly basis, with a reserve maintained for an annual payment in December. Employees were eligible to participate in the scheme after three months service, and their wages and salaries were excluded from the calculation until that time.

The company and the steering committee were hoping the scheme would quickly begin to pay a bonus. But at the end of July 1979 there was a major set back, when a major customer did not give the company an expected order, and further requested price reductions on other products in accordance with their agreement on sales prices. Problems arose in domestic and export markets as a result of the increasing strength of the pound sterling and the price advantage this gave to overseas suppliers. Members of management were called in from holiday in an attempt to work out a plan for the survival of the plant. When the workforce returned from their annual holiday the problem was explained to them. The recently signed wage agreement had to be reconsidered and it appeared that redundancies were possible.

Discussions went on until early October before the position became clearer. The customer decided to take the product in a larger quantity than anticipated in return for price reductions. Estimated redundancies from a workforce of 350 ranged from 120 down to 20 or 30. In fact, no redundancies were made. The union believed that the whole problem had been a carefully planned company strategy to get the new wages deal accepted and relationships were, for that reason, strained. Throughout October and November production efficiencies were down and tonnage output low. The Board expressed dissatisfaction with productivity. The plant responded by increasing production. Efforts were once again aimed at promoting the plant-wide scheme which had received little attention during the company's time of crisis. No bonus was earned for the quarter to December 1979, but in January it was felt the scheme was beginning to work. This generated more interest. A payment of £25–30 was anticipated from January's results, but the effects of the steel strike eroded this to £19. The situation improved later that year, and in the quarter to December 1980 the scheme produced its highest payment of £46 per person, reflecting the increased productivity.

Problems that have Arisen since the Introduction of the Scheme

In practice the scheme had some positive outcomes, for example, great efforts were made to reduce scrap and many suggestions for improvement emerged which might not otherwise have been made. But in the first year of its operation there was little evidence of the major benefits that were expected, particularly the payout. From interviews with management and shop floor committee members as well as the consultants, we collected different perspectives on the scheme and direct and indirect data on the problems which emerged.

Accounting The management accountants were able to shed light on one particular set of problems. There had been difficulties in the calculation of the sales value of production. In adjusting for stocks, the question arose as to what value should be placed upon them. It was decided to adjust for stocks at balance sheet value, at cost, rather than selling price. But it was later decided that a more relevant measure is arrived at by valuing stock at selling price, so giving a truer measure of output performance. But it was then thought too late to change this. A second major accounting problem was the handling of inflation. When comparing the base ratio with actual output at a later date, the prices and costs had inevitably changed. The question arose as to the extent to allow for this, if at all. The decision was made to inflation-proof wages and salaries as fully as possible. (Wages and salaries were the major part of defined costs). The balance of defined costs were not fully inflation proofed, and consequently the calculation was not strictly accurate.

Unless provision is made for inflation, the possibility for earning bonus is reduced, and the scheme will fall into disrepute. For instance, in the first five months of 1979 output went up but profit had fallen simply because selling price increases had not matched cost increases. If adjustments had been made for inflation, a bonus would have been due in recognition of increased output.

Difficulties also arose over the standard ratio. It was thought that the standard should be revised each year; for example, if 1978 is the standard for 1979, 1979 then becomes the standard for 1980. But this approach was later thought to be wrong. If improvements effected in 1979 over 1978 are built into the ratio for 1979, in 1980 even more improvements have to be made before a bonus is achieved, which may well be an unreasonable expectation.

Product mix Product mix and mix changes were also a problem. Changes resulted in a temporary loss of output; and some products required tighter quality control which extended manufacturing times. The volatility of the market for the plant's products made conditions difficult for the Scanlon plan. Stability would have enabled efforts to be focused on controlling those items of cost that were causing problems.

Lack of enthusiasm It would appear that supervisory staff, in particular, had not devoted any real effort to making the scheme work. Initially the scheme generated enthusiasm in the plant generally, but by the end of the first year this had diminished. Efforts were made to reduce scrap and it was shown what a 1% reduction in scrap would generate in terms of bonus. In one three month period there seemed to be promising results in terms of scrap reduction, but the payment in that quarter was relatively small, only £25 per employee. Employees were said to be disillusioned. It was thought unlikely that employees saw the plan as a way of earning significantly more. But at the time of writing, January 1981, a payment of £46 had recently been made, and it was hoped that this payment might improve attitudes towards the scheme.

Understanding of the scheme Despite efforts to explain how the scheme worked there was still lack of understanding. Some expressed the feeling that it was too complicated and had been wrongly described as profit sharing, rather than as an 'efficiency' bonus, which would have made it clearer that profits were not the only criterion.

Problems arose when the accountant notified the workforce about the good progress of the bonus pool over the first six weeks of a particular quarter, then the final calculations produced a lower bonus than had been anticipated.

Communication and organization One of the main problems was lack of communication, between the main committee and the sub-committees and interdepartmental communication and cooperation. There was a mixed response to questions about the following up of ideas generated from the workforce. Some felt it was adequate, and the workforce did not seem very interested in the scheme anyway. Others felt there was a problem in this area. Reasons for not acting on suggestions did not seem to filter back and the result was declining interest in the scheme and disheartenment. A common reaction was 'why suggest things if management does not do anything'. One interviewee commented that it was a struggle to get any changes implemented even if the cost was nothing.

A management scheme The impression came across strongly that this was a management scheme rather than a joint one, and that management were expected to take action on suggestions rather than these being committee decisions. The general manager believed that it was important that people, particularly shift managers, supervisors, and line management were encouraged to make decisions. He also saw the departmental committees as the key to the success, and believed it important that they appreciated their autonomy. At the time of writing (January 1981), there had been no allocation of steering committee Scanlon allowances for productivity improvement plans.

The Scanlon plan embodied a particular managerial philosophy; but some managers viewed it as a secondary productivity scheme. They did not seem to want the scheme integrated into the company's managerial philosophy.

Non-acceptance of Scanlon One major failing of Scanlon plans that is not mentioned in the literature, is that management may not adopt the scheme in a whole-hearted fashion. It was difficult for this particular management to perceive this scheme as anything other than an *addition* to their already existing wage payment systems. The failure of managerial philosophy was expressed by one of the consultants:

> People say here is a business which involves making and selling a product. And then we have a set of obstacles which include people, unions etc. If we can find a way of getting over the obstacles we run the business better. They do not see it the other way round, as a system of people with different perspectives and interests and we have to weld them into a social machine which can run the technology to make the product and sell it. The Scanlon plan may be seen as a way of clearing away some of these obstacles to cooperation and if it doesn't do this then it's a waste of time.

Conclusions

One of the objectives of the scheme was to foster cooperation and improve communication within the plant. Vertical and horizontal communication channels should have been improved by the scheme and this was vital to its success. We found evidence of some improved vertical communication. Departmental committees suggestions were coordinated through a chairman after some initial difficulty in expressing these ideas to the steering committee. However, it was vital that there should be a continual stream of ideas flowing, being processed and decided upon. This, unfortunately, does not seem to have happened. The shop stewards perhaps saw this bonus scheme as a good way of earning money for their members and the workforce were too optimistic that they could gain a substantial bonus with little effort. They could well have felt disillusioned when there was no pay-out on some occasions. The company was having to compete in a market where prices were falling and the workforce had very little power to improve this worsening situation. Interdepartmental communication caused more problems, with delays, poor cooperation, poor information about meetings, and poor results from the scheme.

A great deal of effort went into working out the mechanics of the scheme, but this is not the most vital part. What is more important is for the framework for cooperation to be seen as a total managerial philosophy. This, clearly, had not occurred. All employees must have a clear understanding of the mechanics of the scheme, its objectives, the ways in which they can influence the bonus, and the external influences which will affect it. The indirectness of the bonus makes understanding the scheme of prime importance.

Despite briefing sessions to explain the scheme, the consultants were never quite sure if employees had a grasp of what the principles of the scheme were. They were, however, confident that several influential people understood it. The fact is that it was a very complicated scheme to understand; but it was hoped that the principles could be grasped and this would be sufficient. For instance, there was provision for cost-saving ideas to be implemented without consultation; but even simple ideas were passed to management for assessment. This could either be the result of their lack of appreciation of the autonomy the scheme gave them in relation to work, or unwillingness on their part to accept the responsibility for the decisions coupled with lack of encouragement from supervisors.

Many of the more negative features of the scheme that we have mentioned could be overcome. But the major obstacles were external factors and these factors the company could not control. The market, if not buoyant, can shatter all assumptions about Scanlon.

References and Further Reading

Engineering Employers Federation. *Business Performance and Industrial Relations*, Kogan Page (Associates) Ltd, London, 1972.
Gray, S.J. and Maunders, K.T., *Value Added Reporting: Uses and Measurement*, The Association of Certified Accountants, 1980.
Koestler, A., *The Ghost in the Machine*, Pan Books Ltd, London, 1967.

Marchington, M., 'Worker Participation and Plant-wide Incentives', *Personnel Review*, Volume 16, no. 3, 1977.
Minns, A.S., *Share Aquisition Schemes*, HFL, 1980.
More, B.E. and Ross, T.L., *Scanlon Way to Improve Productivity: A Practical Guide*, Wiley, 1978.
Woodmansey, M., *Added Value: An Introduction to Productivity Schemes*, BIM, 1978.

23

Selecting a Wage System

Angela M Bowey

Previous chapters have described different methods for relating wages and other rewards to the work done by employees. Each has suggested that the characteristics of the situation to which a payment system is to be applied are important determinants of the degree of success that can be expected. How then, can the payment system administrator be sure that the scheme he is proposing to install is suited to the situation in his organization? How can he choose the scheme that is best suited to his organization? Rather than sift through all the case studies that have been written, making notes of similarities to his own case, and listening to the advice given by proponents of each system, and the experience of other companies, we suggest that he should use one of the formal procedures for systematically appraising the relevant features of his organization. These have been developed by Bowey and Lupton (1974) and other members of the reward systems research team at the Manchester Business School, and are based on numerous case studies and the available literature as well as our own experience as advisers to companies wishing to change their payment system.

'Selecting a wage system' suggests that all payment systems are packages and that the task is one of selecting between alternative packages. This, however, is misleading. There are a number of dimensions along which a payment system may vary, and consequently an enormous number of possible different types of scheme, although only a few of these have been given names. The decisions which need to be made about the mechanics of any new payment system are:

1 What sort of variable incentive payments should there be? The choice

lies between: none; a directly proportional scheme, where uniform pay increase are given for each unit of work (however that is measured); a geared scheme where pay increases more rapidly or less rapidly beyond a particular point or points; or a stepped incentive scheme, where specified non-varying levels of pay are given for specified non-varying levels of work.
2   Should incentive payments be based on the work of an individual, a group, a department, the whole factory or the company?
3   How large a proportion of the pay packet should the variable elements make up?
4   What features of the work should the variable pay be related to? For example: effort; output; quality; machine utilization; cost reduction; contribution to profit; profit improvement; added value; merit; cooperation; wastage savings; etc.

Question (4) must be decided from an analysis of the most important aspects of the job from the company's point of view. Questions (2), (3) and the most important part of question (1) (ie whether there should be any incentive at all) can be answered by using a technique for determining the proportion of individual and/or group incentive payments which should be included in the pay packet, developed by Bowey and Lupton (1970).

In order to illustrate the use of the technique, I will describe a case study of a garment factory where difficulties were experienced which were thought to be due to the payment system, and whose directors sought our advice and aid in early 1972.

It is important to bear in mind that recent research has shown that the process of implementation, the care taken to prepare for the change and introduce it, is more important in determining the success of a scheme than the details of the scheme itself. Ensuring that the scheme is appropriate is only a small part of this preparation.

Background to the Study

This factory specialized in producing high quality garments, which were made to order for a design and marketing company, belonging to the same firm, housed in another section of the same building, and administered by the same directors. This design and marketing company was, at the time of the study, very successful. Apart from the garments manufactured at this factory it also placed orders with other garment factories, known as outworkers, and with a second factory, known as the 'Downstairs Factory', belonging to the same company and situated in the same building. In 1972 it was costing the company more to manufacture an order for a number of garments at their own

'Upstairs Factory' (the one studied) than to place the order with an outworker. It had been calculated that provided the Upstairs Factory produced 400 garments per week, it would break even on costs. Beyond 400 garments, it began to make a profit. Production levels were varying between 300 and 450 garments per week, and an additional problem was that the quality of these garments was not as high as the company desired in order to maintain its reputation for quality, and there was a very high reject rate (see Figure 23.2).

It is reasonable to ask why the company did not close the factory, since it had made a loss for about 20 years, and its quality was now so poor as to threaten the company's image. But there were advantages in maintaining their own factory rather than putting all work to outworkers, ie that when the industry was booming (it was weathering a slump at the time of this study) it was not so easy to find outworkers with spare capacity, and also they increased their charges at such times. Another advantage was that when a style or a material was exceptionally difficult to work with, an outworker could refuse to accept the order, but the company's own factories could not.

The manager of the Upstairs Factory had been recruited six months before my study began, on twelve-month's trial. His predecessor was dismissed after many years of inadequate service during which the factory made a continual loss. Only when the composition of the board of directors changed in 1971 did his dismissal become possible. The new manager was cooperative and keen. He had made a number of organizational changes in the factory since he took over the job, rationalizing the meal breaks and the physical positions of the different sections in relation to the work flow.

The employees were mostly female and elderly. Their average length of service was 22 years and their age range (from late twenties to early seventies) was fairly typical of the industry, which fails to attract many young people. These ladies tended to be resistant to change—they downed tools for an hour in protest over the manager's re-organization of their meal breaks.

The Production Process and Associated Behaviour Patterns

The processing of the garments began in the cutting room, where there were four male and two female workers all paid 'standard rates' (the term used in the factory to describe a payment system based on hours worked) for their work. The cutting room supplied the rest of the factory with work, and a bottle-neck here meant that production for the whole factory would be low. This was the only section which had a supervisor (male), as the 62 employees in the other sections were all supervised by the manager himself.

The supervision in the cutting room was slack, and this coupled with the payment structure for cutters which lacked any financial incentive to faster work was contributing to just such a hold-up in the production line. It was also a possibility that the cutting room did not have enough fully skilled staff to keep the factory supplied with sufficient work, but the employees in the cutting room did not complain very much of being short-staffed.

In order to disguise the short supply of work coming out of the cutting room and to provide the factory with a trickle of work rather than a series of spurts and stoppages, the cutters put the work for the machinists into very small bundles. Whereas in the Downstairs Factory the average bundle contained twelve identical garments, and a bundle of seven was regarded as very small, the average bundle in the Upstairs Factory contained only three or four garments, and a bundle of seven was a large bundle. There were other contributory reasons for the smaller bundles in the Upstairs Factory which will be discussed later. The effect of these small bundles was that the machinists took longer to get through the same amount of work. This was because once the work in a bundle had been sorted out and the girl had decided in what order to sew up the pieces, it added little to the total time taken if she then sewed up six identical left seams rather than only three, followed by six right seams and six sleeves, etc. But if she had instead, two bundles of three garments she had to organize and plan the work for each one. They would probably not be from the same cutting lay and might require different adjustments to the seam sizes and so on. They would often be different garments because the factory produced many small runs of particular styles. (A lay is a number of garment sections obtained from one cutting through several layers of cloth. At this factory the cutting machinery was capable of cutting about 40 layers of cloth at a time, and usually the garments were cut in 40-garment lays, before being subdivided into small bundles). So by supplying these small bundles of work the cutting room staff slowed down the production of the factory and there were no hold-ups when pressure might be put on them to increase their output.

From the cutting room the next stage in the production process was the machining, carried out mostly by girls paid piecework rates. In order to minimize arguments and ill-feeling between pieceworkers these girls demanded that the work had to be seen to be shared out fairly between them. This was the second reason for the small sizes of the bundles of work. Since runs of only 40 or 50 garments were quite common and there were 15 pieceworkers, they needed to be as small as three garments per bundle in order to provide each girl with the same kind of work as her colleagues. These pieceworkers were usually vociferously discontent when there was no work for them, and so the trickle of work provided by small bundles caused less conflict than a stop-go situation.

One obvious question is: Why did the manager allow this practice to continue? He had earlier in his career attended a 'human relations training' course where he had been taught that conflict in organizations is dysfunctional and that the elimination of conflict leads to improvements in productivity. The cutting-room supervisor explained to him that the use of small bundles ensured that the piecework machinists did not run out of work and this reduced the conflict between the two departments. To reduce this conflict further the manager had a partition built between the two sections.

Under a piecework system in the garment industry workers are usually motivated to work as fast as they can. The girls in the machining section, therefore, worked rapidly and sometimes with little regard for quality. The quality of their work was also affected by the lack of any machine passing (checking the garments after initial machining before they went to the next process). Machine passing, in turn, was made difficult by the large numbers of small bundles going through the department. Not only did each fault with a particular lay occur in some ten different bundles and probably affect ten different machinists, but other administrative tasks were similarly multiplied and the manager spent much of his time following the work through and coping with problems. And with such a large number of bundles being machined daily, machine passing the first of each bundle would have been very time-consuming.

Because of the poor quality of some of the work, quite a lot of time was spent altering garments previously made-up (an estimated 20% of the garments produced needed alterations later). This also lowered the productivity of the factory.

The other sections in the factory—underpressing, fancy machining, finishing and pressing were not overworked. They were all paid 'standard rates'. If anything, these sections could have coped with more work—especially the pressers. Any bottle-necks which did occur in these sections were due to absence and illnesses and could be avoided or coped with fairly easily by moving staff about to cover for absenteeism or by redistributing the work amongst them. These employees did not object to these demands being made of them. It was often impossible to persuade the pieceworkers to help out on jobs other than their normal tasks, which were highly specialized.

The Payment Structure

The payment structure in the factory was fairly complex. Although the employees in the Upstairs Factory talked about a standard rate there were in fact no two people earning exactly the same pay for exactly the same hours of work. Figure 23.1 shows the earnings per hour for the

Upstairs Factory				Downstairs Factory	
Pieceworkers		Timeworkers		Timeworkers	
Machinist	63.28	Machinist	40.84	Machinist	42.09
Button tailoress	71.70	Fancy machines	39.17	Machinist	47.00
Machinist	40.57	Tailoress	39.59	Cleaner	30.00
Machinist	54.24	Fancy machines	39.17	Finisher	32.82
Machinist	43.15	Fancy machines	38.34	Finisher	46.07
Machinist	48.29	Finisher	38.87	Machinist	32.50
Machinist	78.99	Machinist	37.09	Machinist	52.50
Machinist	62.57	Underpresser	46.92	Machinist	37.92
Machinist	56.06	Cutter	37.09	Machinist	43.50
Machinist	45.90	Machinist	30.00	Finisher	49.80
Button tailoress	71.75	Finisher	44.59	Machinist	46.78
Presser	55.56	Fancy machines	39.17	Machinist	40.00
Machinist	54.13	Tailoress	47.09	Machinist	44.16
Machinist	54.75	Machinist	31.67	Machinist	46.35
Machinist	43.78	Fancy machines	31.76	Machinist	43.34
Machinist	50.23	Underpresser	34.60	Underpresser	40.90
Machinist	60.41	Tailoress	35.84	Machinist	37.92
		Trimmer	40.01	Machinist	33.34
		Machinist	41.25	Finisher	39.59
		Machinist	32.92	Machinist	58.25
		Fancy machines	35.42	Machinist	42.77
		Finisher	46.26	Machinist	37.50
		Finisher	39.39	Fore lady	49.96
		Machinist	35.42	Machinist	54.59
		Passer	43.00		
		Machinist	35.39		
		Finisher	39.50		
		Odd jobs	25.84		
		Tailoress	39.39		
		Finisher	44.59		
		Tailoress	44.59		
		Machinist	43.34		
		Finisher	52.20		
		Finisher	35.01		
		Finisher	42.50		
		Tailoress	44.59		
Average	56.16	Average	39.24	Average	43.90

Figure 23.1   Hourly earnings (averaged over six weeks) of female staff (in pence per hour)

female staff divided into pieceworkers and timeworkers from the Upstairs and Downstairs Factories. The Downstairs Factory was generally regarded as the more successful of the two. It produced better quality garments, made a profit and generally gave rise to fewer headaches for the directors. The manager was a very capable man who was much respected by the directors.

There were 18 pieceworkers in the Upstairs Factory, 17 of them female and 15 of them machinists. All the other sections—cutting, underpressing, fancy machining, finishing, pressing, passing, etc, employed workers who were paid by the hour for their work. The pieceworkers were earning considerably more money per hour than the timeworkers in either factory.

On average they earned 56.16 pence per hour compared with 39.24 pence per hour for the Upstairs Factory timeworkers and 43.9 pence per hour for Downstairs Factory timeworkers. The timeworkers, on the whole, worked longer hours than the pieceworkers, so levelling up their weekly pay to some extent. Figure 23.2 shows the average hours worked over six weeks for the various groups of female employees and also for male employees. The employees were allowed to come to work and to leave at whatever times they wished, and hourly earnings were calculated from their clock cards.

	Female			Male	
	Upstairs Factory pieceworkers	Upstairs Factory timeworkers	Downstairs Factory timeworkers	Upstairs Factory timeworkers	Downstairs Factory timeworkers
Week 1	23.84	32.03	31.89	43.43	43.90
Week 2	26.09	32.15	33.20	45.57	44.09
Week 3	25.25	33.28	32.30	44.14	42.94
Week 4	25.05	32.30	32.39	46.21	43.62
Week 5	25.75	31.30	31.02	45.50	40.34
Week 6	29.02	33.44	31.81	43.61	43.22
Average over 6 weeks	25.83	32.42	32.01	44.73	43.02

Figure 23.2   Average hours worked per week

The pay for pieceworkers in the Upstairs Factory was made up of a price for each garment plus a time-based payment of 17.09 pence per hour. The one and only pieceworker in the Downstairs Factory was paid a price per garment plus 2½ pence per hour. If there was not work available the pieceworkers in the Upstairs Factory were usually given the option of going home or working on an unfamiliar job. For example, if there were no skirts to be made-up, a skirt machinist would be asked to sew jackets or mantles. Some refused because they could not make these garments fast enough to earn what they regarded as a worthwhile rate of pay, and instead they went home when the supply of skirts was exhausted. The girls did not expect to receive 'waiting time' payments because they had never received them in the past, although some thought that they had an ethical right to be paid for waiting time.

The pay for timeworkers (excluding staff) in both factories was calculated from an hourly rate. These hourly rates were based on merit which in most cases were originally assessed from previous pieceworker earnings when the girls were transferred from piecework to 'standard rates'. As Figure 23.1 shows, there were barely two people earning the same rates per hour.

The factory was making a loss and it was hoped that by changing the payment structure the output would be increased, the quality of work improved and the factory would begin to make a profit.

In order to assess the suitability of different types of payment structure for the piecework machinists I used the Bowey-Lupton method (Bowey and Lupton, 1970). This method requires detailed information to be obtained on eight different features of the organization and the jobs. Figure 23.3 shows what those parameters are and how they should be measured.

The first parameter (P_1), replacement time, was scored 7 because it was difficult for this factory to recruit staff who were sufficiently skilled for this work, and those who were recruited usually required training before they achieved average rates of working. On average it took seven weeks to recruit and train a replacement and reading from the top line of the chart, this score indicates the restriction that x_3 (the proportion of total pay which takes the form of a bonus based on the output of the group) should not be more than 40–50% of total pay. The reason that our technique recommends this restriction is that in a situation where it takes seven or eight weeks for group output to recover from one member leaving, a bonus based on group output is likely to produce frustration and low productivity if it makes up more than that amount of total pay.

The second and third parameters (P_2 and P_{2b}) were scored zero. This was because there were no drops in output below some expected norm due to changes in tasks. These machinists were working on a 'make-through' system, ie each garment was machined entirely by one girl, unlike the 'section-work' system used in many garment factories in which one girl makes collars, another sleeves, etc. So changes in style at this factory did not produce such major changes in tasks as would occur in a section-work factory. Also, the number of garments of any one style that a machinist made were small—often only three, partly because of the small orders which this factory supplied. Even when a large order was received for one style, the machinists would be given bundles of other styles interspersed with those for the large order. This meant that no high rates of output were achieved which were

Selecting a Wage System

Maximum recommended amount of pay based on group output (%)		0–10	10–20	20–30	30–40	40–50	50–60	60–70	70–80	80–90	90–100
P_1: Average time in weeks between an employee leaving and his replacement achieving average performance		12	11	10	8 and 9	7	6	4 and 5	3	2	1
P_{2b}: Percentage loss of output per annum due to normal task changes (relearning losses) average per group		90–100	80–90	70–80	60–70	50–60	40–50	30–40	20–30	10–20	0–10
Maximum recommended amount of pay based on individual output											
P_2: Percentage loss of output per annum due to normal task changes (relearning losses) average per individual		90–100	80–90	70–80	60–70	50–60	40–50	30–40	20–30	10–20	0–10
P_4: Maximum possible percentage change in total costs due to increases in employee effort		1	2	3	4	5	6	7	8	9	10
P_5: Comparative frequency and significance of changes in technology		rapid			moderate			slow			
P_6: Average percentage loss of output due to work-flow problems, per employee		20	18	16	14	12	9	6	4	2	0
P_7: Average number of wage bargaining opportunities per annum weighted according to bargaining strength*		100	90	79	68	58	47	36	25	14	3
R: Average total weekly pay as a proportion of the regional pay for similar work	R more than 1½	///	///	///	///	1½–2	2	2½	3	4	7	10 and over
	R less than or = 1½	¾	⅘	1	1½	///	///	///	///	///	///

Sections: Section 1 (top three rows), Section 2 (next three rows), Section 3 (remaining rows).

Figure 23.3 Assessment of suitability of different proportions of incentive pay

*Weight the number of opportunities by raising it to the power N where N is the square of the average pay for this type of work divided by the square of the national average rate of pay for employees.

dependent upon there being no task changes. Another factor which contributed to the lack of impact of style changes on output (and consequently on piecework earnings) was the machinists' use of hours worked as a means of compensating for low output on a difficult style, ie when their earnings per hour were low, these machinists maintained their earnings level by working longer hours. At the time of my study the management allowed them to work as many or as few hours as they wished.

Inserting this score in Figure 23.3 indicates no restrictions to the amount of bonuses which might be included in the pay packet. This was because there would not be any adverse effects on motivation resulting from the use of a piecework payment system with the kind of task changes occurring in this factory.

The next parameter *(P4)* was scored 3.2%. This score was obtained by weighting the effect which these machinists could have on their own output (40% increase) by the proportion of total costs generated by this particular section (8%). When the parameter score was inserted in the table we obtained the restriction that the total of all output-based bonuses should not be more than 20—30% for these machinists.

This restriction implied that there were some advantages which could be gained by motivating these employees to work faster by means of output-based incentives. But that if those incentives made up more than 20—30% of total pay, the advantages gained would be no greater than for a smaller proportionate bonus, and the risks of disadvantages would be greater.

Parameter *P5* was scored slow, corresponding to a situation of very slow technological change. Inserting this score into the figure showed that no restriction was imposed on the use of bonus payments by the rate of technological change. The reasoning behind this result is that technological changes can provide opportunities for re-negotiating piecework rates and for other sources of change in the relationship between output and earnings. Where the rate of change is rapid, therefore, piecework systems have disadvantages. But in this case the rate of change was very slow and no precautions needed to be taken on this account.

The sixth parameter *(P6)*, the output losses due to workflow hold-ups, was approximately 30%. This is a high score which went right off the left-hand end of the scale in Figure 23.3. This kind of result must be interpreted as equivalent to an emphasized zero, ie in this situation there were, most emphatically, no advantages to be gained from using an output-related bonus system. The flow of work was so inadequate that fast work in the machinists' department only meant problems for the management in spinning out the work to keep the girls occupied and devising methods of slowing the girls down. It also meant poorer quality work than might otherwise have been obtained, and frustration amongst the machinists when their efforts to work fast were thwarted.

This result made the restrictions imposed by the previous parameters redundant. The last parameter (P_7), the impact of wage bargaining, was scored zero. Although each new style was an opportunity for bargaining, the bargaining strength of the group was low and very few prices set by the management were seriously disputed by the machinists. And finally, the comparative pay restriction (R) gave the result that basic pay should make up at least 20—30% of total pay. This restriction was also redundant because of the more severe restriction obtained for P_6.

The outcome of applying our technique to the machining section in this factory was that the piecework system was seen to be totally unsuited to achieving the management's objectives of increased output and improved quality. It was recommended that the machinists should be paid hourly rates, and following the tradition in the company, that these should be based on their previous average earnings under the piecework system.

If time and resources had been available for a much larger project, it would have been preferable to involve the labourforce more fully in the analysis of the problems, and allow them and the management to reach conclusions about the changes to be made. This would have required a complete change in management style and workers' orientations, and the directors were not prepared to embark on such an exercise. As a result, some members of the management, and in particular the factory manager, expressed concern about the way these ladies would receive the news that they were to be 'taken off piecework' and paid hourly rates. The author had interviewed all of the machinists at an earlier stage of the project, and had been left in no doubt that some of them would resent such a change very much.

A meeting was held with the machinists at which the above analysis, without too many technical details, was explained to them. They were told that the company was anxious to obtain better quality work from them, and that changes were being made in the cutting room to ensure that in future larger bundles of work would be given to them. The payment system was being changed and they were all to be paid hourly rates in future, and in addition, a quality checker would be appointed to check the first garment from every bundle they began. After this meeting it was planned to negotiate with each individual separately, about her rate of pay under the new system. At this joint meeting of machinists, factory manager and the author, there were divided views expressed by the machinists. Some were clearly quite happy about the new scheme, but others were very discontent. The contented group of machinists preferred to discuss their new rates of pay as a group. They wished to be paid the same rate of pay as one another which meant that those earning high pay accepted a drop in earnings of a penny or twŏ per hour in order to subsidize their colleagues. This they were content to do and the negotiation with this group produced a satisfactory conclusion for all concerned.

The author then negotiated with the machinists who were either indifferent to the change or suspicious that it might prove disadvantageous. Most of these ladies were pleased that the company was prepared to make them what some termed a 'very fair offer'. They also accepted the new scheme with a reasonable amount of enthusiasm. Two would only accept the new scheme if the rate of pay offered were reduced from 71 pence to 60 pence per hour. They said that 71 pence was too much (although this had been their average rate of earnings over the past 12 months). One is left to speculate about the reasons for this behaviour.

This left three machinists who said that the new scheme was totally unacceptable to them. One of them after discussion, agreed to 'give it a try'. The other two threatened that they would leave the company and could not be persuaded to change their minds. However, when the time came these two did not leave.

Follow-up

There was a follow-up three months later to observe the responses to the changes. The manager had responded to the new situation by allocating longer runs of one garment to the same machinists; a 'machine-passer' was appointed (promoted from machinist) to check the quality of the garments; unskilled tasks were transferred to sections which had spare capacity; and the manager, relieved of some of the pressures he previously tackled, had more time to avoid major errors in the manufacturing process. Clearly some of these changes would take time to show their impact on production.

The machinists had all adapted quite well to the new system, although some of them were maintaining behaviour patterns which were devised to cope with the piecework system and appeared to be redundant with the new payment system. For example, they still recorded their output weekly, and engaged in 'cross-booking' in order to offset a good week against a bad one. They still downed tools to help a colleague who had made up a batch of garments incorrectly and would have suffered financially for this under the piecework system.

Figures 23.4 and 23.5 show the effects of the changes on the reject rate and the output rate in the first two months after the change. There had been a fairly drastic reduction in the numbers of reject garments produced, but the impact on output levels was not so striking, although the trend was promising and the average weekly output for the eight weeks in May and June was 390 garments compared with 360 in the previous six months.

Soon after this the manager's twelve-month's probationary period came to an end, and the directors dismissed him and amalgamated the Upstairs and Downstairs Factories under one manager. The reason for this appeared to be to save costs. Results from the factory continued to improve, but the change of manager no doubt had a large impact on this. Two years later the staff of the Upstairs Factory had been reduced to two-thirds of the former figure, the output levels were on average 400 garments per week, and the reject rate had virtually disappeared (one garment per fortnight or so).

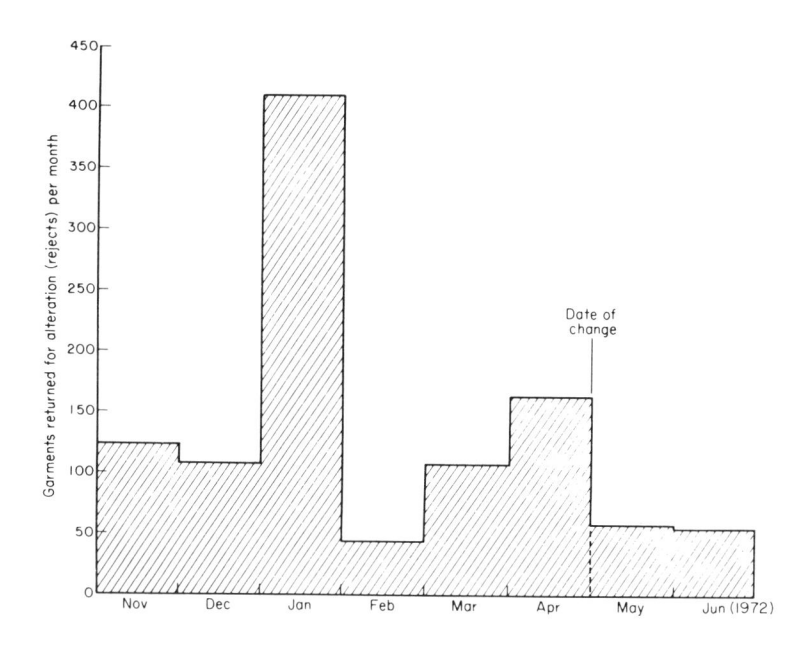

Figure 23.4   Reject rates in the factory before and after the change in the payment system

Conclusion

This case study shows how to use the technique for deciding how much, if any, bonus should be included in the pay packet of a group of employees. It is not put forward as a model either of procedures or of the ideal payment system, since both of these must be adapted to the requirements in any particular situation. In particular, it is the author's opinion that for any production system more complex than this, or group of employees much larger than this (both of which are more usually the case when a company has a wage or salary administrator), it would not be feasible to produce an adequate solution to a payment system problem without the cooperation of workers and managers in a joint exercise to investigate the problems.

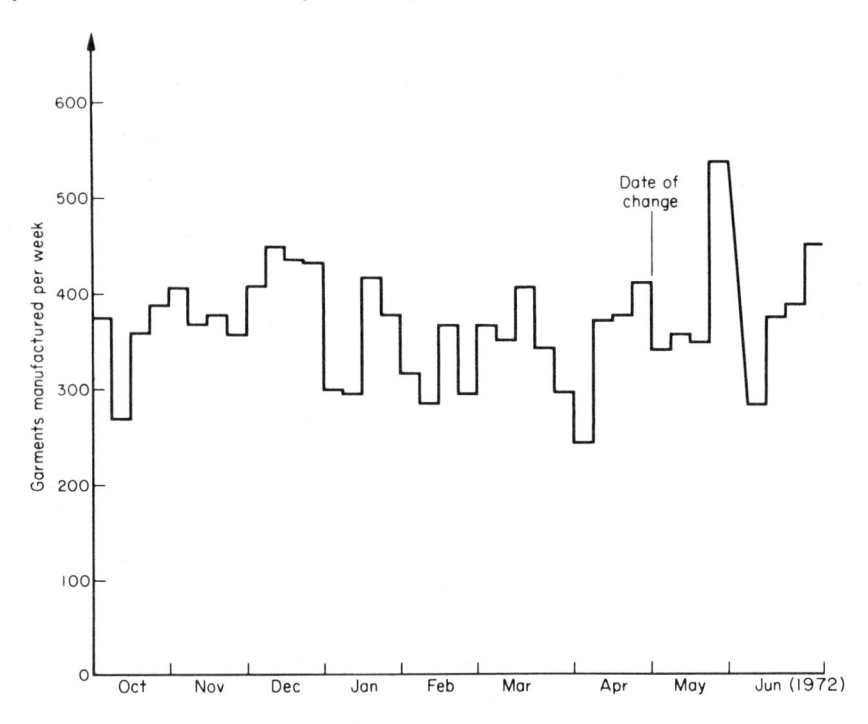

Figure 23.5 Garments manufactured per week before and after the change in the payment system

References and Further Reading

ACAS *Advisory Booklet no. 2: Introduction to Payment Systems*, Advisory, Conciliation and Arbitration Service, London, 1980.

Lupton, T. and Bowey, A.M., *Wages and Salaries*, Penguin, 1974. **(revised 2nd edition, Gower, 1982, forthcoming)**.

Mansfield, D., 'Payment systems in smaller companies: Relationships with size and climate', *Personnel Review*, Volume 9, no. 2, Spring 1980.

Robinson, D. (Ed.), *Local Labour Markets and Wage Structures*, Gower Press, 1970.

Torrington, D. and Chapman, J., *Personnel Management*, Prentice-Hall, 1979.

Part Six

Employee Benefits

Editor's Introduction

In this section separate chapters are devoted to fringe benefits for managers and executives, fringe benefits for manual and clerical workers, and pension schemes.

For a manager or an executive fringe benefits can be an important part of the reward package he receives. In Chapter 24 the various kinds of fringe benefits which a company can utilize are described and appraised; and there is also a discussion of the concept of allowing managers to select from a range of fringe benefits those which they most desire, to make up some specified total allowance.

Similarly Chapter 25 considers the types of fringe benefits typically made available to manual and clerical workers, and the advantages and disadvantages of each.

Pension schemes are a complex topic, involving consideration of government legislation, company funding activities and the desirability of the possible alternative types of scheme from the employees point of view. For this reason a separate chapter is devoted to this one major kind of fringe benefit.

24

Employee Benefits for Managers and Executives

Richard Cockman

This and Chapter 25 define employee benefits as 'those benefits supplied by an employer to, or for, the benefit of an employee which are not in the form of wages, salaries and time-related payments'. This definition makes it possible to consider as benefits profit-sharing, share schemes, bonus payments, etc, as well as pensions, company cars, holidays, etc. Pensions are fully discussed in Chapter 26, and bonus payments, share schemes and profit-sharing in Chapters 22 and 17 so the discussion in this and the next chapter will exclude these.

At first sight, benefits are provided primarily for the benefit of the employee; but, perhaps even more important, they also provide a benefit to the employer in the form of higher motivation, more efficient working, increased cooperation and, generally, a better working atmosphere.

A feature of benefits is that very rarely, if at all, does a company provide a single benefit; they normally come as a package which works alongside, and very closely with, the salary structure that a company operates. The best benefits package is one that provides the optimum benefits to employees with the optimum benefits to the employer.

The prime point when establishing a complete set of benefits is to realize that it will be effective only so long as the salary structure is satisfactory. The best benefits package may turn a suspect salary structure into one which is just about acceptable, but it will not turn a bad salary structure into one which is acceptable. Conversely, a bad benefits package can turn a good salary structure into an unacceptable one.

This chapter considers:

1. The two basic types of benefits which may be included in a total benefits package.
2. The individual benefits which may be provided.

But first there is a discussion of the idea of a complete set or 'package' of benefits.

The Total Benefits/Salary Package

Employers realize that the cost of an employee is made up of three components: salary, benefits and overheads. Disregarding the last, because it is of no benefit to the employee, an employer can see that the cost of providing salary and benefits to an employee is so many pounds per year. Although employees are able to negotiate their salary and some or all of their benefits as individual components, they only rarely, if ever, negotiate the package as a whole.

Companies are increasingly taking the view that they should offer a 'total compensation package', ie the system of setting a ceiling level to an employee's total compensation. For the sake of argument, assume that for a senior manager it is £20000 per year. Within this total certain minima and maxima are set and the following is an example of such annual cost minima and maxima:

Salary	55–100% of the ceiling
Pension contributions	£3000–£9000
Car	£2000–£3400
House purchase	up to £3500
Insurance, medical and otherwise	up to £500
Children's education	up to £1000

Thus an employee with a ceiling of £20000, with two children at school, might choose £1000 for his children's education, £3000 for his car, £1000 for his house purchase, £3000 for pension and £12000 for salary. Whereas his rather older colleague whose children have left school, who wants to purchase a new house and who does not like driving, could choose £6000 for pension, £3000 for his house purchase, £500 for insurance and £10,500 for salary.

The obvious advantage of this system is that each employee can choose the benefits which are of most use to him. An additional advantage is that an employee who has no need of a particular benefit will not feel chagrined if his colleague avails himself of it because he knows that he can take other benefits or a larger salary.

The disadvantages are first, that too much flexibility can create great administrative difficulties and second, an executive who chooses 'unwisely' may feel aggrieved later in his working career. These can be reduced to manageable proportions by reducing the choice within components, eg cars in specific price ranges for a particular grade may be specified and by specifying that the choice may be changed only after a specified length of time, eg cars must be kept for three years, or a particular insurance may not be reduced during its period of existence.

Basic Types of Benefits

In examining the available benefits, it is possible to divide them into two basic types.

1. 'Fringe' benefits which individually are relatively unimportant but collectively may become very important.
2. 'Key' benefits which can be as important as, or even more important than, salary for managers and executives.

It is necessary to examine these two basic types of benefit separately because they play a different role in the management philosophy of a company. Some of them also apply to manual and clerical staff and, where they are more important for these grades, they are examined more fully in Chapter 25.

The benefits which can be incorporated under the heading of 'fringe' benefits are surprisingly numerous and, in some cases, it is clear that their presence is of little direct benefit but their absence could have quite serious negative effects on executives. The following list can never be totally comprehensive, nor will the whole range be applicable to any one company but it does serve to illustrate the scope available to companies and can be subdivided into broad categories which for simple identification can be summarized as status, security and work benefits.

Status	*Security*	*Work*
Cars	Insurance	Office accommodation
Meals	Medical care	Secretarial services
Entertainment facilities	Medical facilities	Company scholarships
Holidays	Children's education	General management training
Foreign travel	Crèches	Language training
Gifts	Home loans/ mortgage support	Sabbaticals
Telephone		

The 'key' benefits are naturally fewer in number but can also be divided into two broad categories, ie non-performance-related and performance-related benefits.

Performance-related   *Non-performance-related*
Share schemes   Retirement counselling
Profit-sharing   House purchase

In examining the individual categories of 'fringe' benefit, it is evident that each group fulfils a different function. All the benefits clearly have a monetary value which is important to the recipients, but their true value bears less relation to this than it does to the intrinsic nature of the benefit. Generalizations are always dangerous but, though the status benefits may not have a direct influence on the performance of an individual manager or executive, their absence is likely to have a far greater counter-productive effect.

'Status' Benefits

Cars

The provision of company cars and a company's car policy is potentially something which can cause the extremes of satisfaction and effectiveness. Apart from office accommodation, no other benefit which an executive receives so easily identifies his seniority. Therefore it is important that a benefit which can be costly to a company achieves its maximum effect. The detail of any successful car policy will obviously depend very much on an individual company's requirements but, wherever possible, the policy should be clearly defined and err, if anything, on the generous side. Flexibility and choice are desirable provided they are consistent with a company's administrative capability. It is much easier to cater for individual desires in a company where only two to three people have cars than in one where there may be several thousand, many of which are 'passed on' with the job. The critical number at which it becomes really necessary to have a defined policy is surprisingly low, probably as few as ten. Below that figure, the administration involved can probably be handled easily by existing administrative staff without any great loss of time. Above that figure, there is still no great time loss provided the whole policy is reasonably automatic but, if a whole series of individual requirements have to be catered for, then it is inevitable that one member of the administrative staff is going to spend a disproportionate amount of time on relatively unimportant niceties. It is much better to have a procedure which is as unrestrictive as possible but that is automatic in that the number of 'special circumstances' are kept to a minimum.

Meals

The provision of meals to executives is another highly sensitive area, particularly to those who just miss inclusion in the executive dining-room. The disadvantages of creating a benefit which is over-elaborate or divisive are obvious but the provision of meals for executives and managers can be an extremely practical benefit. It can be a true saving, it should be a useful meeting ground for managers of different departments and, if it enables visitors to be entertained easily and relatively economically then it is useful.

Entertaining facilities

Entertaining may be an extension of the 'working' arrangements described above, or it can be, for certain executives, a fundamental part of their job involving his home and 'leisure' times. The pressure on many businessmen today has meant that entertainment for entertainment's sake is rapidly declining but that, as a means of finding extra working hours, it is extremely useful.

It is unlikely that many executives who are involved to any degree in entertaining would admit that they found any benefit (other than time utilization) in it, but it is equally true that if they lost the facility to entertain, there would be an immediate feeling of disenchantment.

The cost-effectiveness of entertaining is difficult to determine and perhaps commonsense is the only real guide.

Holidays

Again, holidays are likely to invoke a contradictory reaction from its recipients. Executives will enjoy the reflected status that comes with a large holiday entitlement (although the differential between executive and other employees has or is rapidly disappearing), but at the same time are likely to claim that they are unable to take the time off fully to utilize their allocation. In many cases, this is true and it should cause a company to look hard at its operation because there is growing evidence that holidays, far from being a fringe benefit, are an essential to good health in senior managers. Ways of overcoming this situation are to encourage executives to take holidays, say, at the end of a business trip on which their wives have accompanied them, or to take a sabbatical (see below).

Foreign travel

Like entertaining, travel is probably considered an important benefit initially but loses its glamour when it becomes commonplace. However, absence of business travel can again be counter-productive to an executive who has been used to going abroad regularly in the past. To executives not heavily involved in foreign travel, the occasional trip to overseas customers or overseas offices is a genuine attraction and can be used productively. Once again, it is worth a company considering whether wives can accompany their husbands on the occasional trip as this will lead not only to greater identification of an executive's family with his work but will also provide some compensation for the commitment that he may be called upon to make to his work.

Telephone costs

The payment of an executive's telephone bill can be justified on the grounds that he may have to make out-of-hours telephone calls or should be on call at any time of day or night. It is rare that the need for such action can really be balanced against the cost of paying the full telephone bill and at a time of increasing living costs can be distinctly useful.

Gifts

Gifts are usually not of any great monetary importance to an executive. However, they can provide additional matters by which the company can be seen to be looking after a senior man. The presentation of gifts to an executive (apart from on special occasions, such as 25-years' service or retirement) is purely 'cosmetic'. The concept of giving everybody in the company a present on their birthday is useful again as a means of identifying that person with the company and showing the company cares about him as an individual. However the non-presence of these two benefits is unlikely to be commented upon or affect the company's standing in the eyes of its employees in any way.

Security Benefits

Insurance

The provision of additional insurance cover for executives and managers can be a fairly significant benefit. The insurance cover can be provided as part of the company's pension plan or it can be additional to that. Insurance cover can be operable only when the executive is working on company business, or it can be operable on all occasions. This is one area where the company can get total cost-effectiveness because insurance cover is relatively cheap to provide on a group basis.

In cases where an executive has died in service and his widow, by virtue of the superior insurance cover provided by the company, receives a full and adequate sum of money as provision for the future, the company derives very considerable credit and is seen to be a good employer.

Medical care

There is a rapidly increasing trend for companies to provide facilities by which employees can take out private medical insurance on advantageous terms or where the company pays for the whole insurance. This insurance normally provides the advantages of privacy for executives and can ensure that employees can be treated in accordance with a timetable to suit the mutual needs of the executive and the company. Furthermore, private hospital treatment can allow an executive to carry out important parts of his work from his hospital bed in many instances. In this context, such insurance may be seen to be prudent from the company's point of view.

Medical facilities

On-the-site medical facilities are likely to be of less importance to the average senior executive or manager. However, where he is responsible for a plant or factory which is not in close proximity to widely available medical facilities, such provision can be useful.

Children's education

Few companies are prepared to take the lead in providing direct facilities for the payment of employees' children's school fees and tertiary educational costs. However, many companies' senior management realize that this is one area where executives in the company are likely to be faced with increasing costs. One method by which an executive can be prepared to meet such cost is for the company to arrange for personal financial planning consultants to advise its executives on a group basis with the company paying the consultant's fee. There is definitely a growing trend for this service and it has the advantage of giving the individual freedom of choice but clearly indicating the company's interest in his welfare.

Crêches

The increasing demand for able managers and the greater freedom being demanded by women means that it is very probable that a large proportion of executive positions will be held in the future by women and this trend is likely to be accelerated by the right under Employment Protection (Consolidation) Act for women to return to work after confinement. Many of the women who could make an important and worthwhile contribution to organizations will also desire to become mothers as well as have careers. This can only be achieved if proper child care or crêche facilities are provided which will mean that the mother can return to her work with absolute confidence for the welfare of her child. Therefore it is likely that an increasing number of crêches will be established by companies.

Work Benefits

Office accommodation

Along with the provision of the company motor car, the most visible sign of executive success is the type of office which the executive occupies. The reason that the provision of office accommodation has not been included under the status benefits is that, properly planned, an office can provide tangible work benefits to an executive. There are a growing number of consultants in this field and a company can achieve positive benefit from showing that its office accommodation is as well planned as its factory layouts, etc. However, the cost of providing every executive with all possible accoutrements can be prohibitive, so this particular area has to be carefully considered on a widely planned basis for changes to be made.

Secretarial services

A policy which enables executives and managers of the company to have really good secretarial facilities is of paramount importance. This is included under the section on work benefits because many companies adopt plans which can only be described as providing the minimum acceptable. Where companies decide to provide really well-planned secretarial services, there is an immediate benefit not only on the output of the executive but frequently in the quality of his work as he is allowed to concentrate on the main issues rather than on petty disturbing issues.

Companies scholarships

Company scholarships really fall into two categories—those which are related to an executive's work and those which are not. Clearly, those which are related to his work can have a beneficial effect on the company and an increasing number of companies are realizing the value of sending their key men on carefully selected educational programmes. Equally, however, a number of companies have realized that theory is frequently not as useful as practical experience for people holding key positions. Therefore it is essential that any company sponsored scholarships should be of a very carefully selected nature.

The second category, where the company sponsored scholarship is not work promoted but allows the executive to take a scholarship to read for a qualification which is important to him but does not necessarily have any bearing on his work needs to be considered in a different light. Like sabbaticals, such a programme can have a wider benefit than may at first seem necessary. However, most companies are likely to feel that the provision of some scholarships, if done at all, can be done only on a very selective basis.

General management training

There has been a move away from the practice of sending executives away on frequent vague management training courses or seminars. Companies have found that these are just not cost-effective. However, with more careful selection, or with the use of 'in-house' training, management training can be continued on a more cost-effective basis. Provided the courses are of reasonably short duration, then they are welcomed by managers who feel that their worth as an individual is being increased by the knowledge they acquire on these courses. Recent developments in management training (such as the Manchester Business School's 'Joint Development Activities') indicate that great success can be obtained from a series of short courses with practical project work forming the linking theme between them.

Language training

The need for executives and senior managers to be fluent in more than their mother tongue is rapidly increasing, and therefore language training has potentially a very practical benefit to both employee and employer. It is certainly a benefit which is welcomed by the employee because it increases his worth as an individual. Companies will normally only choose to send employees on language training courses if they feel there is likely to be a need for that executive to use languages during the course of his job. However, many companies who specify the need for someone to be fluent in a certain language before making an appointment are unnecessarily limiting the scope of their choice. In many cases, it may be more worthwhile for the company to recruit somebody who has the practical knowledge necessary to undertake the position well and for the company then to train him after recruitment.

Sabbaticals

The concept of allowing senior executives to go on a sabbatical (ie to be allowed a specific period of leave, eg one year with pay) after they have served a number of years, (typically, 15 or 20) is one that has been adopted for some considerable time in the USA. It is rare for UK companies to provide such a facility. However, as pressure on executives tends to increase, this facility is likely to become more widespread. There are two clear advantages: from the executive's point of view, it enables him to 're-charge' and to come back fresh to his position; from the company's point of view, provided it has some choice on the work undertaken during the sabbatical, there is also the advantage that it prevents the senior managers from becoming too stereotyped and blinkered in their approach to their job.

Key Benefits

Performance-related

Performance-related benefits such as share schemes and profit-sharing are discussed in Chapter 16. Non-performance-related benefits are considered below.

Retirement counselling

In the immediate past period and currently, many of the larger companies have been faced with the prospect of having to retire senior executives earlier than their statutory retiring ages. This has brought home the need for the socially responsible company to prepare its executives for retirement. Therefore it is not surprising that there is a growing amount of work being carried out by independent bodies, by consulting organizations, and by companies themselves to provide a retirement counselling service both at pre-retirement ages and post-retirement.

House purchase

Banks and financial institutions have provided house purchase facilities to their employees for a long time. As house prices have risen dramatically in the last few years and, as companies are demanding that their executives be more mobile, it is becoming necessary for companies to consider whether or not to provide beneficial house purchase facilities to their employees. There is a danger that employees may become 'locked in' to the company by their dependence on such a loan, and consequently resentful. An alternative approach is for a company to give mortgage support and provided care is taken, house purchase schemes can provide a very genuine attraction for the purposes of recruiting and retaining senior men, and it is clearly one which is considered very important by the employees themselves.

Summary

This chapter has examined a wide range of fringe benefits. Clearly, few companies could afford to provide them all and therefore there is the question of how the benefit programme should be constructed.

The two basic steps that a company should take are—first, to define precisely what it hopes to achieve by introducing additional fringe benefits or re-shaping its present programme; and second, to ascertain clearly what it provides at the moment and what the effectiveness of these benefits is. In citing what it wants to achieve, a company has to decide whether it wants its benefits to be linked to the performance of the company or whether it wants to give them as a reward to employees in such a way that it provides them with additional security.

A company should work down from the key benefits to the less important benefits. Thus, if it decides it wants to try to build-up a compensation package which is related to the company's performance, it should be prepared to investigate and have designed either or both share schemes and profit-sharing schemes. If, on the other hand, the emphasis is to be placed on non-performance related benefits, house purchase schemes and retirement counselling must be of primary importance.

Of these key benefits, the house purchase scheme is the only one which is likely to be a cost burden to the company. The others are unlikely to incur heavy costs to the company, since they should be paid for out of additional profits obtained, in part at least, by the effect of introducing the new benefits.

Having decided which of the key benefits should be installed first, the company can then move on to adding the other 'fringe' benefits as they appear necessary and as their budget allows. In order to obtain the maximum effect from the second stage, it is important that the company is aware of the effectiveness of its present benefits programme. To obtain this information an 'audit' may be carried out of the benefits currently provided and how these are received by employees. Difficulties may be experienced in carrying out such a survey objectively, but the use of outside consultants could make this a more feasible operation. A typical programme would involve deciding which benefits should be included in the survey and also any attitudinal points of special interest which should be covered in interviews with a cross-section of recipients and potential recipients. The recipients would then be interviewed to see if they both appreciated precisely what benefits they were receiving and how much these were worth to them and how much they cost the company. Furthermore, they could also be asked what further benefits they would like to receive or would prefer to receive in place of benefits that are already in existence. The results of this survey could be cross-referenced with the cost of a company's benefits programme and a realistic view of the cost-effectiveness of their benefits programme worked out. The company would then be in a position to decide precisely how the programme should be amended or added to and how such a programme should be undertaken. It is vitally important that, once the new programme is introduced, great care be taken to see that its effectiveness is duly checked and, more importantly, that the full impact of the new programme is communicated to the recipients and potential recipients. The continual up-dating can be carried out by having annual surveys or 'audits' carried out to see if the hoped for effect is achieved and whether any failure to achieve this effect is due to the programme itself or to a failure to communicate it properly to employees.

This leads to the importance of communication. Many fringe benefit programmes are introduced extremely badly by companies who content themselves with sending out an explanatory booklet or memorandum which is often in semi-technical jargon which is incomprehensible to the recipients. It would be much better if companies took the time and trouble to make sure that their personnel department, for example, had a specialist person who was responsible for communicating the programme internally within the company.

Thus, a company wishing to up-date its benefits programme should be prepared to take the following steps:

1 Clearly define its aims.
2 Ascertain what it gives and how these are received.
3 Ascertain what employees would like to receive.
4 Work out what it can afford to spend on its benefits programme.
5 Draw up a new benefits programme bearing in mind the vast range of benefits which can be given.
6 Make sure that the programme is communicated fully and efficiently to all recipients.
7 Continually check to see that the benefits programme is achieving its aims or objectives.
8 Be prepared to amend or alter the benefits programme if it is not achieving these objectives.
9 Consider the possibility of giving flexible benefits to employees who can have an element of choice in deciding what they receive.
10 Be prepared to employ specialist personnel both internally and externally to ensure that a benefits programme is properly constructed.

References and Further Reading

Briggs, J.F., *Planning Your Personal Finances*, Ward Lock, 1979.
Cooke, P.N.C., *The Company Car*, Gower, 1975.

Greenhill, R.T., *Employee Remuneration and Profit Sharing*, Woodhead Faulkner, 1980.
McBeath, G., *Management Remuneration Policy*, Business Books, London, 1969.
Murlis, H., *Employee Benefits (Management Report no. 37)*, The British Institute of Management, 1978.
Pilch, M. and Wood, V., *Pension Schemes: a Guide to Principles and Practice*, Gower, 1979.
Swallow, B., 'Sabbaticals—breathing space or nightmare?', *Business Administration*. February, 1973.
Towers, Perrin, Forster and Crosby, *Employee Benefits Communication Practices in the United Kingdom*, London, 1972.
Vinson, N., 'Participation in Profit', *Industrial Society*, August, 1973.

25

Employee Benefits for Non-managerial Staff

Richard Cockman

Chapter 24 examined the differing concepts behind the provision of certain benefits for managers and put forward for consideration the view that managers should have some choice in the way their individual benefit packages should be built up. This chapter differs because employee benefits for manual and clerical staff have been in many cases far less common and therefore to many potential recipients the main question is not one of choice but of whether or not the benefits are offered at all. Information on the subject comes from two surveys (Moonman 1973 and BIM, 1974) and has shown that though manual and clerical employees have lagged behind managers in the receipt of many benefits the position is rapidly changing.

Perhaps the major difference between the positions of managers and of manual and clerical workers is that whereas benefit programmes for the former are usually set up on a very individual and frequently discretionary basis, for the latter they are increasingly becoming part of a negotiated package. This means that unions and staff committees are far more involved in the establishment and improvement of benefits and will be increasingly involved in the future, as with industry associations they agree the basic terms for any particular form of employment.

The second major difference is likely to be the fact that benefits for manual and clerical employees are more related to 'basic rights' schemes and so have a strong emphasis on security whereas additional benefits for managers can, perhaps, be considered as the 'icing on the top' necessary to compensate for the huge commitment to his work often demanded of the modern professional manager.

It is possible to divide the benefits available into broad categories which can be summarized as 'statutory', security, welfare and work benefits.

1 'Statutory'
   (a) Pensions
   (b) National insurance
   (c) Redundancy payments
   (d) Holidays
2 Security
   (a) Sick pay
   (b) Insurance
   (c) Medical facilities
   (d) Crêches
3 Welfare
   (a) Subsidized meals
   (b) Sports/social facilities
   (c) Discounts on products
   (d) Housing
   (e) Assistance with education
   (f) Retirement counselling
4 Work
   (a) Bonus/profit-sharing schemes
   (b) Share schemes
   (c) Long-service payments.

Statutory Benefits

Holidays

Pensions are discussed in Chapter 26 and national insurance benefits require no further examination. Therefore holidays are the only benefit included in this category. However, in the UK the only statutory holidays are the Bank Holidays whereas in some other countries there is legislation enforcing a prescribed minimum number of holidays. Though proposals for similar arrangements have been made in Britain, these have been rejected on the grounds that holidays should be a matter for negotiation.

Until recently manual workers have compared unfavourably with salaried employees but this inequality is being rapidly diminished. The norm nowadays is four weeks to start with and many industrial workers are set to achieve five weeks. A substantial number of clerical workers have benefitted for some years from arrangements which entitled them to five weeks or more on achieving certain length of service. Though, on average, British workers do not get as much holiday as the EEC counterparts they appear to be treated better in this respect than their

American counterparts. However, a straight comparison is not always valid because there are more public holidays in America and there is a growing trend for certain large American companies to allow employees preferential terms in holiday centres in which the company has an interest.

Many companies do not assess the cost of holidays in their benefit programme but they are (with pensions) one of the most expensive items in a programme. It has been established in a private survey carried out amongst 30 of the larger companies in the UK that the average cost of holidays is equivalent to 0.4% of pay for each day of holiday.

Security Benefits

Sick pay

In line with the trend for more security benefits for manual and clerical employees, sick pay schemes in addition to national insurance benefits, have been the cause of one of the largest increases in expenditure on employee benefits over the last two decades.

Once again staff employees are treated better than non-staff employees but here, too, the differentials are being lessened though it is still common for bonus and overtime payments to be excluded when calculating a non-staff employee's sick pay. Furthermore, though there are many different schemes in operation, there are two widespread shortcomings. First, the actual payments made to employees who are ill are often inadequate and cause a reduction in standard of living. Second, very few companies make realistic provisions for long-term illness. As in the vast majority of cases absences through illness are relatively short term it should be possible for companies to amend this second point at little additional cost. Trade unions have put considerable emphasis over the last few years in efforts to obtain sick pay in addition to national insurance payments so that the aggregate payments are as near to average pay as possible.

Insurance

There are usually two main ways in which a company provides benefits in this area. First the company pays for the insurance and second it arranges facilities by which employees can take advantage of group rebates. The first instance naturally includes works liability cover for employees whose work may involve special risks and for travelling on behalf of the company. Additionally there is an increasing trend for companies to provide 24 hour insurance cover for its employees even for accidents totally unconnected with their work or place of work with death benefits being provided as part of the pension package.

Group rebate schemes enable employees to take out additional cheaper insurance on themselves and in some instances on their families. These schemes frequently include insurance for medical treatment though participation in these arrangements is rare for manual workers.

The overall cost of providing insurance cover is low and is in the region of 0.5% of payroll.

Medical facilities

It used to be rare for manual workers to be involved in medical insurance schemes but certainly one major national trade union has negotiated such cover with the employers, covering substantial numbers of workers. But it is fairly common for a company to provide facilities by which employees can get treatment for minor illnesses and injuries on site.

Redundancy payments

These benefits could fall into the statutory category because as a result of the Employment Protection (Consolidation) Act, 1978 companies are bound to make certain minimum provisions for employees who are made redundant. However, they are included under the security category because many companies realize the need to give payments which are more generous than the act if their employees are to feel a real sense of security.

The people who normally suffer first from redundancy are part-timers, newcomers and employees with no domestic responsibility. Therefore it is feasible for companies to be generous to long-serving loyal employees without such action being too costly.

It is difficult to quantify the costs of providing for redundancy because the measures taken can vary widely. Not unnaturally the more successful a company is the less likely it is to see a need to make greater provision for redundancy though it may provide more than required under the 1965 act. This is where such benefits as well-arranged company pension schemes and share schemes can play a vital part. The former give long-term security and the latter can provide an incentive if the company continues to do well and a solid buffer if any unfortunate circumstances arise.

Crêches

As discussed in Chapter 24 companies are likely to have an increasing need to utilize women who are capable of undertaking executive responsibility and the same is true at clerical and shopfloor level as well. Indeed the case is possibly more pressing at these levels, and additionally legislation introduced in the Employment Protection (Consolidation) Act 1978 gives women the right to return to work after confinement. Fiat in Italy have long provided facilities by which female workers can leave their children in crêches or nurseries when they return to work and this is a relatively inexpensive and socially attractive way by which companies can go towards overcoming shortage of labour problems.

Welfare Benefits

Subsidized meals

The provision of canteen facilities has been one of the longest established fringe benefits for manual employees. They are popular benefits with employees because of the provision of economical easily obtainable meals. Indeed the Industrial Society produced a report in 1971 which indicated that 37% of all employees take their main meal of a day in the company canteen. Though the original intention was to ensure that workers obtained an adequate diet, the provision of these facilities are advantageous from a company's point of view today because they ensure prompt after-lunch attendance. The cost on average has been calculated as being 1.8% of payroll because few companies are able to run canteens economically but such a cost is usually acceptable in view of the benefits conferred.

Sports/social facilities

Like canteens, sports and social facilities are also long-established fringe benefits. They are one of the best ways by which identification with a company can be achieved by an employee and his family and such facilities are normally well accepted. Two problems arise. First, when introducing such facilities some companies make the mistake of trying to over-economize and thereby produce facilities which are unattractive in comparison with similar 'outside' facilities and second, in the large conurbations the location of these facilities can be out of reach for perhaps two-thirds of the workforce. In such instances, it is possibly better to concentrate on producing really first-class social facilities close to the place of work.

Discount and company purchase plans

Many companies take advantage of their purchasing power or of trade inducements to provide facilities by which employees can purchase certain goods and/or at certain places at favourable prices. While such arrangements are pleasant they are unlikely to provide more than a minor contribution to an employee's loyalty or willingness to remain in a particular job except in exceptional cases, eg in some of the major car manufacturers where employees can purchase motor cars at highly attractive rates.

Assistance with housing

There are three main ways in which companies can provide facilities in this area, ie company-owned houses, house-moving expenses and assistance with house purchase.

The provision of company-owned houses is falling out of favour socially because it ties employees and their families firmly to a company. However, it must be stated that in practice the author has found that people living in such accommodation are very satisfied and that the companies providing such accommodation are and were not attempting to exploit the fact that these employees were in a sense 'tied' to the company. It is unlikely that such schemes will be expanded and therefore housing assistance in the future is likely to be confined to the other two ways.

Assistance with house-moving expenses has been a natural consequence of the growth of large groups of companies who have a need to transfer staff at all levels and also because some companies have found it economical to move out of areas of concentrated population. In the latter case companies can both give direct assistance and arrange for assistance with housing to be given by the local authority.

The last alternative, of companies giving direct assistance with house purchase, is relatively unusual for employees at manual and clerical levels except in the case of finance houses such as banks and insurance companies. However, with the difficulty lower income groups are having in obtaining mortgages in certain areas there is likely to be an increase in such arrangements. Direct assistance with low interest company loans means that the whole purchase price of a house can be a heavy extra cost for companies and there are tax complications. Many companies prefer to provide bridging loans or to make up the shortfall between a mortgage and the house price or to arrange connections with mortgage companies. In this context the operation of a savings-linked share scheme in conjunction with a building society can be useful to the participating employees.

Assistance with education

Assistance with education has two aspects—the first deals with assistance for employees themselves and the second with the education of their children. Assistance with the education of employees is rare and is usually confined to training connected with the employees' specific jobs and there are virtually no instances of providing educational assistance for the children of manual and clerical workers except in the case of schools connected with specific trades. There is, however, no reason why companies should not consider providing assistance either directly to employees or in the form of a bursary to selected or local schools.

Retirement counselling

As this type of benefit is not widespread for managers it is not surprising that it is a relatively rare benefit for manual and clerical workers. However, it is a really useful perquisite that could be provided relatively inexpensively by a company. Areas where the counselling may be most useful is in giving employees advice on financial planning, on the company's pension scheme and other benefits which may be available.

While dealing with the subject of retirement it should be noted that some companies allow employees nearing retirement age to go into 'gradual retirement' by progressively reducing the number of days worked over a period prior to retirement.

Conclusions

The most illuminating factor in examining company remuneration programmes is the discrepancy that exists in most companies between hourly paid and salaried employees. It is inevitable that these discrepancies will be eroded rapidly over the next few years. This is to be welcomed because unless such a change takes place there is little hope for improving industrial relations. There are always likely to be additional benefits made available to senior managers because of the enormous commitment they are increasingly being asked to make to their work; but below that level the trend must be for equality.

As discussed in Chapter 24, if a company is going to significantly increase its benefit programme it should only do so in a planned and defined manner. It is even more important below management level for the full importance and value of benefits to be completely understood. Therefore it is essential that great care is taken to explain thoroughly all existing and new benefits and to monitor employee reaction to them. Otherwise much of the total cost of a benefit programme, which, including pensions, will be 20—40% of the payroll, will be wasted.

References and Further Reading

Beecham, R.H.S., *Pay Systems: principles and techniques*, Heinemann.
BIM, *Employee Benefits Today*, BIM Management Survey Report 19, 1974.
Greenhill, R.T., *Employee Remuneration and Profit Sharing*, Woodhead Faulkner.
Jago, A., *Sick Pay Schemes*, The Institute of Personnel Management, 1979.
Moonman, J., *The Effectiveness of Fringe Benefits in Industry*, Gower, Epping, 1973.

26

Company Pension Schemes

Michael Pilch

Pension schemes form an essential part of any modern pay structure in the UK. They come in all shapes and sizes—from one-man pension arrangements to mammoth funds covering thousands—but all have been designed to fulfil some basic purpose other than the mere provision of a pension.

Objectives

What does an employer hope to gain from the introduction of a pension scheme? Among possible objectives are:

1. To make employment with the firm or company more attractive and thus make it easier to recruit new employees of high calibre.
2. To encourage existing employees to remain and thus to reduce the costs of labour turnover.
3. To remove promotion bottle-necks by providing for the orderly retirement of older men and women.
4. To satisfy any legal or moral obligations of the management towards employees or their dependants.
5. To help employees spread their earnings over the whole of their lives to best advantage instead of having them confined to their working lives.

Most of these elements will be associated with any occupational pension scheme in some degree. Differences in design will depend on which particular objective predominates. The key item may well be the last one. The concept of the pension as deferred remuneration is now generally accepted. In other words, an employee's pay consists of two parts—immediate salary or wages and a deferred portion which is set aside for his benefit in retirement or the protection of his family if he dies beforehand.

The success of a pension scheme must, in any case, depend on the extent to which it meets the needs of the employees. Any benefit obtained by an employer as a result of setting up a scheme can only stem from acceptance and appreciation of its provisions on the part of the members. A complex scheme may therefore fail, however generous the benefits may be; while a simpler, even if more modest, arrangement may evoke a better response and prove a more rewarding investment to the employer.

Types of Benefit

A simplified approach to pension plan design, avoiding technicalities, is to regard it as an architectural problem in which three different basic types of building brick are available—the problem being to combine them into a harmonious design which will be attractive to a particular purchaser, in this case the prospective members of the pension fund.

The three basic components are:

1. Retirement pension
2. Cash lump sum at retirement
3. Death benefit.

There are other circumstances in which benefits may be payable—eg on leaving the employment or disablement—but the above are the main ingredients in the pension scheme mix. The appeal of the retirement pension is clearly to the older man or woman, while the younger members are more likely to value the protection given by the scheme to their dependants. The cash lump sum at retirement is especially attractive, both because of the flexibility that it gives to the scheme (because each member can use it to buy the kind of benefit he wants) and because it confers a tax advantage on the recipient. Each ingredient therefore appeals to a particular section of the membership, and the secret of successful pension planning is to balance the proportions in such a way as to maximize the attractions of the scheme to employees, bearing in mind the objectives set out above.

Retirement pension

Pensions may be subdivided in four ways—according to recipient, manner of calculation, method of payment and degree of dynamism.

Apart from the retirement pension payable to the member, the scheme may provide a pension payable to his widow or other dependant on his death in retirement.

Formulae for calculating the pension include the following:

1. *Final salary*. The pension is expressed as a fraction of the member's earnings at or near retirement age, eg 1/60th of final earnings for each year of service. This is much the most common basis for a modern scheme.
2. *Salary grade* or *average salary*. Units of pension are earned each year, eg 2% of salary, and added to give the final pension.
3. *Money purchase*. There is no fixed scale of pension. Instead, a fixed rate of contribution is paid and the benefits depend on what that will buy at any given age.
4. *Flat rate*. Pensions do not vary with earnings, though they may depend on length of service, eg a pension of £6 for each year of service.

Methods of payment vary greatly. Pensions may be paid monthly, quarterly or annually, in advance or in arrears. They may be paid for the lifetime of the person only, or for a fixed period, or for life with a guaranteed minimum number of payments. The usual guaranteed minimum period of payment is 5 years, though 10 years is not unknown.

Many pensions are fixed in amount, but others vary during the payment period. The main ways of adding dynamism, inflation-proofing or escalator provisions, as they are variously described, to pensions are as follows:

1. Pensions in payment may be increased at a fixed rate, usually 3% or 5% a year.
2. Pensions may be linked to a cost-of-living index.
3. Pensions may be increased on an unspecified basis, at the discretion of trustees or the employer, depending on the investment performance of the pension fund or insurance company.

Cash lump sum

Provided the rules of the scheme permit, a part of the member's total retirement benefit may be taken as a lump sum, free of tax. Strict limits are imposed on this concession by the Inland Revenue (see p. 390 and Figure 26.2).

Death benefit

The benefit paid by the scheme on the death of a member before retirement may take the form of a lump sum, or a pension, or a mixture of the two. Pensions may be payable to widows, widowers or other dependants. It is usual for trustees, wherever possible, to be given discretionary powers over the disposal of death benefits for three reasons:

1. This arrangement will normally ensure that no capital transfer tax is payable.
2. It allows benefits to be paid without waiting for probate or letters of administration.
3. It introduces a degree of flexibility so that benefits can be tailored to the needs and circumstances of dependants.

Legislation

Two serious warnings must be given. Pension legislation is complex and changes frequently. Eleven out of the last twenty years have witnessed Acts of Parliament affecting either state or occupational pension schemes or both. Thus, no discussion such as this one can be expected to do more than give a very brief outline of the legal aspects and the information should be verified before action is taken in view of the constant possibility of changes in the law or—more importantly—Inland Revenue practice.

In any case, no book on a subject of this kind can be regarded as a substitute for professional assistance. Pension schemes are no field for the do-it-yourself enthusiast. Mistakes are likely to prove far too costly: the fees charged for expert advice are, by comparison, modest.

There are two main areas of legislation—the Finance and Tax Acts, which impose upper limits on the benefits that can be provided under an approved pension scheme (approved for tax purposes, that is), and the National Insurance and Social Security Acts, which set minimum standards for schemes in certain circumstances.

Inland Revenue approval

All new pension schemes nowadays need to be approved under the Finance Acts of 1970 and 1971. Transitional concessions may be applicable to benefits secured by schemes approved under earlier legislation, but for the sake of simplicity no further reference will be made to them. The rest of this chapter will be concerned with the conditions laid down by legislation, as currently interpreted in terms of day-to-day practice by the Superannuation Funds Office, for the purposes of Inland Revenue approval.

If a scheme is not approved by the Inland Revenue, the consequences are not confined to disallowance of tax relief. An employee may find himself assessed for tax on actual or notional premiums paid to secure benefits for him by his employer.

If a scheme is approved, however,

1 Employees' contributions are an allowable expense for tax purposes.
2 Employers' contributions are normally allowable as an expense of the business.
3 Investment income of the pension fund is generally free of tax and no capital gains tax is payable.

The main limits imposed are on retirement pensions, cash lump sums and death benefits.

Figure 26.1 shows the maximum pension that may normally be provided for any member of the scheme who will have completed less than 10 years' service by normal retirement age. Any pension benefits retained from previous employment must be taken into account to the extent of ensuring that the combined total retirement pension does not exceed two-thirds of final earnings.

Total years of service	Number of 60ths of final earnings	Total years of service	Number of 60ths of final earnings
1	1	6	8
2	2	7	16
3	3	8	24
4	4	9	32
5	5	10 or more	40

Figure 26.1   Limits on pensions

In addition, a pension may be provided for a widow or widower on the member's death in retirement of up to two-thirds of the member's pension.

Provision may be made for all pensions to increase in retirement at a rate not exceeding any rise in the cost of living during the same period.

Figure 26.2 shows the maximum lump sum that may normally be paid, free of tax, to a member at normal retirement date. It will be noted that an employee must have completed 20 years' service to qualify for the maximum lump sum payment of 1½-times final yearly earnings, as compared with the 10 years required to qualify for maximum pension.

The lump sum forms part of the total retirement benefit and the pension equivalent to it must therefore be included when measuring total pension against the limits set out in Figure 26.1.

Finally, death-in-service benefits may be provided up to the limits shown in Figure 26.3. Pension benefits at the level indicated may be paid in addition to the lump sum death benefits.

It must be stressed that these figures all refer to upper limits on

Total years of service	Number of 80ths of final earnings	Total years of service	Number of 80ths of final earnings
1	3	11	42
2	6	12	48
3	9	13	54
4	12	14	63
5	15	15	72
6	18	16	81
7	21	17	90
8	24	18	99
9	30	19	108
10	36	20 or more	120

Figure 26.2   Limits on lump sums

benefits. What is actually paid depends on the rules of the scheme and will often be much less, since the main constraint on the generosity of employers is not the law, or the Inland Revenue, but cost.

Lump sum benefits

A refund of the employee's contributions, with or without interest, plus either

(a) twice the employee's yearly earnings

or

(b) £5000 or four times yearly earnings, whichever is the greater, less any lump sum death benefit (exceeding £500) retained from previous employment.

Pension benefits

Pensions payable to a widow and other dependants not exceeding in total the maximum approvable pension that could otherwise have been paid to the member at normal retirement date based on his earnings at the date of death but with service taken forward to normal retirement date. The pension payable to a widow or widower must not exceed two-thirds of the total figure.

Figure 26.3   Limits on death benefits

Contracting out

After many false starts, a comprehensive earnings-related state pension scheme reached the statute book in the shape of the Social Security Pensions Act 1975, which came into effect on 6 April 1978.

Provision was made in the legislation for employers to contract out of part of the state scheme on condition that they offered equal or better benefits to their employees through occupational pension schemes. According to the latest estimates, more than 10 million employees have been contracted out on this basis. Contracting out is supervised by a body known as the Occupational Pensions Board. The conditions which have to be satisfied are complex, but the main requirements may be summarized as follows:

1. The scheme must offer a scale of personal pension which is at least equal to 1/80th of final salary (or average salary revalued in line with national average earnings) for each year of service.
2. It must also guarantee a minimum pension for each member which is not less than the amount forgone under the state scheme.
3. Pensions must be available not later than age 65 for men or age 60 for women.
4. The scheme must provide for a widow's pension on the death of a male employee or pensioner before or after retirement, equal to one-half of the personal pension earned by the member on bases (1) and (2) above.
5. A member leaving the employment must be assured of a preserved pension which is not less than the amount of the guaranteed minimum pension for the relevant period of contracted-out service, revalued to retirement age in line with any change in national average earnings.
6. Where payment of pension is deferred beyond the ages set out in (3) above, the guaranteed minimum pension must be increased by 6½ per cent for each year of deferment.

Where these conditions can be satisfied, the employer and employees both qualify for a reduction in national insurance contributions—the rebate currently standing at 4½ per cent of the relevant band of earnings for the employer and 2½ per cent for the employee.

A further requirement imposed by the 1975 Act, irrespective of whether a pension scheme is used for contracting out or not, is that men and women doing comparable work must be admitted to the scheme on equal terms, as regards entry age, period of qualifying service and whether entry is voluntary or compulsory.

Designing Schemes

It might be thought that the prescribed maximum and minimum benefit levels laid down for approval and recognition respectively left very little room for manoeuvre when designing pension schemes, at least in the case of contracted-out schemes, but the reverse is true. The employer is still free to choose who should come into the scheme and who should not; the ages at which employees should be expected to retire; whether or not they should contribute towards the cost of the benefits; the amount of pension to be provided and how it should be calculated; whether a cash retirement benefit should be included; the form of the benefit payable on death in service, whether pension or lump sum, and the amount; the type of widow's pension payable on death in retirement; whether or not pensions are to be protected against rises in the cost of living and, if so, the form which such protection should take. He is free to pick the method of costing which is most suitable for his purpose (see below). He can also choose between an insured scheme and a privately invested fund, with in each case a wide range of alternative investments open to him.

Apart from these more or less technical choices, an employer setting up a pension scheme is confronted with a number of other, more fundamental problems to resolve. For example, if he employs manual workers, will he treat all grades alike for pension purposes or will he operate separate pension arrangements for white-collar workers? Will he follow the pattern of the state pension scheme by differentiating between men and women or will he try to give similar pension treatment to both sexes?

These questions—both technical and fundamental—can only be answered correctly in the light of the employer's particular circumstances and objectives, as set out. Further advice is therefore beyond the scope of this chapter, but the variety of occupational schemes in existence is sufficient evidence of the diversity of answers possible.

Paying for Pensions

Small pension schemes, covering up to 50 members say, are mostly insured and are usually based on either single or annual premium costing. In the former case, the exact cost of the benefits earned in each year is paid. This cost rises for each member every year as he grows older (though the cost for a group of employees will not necessarily rise if older members leave and are replaced by younger ones). The annual premium method of costing spreads the cost of a given benefit for any member forward so that it remains constant throughout his membership. Nevertheless, the cost for a group of employees will vary as benefits alter, new entrants join and existing members leave, die or retire.

Controlled funding which, in one form or another, is the basis used nowadays to cost most larger schemes, whether insured or privately invested, makes assumptions about all the factors likely to affect future costs. These include, for example, mortality of employees and pensioners, rates of salary and wage increases, investment yields on the pension fund and expenses of administration.

The cost is then usually assessed as a percentage of the salary roll of members of the pension scheme and reviewed at regular intervals when it may be revised in the light of experience. The method is flexible, since the cost depends largely on the assumptions made about the future, and in practice allows the employer to exercise a fair degree of control over the incidence of cost—ie whether to pay more now and less later or vice versa.

Sources of Advice

All pension schemes need to be reviewed from time to time, to make sure they are still serving the purpose for which they were originally established. Employers often find it difficult to obtain impartial advice because of the confusing array of experts claiming to offer it. Nobody would buy fish from a butcher or ask a vet to take out their appendix: the expertise has to be relevant to the subject-matter. Insurance brokers know about insured schemes. Consulting actuaries are mainly concerned with privately invested schemes. The larger firms of pension consultants have experience of both.

Reference to the relevant professional bodies will produce informative, if not particularly helpful, lists of member firms. Alternatively, the most practical way to find a good adviser, if you do not have one already, is to ask other employers of a similar size in similar businesses to recommend one to you.

References and Further Reading

Code of Practice on Information to Members of Pension Schemes, National Association of Pension Funds, 1980.
Equal Status for Men and Women in Occupational Pension Schemes, report of the Occupational Pensions Board, Cmnd. 6599, HMSO, 1976.
Occupational Pension Schemes 1975, Fifth survey by the Government Actuary, HMSO, 1978.
Occupational Pension Schemes: the Role of Members in the Running of Schemes, Cmnd. 6514, HMSO, 1976.
Pension Schemes, Michael Pilch and Victor Wood, Gower, 1979.
Solvency, Disclosure of Information and Member Participation in Occupational Pension Schemes, report of the Occupational Pensions Board, Cmnd. 5904, HMSO, 1975.
Survey of Occupational Pension Schemes—1980, National Association of Pension Funds, 1981.

Part Seven

Administering Policy and Planning

Editor's Introduction

In this section, the administrative problems, policy decisions and planning activities of the salary and wage system administrator are considered.

Chapter 27 considers the problems involved in ensuring that an existing salary or wage system is still reasonably well suited to the needs of the organization; deciding what steps are necessary if it is not; and determining the circumstances in which a major revision of a payment system would be desirable.

Chapter 28 considers various methods of budgetary control procedures and their impact on the effectiveness of salary and wage systems. These control procedures are often designed without reference to the financial reward systems in use, with the result that the same activities are being influenced by two different control procedures, and neither works effectively.

The sources of information which can be used in the field of wage and salary administration are covered in Chapter 29.

27

Operating, Developing and Adjusting Reward Systems

John F Percival

In previous chapters various wage and salary systems have been described. In all cases, the objectives of these systems went beyond that of providing a mechanism for passing money or other reward from employer to employee. Other objectives were:

1. The relationship between the rewards for different jobs.
2. Determining and controlling the proportion of the remuneration which should be in the form of:
   (a) Cash—fixed and variable.
   (b) 'Fringe' cash benefits, eg sickness pay and pensions.
   (c) Other 'rewards', eg holidays, perquisites, etc.
3. Motivating the employee, in some cases, to maintain or improve the pay/work relationship and provide the means to monitor this. This is applicable not only in the traditional hourly-paid situation of payment by results, but also in the area of objectives/task setting in the management environment.
4. Ensuring that the method of reward is appropriate to the nature of the work done or tasks performed.

In many cases, there will have been more local objectives to be met also, concerned with the current trading position of the company, the local requirements of the unions, shift working, etc.

This chapter considers salary and wage systems in three senses. First, in the short term, ensuring that the system does operate to meet the above objectives; second, in the medium term, identifying whether the underlying circumstances, which determined the original system design, are still relevant; and third, in the light of the above, determining what action can and should be taken to improve the system by adjustment and by design change (hopefully evolutionary). In each case the original objectives and circumstances will be related to those current at the time under discussion.

Monitoring in the Short Term

Short term in this context is taken to mean a period after which minor routine changes in remuneration can be expected, or in which changes in operating performance of the individuals or groups concerned can be detected. With a payment by results scheme, for example, monitoring is likely to be required on a weekly or monthly basis, depending on the bonus period used. In the case of a management by objectives scheme, operational monitoring may be quarterly, but salary reviews may well be annual.

The close link between operational and remuneration monitoring must be recognized; they are interdependent and are usually based on the same factual data. Though this handbook is not concerned directly with operational matters, it is clear from the objectives set out on the previous page that many of them are closely related to the performance of designated tasks. Two examples show how wrong conclusions may be drawn by considering pay and salary details only. The control data needed in practice have been discussed in the chapters on individual systems. Here we are concerned with interpretation.

The first example concerns an assembly department which operates a payment by result scheme. Key figures over six periods were as shown in Figure 27.1. Looked at from the pay point of view alone unit cost per attendance hour has dropped and bonus has remained at an acceptable level, even if it has dropped somewhat. All in all, there is not a great deal for the management to comment upon. However, if one considers the pay and operational data together (Figure 27.2) a number of potentially serious questions must be raised:

1 Output targets are not being met (cf budgeted hours) and sales may be affected.
2 Absenteeism has risen sharply—in the absence of an obvious explanation such as a flu epidemic, this deserves further investigation. Is absenteeism affecting bonus percentage, or perhaps vice versa?
3 Overtime has reached a plateau despite pressure of output need; why? There is probably a reason which deserves recognition.
4 The current bonus at 25%—against the 30% in the system design—suggests it is not producing the motivation intended.

Superficially, all was well in this shop, but the full figures suggest a

Period	Actual hours	Total pay (£)	Cost per attendance hour (P)	Bonus (%)
1	952	1542	162	32
2	968	1560	161	29
3	1014	1623	160	29
4	1040	1640	158	27
5	1020	1584	155	24
6	1056	1616	153	25

Figure 27.1 Pay data from assembly department

Period	Budgeted hours	Actual clock hours	Absentee hours	Over-time hours	Total pay (£)	Cost per attendance hours (P)	Bonus (%)
1	960	952	68	60	1542	162	32
2	960	968	76	84	1560	161	29
3	1040	1014	100	84	1623	160	29
4	1120	1040	156	76	1640	158	27
5	1120	1020	140	80	1584	155	24
6	1120	1056	156	76	1616	153	25

Figure 27.2 Pay and operational data from assembly department

need for investigation and explanation; this is only apparent when one looks at the pay and operational factors together.

In the second example, a computer operations manager has the following item set out and agreed in his objectives:

'To implement computer operation of the proven stock control routines for two stores.
Target time—3 months.
Resources required—4 punch operators (to be engaged and trained)
　　　　　　　　—1 systems analyst (part-time).'

The results achieved at the next review were:

1　One store only applied despite excellent data being available and good cooperation of all stores staff.

2   6 punch operators engaged and trained, 2 have left and 4 are still working.
3   Staff costs exactly to budget (staff and manager's salaries contain no variable bonus element).
4   Failure to achieve objective was put down to the shortcomings of the punch operators.

From the remuneration point of view, there appear to be no questions to ask about the punch operators; their costs are to budget, their rates of pay are in accordance with the company scales. In practice, however, there are a number of questions about the pay and operational arrangements to be asked:

1   How do company pay scales relate to the local market for this type of staff?
2   Is the quality of training satisfactory? Of supervision?
3   Is a flat salary, plus other company pay conditions (sickness, holidays, etc) adequate motivation for this type of work. Would a variable element, dependent on output, produce better results? Would status promotion offer a more appropriate form of motivation, eg being taken on as trainee operators, appointed to grade I after training, to grade II after four weeks' satisfactory service and perhaps grade III after further training and after showing demonstrable skill, flexibility, enthusiasm and time-keeping?

It is insufficient to blame the failure on four substandard punch operators. The remuneration arrangements may play a key part in determining their apparent skill and their output. The control data should be re-examined as staff costs alone do not provide an adequate basis for judgement. What about the computer operations manager? He has failed to meet his objective. Is he to blame? Should it affect his salary at the next review?

These two examples illustrate the need to monitor remuneration arrangements and how difficult this is unless the criteria used concern both operational and remuneration matters. No hard and fast rules can be laid down for short-term monitoring but in general:

1   It should be done frequently enough to permit local short-term correctable faults to be acted upon.
2   Decisions on the necessary action usually need to be based on remuneration and operational data taken together.
3   If the objectives of the reward system are clearly set out the data required to judge their short-term effectiveness will not be hard to identify. If they are not so set out, too much or too little data are almost inevitable.

Adjustment and Development in the Medium Term

Reasons for development and adjustment

The examples given above required action of a local nature in order to correct a fault which was apparent within the period of review. In the short term, it would be impractical to attempt to modify the whole remuneration system of an organization due to discrepancies of a local nature. However, there are two other main types of reason why remuneration systems may require modification or development. First, any reward system is designed and introduced within the circumstances and constraints appertaining at that time. These will change. Second, the original design may be part of an evolving policy and at some point it will be appropriate to actuate the next stage.

If events take place for either reason and no action is taken to modify or redesign the system, it is highly probable that one or more of the objectives set out at the beginning of this chapter will cease to be met. This implies that the system will be ineffective to a degree; in the short term this may be unimportant but the inadequacies tend to accumulate to the point that positive 'decay' of the system becomes apparent.

The cause and degree of ineffectiveness must be determined if remedial action is to be taken. Some of the more common causes of change are examined in greater detail below.

Changing circumstances

In considering these, it should be noted how a simple change can have a wide effect, as when a stone is thrown into a pond the ripples spread to all parts. Secondly, some of the changes will produce dramatic and obvious effects in one part of an organization but in other parts only small ones which may be difficult to detect.

Technology Take for example the replacement of a traditional production machine by a numerically controlled one. The job content and probably remuneration can be expected to change and to affect at least the following people:

1. Machine operator: machine setting must, in future, be to a prescribed pattern and not reflect his own work patterns or skills. New operating role is more akin to machine minding, ie job is de-skilled. Ability to influence output by increased effort is at a minimum, hence individual bonus system will probably be inappropriate in the future. Additional skills associated with quality and reliability, may be added to the job.

2. Engineering planner: needs retraining to plan and program for numerically controlled operations. New and higher skills required.
3. Designer: requires retraining to design for this form of manufacture; additional skills required.
4. Maintenance electrician: requires training as an electronic technician if he is to be involved in the maintenance of the control mechanisms. Additional skills required therefore.
5. Foreman: requires training in the new technology if he is to appreciate the design, engineering and other changes involved. Change in man management requirements if the operator is to cease to be paid by payments by results.

No one of these changes in role may call for change in the reward system as a whole. If more such machines are installed, however, the whole job a man does may alter and new forms of remuneration may be needed.

Comparable ripple effects can be traced if, for example, the payroll is to be done on a computer rather than manually, if palletization is to be introduced into a bin store and in many other situations where a change of technology is involved.

Finally under this heading, reference must be made to 'method creep', ie small-scale changes in methods of working or allocation of tasks which gradually change the nature, skill or responsibility of a job. These occur not only on the shopfloor but in office situations, whether it be through form re-design, fresh appointments or modifications of procedure.

Trading policy The introduction or elimination of a service or product normally will affect personnel in the sales and other operating areas of an organization. Smaller variations in the mix of products or services also may lead to an imbalance of resources necessitating overtime or short-time working in selected areas with distorting effects on the wages. Permanent movements of this nature must be recognized and acted upon.

Trading conditions These also can greatly affect overtime working. However, more fundamental change may also be needed. For example, a wage agreement may be made in the expectation that increases in productivity will be absorbed by increased product demand on the company. If the expansion does not take place, then the basis of the agreement will be undermined.

Legislation The implementation of the Equal Pay Act is an obvious example in this area. Less satisfactory examples arise from the repeated attempts by government to control incomes; each such attempt has called for different action to remain within the law.

Mergers and acquisitions Either partner in these circumstances may find it necessary to alter the reward systems and so remove anomalies between them.

Personnel changes The arrival or departure of a single person of authority, be he employer or employee, who holds strong views on wage matters, can have a determining effect on the reward system. There are those who advocate payment by results, there are those who abhor it, for whatever reasons. Changes in people and roles can open and close opportunities and this must be recognized.

Summary

In many cases the changes described do not take place dramatically but quietly and gradually. A single change may be of little consequence; taken cumulatively over a period they can damage irreparably a well-designed system of reward.

The examples given under the short term were of a local character and needed local correction. However, in the medium term, the cumulative effect of such corrections and any new circumstances or objectives must be recognized and evaluated. More substantial revision of the systems may be indicated.

Evolving policy

The last section dealt with changes which 'happen' and cumulatively may have a significant effect on the payment system. However, further development of a remuneration system may be preplanned as part of a policy, even though the precise form this should take cannot be determined in advance. Examples from the wage and salary fields illustrate this.

A factory manufactures joinery products. A flat rate was paid to all workers, but wages were below those for the surrounding district. Following changes in the market and on the board of the company, it was decided to overhaul the production methods and factory layout over a period of two years. This called for considerable change by the workforce in terms of the jobs they did, their skills and the mix of labour required. Apart from these management-based changes, however, the rate of working of the labourforce could also be improved.

It was recognized that the rate of improvement in productivity would be heavily dependent on the attitude and cooperation of the employees. The immediate objectives in relation to the employees were that action must be taken such that:

1   The attitude of labour to physical changes in its many forms would be sympathetic.

2　Flexibility of labour would be enhanced, including re-deployment and retraining where required.
3　The engagement of fresh labour of the right quality would be possible to re-balance the skills and jobs in the new situation.

Ignoring here all but the pay aspects, it was decided, in consultation with the men, that the differential between the factory rates and those outside could be partially closed by a direct increase in wages. Secondly, a low geared productivity bonus would be introduced, calculated across the whole factory and based on changes in the added value of the products per employee hour.

These arrangements were designed specifically to meet the short-term objectives and it was recognized that they would not provide the necessary motivation to increase the personal rate of working. It was anticipated, therefore, that a further change in pay arrangements would be required to effect this but it would be pointless, and indeed damaging, to attempt to introduce this until stable working conditions had been created.

In the event, the rate of change in productivity was monitored and levelled off after some 18 months. As the departments completed their re-organization, proper work standards and records of the methods employed were created and more highly geared departmental productivity schemes were negotiated.

The important points from this example are that the objectives of the original scheme were clearly stated and the need for change, as a matter of evolving policy, had been foreseen. The nature of the final arrangements had not been laid down as they could have taken many forms, depending on the circumstances ruling at that time.

On the salary front, comparable situations can arise. For example, it was decided to offer special commission to a re-organized sales force for business secured from any new account during its first year. Such a drive for new account business in a stagnant situation can be very beneficial under the right circumstances but competition and the sheer availability of suitable accounts will diminish the opportunities in time. Though, therefore, such a scheme may be introduced as a deliberate act of policy, designed to widen the account base, clearly it must be replaced, also as an act of deliberate policy at the appropriate time.

A second example from the salary area concerns the temporary imbalances which can occur in a particular manpower market. For instance, in the mid-1960s, if one wanted to employ well-qualified and experienced systems analysts or computer programmers, one had to pay their price. In many companies, this introduced serious anomalies into the salary scales. However, technical and operating advances in the computer world and the increase in the number of people available in this market, brought the price back to a more normal level after a few years. A wise salary administrator will have monitored this situation as it unfolded and altered the arrangements accordingly. Such examples are repeating continuously as technology and practices advance and, from time-to-time, accountants, electronic technicians, practical OR men and behavioural scientists have all commanded disproportionate values in the writer's experience.

Summary of medium-term changes

From what has already been discussed in this chapter, it may appear that the wage or salary administrator must be extremely perspicacious, be admitted to a wide spectrum of company policy-making and probably have a first-rate crystal ball. He must constantly be recognizing short-term anomalies and the cumulative effect of changes in many areas inside and outside his organization. Above all, he must convince his management that his views are sound and often that action must be taken, despite the lure of *laissez-faire*.

All this is reduced to a more practical level if a systematic and quantitative review of the facts of the wage and salary situation is undertaken on a regular basis. Such a review will be referred to as an audit and it is strongly recommended it should be undertaken annually and formally reported upon to the chief executive of the organization.

Wage and Salary Audits*

The mechanism of a wage audit will be described in terms of hourly-paid employees in manufacturing industry and differences in detail, though not in approach when applying it to salary and other situations, will then be made.

A wage audit has two distinct elements. First, specific criteria are used as the basis of factual comment on the current situation (this may be compared in the financial audit with the balance sheet and profit and loss account). Second, informed comment is made to the board of a company based on an interpretation of the facts and the changes needed in the light of developing trends. The actual criteria used in an audit must be constructed to suit the particular needs and circumstances. The elements to which they are applied for hourly-paid staff will normally include:

---

* This section contains major extracts from the writer's original work on this subject, 'Towards a Wage Audit', published in *Enterprise* (the magazine of the P-E Consulting Group), Spring, 1970 and subsequently in Lupton, Tom (Ed.) *Payment Systems*, Penguin, Harmondsworth, 1972.

1. Unit cost of labour per hour.
2. Percentage overtime worked.
3. The average performance level achieved by operatives per month or similar period.
4. Percentage 'covered' time, ie that time not worked under a bonus arrangement where bonus is applicable.
5. Percentage shift premium in total pay.
6. Percentage bonus in total pay.
7. The spread of earnings between departments.
8. The spread of earnings within departments.
9. The principal items of unproductive time.
10. Average earnings as related to the salary scales of first line supervision.

Board report

Specific measurements of these elements, made usually in each department, are reinforced by and interpreted through selected interviews with key personnel. The resulting report to the board would typically incorporate:

1. An analysis of the specific figures in the light of the criteria agreed with the company as appropriate for its needs.
2. Comment on these figures with special reference to changes and trends observable.
3. Comparison of total earnings with:
   (a) Other rates in the district
   (b) The national growth in related earnings during the period.
4. The continued effectiveness of the job evaluated wage structure where applicable.
5. Comment on the prevailing industrial relations climate in the light of current wage policies.
6. Comment on the continuing relevance of the company's training programme for supervision and other personnel concerned.
7. Comment on other factors arising from the specific figures, as for example, the effect of production planning on waiting time, the validity of the figures, or the booking system employed.
8. Comment on the effects of plant investment programmes, other proposed technological changes or re-organization.

Typically an annual wage audit based on sound data in a company employing 1000 hourly-paid staff takes between four and five days. In the first instance, however, when the need is to establish in detail the quality and quantity of the information to be collected, more time will be necessary. The precise definition of information requirements provides a sound basis both for future audits and for improved day-today control by management.

Looked at superficially, the relevance of the above to clerical workers or, even more to salaried grades of employee, may be small. However, the words used to describe the likely report to the board are equally applicable with only the most minor changes, eg salary structure for wage structure in (4).

Three other concepts implicit in the hourly-paid situation are emphasized as having direct counterparts in the white-collar and salary fields. First, the concept of measurable output which is common in manufacturing organizations is analagous to the concept of measuring output, task or objective achievement, whether this is through clerical work evaluation, management by objectives or some other type of formal assessment.

Secondly, overtime is a concept normally related to hourly or weekly paid employees and their immediate supervisors. But, how many hours per week can an executive work under high pressure? 30, 50, 70? It is not relevant to attempt to answer this question here, but the relationship between contractual and actual hours worked is vital to an audit in either the wage or salary fields.

Finally, the question of shift working must also be faced in an increasing range of commercial and industrial sectors. Traditional multi-shift industries such as mining, steel and chemicals, have tackled the problems of proper management 'cover' other than on days. Many more industries are coming to recognize the need to man and use assets on a multi-shift basis, eg computers, expensive machine tools, etc. The adequacy of management cover may be considered during an audit, the pay or salary arrangements must be adequate if shift working of management personnel is to be effected.

Overtime and shiftworking

It is worth looking in more detail at typical situations in the two areas of overtime and shift working which are often brought to light when the wage audit procedure is applied.

On the question of overtime, a root cause of much industrial unrest is the presence of anomalies in the take-home pay packets of employees within departments, between departments, or between the company and its employing neighbours. Overtime, rarely spread evenly throughout an organization, has two main causes, both of which lead to its uneven application. It may, in the first place, be the outcome of a genuine need—temporary overload situation arising from an influx of orders, or perhaps a temporary imbalance in the capacities of the plant. In either case, it would be most unlikely for the extra work to be shared equally between different departments—production and service, for example. Second, and much more often, overtime is used deliberately in order to raise a low wage to a rate which is implicitly accepted to a greater or lesser extent by both management and work people. Rarely, if ever, is this official policy, but rather a *de facto* arrangement 'negotiated' at departmental level, which is not only bad in itself but also shows up management in an unfortunate light. From the work people's point of view, the arrangement will of course depend on their local bargaining strength with their own supervisors, and this, with corresponding levels of overtime, will vary from department to department. The wage audit procedure, by throwing the spotlight regularly on such situations, can contribute to getting both the uses and abuses of overtime into perspective.

The impact of shift arrangements on overtime illustrates another distortion which a wage audit can often isolate. For example, in many industries the premium for three-shift working is still barely 15% of the forty-hour pay of a day worker, who can easily exceed this additional inconvenience payment by working an extra few hours, say on a Saturday. In other words, the reward is not truly related to the degree of social disturbance in each case. Yet the rapid rise in the capital intensity of industry leads to the desirability of maximum plant utilization through multi-shift working; in some process industries seven days a week, twenty-four hours a day working is essential. If shift premiums are not large enough to compensate for social disturbance—much depends here on the history of a locality in regard to shift working—the result is often a serious inability to recruit enough shift labour. In such circumstances, overtime on a massive scale may be management's only recourse, though it may be a disastrously costly one and damaging to the whole structure. Here again a wage audit can help in pinpointing the situation at an early stage.

Taking Action

Clearly every wage and salary situation, irrespective of the commonality there may be in the design of the structures and systems employed, is unique and can only be dealt with on its own merits. Whether the need for action arises from adjustment, development or simply making the best of an unsatisfactory remuneration system, the wage audit will highlight the facts and hence the sort of action required. It is necessary to control the physical background since here lie frequent causes of failure. Key areas to check include:

1. Job descriptions in existence and up-to-date.
2. Method control in existence and up-to-date.
3. Flow of work; peaks, troughs, gaps.
4. Extraneous and unplanned work; fetching, waiting, additional operations.

5 Output and time booking systems not abused.
6 Supervision is adequate and respected as competent.

Having established the facts of the current situation, what sort of action, short of major redevelopment, can be contemplated?

Wage freezing

Whether applied nationally or locally, to earnings, overtime or bonus schemes, wage freezing achieves only one objective; it buys a little time. It makes no constructive contribution to the solution of the underlying problem and usually causes resentment and frustration which will lead to evasive action by employees if it is applied for more than a short time. It should be a last resort when more constructive action is impossible.

Consolidation of bonus earnings

When an individual or small group incentive scheme has been running for a year or two, it is often said to have 'run out of steam', ie the motivating effect has declined. It is important for the administrator to find out why this has happened, but one way of re-injecting some stimulus is to consolidate part or all of the variable element of pay into the base rate. Two preconditions are vital. First, the control and recording of job method must be good, ie the system must be under control. When consolidation takes place, many job standards may require revision, however, since method creep will almost certainly have taken place. Second, the quality of supervision must be adequate to maintain full control, particularly of quality and the flow of work to the employees.

Given these conditions, the workforce will frequently respond and regenerate the bonus element on top of the new base rate through a mixture of increased effort and cutting fresh corners, hence the accent on quality. This action is also useful if indirect remuneration and other elements dependent on base rate are falling behind.

Ratchet mechanisms

Ratchet mechanisms are usually associated with stepped measured daywork. Once employees have achieved a given level of activity, or reached a given step, they are guaranteed that level of earnings thereafter, even if their activity drops. The following conditions are essential:

1 Management must be in a position to control and provide adequate work opportunity.

2   Disciplinary procedures must be sound and used in practice.
3   The employees should prove their capability of maintaining the output over a reasonable period before the ratchet operates (eg 1–3 months).
4   Real mutual respect between employer and employee must exist since a high level of mutual trust is involved.

The procedure can be useful as a stepping stone on the path from incentives to, eventually, a high day rate or staff structure.

Change of bonus review period

If the period is increased, it smooths out variations in earnings, or conversely, if the period is shortened, it accentuates them. The effect, therefore, is to sharpen or blunt the motivating effect. It is dangerous to use it to hide bad management if that is the cause of variation but it can be useful, for example, to smooth the effects of product mix changes over the short term.

Summary

Many variations and combinations of possible actions could be listed but it is of little value having a set of solutions looking for a problem. In a handbook of this nature therefore, it is only possible to give general guidance which may help the practitioner to monitor and develop such systems.

Objectives

This chapter opened with a list of some of the more likely objectives and constraints under which a remuneration system will have been designed. If these have not been set down at the time the observer comes to look at a situation, it is worth trying to reconstruct them. This may sound pedantic but the crux of the matter is that the change of significant objectives, or a system ceasing to fulfil an objective, should be the only real determinant for a change in that system of remuneration.

Such phrases as 'the system has run out of steam' or the 'salary procedures are hard to explain' must be challenged and the logic of the arrangement made clear. This is not only theoretically possible, it is practical, illuminating and essential if the extent and nature of any necessary change is to be determined.

Facts: the wage and salary audit

Qualitative arguments concerning a remuneration system are valuable.

They must be supported by facts; not just any facts but the facts which will throw light on the original and present objectives. As has been inferred, the facts in the appropriate form may not always be readily available in an organization. If they are not, then it suggests that the designer of the controls was not clear on the objectives of the arrangements in the first place. Not all objectives are fully quantifiable but it is rare that factual data cannot be found which throw light on objectives even if they do not measure their achievement precisely.

When the objectives and facts are set down as outlined in this chapter, it is rare that the need for and the main options for change which are open will not become apparent. This is not to suggest that the administration and development of wage and salary systems can be reduced to a mathematical analysis. One is dealing with human beings who have feelings, attitudes, prejudices and rights, real or imaginary. One may disagree with the views expressed by employees but there is no point in ignoring them; they will neither go away nor change unless there is a positive agent of change. That agent should be management, if the latter is to fulfil the role implied in the word 'manage'. This point leads to the third principle.

Tactics of development and adjustment

The tactics adopted by management in this context must be heavily dependent on its own personal style, on the relationships which may exist between employer, employee and their representatives and on external factors such as legislation. No attempt to categorize or define the nature or importance of these factors would be useful since they will be unique in themselves and in combination in any given situation. In determining tactics to be adopted however, there are two further underlying facts which the practitioner will ignore at his peril.

On one level, pay and conditions of service are the basis of the contract of employment. At a different level, that of the individual, they are the things which determine the material side of his life. They are immensely important to him. Treat them as such. Understand the individual's objectives, his attitudes, however much effort this may cost. The development or adjustment of a wage or salary system must clearly be compatible with the facts of the situation as determined by an audit and with management's objectives. However, if the changes are not also compatible with the objectives and attitudes of the employees concerned, then the change will fail.

Secondly and finally, if matters of wages and salaries are important and the employee does hold definite views, which he will, there is nobody better placed to express those views than the employee. It is too late if these views are expressed explicitly or implied around the negotiating table. They must be sought out by a continuing consultative process so that they can be taken into account at the time when change is contemplated and designed.

Clearly the administration, development or adjustment of salary and wage systems has one foot in the systems themselves, the other is firmly in the field of industrial relations and account must be taken of both.

References and Further Reading

Armstrong, M. and Murlis, H., *Salary Administration: A Practical Guide for Small and Medium Sized Organisations*, British Institute of Management Foundation, London, 1977. (Management Survey Report no. 36).

Bowey, A.M. and Lupton, T., *Productivity Drift and the Structure of the Pay Packet*, Manchester Business School, 1971.

Lupton, Tom (Ed.), *Payment Systems*, Penguin, Harmondsworth, 1972.

McBeath, G. and Rands, N., *Salary Administration*, Business Books, 3rd Edition, London, 1976.

Robinson, D., (Ed.), *Local Labour Markets and Wage Structures*, Gower, Epping, 1970.

Schofield, A. and Husband, T., *The Wage and Salary Audit*, Gower, London, 1977.

28

Budgetary Control of Salaries and Wages

Anthony G Hopwood

Budgeting now occupies a central position in the design of most systems for influencing managerial and employee behaviours. Almost regardless of the type of enterprise, the nature of its problems and the other means for influencing behaviour, the preparation of a quantitative statement of expectations regarding the allocation of the enterprise's resources tends to be seen as an essential, indeed indispensable, feature of the battery of administrative controls. However simple the procedures of budgeting may be in conception and design, and very often their practical complexity reflects the intricacies of organizational structure and technology rather than of budgeting itself, they are now recognized as providing a vital basis for planning and control.

One reason for the practical significance of budgeting is that it is capable of serving a wide variety of important organizational functions. By trying to encourage an active concern with the future, budgets help to structure some elements of the wider decision-making process. Some of the estimates which they provide are used directly in costing, pricing and scheduling, but, by providing a framework within which subsequent delegation of authority takes place, the budgetary system also plays a part in the process by which influence is distributed within the enterprise. Budgets thereby serve as communication devices by which it is possible to relay top management style and authority, and to establish a particular organizational ethos. And at the same time, the process by which they are established often provides a means for attempting to reconcile some of the conflicts between diverse components of the enterprise so that they move in a more coordinated manner towards management's conceptions of the wider organizational purposes.

Once formulated, budgets also can help managers and employees to be more effective in their own jobs. They can clarify direction and purpose, so enabling the members of the enterprise to better comprehend where they are going and whether they are getting there. Budgets are also used to motivate superior performance by serving as targets and mechanisms for gaining commitment and involvement. To this end, a budget provides a means for measuring accomplishments against objectives and the budget reports are used in measuring the performance of not only the components of the enterprise, as economic entities, but also of the managers responsible for their administration. Accordingly they can form an important part of the logic of both superior evaluation and self review and control. With a successful budgetary system, the communication of knowledge of results can reinforce or discourage previous behaviour, stimulating a learning and adaptive organizational atmosphere.

However, if budgets are seen as ends in themselves rather than as mere means to a wider end, they can easily result in a concern for the immediate present to the detriment of their avowed future, stimulating rather than reconciling conflicts and stifling rather than encouraging initiative and creative action. The prevention of these undesirable outcomes depends upon budgeting being seen quite explicitly as a management rather than a financial activity. Not only must it be recognized as an integral part of the management process rather than a once-and-for-all exercise in extrapolative and financial skills, but all managers must have an appreciation of the procedures so that they can participate fully in their construction and subsequent use. This is no less true for the personnel manager as it is for his or her production, marketing and financial colleagues.

The Technical Framework of Budgeting

All forms of management control need to be based upon an understanding of the factors which influence and constrain the behaviour of the phenomena to be controlled. For budgeting, this means that budgets must be constructed upon the basis of a detailed appreciation of the environmental and organizational factors which influence how all forms of revenues and costs are incurred.

When an accountant speaks of patterns of cost behaviour, he is usually concerned with the way in which costs systematically vary in response to two factors: changes in the level of the enterprise's activity and the passage of time. Three categories of cost with respect to the level of activity are usually distinguished:

1. Variable costs vary directly and proportionately with volume. Direct material is obviously an example of a variable cost. Direct

labour is frequently cited as another example and often treated as such in designing budgeting systems, but in many enterprises this is increasingly becoming a questionable assumption over quite significant ranges of output.
2 Semi-variable costs vary with volume, but neither directly nor proportionately. They may, for instance, increase in a step-like manner. It is often thought that semi-variable costs increase less than proportionately than the corresponding volume increase, but it is not difficult to envisage situations where they increase more rapidly than the increase in volume. This is particularly true for wages when the enterprise is already operating at a level close to its practical capacity.
3 Fixed costs do not vary in response to volume in the time period under consideration.

Patterns of cost behaviour should not, however, be regarded as being determined by an accountant's declaration. On the contrary, although an accountant always has a responsibility to suggest and influence, his or her primary responsibility is to reflect as accurately as he or she can the underlying environmental, technological and managerial factors which influence how costs are incurred. Some of these factors must obviously be accepted as constraints, but to some extent managers have the discretion to decide whether particular costs are fixed or variable because they have been observed to behave in that way in the past or because management decides that is the way they are to behave. From the point of view of an observer, the question may be tautological, but the issue is real enough in practice because many important elements of cost are neither fixed nor variable (nor even semi-variable) in the sense described above.

Advertising, research and development, and possibly repairs and maintenance costs come to mind. Whilst these types of cost need not vary in relation to output, there are obvious dangers in regarding them as truly fixed. Yet for the purposes of many cost analyses, this is frequently done. Such costs are, however, certainly subject to management influence and control on a continuous basis, but the influence must be explicit and planned. For this reason, such items of cost are frequently termed policy, programmed or managed costs. Surprisingly, at least for many non-accountants, the design of accounting and budgetary systems for the control of these important elements of costs is still in a rather primitive state, although some progress is beginning to be made (Dewhurst, 1972; Phyrr, 1973).

Many salary and wage costs are increasingly of a programmed nature. Due to governmental, union and managerial decisions, they quite frequently depart from the strict definition of variable costs, at least for quite significant ranges of output. Even where there is an element of variability, some part of it is often influenced by the choice of wage and salary systems which are themselves subject to management influence. Yet salary and wage costs can and do change, and control certainly needs to be exercised. The control must, however, be anticipatory in nature, being viewed in relation to the wider organizational objectives which the expenditures are designed to serve. It needs in other words, to be exercised within the context of a budgetary framework where costs can be weighed against benefits, even though the latter need not necessarily be considered in financial or even readily quantifiable terms.

Budgets are designed to assist in arriving at such cost-benefit assessments, and thereafter, to provide a basis for monitoring and review. For these purposes, budgetary control procedures need to be oriented towards the decision needs of managers and designed to respond in a flexible manner to changing and often unanticipated circumstances. Increasing use is therefore being made of flexible rather than static budgets.

Static budgets are framed exclusively around one single forecast of output and compare subsequent achievements with this budget regardless of the actual level of activity. But the idea of comparing performance at one level of activity with a budget that was developed at some other level is nonsense from the point of view of judging how efficiently any given output has been produced. The comparison is meaningless since if there is any variable element of cost, we would expect actual expenditures to differ from the budget as output varies. Flexible budgeting, on the other hand, provides a means for constructing budgets which are tailored to any level of activity. During the course of the year, as activity levels deviate from those originally anticipated, so do the budgets used for comparison purposes. In this way, by using a budget formula rather than a static amount, flexible budgeting makes it easier for managers to judge the efficiency of their expenditures at the actual level of operations.

The flexible budgeting approach emphasizes the importance of making an accurate breakdown of costs into their fixed and variable components. If the underlying assumptions about cost behaviour are incorrect, the subsequent comparisons and control can be misdirected. Yet, in many cases, there is a tendency to underestimate fixed costs when budgeting. Labour costs, for instance, are often treated as variable even when for union, management or other reasons they are effectively fixed from month-to-month. If this mistake is made, however, even though total costs may be correctly budgeted at a forecast level of activity, performance measures can be seriously biased if this level is either not attained or surpassed. As can be seen in Figure 28.1, an underestimation of fixed costs can result in an efficient operation failing to meet its budget if it produces less than was anticipated or performing better than the budget if it produces more than was anticipated.

Such problems are not uncommon even with the most sophisticated budgetary control systems. For although the conceptual framework of budgeting may be fairly simple, severe practical difficulties place limits on its implementation. It is easy enough to talk of the various cost categories, for instance, but even without considering the increasing uncertainty inherent in today's business and economic environments, they can be difficult, if not impossible, to precisely measure in complex enterprises. In practice therefore, if the technical limitations are not to interfere with the purposes of any budgetary control system, the problem becomes one of gaining the most effective managerial utilization of imperfect but nevertheless valuable procedures.

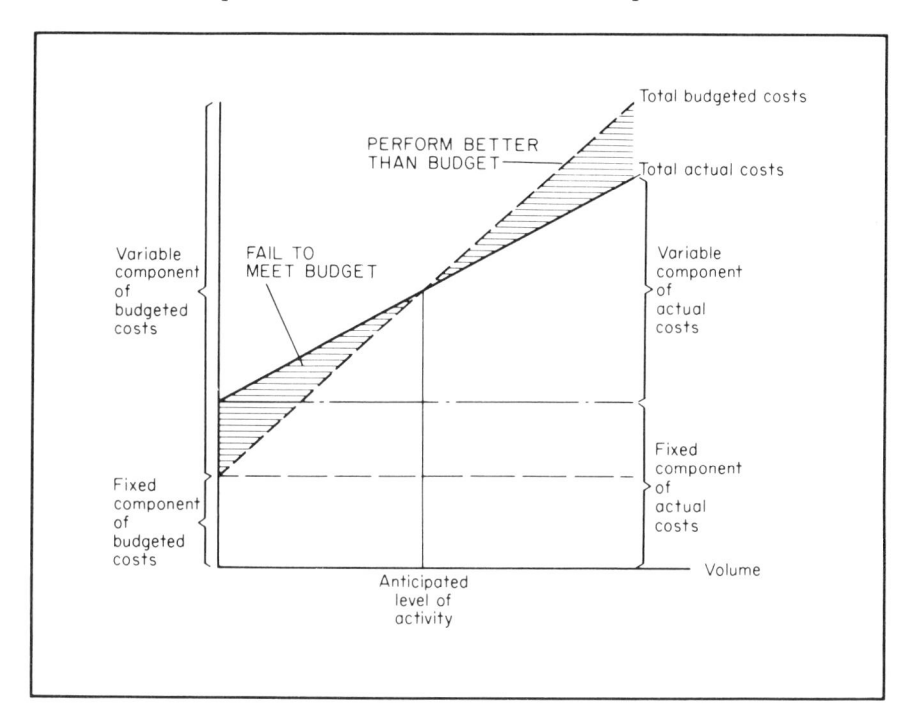

Figure 28.1   How the under-estimation of fixed costs results in budget bias

Using Budgets as Targets

One of the most controversial uses of budgets is as targets for encouraging superior performance. Although there is considerable evidence that budgets can indeed serve this purpose, some people still argue for and against it. And those that are in favour of placing at least some emphasis on this function are often unsure as to the type of budget which should be used.

In general, the relationship between the level of budget difficulty and subsequent performance follows the bell-shaped curve shown in Figure 28.2. Whilst there is always some motivation to meet the budget, the motivation is strongest for the budget which is seen as being of intermediate difficulty. If a manager were presented with either a more difficult or an easier budget, the strength of overall motivation to meet it, and hence the final level of performance, would be less.

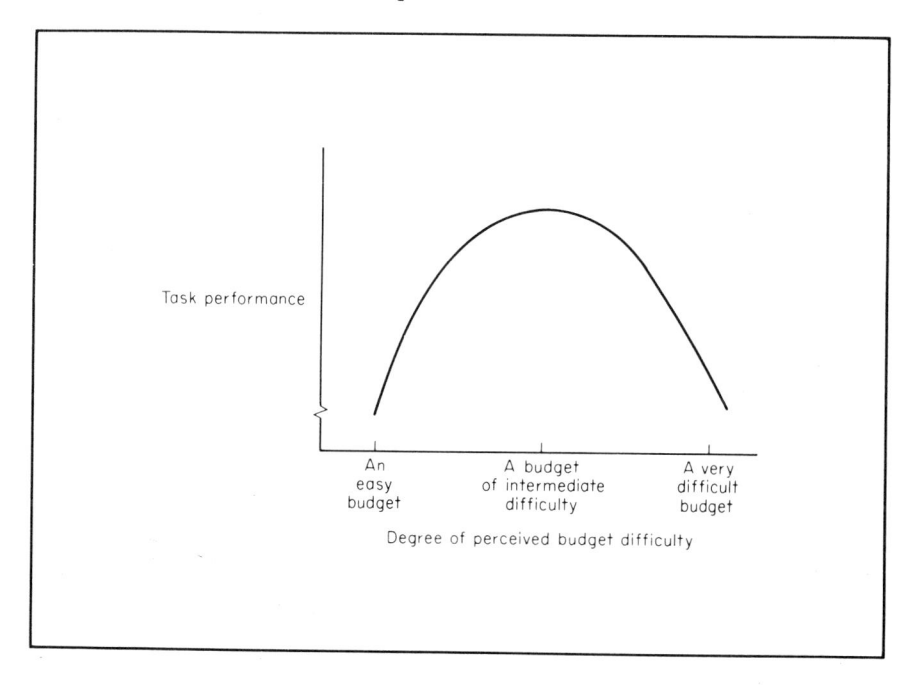

Figure 28.2 Relationship between degree of budget difficulty and task performance

However, caution is required before too readily proceeding with setting motivational budgets. For one thing, the relationship between budget difficulty and performance is stated in terms of perceived difficulty. Hence there is a strong suggestion that such budgets need to be attuned to individual managers as much as they do to the situation. But in addition, the budget resulting in the best performance is one that is unlikely to be achieved. It is, in other words, a pulling budget stated at a level higher than expected performance.

In practice, this problem presents a serious dilemma to management. While budgets which are best for motivational purposes may need to be stated in terms of aspirations rather than expectations, the budgets which are so necessary for planning and decision purposes need to be stated in terms of the best available estimate of expected actual performance. So even though budgets are used for both purposes in many organizations, the types of budget which are necessary to achieve the separate ends are in conflict. Ideally there is a need for separate budgets for the different purposes. Of course, there are difficulties in implementing such an idea since it would require an enormous educational effort and a lot more careful attention would have to be given to budgeting itself. But there are benefits as well as costs, and where the underlying problem is sufficiently important, the overall benefits which may be derived may justify the costs involved. Certainly a number of British companies are now making practical experiments in the area. If managers are unwilling to move in this direction, however, it should be realized that whilst budgets are only one of the many ways of motivating performance, as a future-oriented decision tool, their role is unique. Should this unique role be endangered because of an emphasis on their motivational potential?

One final difficulty needs to be mentioned. The bell-shaped relationship between budget difficulty and performance presumes a positive and intelligent use of the budget reports, but we all know that budgets can be used in a more negative and punitive sense. A small cost overrun can be immediately questioned by some managers, almost regardless of reason, while a large cost saving may receive an eventual comment, if that is, it is not used as evidence for cutting next year's budget. But what happens to the motivational role of budgets when senior managers use the reports in this way? Since it implies an unbalanced reward structure, a punitive use of budgets can result in an inversion of the relationship between budget difficulty and performance such as is shown in Figure 28.3. Given the strong need for managers to avoid failing to meet their budgets, the motivation to perform is strongest for very low levels of perceived difficulty and weakest for budgets of intermediate difficulty. Yet, in practice, those intermediate budgets may well be the ones which are associated with the overly negative use of budgets as pressure devices!

Budgets can be used as targets, but the numerous practical problems serve to emphasize that this is far from being a simple mechanical activity for which commonsense is a sufficient guide. Careful consideration needs to be given not only to the nature of the task but also to the personalities and needs of the individual managers, the way in which budgets are used and the social climate which they create, and the other purposes served by the budgetary controls. Such requirements make budgeting a much more demanding endeavour, but without due care, purposes can conflict and budgets which are intended to stimulate active performance can have the opposite effect. For a more detailed discussion of the use of budgets as targets see Hopwood (1974; 1980) and Hofstede (1967).

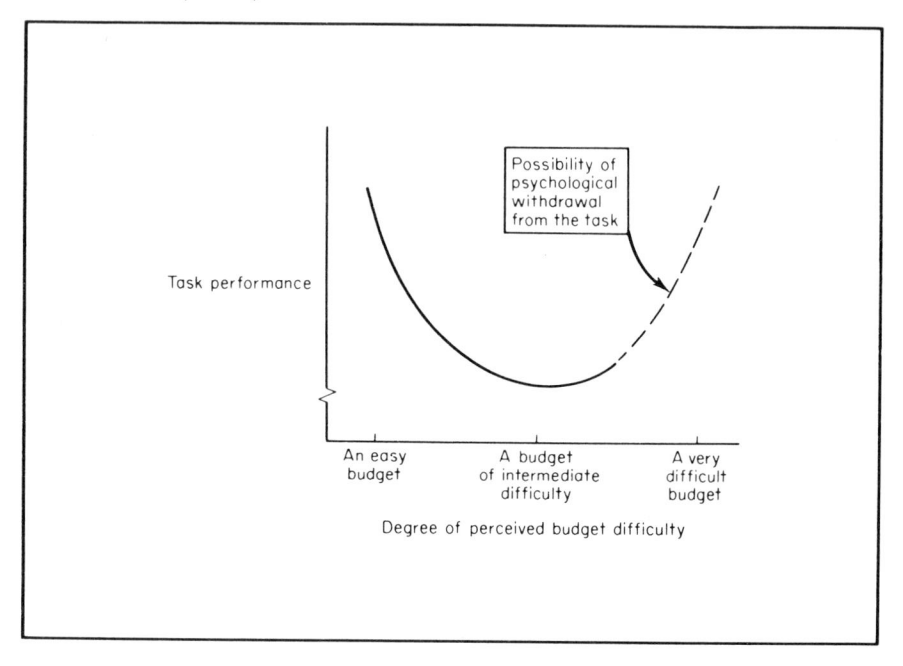

Figure 28.3   Relationship between degree of budget difficulty and task performance when the budget is used in a punitive manner

Managerial Uses of Budget Reports

Despite the many admirable reasons which are used to justify the implementation of any budgetary control system, it is known that some managers react to budgets by deliberately manipulating the reported information and by taking short-term decisions almost regardless of their longer-term consequences. The budgets themselves can also be biased, and on occasions, the pressures which they induce can result in interdepartmental conflict and rivalry as managers seek to protect their own departmental reports.

Such undesirable reactions can be as important as the anticipated outcomes of the control procedures. Invariably, however, they reflect the way in which budgets are used rather than their technical design. Since few, if any, budgetary control systems ever achieve a perfect representation of the underlying structure of economic and financial events, a careful and considerate use of the information is always essential to compensate for its many unavoidable inadequacies. If managers use the information in an inappropriate manner, attributing too much, or even too little, validity to it or being unaware of its intended purposes, the value of the systems may be questionable.

However, while a great deal of attention has been devoted to different ways of designing budgetary control procedures, comparatively little consideration has been given to the different ways of using them. Any appreciation of the different managerial uses of information must, however, be based upon an understanding of the human context in which the use occurs. The interpretation and use of information is the outcome of a personal and social process which is sustained by the meanings, beliefs, pressures and purposes that are brought to bear by managers. In of necessity providing it with a personal significance and placing it in their own wider context, managers are able to use information, perhaps without reflection, in a variety of ways—appropriate and inappropriate.

The importance of considering the different ways in which budget reports are actually used is illustrated by research on the use of budgetary information in managerial performance evaluation (Hopwood, 1973). Three distinct ways of using the information were distinguished:

1 *Budget-constrained style*
   Despite the many problems with using budgetary information as a comprehensive measure of managerial performance, the manager's performance is primarily evaluated upon the basis of his or her ability to continually meet the budget on a short-term basis. This criterion of performance is stressed at the expense of other valued and important criteria, and the manager will receive unfavourable feedback from his or her superior if, for instance, his or her actual costs exceed the budgeted costs, regardless of other considerations.
2 *Profit-conscious style*
   The manager's performance is evaluated on the basis of his or her ability to increase the general effectiveness of the unit's operations in relation to the long-term purposes of the enterprise. For instance, at the cost centre level, one important aspect of this ability concerns the attention which he or she devotes to reducing long-run costs. For this purpose, however, the budgetary information has to be used with great care in a rather flexible manner.
3 *Nonaccounting style*
   The budgetary information plays a relatively unimportant part in the superior's evaluation of the manager's performance.

Unlike a budget-constrained evaluation, a profit-conscious evaluation is therefore concerned with the wider information content, or lack of it, of the budget reports, and not with just a rigid analysis of the direction and magnitude of the reported budget variances. The budget is, in other words, seen as a means to an end rather than an end in itself.

Empirical evidence indicated that both the budget-constrained and profit-conscious styles resulted in a higher degree of involvement with costs than the nonaccounting style. Only the profit-conscious style, however, succeeded in attaining this involvement without incurring either emotional costs for the managers in charge of departments or defensive behaviours which were undesirable from the company's point of view. The budget-constrained style resulted in a belief that the evaluation was unjust and widespread tension and worry on the job. It was hardly surprising that such a single-minded concern with the budget was met with manipulation of the accounting reports and even decisions which increased the total processing costs for the company as a whole. The managers' relationships with the budget-constrained supervisors were also allowed to deteriorate, and with the rigid emphasis on the short-term budget results serving to highlight the interdependent nature of their tasks, the immediate instrumental concerns easily permeated the patterns of social relationships amongst colleagues. When the managers were continually asked about budget variances over which they often had little or no control they each went out to improve their own reports regardless of the detrimental effects for the organization as a whole. Yet the ensuing rivalry often impeded the cooperation which was so essential for controlling their interdependent activities.

In contrast, the profit-conscious style resulted in similar levels of tension, supervisor satisfaction and cooperation amongst colleagues as prevailed under a nonaccounting style. And there was little or no fiddling of the reports. But while the style was accepted, even respected, it was certainly seen as very demanding.

A manager is not therefore faced with a simple choice of using or not using budgetary information in evaluation and feedback. Instead he can reap many of the benefits of a budgetary control system by stressing factors which it attempts to measure without this resulting in defensive behaviour. To do so, however, consideration needs to be given to the precise manner in which the information is used. But to what are the various styles of using the information related? Certainly it is not sufficient to merely acknowledge their presence. It is also necessary to consider the factors determining the styles because a systematic understanding of their nature is an essential prerequisite for the intelligent management of change and improvement.

No doubt due to the arithmetical nature of budget reports, the budget-constrained style, unlike either of the other two styles of using budgetary information, was difficult to resist passing down once it had been established at one level in the organizational hierarchy. More importantly, however, the ways in which the budget reports were used were very clearly associated with much more widespread differences in management style. Using the well-accepted dimensions of managerial style developed at Ohio State University, ie initiation of structure and consideration, it was found that both the budget-constrained and profit-conscious supervisors, unlike those using a nonaccounting style, were seen as trying to create a structured job environment. The profit-conscious supervisors, however, were also seen as maintaining a warm and friendly atmosphere which was supportive and conducive for mutual trust and respect. In this regard they were similar to the non-accounting supervisors but very different from the budget-constrained ones. Without the moderating effect of the considerate attitudes towards the subordinate managers, the concern for the budget reports was seen as threatening and stressful, and served as a trigger for defensive and often undesirable behaviour.

The budget reports were one vehicle through which the managers were able to express their more general approaches to the job. The way in which they were used was, in fact, a good enough indicator of the managerial ethos which pervaded any section of the company. The profit-conscious style, for instance, appeared to be only one aspect of a problem-solving approach to management, as distinct from an approach which attempted to impose a false measure of simplicity onto a complex and highly interdependent series of activities. The evaluation of performance was itself of primary importance with the budget-constrained style, influencing all aspects of the managers' behaviours. Evaluation was not viewed as an ongoing part of the managerial process, interrelated with other important aspects of the job. Rather it was seen as a distinct and dominant activity, and the primary source of influence and control, overshadowing other vital elements of the process. The budget became not an aid to management but a constraint upon it.

These findings emphasize the vital importance of considering the precise manner in which budgets are used by managers. It is never a simple matter of merely getting them to use the information in any way. Budgets, like salary and wage systems themselves, are quite capable of helping to gain involvement and concern. But they also share with other management procedures the problems of being partial and imprecise. The real challenge comes in trying to achieve an effective utilization of imperfect but nevertheless valuable procedures. Such a challenge is only just being acknowledged in many enterprises.

The Way Ahead

The problems described in this chapter point to the necessity for all managers to move beyond questions of the design of budgetary control procedures to gain a systematic understanding of the wider human and organizational factors which influence their effective use in large enterprises. While the technical procedures are undoubtedly important, they are designed to serve organizational purposes and they are embedded in rich and varied organizational settings. Yet all too little consideration is given to how they are actually used and function within real enterprises.

Personnel managers have a particular responsibility in this respect. For one thing, they can help the accountant with the enormous educational effort which is required in most enterprises. With the increasing complexity of budgetary procedures, it is unrealistic to expect managers at any level in an enterprise to use the information in an appropriate manner without adequate preparation and training. However, managers need to be informed not only of the objectives and advantages of budgeting, real though they may be, but also of the inadequacies of the information and the consequences of attaching too much importance to the short-term reports. They need, in other words, an appreciation of how to confidently integrate the financial aspects of their jobs with their own managerial understandings.

But even the most carefully designed educational programme is neither an easy nor the only solution to the problem because the way in which budgets are used is not simply based on ignorance. The real need is for a view of budgeting which sees it as a part of a much more complex process for influencing behaviour. Not only does budgeting represent only one means of control but also its final effectiveness is dependent upon how it interacts with the other approaches to the control problem. The behaviours so inadequately reflected within the dimensions of managerial style are, for instance, also trying to influence behaviour. And the effects of just these two approaches, let alone salary and wage systems, certainly do not occur in isolation.

It is all too easy to concentrate on separate mechanisms for influencing behaviour, perhaps even achieving some satisfaction in the individual situations, but by not taking an integrated view of them as a whole, still fail to achieve their full potential. As the emerging specialists in management and organizational development, personnel managers may be in a unique position to provide some of the overview which is so necessary. Such a task would certainly be a difficult one, but there is no doubt that the problem is sufficiently important to warrant serious consideration.

References and Further Reading

Arnold, J., 'Budgets for Decisions', in J. Arnold, B. Carsberg and R. Scapens, (Ed.), *Topics in Management Accounting*, Philip Allen, 1980.

Beyer, R., and Trawicki, D., *Profitability Accounting for Planning and Control*, 2nd Edition, Ronald Press, 1972.
Caplan, E.H., *Management Accounting and Behavioural Science*, Addison-Wesley, Reading, Massachusetts, 1979.
Dermer, J., *Management Planning and Control Systems: Advanced Concepts and Cases*, Irwin, 1976.
Dewhurst, R.F.J., *Business Cost-Benefit Analysis*, McGraw-Hill, New York, 1972.
Flamholtz, E., *Human Resource Accounting*, Dickenson Publishing Company, Encino, California, 1974.
Garbutt, D., *Training Costs*, Gee and Co., London, 1969.
Hofstede, G.H., *The Game of Budget Control*, Van Gorcum, Assen, The Netherlands, 1967.
Hopwood, A.G., *An Accounting System and Managerial Behaviour*, Gower, 1973.
Hopwood, A.G., *Accounting and Human Behaviour*, Haymarket Publishing Company, London, 1974.
Hopwood, A.G., 'Organizational and Behavioural Aspects of Budgeting and Control', in J. Arnold, B. Carsberg and R. Scapens, (Ed.), *Topics in Management Accounting*, Philip Allen, 1980.
Phyrr, P.A., *Zero-Based Budgeting: A Practical Tool for Evaluating Expenses*, Wiley, 1973.
Sizer, J., *An Insight Into Management Accounting*, Penguin, Harmondsworth, 1979.
Tricker, R.I., *The Accountant in Management*, Batsford, London, 1967.
Welsch, G., *Budgeting: Profit Planning and Control*, 4th Edition, Prentice-Hall, 1976.

29

Survey of Sources of Information

Anthony Barry

Information on wages, salaries and other terms of employment may be needed for varying purposes: eg establishing new rates as part of a whole new pay structure; or wage or salary bargaining for particular groups; or to check that comparable amounts are being paid for employees in particular jobs. Thus different sources of information are useful at different times. The main sources of all types of information on pay are discussed below and their use for particular purposes and overall value are considered.

Official Statistics

There is a whole range of official data on pay, most of which is collated by the Department of Employment (DE). The main data are:

Department of Employment indices

The monthly *DE Gazette* publishes indices on basic weekly and hourly rates of wages for manual workers, on average salaries and average earnings. The wage rate and earnings indices are also broken down by industries, but they are only of practical use in showing general trends in pay and are of little help in setting actual rates. The wage indices are of limited value in that they are not based on actual rates of pay, but only represent 'minimum entitlements' which in practice mean a mixture of basic wage rates, minimum earnings levels, etc. While in some cases they correspond with actual pay, in the majority of cases they do not. Moreover, movements in the wage rate index have to be looked at in relation to recent settlements: major ones such as the national engineering agreement are obviously going to have a big impact on the index. Back-dating of major settlements can also have an unexpected retrospective effect on the indices.

DE average weekly and hourly earnings statistics

These are actual figures of average earnings broken down by industries (under the standard industrial classification) and are published monthly in the *DE Gazette*. Since they show the general trends in earnings for an industry or occupation they may be used in wage bargaining—particularly when taken with the DE's monthly figures on hours of work. These figures and NES statistics (discussed below) are often used to draw up 'league tables' of the group of employees' earnings and these feature in a number of pay negotiations at national level. But these statistics have two grave limitations. First, they are only average statistics and cannot be used for realistically comparing pay of workers in different industries as they do not relate to comparable jobs or take account of wide variations in proportions of skilled workers between different industries, or of varying opportunities for overtime or extra pay from payment-by-results systems. The Department itself recognizes the statistics' limitations in stating that: 'the difference in average earnings should not be taken as evidence of, or as a measure of, disparities in the ordinary rates of pay prevailing in different industries for comparable classes of workpeople employed under similar conditions'.

Second, these average figures do not give any information on the make-up of the pay packets of workers: this is an important factor in real pay comparisons, as Bowey and Lupton (1973) have shown in advocating the need for comparisons based on weighted or 'compounded' earnings tables.

New earnings and manual workers' earnings surveys

These surveys published annually by the Department of Employment provide data on the previous year's levels and distribution of earnings. The first results of the April NES survey begin to appear in *DE Gazettes* from October or November of the same year. The main data are of weekly and hourly earnings broken down by industries (standard industrial classification), occupations, negotiating groups, regions and ages. Total gross earnings are also subdivided to show overtime earnings, payments-by-results and premia for shift- and night-work.

Because of the detail available, these statistics provide extremely useful information for making regional comparisons of earnings, for examining the make-up of pay in a particular industry or occupation. But their usefulness is limited when it comes to setting actual rates of pay for jobs, because the job descriptions are usually too general; eg 'office supervisor', 'clerk—routine or junior level'. It would thus be impossible to know that jobs were truly comparable. The timing of settlements can also have a distorting effect as increases agreed before April which do not come into effect until later will not show in the figures.

The NES also suffers from the same basic defect as the manual workers' earnings survey—known as the October survey—in that they both contain data about only one pay week of the year. The October survey of earnings and hours of work of manual workers in manufacturing and some other industries are published in the *DE Gazette* of the following February. The data is very much less detailed than in the NES and it only gives total gross average earnings. An additional weakness is that through being carried out in October, the survey runs into the problem of coming at a time when the pay round is in full swing and it may therefore not give an accurate reflection of pay settlements.

Other DE earnings surveys which are produced regularly cover specific groups of employees. These include the June survey of manual workers' earnings and hours of work in the engineering, shipbuilding and chemical industries, published in the November *DE Gazette*; the April DE survey of manual workers' in aerospace equipment manufacturing and repairing (which usually includes other industries such as biscuit manufacturing and pharmaceuticals), published in the August *Gazette*; and the October survey of non-manual workers' earnings, published in the April *Gazette*, which is limited to gross weekly earnings by broad industry groups.

Time rates of wages and hours of work

This annual DE publication contains data on minimum or standard rates of wages fixed by national agreements or wages councils, and also lists the normal weekly hours (exclusive of mealtimes) for which these rates are paid. Additional information includes some basic piece rates and premia for shift- and nightwork. The data are for April of each year, though it is updated in a monthly supplement giving changes in rates and hours of work.

Useful as this information can be, since a large number of firms pay more than the minimum rates for their industries, it cannot serve as a guide for setting rates of pay for particular jobs.

Other official data

Details of the pay of particular groups—*Doctors' and dentists' remuneration*, *Armed forces pay* and *Top salaries* (eg the chairmen of nationalized industries)—are given in the reports of three official review bodies. First set up by the government in 1971, they recommend new pay scales for these groups, partly based on comparisons with other specified groups, but the reports only give statistics on the current pay and recommended scales of the groups reviewed. Discussion of the comparisons made may, however, be of some interest.

Pay Agreements

Details of both national and company level pay agreements are obtainable from *Incomes Data Report*. This gives full details of currently negotiated basic rates of pay and also of the other terms and conditions of employment contained in collective agreements. *Incomes Data Studies* gives a much broader picture of the pay and conditions of certain industries and groups of workers, eg clerical workers, manual workers in heavy chemicals, drivers, etc, and other studies have examined particular areas such as incentive payments, shiftwork, sick pay and holiday entitlements. The studies usually contain a selection of pay agreements.

These publications are invaluable sources of information on rates of pay and they are often used by both sides for making comparisons in pay negotiations. This is a considerable advance on relying purely on official statistics, and their prime value is to show not only actual levels but also the movements in pay which are of prime importance in bargaining. But they have two main limitations. First, although some details of job grades and job descriptions are often given, they are inadequate for making effective comparisons: certainly no comparisons based on 'benchmark' jobs are possible in the way discussed in Chapter 8. Secondly, no information on actual earnings is given. This means that true comparisons of pay cannot be made, as the actual make-up of the pay packet is unknown.

Surveys

Wage and salary surveys are one of the most useful and most popular methods of obtaining detailed information on current rates of pay. There are three main types of survey—informal, external and commissioned.

Informal surveys are conducted in an informal way and can vary from personal contacts to specific arrangements for exchanging information with a number of local companies, or with companies in a particular industry, or even with a wide cross-section of firms. This method has won wide favour in industry and commerce and a BIM survey (Cothliff, 1973) discovered that 83% of 216 participating companies found it the most valuable method of obtaining the information on salaries which they require.

The exchange method of obtaining data clearly has major advantages. It can provide exactly the type of information on existing rates of pay which firms seek, as well as giving them an indication of the likely trends in increases of pay during the year. But the reliability and real usefulness of the information depends in the first instance upon the type of arrangements for exchange and secondly on the information obtained.

Reliance upon an old boy network would have very restricted use, as the information would be unlikely to be sufficiently comprehensive or structured. What is really required is an arrangement for a regular exchange of information, preferably with periodic meetings, between companies in the same location and in the same line of production or service and possibly others also. The information exchanged should cover full details of rates of pay, other terms and conditions of service, together with detailed job descriptions and ideally 'benchmark' jobs, plus some guide to future pay policy. One company in the BIM survey did make such arrangements for exchange of information on salaries and the data on salary ranges were related to standard benchmark descriptions.

External surveys are almost entirely confined to salary earning groups. Few comparable surveys of wage earners are produced which are generally available. A large number of salary surveys are produced however, many of them annually and some every three years. They fall into three main categories. First, those produced by professional bodies about their own members' pay. Secondly, those which management consultants and other management bodies prepare as a sideline to their other activities—these are mainly on either a range of management posts or on a particular area, eg office or computer staff. Thirdly, some employment agencies and career registers publish surveys based on applicants' salaries.

So many surveys are produced and by such different methods and presented in varying format that it is difficult to generalize about their worth. Fortunately, *Guide to salary surveys 1980* gives some idea of the usefulness of the surveys listed.

In general, salary surveys are widely used and Cothliff (1973) found that they were next in popularity to the informal surveys, with 76% of its sample making use of them. But while many firms considered that they gave good guidance, their limitations were generally recognized. One of the weaknesses of some surveys is that they give insufficient—or even no—information on survey methods, the sample, etc, which are important in assessing the results.

Using the surveys can present other problems. They frequently provide different results and, because of sample and other differences, they often are not directly comparable anyway. Use of survey figures in making comparisons with particular salaries in an organization is therefore doubly difficult and has to be approached with great caution.

The most reliable method of obtaining the wage and salary data required is for a company either to commission management consultants to carry out a survey or to organize its own survey. Cothliff (1973) found that 27% of the companies in his inquiry had instigated their own formal surveys, although their scope and sophistication varied considerably. They are, however, expensive.

Surveys may of course have very different aims. They can be major surveys for examining the whole pay structure or they may be concerned solely with the pay and conditions of a particular group or groups of employees, or even just a particular fringe benefit. Once a major survey has been carried out it should not need to be repeated for at least two or three years. It can be updated in particular areas as necessary by minor surveys, or even by the informal methods discussed on the previous page.

While such surveys can be enormously useful, it is crucial that they ask the right questions in the first place. Once having decided on the area of pay and conditions to be surveyed, the starting point is in choosing the companies to be asked to supply information. Some surveys cover other large firms or a cross-section of industries without selecting on the basis of real relevance to the firm's needs, which is not going to produce a really useful survey. The companies in the survey need to be carefully selected and should include not only firms in the same industry, but others which compete for employees. Local firms will clearly be of major importance here. The number of participating companies is also important, too, since too small a sample means that one firm's rates of pay exert too big an influence on the total results: 20—30 companies is often considered an ideal number, although it may be more in a major survey.

Another key factor is the selection of a number of benchmark jobs (see Chapter 11), so that not only is pay data obtained on the key jobs, but effective pay comparisons can also be made with these data. This increases the importance of a survey not only being confined to a questionnaire but also including some visits to other plants.

Surveys are especially valuable when the data is expressed in common terms—eg a basic rate of pay (or basic earnings in the case of workers on PBR) with comprehensive data on the make-up of earnings, plus fringe benefits, in order to make realistic pay comparisons possible.

Comparability—the CSPRU

Surveys should produce sufficient data about earnings to enable comparative tables of earnings to be drawn up, along the lines of the comparative earnings tables (which weight earnings to allow for variability of elements in the pay packet) recommended by Bowey and Lupton (1973). A similar method is used for non-industrial employees in the civil service. Re-established with a new structure in 1979, after a period of suspension due to incomes policy, the Civil Service Pay Research Unit is one of the major statutory bodies which uses comparability for determining pay in the public sector. Like the three review bodies mentioned above, and the Standing Commission for Pay Comparisons (better known as the Clegg Commission), which was abolished in 1980, it uses comparability as a way of dealing with the difficulty of setting rates of pay in the public sector where normal labour market forces tend not to operate.

Although the CSPRU does not make recommendations about the level of pay increases, which is left to the negotiators, it supplies data on pay, bonuses, fringe benefits and conditions of service from a data bank of jobs in around 300 organizations. These are judged to be 'broadly comparable' with selected benchmark jobs which the CSPRU uses under its 'jobs-for-jobs' comparisons approach to comparability.

Particularly valuable is the 1979 report in which the CSPRU detailed its comparability procedures. A similar report was also published by the Clegg Commission, which adopted the factor analysis method of comparability—a type of points rating system of job evaluation. And although the Clegg Commission has now been disbanded, it left behind a very detailed discussion in its first report of the various methods of making comparisons, together with the pros and cons of each, as well as setting out in some detail the figures on which it based its own comparability exercise (see Chapter 12).

Other Sources

The other main sources of information on rates of pay are newspaper advertisements and employment agencies. Despite the severe limitations of advertisements, they remain a popular guide to current rate of pay. Cothliff (1973) found that almost 50% of the companies surveyed used them. There are two main weaknesses. First, the advertisements often only quote ranges, not the actual rate for the job, and these may be inflated for 'poaching' purposes. Secondly, the job descriptions are usually so brief as to be unreliable for making comparisons.

Rates quoted by employment agencies are also doubtful guides, since they may be inflated and they usually give only a basic rate, rather than a full pay packet.

The other side of the coin—prices—is of course equally important in pay bargaining. The Retail Prices Index, published monthly by the Department of Employment, is the key statistic here, although it has a number of weaknesses such as excluding a number of items on which people regularly spend money, including national insurance contributions, and questionable expenditure patterns based on a 'general household'. There are also other useful sources of price information, particularly the regional cost of living indices published by Reward Regional Surveys.

References and Further Reading

Armstrong, M. and Murlis, H., *A Handbook of Salary Administration*, Kogan Page, London, 1980.
Bowey, A. and Lupton, T., *Job and Pay Comparisons*, Gower, Farnborough, 1973.
Cothliff, J.S., *Salary Administration*, British Institute of Management, London, 1973.
Department of Employment, *New Earnings Survey 1979*, HMSO, London, 1980.
Department of Employment, *Changes in Rates and Hours of Work*, HMSO, London, published monthly.
Department of Employment, *Time Rates of Wages and Hours of Work*, HMSO, London, published annually.
Department of Employment Gazette, HMSO, London, published monthly. (Giving basic wage rates, average earnings and retail price index).
Genders, P., *Wages and Salaries*, Institute of Personnel Management, London, 1981.
IDS Study No. 233., *Salary Surveys 1981*, Incomes Data Services Limited, London, January 1981.
Incomes Data Report, Incomes Data Services Limited, London, published twice monthly.
IDS Study No. 231., *Pay and Price Statistics*, December, 1980.
IDS Studies, Incomes Data Services Limited, London, published twice monthly.
Industrial Relations Review and Report, Eclipse Publications Limited, London, published twice monthly.
MacBeath, G. and Rands, D.N., *Salary Administration*, Business Books, London, 1976.
Murlis, H., 'Making Sense of Salary Reviews', *Personnel Management*, Volume 13, no. 1, January, 1980.
Pay Board Advisory Report No. 2, *Relativities*, HMSO, London, 1974.

Review Bodies on *Armed Forces Pay, Doctors' and Dentists' remuneration*, and *Top Salaries*, HMSO, London, all three publications are published annually.
Regional Cost of Living Reports, Reward Regional Surveys, Stone, Staffs. Published quarterly.
Report of the Civil Service Pay Research Unit Board and the Civil Services Pay Research Unit, 1979, HMSO, 1979.
Schofield, A. and Husband, T., *The Wage and Salary Audit*, Gower, Farnborough, 1977.
Standing Commission on Pay Comparability, *Report No. 1, Local Authority and University Manual Workers; NHS ancillary staffs; and ambulancemen*, HMSO, 1979.

Index

Adamson Company 323
Advisory, Conciliation & Arbitration Service (ACAS) 28
Added value plan 323
Added value schemes 22
  effect on employees 22
  performance related bonuses 22
  productivity measured 33
Administration, facets of, in wage & salary structures 3—8
Agricultural Wages Act 189
Allport (1968) 318
American Management Association 'package' 226
American Telephone & Telegraph Company 226
Anderson (1980) 198
Anstey (1976) 231
Appeals Committee 100
Appraisal *see* Management by Objectives; Performance Appraisal Review
Assessment centres 226—30
Autonomous group development 4

BSI 153
Babbage, Charles 104
Bargaining
  levels; units; forms or scope 38
  strategy & tactics 173—83
    analysing & selecting negotiating tactics 179—80
    developing a negotiating strategy 174—9
    negotiating team 179
    objectives 173
    training for bargaining 180—3
Bargaining structure
  development 41—2
  effect of decentralisation 51
  efficiency 48
See also Collective bargaining
Barnison (1979) 220
Bass & Ryterband (1979) 207
Beaumont, Thomson & Gregory (1980) 39
Bedaux, Charles E. 106, 286
Beenstock & Emmanuel (1979) 170

Benefits *see under*
  Employee benefits for managers and executives;
  Employee benefits for non-managerial staff
'Best-fit' line 5
Bethlehem Steel Works 106
Bonus
  based on company performance 321–61
    added value schemes 329
      calculations 331, 333
    advantages & disadvantages 325–6
      relative merits 325
    objectives of bonus schemes 321–2
      socially integrative appeal 321
    payment system 334–7
      maintenance 336
    Scanlon plans 333
    types of scheme 322–6
  formulae 259–62
  reward payment 287, 299
Bowey (1978) 138
Bowey & Lupton (1970) 350
  (1973) 166, 430
  (1974) 349
See also Lupton & Bowey
British Institute of Management (BIM) (1977) 28; (1976) 120; (1967) 203, 331; (1974) 379
British Standard (1979) 107
British Steel Corporation 121
Brown (1980) 43
Brown & Sisson (1975) 160
  (1979) 43
Brown & Terry (1978) 46
Budgetary control of salaries & wages 415–27
  budgets as targets 419
  managerial uses of budget reports 422
  non-accounting style 424
  use of budgetary information 423
  technical framework 416–19
    cost categories 416–17
  the way ahead 425–6
Bullock Report 51
Bureau of National Affairs (USA) survey 230

Canada
  strikes 51
Case Studies of job restructuring 74
Central Arbitration Committee (CAC) 102–3
China
  Royal Enfield 125
Civil Service Pay Research Unit (CSPRU)
  26, 159–69 *passim*, 435
Civil Service Selection Board (CSSB) 226
Clegg (1976) 47
  (1980) 79
Collective bargaining 6, 37–53
  British system's weaknesses 40
  fragmentation of 39
Company
  case study one 30–3
  case study two 33–6
  changes, supporting 61
  company-wide incentive system 6
  pension schemes 387–95
Comparability 159–72, 435
  factor job comparisons 164
  methods of making comparisons 162
Comparability Commission 26
See also Standing Commission for Pay Comparisons (Clegg)
Confederation of British Industry (CBI)
  guidelines 52
  proposals on pay determination 37

support for added value schemes 324
Conflict clear/firm 175
Conflicts about outcomes 11–13
Control systems 55
Cothliff (1973) 433, 435
Currie, Russel M. 106 (1972) 121

Department of Employment 34
   definition of structure 38
   New Earnings Survey 44–6
Department of Employment Gazette 429
Department of Employment indices 429
Design & administration of pay systems 15
Desirable job attributes 68
Dewhurst (1972) 417
Differentials 25
   'correct' hierarchy of 25
   instability of 26
Disclosure of information 103
Donovan Royal Commission on Trade Unions & Employers' Associations (1968) 37–52 *passim*
   analysis of problem 41
Drucker, Peter 207

EEC 7, 380
Edmund Davies Committee 162
Edward N. Hay Associates 236
Employee 234
   assessing potential of 220
   Donovan report on 37
   new 196
Employee benefits for Managers & Executives 365–78
   basic 367–8
      'fringe' 367
      'key' 367

key 374
   security 370–2
   status 368–70
   total benefits/salary package 366–7
   work benefits 372
Employee benefits for non-managerial staff 379–86
   benefits available 379–80
   security 381
   statutory 380
   welfare 383–5
Employment Appeal Tribunal, 99, 101
Employment Protection Act 103, 160
   (Consolidation) Act (1978) 371, 382
Engineering
   Case Study 33
Engineering Employers' Federation 323
Engineering Industry 157
Equal Opportunities Commission (EOC) 89 n
   (1981) 79
Equal Pay Act (1970) 89, 101, 160, 310, 404

Factories
   Case Study One 32
Fair Wages Resolution 103
Fallback rates 34
Finance Acts (1970) (1971) 390
Forced distribution method 202
Fournies (1973) 199
Fox & Flanders (1969) 39, 41
Free collective bargaining 29

Garrett (1930) 237
General Electric 226
Glacier Metal Company 84
Gilbreth, Frank 106
Gill (1977) 198, 224, 231

Gill, Ungerson & Thakur (1973) 198
Goldthorpe *et al* (1968) 68
Government policy 19—36
  differentials 25
  incentive schemes 19—25
  incomes policy 23
Greene & others v. Broxtowe District Council 101
Group targets 4
Guide to salary surveys (1980) 433

Hay Company Limited 83
Hay Consultancy Company 186
Hay-MSL Limited 153, 236, 317
Hay Guide-chart Profile Method, 186, 235—48
  development of method 236—45
    factor rating system 236
    guide-chart construction 238
  installing the system 239, 246—7
    job evaluation 239
    management 247
  needs of employers & employees 235
    pay structure basis 235
  summary of objectives 247—8
Hart & Thompson (1979) 229
Health & Safety Committee 177
Hirsch (1977) 125
Hopwood (1973) 423
Horizontal job enlargement 4
Housing 384

IBM 226
ICI
  Central Work Study Dept. 106
  share incentive scheme 330
Incentive bonus schemes 12, 19, 34, 249—64
  Government policy's effect on 19—25
  Management schemes 249—64
    key questions 252
      cash or capital 255
      performance measurement 255
    major types of scheme 250—2
      distinctions 251
      incentive 251—2
    policy questions 249—50
  technical problems in management incentives 259—63
    bonus formulae 259—62
    circumstances for intervention 263
    monitoring effectiveness 262
    provision for flexibility 262
  See also Bonus
Income Data Service (1970) 188
Incomes Data Report 432
Incomes Data Studies 432
Incomes policies 23
Industrial democracy 51
Industrial Market Research survey (1980) 220
Inland Revenue 390
Institute of Personnel Management (1967) 203
  (1973) 198
  (1980) 220
Institute of Social Research Michigan 143
Insurance 381
Interview 215
International Labour Organisation (ILO) 106
Introduction to Work Study 106

Jacques (1979) 77, 84
Job context & measurement 63—4
Job design & work organisation 65—76
Job enlargement & work rotation 70

Job enrichment
  horizontal & vertical 71
Job evaluation & sex
  discrimination 89–103
  different schemes 92–8
  excluding certain groups 98
  formulating scheme 90–2
    composition of committee 90
    discriminatory titles 92
    job description & analysis 90–2
  implementing scheme 99–100
    appeals 100
    red circle cases 99
Job evaluation 4, 7, 26, 28, 77–88, 147–58
  decision to use job evaluation 85–6
  main techniques 78–83
    factor comparison 80–2
    points rating 78, 82–3
    ranking 79
  new basic rates 86
  new techniques 83–5
    guide-chart 83
    job profile 83
    time span of discretion 84
  related to wages 147–58
  techniques 77–88
  See also Wages; Work measurement
Job Evaluation Committees 90
Job rationalisation 4, 66–9
  design of workgroup activities 69
  undesirable characteristics 68
Joint Representation Committee 51
Joint Steering Committee 339
Journal of Management Studies 16n

Key benefits 374
Koestler (1967) 321

Leaderless group exercise 227

Legge (1978) 318
Life Magazine 323
Lipsey (1979) 122
Locher & Teal (1977) 199
Locke, McGregor & Maslow 208
Lockyer (1979) 28
Lott, M.R. 82
Lupton (1963) 318
Lupton & Bowey (1974) 5, 60, 278, 349
Lupton & Gowler (1969) 290, 309

McCormick (1977) 126
Mcdougall (1973) 272
Management assessment programme 226
Management by objectives (MBO) 6, 25, 61, 185, 207–13, 258, 271
  advantages 209
  appraisal interview 213–19
    objective in conducting interview 214
  basic technique 208
  present performance assessment 212
  overall appraisal 213
  review 211
  total concept 207
Management Centre Europe 226
Manchester Business School 349
  'Joint Development Activities' 373
Margerison (1979) 222
Mason, Thomas 104
Measured daywork schemes 10
Medical facilities 382
Merit appraisal techniques 6
Method Study 104, 108–12
  defining objectives 108–9
  developing better method 110
  examining facts 109–10
  installing & maintaining new method 110–12

recording facts 109
Methods time measurement (MTM) 290
Monitoring effectiveness 262
Moonman (1973) 379
Motion study 106
Motivation 271
Muczyk (1979) 207, 210

National Board for Prices & Incomes (1968) 26, 77
National Coal Board 80
National Health Service (NHS) 167
Negotiation
  negotiating exercise 227
  negotiating team 179
  process 5
New Earnings Survey
  (1977) 24
  (1973) (1978) 44–6
  (1979) 187, 189
New payment system 60
New Zealand Forest Products 140
Non-performance-related benefits 374
Norman & Bahiri (1976) 135
Novit (1976) 121

OECD
  national structures 47
Occupational Pensions Board 393
Operating, developing and adjusting reward systems 399–414
  adjustment & development in medium term 403–10
    changing circumstances 403–4
    legislation 404
    mergers & acquisitions 405
    personnel changes 405
  monitoring in short term 400–2
  objectives 399–400
  summary 412–14
    tactics 413
    wage & salary audit 412
  taking action 410–12
    bonus earnings 411
    change of bonus review period 412
    wage freezing 411
  wage & salary audits 407–10
    board report 408
    hourly-paid staff 407
    overtime & shiftworking 409–10
Oral expression exercise 227
Overtime pay 24
Owen, Robert 104

Paterson (1972) 77, 82
Pay Board 162
Pay & Rewards Research Centre 131
Pay structures (conflicts about outcomes) 13–16
Pay systems 9–11
Payment by result (PBR) systems 285–96
  bonus reward 287
  piecework & flat day rate 285–6
Payment by time systems 297–308
  effect on performance & labour cost 306–7
  measured daywork 299–300
  philosophy of time-based systems 300
Performance appraisal & review 197–232
  assessment centres 226–9
    management assessment programme 226
  assessing employee potential 220–6
  IPM survey 199
  management by objectives (MBO) 207, 213
  objectives 199

PBR scheme, economics of 293–4
personnel work areas identified 200
procedures 201–7
salary review 230
Performance evaluation monitoring system (PEMS) 201
Performance related bonuses 22
Perronet, Jean 104
Personality trait rating 203
Phyrr (1973) 417
Potential, identifying for further development 6
Predetermined motion time systems (PMTS) 112, 117, 290
Productivity bargaining 6
Productivity measurement 119–44
  complexity of measurement 121–6
  market position 135–7
  organisation location 137–40
  partial measures 120–1
  total measures 131–5
Process allowance 5
Production Efficiency Board 106
Production managers 22
Profit sharing 22
Progression curves 195–6

Randell *et al* (1974) 197
Rated Activity Sampling 33
Rating 291–2
Rates 206
Rating form 205
Redundancy pay 28
Reif & Bassford (1979) 207
Results orientated schemes 203
Review Body on Pay of Armed Forces 161
Reward Regional Surveys 436
Reward system design 3
Royal Enfield motorcycle 125

Salaried employees
  annual review 6
  motivation of 6
Salary bands & progression curves 187–96
  designing bands 189–92
  progression methods 193–4
Salary review 205
Salary & wage systems
  installation of 55–62
  change, strategy for 57–60
  control systems 55
  new system criteria 60
  See also Budgetary Control of Salaries & Wages
Salary system selection 265–81
  matching remuneration to motivation 271
Salaried employees 6
  See also Payment
Scanlon plan 6, 323
Schick (1980) 201
Schumacher (1973) 125
Sears Roebuck 226
Self-financing productivity bonus 24
Self-financing productivity schemes 22
Self-rating methods 202
Semi-autonomous Group Working 72
Sex Discrimination Act (SDA) (1975) 90, 102
  See also Job evaluation
Shift premiums 24
Sick pay 381
Sneath, Thakur & Medjuck (1976) 225
Snoxall & Davies v. Vauxhall Motors Ltd. (1977) 100
Social Context of Work 9–17
Social security benefits 29
Social Security Pensions Act (1975) 392

Sources of information 429
Standing Commission for Pay Comparisons (Clegg Commission) 159–70 *passim*, 435
Statistical Profile 42–6
Status 6, 368
Status, effort & reward 309–19
   status/reward relationship 317
Steers & Porter (1979) 208
Strathclyde survey 24–5
Strikes 34, 51
Success factors 222
Superannuation Funds Office 390

TUC (1973) 51
Tavistock Institute of Human Relations 84
Taylor (1947) 66
Taylor, F.W. 106
The Times 198, 324
Timed studies 104
Tools of Social Science 16n
Torrington & Chapman (1979) 200
Total productivity measure (TPM) 140
Towards a Wage Audit 407n
Towne's gain-sharing scheme 324
Trade Unions 29, 35, 37

Ullman (1974) 48
Unemployment 29
United States 199
   appliance manufacturer 74
   compared with Britain 126
   IBM machine operators 75
   performance appraisal & review 230
Scanlon plan 323
strikes 51
use of money incentives 126
Urwick, Orr Partners Limited 83

Vertical job enrichment 4
Volvo car assembly
   Case 1   74
Vroom & Yetton (1973) 141

Wages & salaries
   administration 3–8
   audits 407
   bargaining 28–30
   freeze 29
   systems 283
      selection 350–60
Wages Councils Act 189
Wages related to job evaluation & work measurement 147–58
Wages surveys 187–9
Walker & Guest (1952) 68
Warwick University Survey 43–4
Whitley Committee 41
Wild (1980) 138
Work
   assessment 4
   benefits 372
   measurement 104, 112–15, 153–8
Work Study 104–7, 115–17
Work Study 106
Works council 33